# MENTAL HEALTH CONCEPTS
## THIRD EDITION

**Natalie Kalman,** M.S.N., M.S.Ed., B.S.N.

•

**Claire G. Waughfield,** M.S.N., C.S., B.S.N

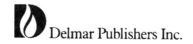
Delmar Publishers Inc.

# MENTAL HEALTH CONCEPTS

**Delmar Publishers' Online Services**

To access Delmar on the World Wide Web, point your browser to:
**http://www.delmar.com/delmar.html**

To access through Gopher:  gopher://gopher.delmar.com
(Delmar Online is part of "thomson.com", an Internet site with information on
more than 30 publishers of the International Thomson Publishing organization.)

For information on our products and services:
email: info@delmar.com
or call 800-347-7707

## NOTICE TO THE READER

Cover design by Nancy Gworek

*Delmar Staff*
   Executive Editor: David Gordon
   Administrative Editor: Marion Waldman
   Project Editor: Carol Micheli
   Production Coordinator: James Zayicek
   Design Coordinator: Karen Kemp
   Art Coordinator: Judi Orozco

Copyright ©1993
by Delmar Publishers Inc.

6 7 8 9 10 XXX 99 98 97 96

Printed in the United States of America
published simultaneously in Canada
by Nelson Canada,
a division of The Thomson Corporation

Library of Congress Cataloging-in-Publication Data

Kalman, Natalie.
   Mental health concepts / Natalie Kalman, Claire G. Waughfield. —
3rd ed.
      p.   cm.
      Includes bibliographical references and index.
      ISBN 0-8273-4980-7 (textbook)
      1. Psychiatric nursing. 2. Mental health. I. Waughfield, Claire
G. II. Title.
      [DNLM: 1. Mental Disorders—prevention & control—nurses'
instruction. 2. Mental Disorders—therapy—nurses' instruction.
3. Mental Health—nurses' instruction. 4. Stress. Psychological—
prevention & control—nurses' instruction. WY 160 K145m]
RC440.K28  1993
616.89—dc20
DNLM/DLC                                                        92-49881
for Library of Congress                                              CIP

*The book is dedicated to John Kalman, and Richard, Anne, Marcus, and Jané Waughfield.*

# CONTENTS

# PREFACE

MENTAL HEALTH CONCEPTS, Third Edition, fills the need for a comprehensive and useful text on mental health written specifically for the beginning health care professional. The text is based on the theory that the ability to cope with stress is the most important factor in mental health. This is only one theory, but it provides a useful framework for planning and providing care. It is the authors' belief that mental health is an integral part of the total care of the client/patient.

A major contribution to health care is the concept of holistic beings and the dedication of the health field to a high degree of wellness. A great deal of emphasis has been placed on understanding the reactions of self and others under stress, and on the prevention of mental illness. An attempt has been made to relate this text to the needs of any person under stress, whether this person is the care provider, member of the care provider's family, a neighbor, or patients in a clinic or hospital setting.

In the past, many psychiatric texts were based on the Freudian psychoanalytical model. There is now an increased interest in other types of psychotherapies, especially Gestalt therapy and behaviorism. Therefore, a chapter covering the more common psychotherapies is presented. Previously, information on therapies had to be obtained on the job or through supplementary books.

Topics covered in the text include maladaptive behavior, anxiety, aggression, assertiveness, and mental mechanisms. The topic of stress, a malady of the twentieth century, is covered thoroughly. There is specific information on helping people who are suffering from stress caused by the death of others, pain, and sexual problems. Two other major problems, alcoholism and drug abuse, are discussed in detail. Extensive coverage is given to therapeutic communication since communication is the basic therapeutic tool of the mental health professional. Students are encouraged to practice these therapeutic communication skills. Also discussed are ways to alleviate the problems of re-entry into the community faced by patients who have been hospitalized for mental illness.

Each chapter contains objectives, suggested activities, and review questions which reflect the objectives and reinforce learning. Throughout the text, the pronoun *she* is used to designate the health care professional and the pronoun *he* refers to the patient. This has been done in an effort to prevent awkward sentences and is not intended to show any type of discrimination.

It is hoped that the third edition of MENTAL HEALTH CONCEPTS will help health care professionals gain a better understanding of mental health and the people for whom they care. This understanding should, in turn, lead to more effective mental health care.

## About the Authors

The authors have each had many years of varied academic preparation and nursing experience. Natalie Kalman is experienced in counseling, teaching student nurses, and caring for persons with psychotic and alcoholic problems in a locked ward situation. She has taught in, or been the director of, a practical nursing program for fourteen years. Mrs. Kalman received a Bachelor of Science in nursing from Loyola University and a Master of Education with a counseling major from Eastern Illinois University. She also received a Master of Science degree with a major in nursing from Northern Illinois University. In addition, Mrs. Kalman has taken courses in school psychology at the University of Arizona at Tucson.

Claire Waughfield has many years of experience in teaching mental health concepts to nursing students and practicing psychiatric nursing from both a clinical practice and management perspective. Currently, she is a clinical nurse specialist in the mental health outpatient clinic and co-chair of the quality improvement nursing council at the Richard L. Roudebush Veterans Affairs Medical Center, Indianapolis, Indiana. Ms. Waughfield is also an assistant clinical professor at the Indiana University Graduate Program for Psychiatric/Mental Health Nursing. Prior to this, she was the unit director of the inpatient psychiatric unit at Indiana University Hospital, Indianapolis, Indiana and a former coordinator of the nursing program at Danville Area Community College, Danville, Illinois. Ms. Waughfield has received a Bachelor of Arts degree from Eastern Illinois University, a Bachelor of Science in Nursing degree from Governor's State University, Park Forest South, Illinois, and a Master of Science degree with a major in Psychiatric/Mental Health Nursing from Indiana University, Indianapolis, Indiana. Ms. Waughfield has certification as a Clinical Specialist in Adult Psychiatric and Mental Health Nursing.

## Acknowledgments

No book is ever written by the authors alone. It takes a great many people to put it together. Our sincere thanks go to Jim Norman, J. Scott Brown, and Robert Wilson for the photographs; to Frank Serio, Joan Serio, Pat Westphal, Patricia Duffy-Cunningham and Charles Elston, who gave us many helpful suggestions; and to Arizona ELK's major project for graciously allowing us to use their facilities.

Without the support and encouragement of our families, co-workers, and friends, this book could not have been written.

# CHAPTER 1
# HISTORY, TRENDS, AND STANDARDS

## OBJECTIVES

After studying this chapter, the student should be able to:

- State the changes in attitude and treatment concerning the mentally ill that have occurred from primitive times to the present.
- Match pioneers in mental health care with their contributions and beliefs.
- Identify legislation enacted to improve mental health care.
- List five services offered by comprehensive community mental health centers.
- Explain how the changes in mental health care affect the role of the nurse.
- Explain the purpose of standards for nursing care.
- Identify legal rights of mental patients.

It is impossible to estimate the extent to which mental illness affected primitive people. However, there is evidence that it did exist and that attempts were made to treat it. Mental illness was thought to be caused by evil spirits entering and taking over the body. Medicine men attempted to drive these evil spirits from the body through the use of incantations and magic, Table 1-1.

Some primitive tribes rejected their mentally ill and drove them from the community. Other tribes allowed the mentally ill to stay as long as they were not completely incapacitated or their behavior did not create fear. Some tribes encouraged disturbed individuals to act out their difficulties and to confide in the witch doctor.

## TABLE 1-1  Concepts of Mental Illness

| TIME PERIOD | CONCEPTS OF MENTAL ILLNESS |
|---|---|
| PRIMITIVE TIMES | Evil spirits possessed the body and must be driven from the body. |
| ANCIENT CIVILIZATION | Thought to be natural phenomenon; humanistic approach. |
| MIDDLE AGES | Superstition, witchcraft, and torture. |
| RENAISSANCE | Decline in belief of possession by evil spirits. |
| | Mental problems irreversible. |
| | Scientific inquiry; humanism. |
| EIGHTEENTH CENTURY | Reform movement; chains removed. |
| | Need for medical care recognized. |
| | First mentally ill patient treated in hospital. |
| NINETEENTH CENTURY | Research began. |
| | Legislation concerning mental health enacted. |
| | Hospitals for mentally ill established with long-term custodial care. |
| | First psychiatric training school in United States established. |
| TWENTIETH CENTURY | Start of mental health movement. |
| | Large state hospitals built. |
| | Psychoanalysis. |
| | More legislation concerning mental health enacted. |
| | Community health care centers established. |
| | Holistic concept of care and short-term care introduced. |
| | Goal to return patient to society. |
| | Human services programs established. |
| | Focus on prevention. |

## ANCIENT CIVILIZATION

The ancient Greeks, Romans, and Arabs viewed mental deviations as natural phenomena and treated the mentally ill humanely. Although emotional problems were thought to be related to disturbances in the brain, some distinction was made between functional and organic disorders. Care consisted of sedation with opium, music, good physical hygiene, nutrition, and activity. The Greek philosopher Plato (429–348 B.C.) and the Greek physician Hippocrates (460–377 B.C., known as the Father of Medicine) were concerned about the treatment of the mentally ill. Hippocrates described a variety of personalities and attempted to classify people according to their behavior. Aristotle (354–322 B.C.), a Greek philosopher, studied anatomy and concluded that the mind was associated with the heart. Galen, a Greek physician and writer during the second century A.D., disagreed with Aristotle. In his writings, Galen declared the mind to be associated solely with the brain.

## MIDDLE AGES (A.D. 500–1450)

When the Roman Empire fell in A.D. 476, the humanitarian ideas concerning the mentally ill were forgotten. The world reverted to superstition, mysticism, witchcraft, and magic. Little was done to treat mental illness. Sometimes, patients were humanely cared for by members of religious orders. However, the mentally ill were usually locked in asylums where flogging, starvation, torture, and bloodletting were common. Within families, the mentally ill were hidden or banished to roam the streets.

## THE RENAISSANCE (Fourteenth to Seventeenth Century)

The belief that mental illness was caused by evil spirits possessing the body continued for much of the Renaissance period. If the mentally ill were considered a menace to society, they were put in prison. Otherwise, society protected itself by locking the mentally ill in asylums where non-professional people were paid to care for them. Mental illness was considered irreversible. The mentally ill were beaten for disobedience and confined to cages or closets. They were often subjected to cruel forms of torture.

Generally, mental patients were viewed as incompetent, defective, and potentially dangerous. They had no rights and were left in social isolation to communicate primarily with other mentally ill patients. Their caretakers were untrained and often punitive. As a result, the mentally ill tended to become more ill and less able to function in society.

The Bethlehem Royal Hospital, the first mental hospital in England, was opened during the seventeenth century. It was the second such hospital in Europe. Patients were treated as animals and were kept chained in cages. For a small fee, the public was allowed to wander through the hospital and view the patients. "Bedlam," as it was called, is the Cockney pronunciation for Bethlehem. The meaning of the word *bedlam* is tumult or frenzy.

A Swiss physician named Paracelsus (1493-1541) rejected the belief that evil spirits caused mental illness. Like the ancient Greeks and Romans, he believed that mental illness was a natural phenomenon. The idea that evil spirits possessed the body began to decline. Scientific inquiry, along with objective study of behavior, began to grow. A rational explanation for irrational behavior was sought. Authorities were divided into two groups—the psychics and the organics. The psychics believed that mental illness was a result of personal guilt; it was a possible atonement for sin. The organics felt that mental illness was caused by internal organs and that bloodletting would release enough blood and pressure to change behavior. It was not until the middle of the eighteenth century that any real advancement was made in the treatment and care of the mentally ill.

## THE EIGHTEENTH CENTURY

Franz Mesmer (1733–1815), an Austrian physician, was a pioneer in the therapeutic approach to maladaptive behavior. He believed that the universe was filled with magnetic forces. Mesmer professed that the mentally ill could be cured by having them hold rods filled with iron filings in water. This supposedly brought people into balance with the universe. Although Mesmer's techniques were later revealed as false, his idea of suggestive power has carried over to some modern psychotechniques. The term *mesmerized* is from Mesmer. To be mesmerized is to be placed in a hypnotic trance.

A French physician, Philippe Pinel (1745–1826), began the movement toward more humane treatment of the mentally ill when he removed the chains from twelve male patients at Bicêtré Hospital near Paris in 1792. Pinel disavowed punitive treatment of mental patients. He recognized the need for medical care and advocated freedom, useful work, and kindness for these individuals. He attempted to classify the mentally ill according to their observable behaviors and sought to devise specific treatment for each classified type.

During colonial times in America, the mentally ill were punished at the stocks or whipping posts. Often considered witches, they were burned at the stake, hung, or tortured.

During the Revolutionary War period, the mentally ill in America were treated for the first time as patients in a hospital setting. The first hospital in America to admit mental patients was The Pennsylvania Hospital located in Philadelphia. The first American textbook on psychiatry was written during this period by Benjamin Rush. Rush (1745–1813) was a physician who used a humanistic approach in the treatment of mental illness. Rush, who was also a signer of the Declaration of Independence, is considered by many to be the Father of American Psychiatry.

## THE NINETEENTH CENTURY

Jean Martin Charcot (1825–1893), a French neurologist, was a major influence during the nineteenth century in the treatment of the mentally ill. Charcot used suggestive power in the form of hypnotism to treat hysteria, Figure 1-1. He also diagnosed and located neurological disturbances in patients.

The establishment of American hospitals for the care of the mentally ill was due largely to the work of Dorothea Lynde Dix. Dorothea Dix (1802–1887) was a Boston school teacher who spent much of her life working for better conditions for the mentally ill. She traveled throughout the country in an effort to have legislation enacted for improved care for mental patients. As a result of her efforts, many hospitals were built in the United States, Canada, and other countries.

Fig. 1-1  Charcot demonstrating hypnotism in treatment of hysteria about 1887 at Salpêtrière. (Photo painting by A. Brouillet, National Library of Medicine, Bethesda, Maryland)

Humane treatment of the mentally ill became more widespread in the late nineteenth century. Nurses showed interest in improving the care of the mentally ill. Research on how syphilis affected the mind was begun. It was also discovered that some bizarre behavior was due to vitamin deficiencies. With advances in medicine, the concept of mental illness and those afflicted with it became more accepted and tolerated.

The first psychiatric training school in the United States was established in 1882 at McLean Hospital, Waverly, Massachusetts. However, in 1939, only half of all nursing schools provided psychiatric nursing courses. Participation in a psychiatric nursing course did not become a requirement for a nursing license until 1955.

## THE TWENTIETH CENTURY

Twentieth-century reforms in psychiatric care began in 1908 with the publication of a book entitled *A Mind That Found Itself*, by Clifford Beers. In the book, Beers describes his experiences and observations during his three years in mental institutions. The suffering of the mentally ill as portrayed in the book promoted the mental health movement. It made the public aware of the need for better care of the mentally ill. Beers came from a wealthy and influential family. In 1909, he used this influence to organize the National Society for Mental Hygiene (now known as the National Association for Mental Health).

Large state hospitals were built as a result of the public's increased awareness of the problems of the mentally ill. These state hospitals usually were established away from large cities, where patients could receive fresh air and sunshine. Few people were released from the hospitals once they were admitted. However, the public's conscience was eased.

In 1920, an Austrian neurologist, Sigmund Freud (1856–1939), made a significant contribution to the understanding and treatment of mental illness. Freud conducted a series of studies and determined a need for deeper probing into the psychological side of the individual. His belief in the power of unconscious memories and repressed emotions led him to develop the theory and practice of psychoanalysis. Because of his work, he is called the Founder of Psychoanalysis. Freud believed that each life event was determined by prior mental events. He studied the dreams, memories, and fantasies of his patients in a search for unconscious impulses and conflicts. Freud identified three major divisions of the self or mind:

the id, superego, and ego. Freud also presented a theory of psychosexual personality development. (See Chapter 5.)

In 1937, an International Committee for Mental Hygiene met in Paris, France, marking the beginning of international concern for mental health. The World Federation for Mental Health was formed in 1948. By 1961, The World Psychiatric Association was organized.

World War II brought the immensity of the mental health problem into view. The public was shocked when vast numbers of young men were rejected for service and many more were discharged because of mental problems. Also, many veterans returning from the war required treatment for mental problems. State hospitals were grossly inadequate. Obviously, new and better treatment was needed.

## Mental Health Legislation

Following World War II, the Hill-Burton Act, which allotted funds for building psychiatric units, was passed by Congress. In 1946, the National Mental Health Act provided federal funds to begin training programs for mental health professions. This act established the National Institute for Mental Health (1948) and provided grants for education and research, Table 1-2.

In response to the public's new interest and concern about mental illness, Congress created the Joint Commission on Mental Illness and Health in 1955. This commission studied and evaluated the needs of the mentally ill and the resources available for coping with the problem. The report submitted by the commission to Congress in 1961 revealed three distinct areas of concern: manpower, facilities, and cost. The commission also made recommendations for solving these problems.

In 1963, Congress enacted the Mental Retardation Facilities and Community Mental Health Centers Construction Act. This act authorized federal funds to match local and state monies to build community health centers. It was believed that community agencies could more easily locate and treat people with mental problems by decentralizing mental health care and bringing services closer to the people. Community health centers were designed to offer such services as inpatient and outpatient treatment, partial hospitalization, emergency services, and consultation and educational services, Figure 1-2. Centers were considered comprehensive if they also offered additional services such as diagnosis and rehabilitation care before and after hospitalization, training of professionals and paraprofes-

## TABLE 1-2  Mental Health Organizations and Legislation, 1909 to 1975

| | |
|---|---|
| 1909 National Society for Mental Hygiene | Studied nursing care of insane<br>Provided reforms in psychiatric care<br>Set up programs to treat afflicted servicemen |
| 1937 International Committee for Mental Hygiene Hill-Burton Act<br>1946 National Mental Health Act | Sparked international concern for mental health<br>Provided funds for building psychiatric units<br><br>Provided funds for professional training programs |
| 1948 World Federation for Mental Health | Provided grants for education and research |
| 1948 National Institute of Mental Health | Provided grants for education and research |
| 1955 Joint Commission on Mental Illness and Health | Studied and evaluated needs and resources available |
| 1961 World Psychiatric Association | Looked at social consequence of mental disorders |
| 1963 The Mental Retardation Facilities and Community Mental Health Centers Construction Act | Federal funds provided to match local and state monies; purpose was to decentralize mental health care |
| 1964 Economic Opportunity Act | Designed to help the poor and disadvantaged reach their full social potential<br>Emphasized improved social environment to prevent mental health problems |
| 1967 Mental Health Amendment | Provided grants for construction and staffing of mental health centers |
| 1968 Community Mental Health Centers Act Amendment | Provided community services and facilities for treatment of drug addicts and alcoholics |
| 1968 Alcoholic and Narcotic Addiction Rehabilitation Amendment | Provided funds to develop treatment and rehabilitation for alcoholics and drug abusers<br>Provided grants for special training |
| 1970 Community Health Centers Amendment | Provided for extended programs, construction gants, and increased construction through acquisition of land |
| 1975 Community Health Centers Amendment | Community mental health programs to include special programs for children and the elderly<br>Continuation of funding for existing mental health centers |

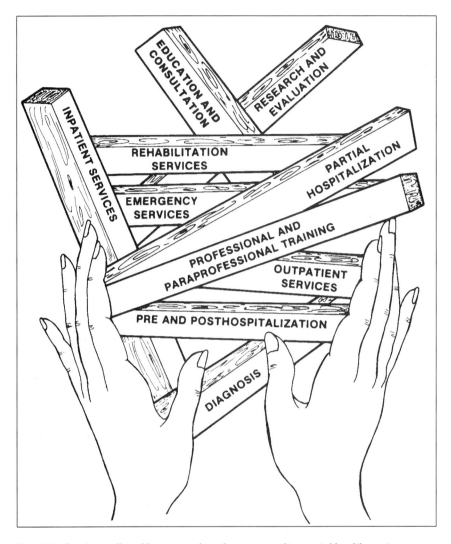

**Fig. 1-2  Services offered by comprehensive community mental health centers.**

sionals, and research and evaluation. Because of limited monies, however, few of the agencies existing today are actually comprehensive.

Later legislation provided added funds to help staff the centers. In 1968, amendments were added to the Community Mental Health Centers Act to provide funds to develop community services and facilities for treating and rehabilitating drug addicts and alcoholics.

The Economic Opportunity Act of 1964 was designed to help the poor and disadvantaged reach their full social potential. This was a step toward placing full emphasis on the prevention of mental disorders through improvement of the social environment. The development of social psychiatry added the public health point of view to psychiatry. Social psychiatry closely examines the social environment of people who are mentally ill or who have a high potential for mental illness. The goal is prevention.

In the early 1970s, care of the mentally ill shifted from the hospital to the community. Community mental health services included:

- Foster homes
- Crisis centers
- Hot lines
- Counseling centers
- Therapeutic communities
- Halfway houses
- Day-care centers

Private psychiatric hospitals were established and units for psychiatric services were developed in general hospitals. Some private insurance companies established coverage for psychiatric care.

Much has been learned since 1970, especially in the area of chronic mental illness. Several very effective drugs have been developed. Although there are serious side effects, drugs along with counseling and supervision offer the best hope for the long-term mentally ill. New theories about the cause of mental illness have been presented. The most prevalent theory today is that mental illness is initiated by some stressor in a genetically disposed person.

## Current Trends

Releasing the mentally ill from state hospitals was based on humanitarian ideals. It was to provide more personalized and humane care to persons whose civil rights had long been denied. However noble the move was meant to be, it has not proven to be totally successful. Some people adjusted very well to the community after being discharged from state institutions, but for some others the quality of life did not improve. Some former patients went home until their families burned out and they were turned into the streets. Some went into their own apartments but were later evicted because of failure to pay rent or because of bizarre behavior that bothered other residents. Many of those who got jobs soon lost them because of their behavior or because of excessive time off.

Unfortunately, the mentally ill do not always recognize their problems and tend not to seek help. Because of current legislation, there is no way to force treatment and there is no control over those who periodically do come to a mental health center. If medication is given to them, there is no way to be certain how it is taken or even if it is taken. As a result, many of today's street people are actually chronically mentally ill. Only a small percentage of the 2.5 million chronically mentally ill are being treated on a regular basis.

Deinstitutionalization has fallen far short of its goal, and there is a current trend to return the mentally ill to the institutions. The fault, however, is not totally with the idea of deinstitutionalization. Many communities were ill prepared to cope with the former patients. They offered few actual services and insufficient housing for low-income people.

In 1980, Congress passed the Mental Health Systems Act, which called for more money for the community centers and for specialized services for the mentally ill. The next year they passed the Omnibus Budget Reconciliation Act, which lumped all mental health services together with alcohol and drug programs. Later, all mental health funding was cut by 30 percent. This meant that there were no funds to carry out the Mental Health Systems Act of the previous year. Even though a small percentage of patients are still hospitalized, many states continue to send the major portion of all funding for mental health to the state institutions.

Since the mentally ill do not readily seek help, the problem will remain even if funding becomes adequate. Mental health services will have to be provided in a more imaginative and progressive manner.

The mentally ill need a satisfactory and useful life within their own social environment. Therefore, emphasis is being placed on community living for mental patients. The mentally ill are helped to participate in a variety of activities. Reality living patterns become a part of the hospitalized patient's life. Patients are taught reality living activities such as dressing, grooming, and manners. This new approach improves patients' morale and increases cooperation. Individual counseling is initiated and supportive contact is made with patients.

The approach to mental health has been redesigned to emphasize human services programs. Training procedures and use of personnel were reassessed. In order to provide services to all levels of the population, it was necessary to recruit and train workers. This led to the *paraprofession-*

*al* (a trained aide who helps a professional person). It has even been suggested by some authorities that mental health workers will have to go into the community to find and treat patients if deinstitutionalization is to work.

With changes in mental health care, the role of the nurse has also changed. The nurse is now a more involved member of the health care team. The nurse in mental health is involved in an *eclectic approach*; that is, she draws from various sources for the best care for the patient. The nurse develops open communication with a variety of people: the professional nurse, psychiatrist, clinical psychologist, social worker, physical therapist, and occupational therapist. She utilizes available therapeutic services. She also expresses her feelings and her findings and draws from her own experience to help develop patient care plans.

Today, mental health nursing is concerned with the whole person. Custodial care is no longer the only nursing concern. Mental health nursing permeates all settings and recognizes the diverse needs of the patients, Figure 1-3.

| CONTINUITY | CONSTANCY | CONSISTENCY |
|---|---|---|
| ASSESSMENT | physical, psychological, social | |
| INTERVENTIONS | provide coping strategies<br>explore problem-solving techniques<br>symptom recognition<br>environmental limit-setting<br>foster positive experiences | |
| EDUCATION | for patient & family/significant other<br>understanding of diagnosis<br>recognition of the symptoms of relapse<br>knowledge of medication & side effects<br>provide support group information | |

Fig. 1-3  Comprehensive care of mentally ill.

## STANDARDS OF CARE

The nurse's responsibilities are determined by legislation, agency policy, and standards set by the profession. Legislation is enacted to provide safe practitioners. Standards focus on practice and fulfill the profession's obligation to provide service and to continually improve that service. Standards provide a means of determining the quality of nursing which the patient receives, whether such services are provided by the professional nurse, the practical nurse, or the nursing assistant. The nurse, working in a mental health care setting, is responsible for providing high-quality care as identified by the standards of psychiatric nursing within the nurse's legal role. The American Nurses' Association's booklet *Standards of Psychiatric-Mental Health Nursing Practices* (Kansas City, MO: American Nurses' Association, 1982) lists eleven standards of psychiatric-mental health nursing practice.

| | |
|---|---|
| Standard I—<br>Theory: | The nurse applies appropriate theory that is scientifically sound as a basis for decisions regarding nursing practice. |
| Standard II—<br>Data Collection: | The nurse continuously collects data that are comprehensive, accurate, and systematic. |
| Standard III—<br>Diagnosis: | The nurse utilizes *nursing diagnoses* and standard classification of mental disorders to express conclusions supported by recorded assessment data and current scientific premises. |
| Standard IV—<br>Planning: | The nurse develops a nursing care plan with specific goals and interventions delineating nursing actions unique to each client's needs. |
| Standard V—<br>Intervention: | The nurse intervenes as guided by the nursing care plan to implement nursing actions that promote, maintain, or restore physical and mental health, prevent illness, and effect rehabilitation. |
| Standard V-A—<br>Psychotherapeutic<br>Interventions: | The nurse (generalist) uses *psychotherapeutic interventions* to assist clients to regain or improve their previous coping abilities and to prevent further disability. |
| Standard V-B—<br>Health Teaching: | The nurse assists clients, families, and groups to achieve satisfying and productive patterns of living through health teaching. |
| Standard V-C—<br>Self-Care Activities: | The nurse uses the activities of daily living in a goal-directed way to foster adequate self-care and physical and mental well-being of clients. |
| Standard V-D—<br>Somatic Therapies: | The nurse uses knowledge of somatic therapies and applies related clinical skills in working with clients. |
| Standard V-E—<br>Therapeutic<br>Environment: | The nurse provides, structures, and maintains a therapeutic environment in collaboration with the client and other health care providers. |

| Standard V-F— Psychotherapy: | The nurse (specialist) utilizes advanced clinical expertise in individual, group, and family *psychotherapy*, child psychotherapy, and other treatment modalities to function as a psychotherapist and recognizes professional accountability for nursing practice. |
|---|---|
| Standard VI— Evaluation: | The nurse evaluates client responses to nursing actions in order to revise the data base, nursing diagnoses, and nursing care plan. |
| Standard VII— Peer Review: | The nurse participates in peer review and other means of evaluation to assure quality of nursing care provided for clients. |
| Standard VIII— Continuing Education: | The nurse assumes responsibility for continuing education and professional development and contributes to the professional growth of others. |
| Standard IX— Interdisciplinary Collaboration: | The nurse collaborates with interdisciplinary teams in assessing, planning, implementing, and evaluating programs and other mental health activities. |
| Standard X— Utilization of Community Health Systems: | The nurse (specialist) participates with other members of the community in assessing, planning, implementing, and evaluating mental health services and community systems that include the promotion of the broad continuum of primary, secondary, and tertiary prevention of mental illness. |
| Standard XI— Research: | The nurse contributes to nursing and the mental health field through innovations in theory and practice and participation in research. |

## LEGAL RIGHTS OF PATIENTS

Most states have revised laws to protect the rights of the mentally ill. For example, in 1977, the state of New Mexico enacted the Mental Health and Developmental Disability Code. This code revised existing state laws for hospitalization and treatment of the mentally disabled. The code specifically states patient rights; what is to be included in treatment plans; steps to be followed in an involuntary admission; the rights of the person who voluntarily admits himself; consent of treatment; treatment of minors; the meaning of confidentiality; and the right to obtain care, regardless of ability to pay. Other states have similar laws. Although most admissions to mental health facilities are now voluntary, patients can still be committed by the courts. Commitment is sought when a patient is assessed as being of potential harm to self or others. Recent violent acts or threats of violence to self (suicide) or others (homicide) are reported. If a person presents as a danger, anyone can initiate the commitment process. This will place a hold on the person for a number of hours (24) until a hearing on the commitment is held. This is called an involuntary commitment. However, just because someone is known to be mentally ill, he/she cannot be picked up and placed on a mental ward. Regulations are now more stringent. The individual committed by the court has a right to treatment—not just custodial care. The health care facility can be held liable if treatment is not provided. Court cases showing that treatment was not provided have resulted in the release of the patient. The courts can look at competency versus incompetency of the individual. Competency is defined as the capability of making a decision. At times, the court may appoint a guardian or conservator. A guardian is legally responsible for the physical needs of another, in this case the patient. A conservator is a person who has the legal responsibility for another's finances. The conservator disperses money to the patient and keeps accurate records of expenditures.

Patients have a right to refuse treatment. All health care facilities must obtain informed consent from the patient before beginning treatment. The patient must be provided with information which will enable him to make a valid decision concerning any proposed treatment. Commitment to an institution does not automatically mean loss of the right to make a valid decision.

Patients have a right to humane treatment. This means they have the right to receive quality care in an environment that promotes their recovery. They also must be treated with respect and dignity. Personnel are legally liable for acts that do not conform with these rights. A nurse who observes cruelty to a patient or other degrading acts and does not report them is as legally liable as the person committing the act. Currently, there are clear, well-defined patient abuse guidelines that are closely adhered to in hospitals and mental health facilities.

Patients have the right to be treated as individuals. Some states have proclaimed that patients legally have the right to their own clothes and belongings while hospitalized. Clothes and belongings help the patient to maintain identity. Maintaining identity is important when everything around the patient is changing. It is an accepted fact that change itself causes stress. When dealing with a person who is already overwhelmed, it is imperative that care be taken by health care workers to avoid creating more stress.

## SUMMARY

Mental illness has existed from primitive times. It was once thought to be caused by evil spirits entering and taking over the body. Medicine men, through incantations and magic, sought to drive the evil spirits from the body. Ancient Greeks, Romans, and Arabs believed that mental illness was a natural phenomenon and treated the mentally ill humanely. After the fall of the Roman Empire, humanitarian ideas gave way to mysticism, witchcraft, and magic. Little was done to treat mental illness. Patients were locked in institutions where flogging, starvation, torture, and bloodletting were common. Toward the end of the Renaissance, the belief that evil spirits possessed the body began to decline and scientific inquiry increased. Objective study of behavior grew.

Philippe Pinel began the movement toward more humane treatment of the mentally ill when he removed the chains from mental patients and advocated freedom, useful work, and kindness for the patient. Dorothea Lynde Dix was instrumental in having legislation enacted to improve conditions for the mentally ill in America.

During the Revolutionary period, Benjamin Rush wrote the first American textbook on psychiatry. He is often referred to as the Father of American Psychiatry. The first psychiatric training school in the United States was established at McLean Hospital in Massachusetts in 1882. Early in the twentieth century, large state hospitals were built to house the mentally ill. These hospitals provided fresh air and sunshine but little cure. In 1920, Sigmund Freud made a significant contribution to the understanding and treatment of mental illness with his work in psychoanalysis.

World War II brought the immensity of the mental health problem to the public's attention. Legislation was enacted to meet the need for better mental health care for returning veterans. The early 1960s saw an increased focus on the establishment of better care for the mentally ill. Human services programs were introduced. Community health centers were provided to take the place of the obsolete state hospitals. Care of the mentally ill shifted from the hospital to the community. Recent trends provide for the prevention as well as the treatment of mental illness. With the recent changes has come a change in nursing. The nurse has become more involved as a member of the health care team. Mental health is now concerned with the whole person. The goal is to restore the mentally ill to an adequate level of functioning so that they may have satisfying and productive lives.

Nursing responsibilities are determined by legislation, agency policy, and standards of care set by the profession. Standards are set to continually improve practice. The nurse caring for mentally ill individuals has an obligation to give high-quality care as identified by the standards of psychiatric nursing within her legal role. The American Nurses' Association gives eleven standards for psychiatric-mental health nursing practice.

The mentally ill are demanding their rights. Many states have enacted legislation protecting the rights of the mentally ill. Patients have the right to therapeutic treatment, informed consent, humane care, and to be treated as individuals. As expanding knowledge of the brain continues, two pertinent areas of serious challenge remain: the provision of quality health care for the mentally ill and the accessibility of that quality care to all people.

## SUGGESTED ACTIVITIES

- Assess your own attitudes concerning the mentally ill. Include personal feelings and stereotypes.
- Evaluate your local hospital's care of the mentally ill. Write your impressions in one or two paragraphs.
- Read about the life of Pinel, Dix, or Beers and plan a panel discussion in class.
- Write a report on legislation passed in your state that has affected the care of the mentally ill.

## REVIEW

A.  Multiple choice. Select the best answer.

1.  Mental illness has existed since
    a. World War I.
    b. the fall of the Roman Empire.

    c. primitive times.

    d. medieval times.

2.    The Father of American Psychiatry is

    a. Hippocrates.

    b. Sigmund Freud.

    c. Benjamin Rush.

    d. Philippe Pinel.

3.    The physician who attempted to classify behavior in ancient times was

    a. Pinel.

    b. Rush.

    c. Hippocrates.

    d. Galen.

4.    The first psychiatric training school in the United States was established in

    a. Connecticut.

    b. Massachusetts.

    c. New York.

    d. Illinois.

5.    The ancient Greeks, Romans, and Arabs thought that mental illness was

    a. caused by evil spirits entering the body.

    b. a punishment for sins.

    c. a natural phenomenon.

    d. the result of witchcraft.

6.    Post World War II legislation that allocated funds for building psychiatric units was the

    a. National Mental Health Act.

    b. Economic Opportunity Act.

    c. Mental Retardation Facilities Act.

    d. Hill-Burton Act.

7.    Community mental health centers were established to

    a. offer consultation and educational services.

    b. offer outpatient care.

    c. bring mental health care closer to the people.

    d. all of the above.

8. Legislation that authorized federal funds to match local and state monies to build community health centers is the
   a. Mental Retardation Facilities and Community Mental Health Centers Construction Act.
   b. National Mental Health Act.
   c. both a and b.
   d. none of the above.

9. Legislation designed to help the poor and disadvantaged reach their full potential is the
   a. National Mental Health Act.
   b. Economic Opportunity Act.
   c. Mental Retardation Facilities Act.
   d. none of the above.

10. Recent trends in mental health care place emphasis on
    a. prevention of mental illness.
    b. returning the patient to an adequate level of functioning.
    c. community care.
    d. all of the above.

11. A nurse who observes cruelty to a patient and does not report it is
    a. legally guilty of cruelty.
    b. morally guilty of cruelty.
    c. just minding her own business.
    d. morally responsible to stop the cruelty herself.

12. A patient who is legally committed to an institution
    a. has the right to treatment.
    b. automatically loses his right to make decisions.
    c. must accept prescribed treatment.
    d. may receive only custodial care.

B. Match the contribution in column I with the name in Column II

| Column I | Column II |
|---|---|
| 1. published the first American textbook on psychiatry | a. Clifford Beers |
| 2. believed all illness was controlled by the stars and planets | b. Jean Martin Charcot |
| | c. Dorothea Lynde Dix |
| | d. Sigmund Freud |

| Column I | Column II |
|---|---|
| 3. used hypnotism to treat hysteria | e. Franz Mesmer |
| 4. worked for passage of legislation to improve care of the mentally ill in America | f. Paracelsus |
| | g. Philippe Pinel |
| 5. authored a book that made the public aware of the need for better care for the mentally ill | h. Benjamin Rush |
| 6. developed a technique called psychoanalysis | |
| 7. believed that the universe was filled with magnetic forces and that the mentally ill could be cured by bringing them into balance with the universe | |
| 8. began the movement toward humane treatment of the mentally ill by removing chains from patients | |

C. Briefly answer the following:

1. How do the changes in mental health care affect the role of the nurse?

2. Explain the purposes of standards for nursing care.

3. Explore the quality and the accessibility of care for the mentally ill in your particular community. Prepare a brief report and include proactive plans.

# CHAPTER 2
# STRESS AND
# MENTAL HEALTH

## OBJECTIVES

After studying this chapter, the student should be able to:

- State the characteristics of a healthy personality.
- Name the three stages of the General Adaptation Syndrome.
- List four factors that affect a person's ability to cope with stress.
- Name four rules of good health that help to maintain coping ability.
- Identify classifications of mental illness.

There are two major contributions of nursing to the health care system: the concept of holistic beings and a dedication to the promotion of a high degree of wellness. Nurses who are committed to these ideals, whether primarily engaged in mental or physical care, accept responsibility for fostering mental health and preventing mental illness. This is not an easy task, and it is made even more difficult because of the lack of a single definition for mental health. The factors which promote mental health are disputed even more. Many authorities even deny the existence of mental illness unless there is a definite change in the brain cells. Some authorities define mental health as a responsibility. They consider a person who accepts responsibility for his or her own behavior to be mentally healthy. Other people relate mental health to self-awareness. Still others consider mental health to be learned behavior. There is also disagreement on what may be termed healthy behavior. Acts that are unacceptable at one time may be considered acceptable or normal at another time. What is punished by one group may be approved by another group.

Even though mental health cannot be universally defined, most agree that it is a positive state. This means that it is more than the absence of disease. The person with mental health usually is considered to be self-directive. Generally, the person has a feeling of well-being, is productive, and enjoys life. He or she sets goals and realistic limits for activities.

Healthy people have the ability to accept and express love freely. There is a reaching out to help others. These people can stand alone when necessary or accept help from others without losing independence. Flexible and willing to try new things, they are eager to learn about themselves and the world around them.

Two factors influencing the way an individual functions are inherited characteristics or potential and the psychosocial environment, which includes nurturing received in childhood and circumstances encountered in life. Almost everyone displays some characteristics that would be considered unhealthy under certain circumstances. Occasionally, everyone becomes depressed, dependent, or loses enthusiasm. To be considered ill, however, the individual must display more of the abnormal behaviors and display them more consistently than most people.

Other mental health difficulties that pose major social, health, and economic problems in the United States include alcoholism, alienation, rebellion, drug abuse, racism, violence, and suicide. Many people need help in coping with the added stresses of disease or disaster. Millions of others, though not considered mentally ill, consistently function under anxiety.

## CLASSIFICATION OF MENTAL ILLNESS

For ease in studying, mental disorders are usually classified. For many years, all mental disorders were covered in the following general categories.

Mental Retardation encompassed all developmental disabilities.

Organic Brain Syndrome included conditions resulting in behavioral changes that could be traced to organic causes. Alzheimer's disease is one example.

Psychoses included diseases that resulted in severe abnormal behavior accompanied by a withdrawal from reality.

Psychoneuroses included forms of abnormal behavior milder than psychosis. The person with a neurosis was more in contact with the real world than was the psychotic individual.

Personality Disorders, or dysfunctional behaviors, were behaviors which interfered with the individual's ability to function effectively in society. They included such conditions as sexual deviation, abusive and violent behavior, alcoholism, and drug abuse.

Psychophysiological Disorders included conditions in which physical symptoms developed because of emotional problems.

These categories caused some difficulties because the boundaries were not clear and symptoms overlapped.

In 1980, the American Psychiatric Association published a new *Diagnostic and Statistical Manual (DMS-III)* that lists new classifications for mental disorders. Following is a *partial list* of the new classifications and some subtypes:

Disorders Usually First Evident in Infancy, Childhood, or Adolescence
    Mental Retardation
    Attention Deficit Disorder
    Conduct Disorder
    Anxiety Disorders of Childhood or Adolescence
    Eating Disorders

Organic Mental Disorders
    Organic Brain Syndromes, substance induced
    Organic Brain Syndromes, resulting from unknown causes

Substance Use Disorders
    Alcoholism
    Drug Dependence

Schizophrenic Disorders

Paranoid Disorders

Psychotic Disorders Not Elsewhere Classified

Affective Disorders

Anxiety Disorders

Somatoform Disorders

Dissociative Disorders

Psychosexual Disorders

Factitious Disorders

Disorders of Impulse Control Not Elsewhere Classified

Adjustment Disorders

Psychological Factors Affecting Physical Condition

Personality Disorders
    Antisocial
    Histrionic (Hysterical)
    Compulsive
    Passive-Aggressive
    Narcissistic
    Dependent

Conditions Not Attributable to a Mental Disorder
    Malingering
    Occupational Problems
    Marital Problems

Both the old and new terms undoubtedly will be used for some time.

## STRESS THEORY

According to Hans Selye, *stress* is a nonspecific response to any demand made on the body. Demands may range from a disappointment to a severe illness. Some stress is necessary, but too much stress may send the body into a state of exhaustion. Coping with stress requires a great deal of energy; the supply of this energy is limited.

A person's response to stress is only one theory used to explain mental illness. However, it provides a useful framework for the study and practice of mental health nursing. The theory of stress developed by Hans Selye provides the framework for this book. The stress framework is based on these assumptions:

- People are unique. Although people have the same physiological reactions to stress, they differ in their use of coping energy, the amount of energy available, their coping mechanisms, and available support.
- People become conditioned to coping with stress. Therefore, more effective coping methods can be learned.
- People are holistic. They are unified biological, spiritual, and emotional beings. Psychological and physical stress cannot be separated. What affects one aspect of an individual affects all other aspects.
- The person's internal and external environments are constantly changing. To remain in physiological and psychological balance, one must constantly adapt to these changes.

- Illness is a result of disruption in the stress adaptation mechanism (the person's ability to adjust to change).
- It is the nurse's responsibility to teach effective coping skills, provide physical and emotional support, and minimize stress in the patient's environment.

## Physiological Effects of Stress

The term *adaptive energy* was coined by Selye to indicate a force that the individual uses to adapt to stress. Adaptive energy is different from caloric energy, which is replenished by food. Selye found that demands, which he called *stressors*, cause chemical and structural changes that are manifestations of the body's attempt to maintain homeostasis, Figure 2-1. According to Selye, these variations represent the General Adaptation Syndrome (G.A.S.), which responds to any stimulus. He divides the General Adaptation Syndrome into three stages: the crisis stage, the adaptation stage, and the exhaustion stage.

In the crisis or alarm stage, the body mobilizes its forces to handle the stressors. The sympathetic nervous system is stimulated. Almost immediately, large amounts of the neurohormones epinephrine and norepinephrine are secreted into the bloodstream. The adrenal medulla is also stimulated, increasing and prolonging the epinephrine in the bloodstream. The heart rate increases and the blood vessels constrict to maintain adequate pressure. The respiratory muscles relax to increase the oxygen supply, and the digestive system, temporarily unneeded, decreases activity. These actions are presumably to save energy, but they may result in some annoying symptoms such as pale, cool skin; shivering; and sweating of the palms and soles. The person under severe stress may experience a pounding heart dilated pupils, insomnia, a dry mouth, nausea, and diarrhea.

In the adaptation or resistance stage, the adrenal cortex secretes increased amounts of glucocorticoids and mineralocorticoids. The mineralocorticoids help save fluids and sodium. The glucocorticoids suppress inflammation, mobilize fatty acids, and increase glucose levels providing fuel for energy. Protein is broken down and changed to amino acids and the lysosome membrane is stabilized to prevent cell destruction. If stress is prolonged or overwhelming and the adaptive energy is insufficient, the body enters into the third stage, exhaustion. The symptoms in this stage are similar to those in the alarm period. The body's ability to adjust is gone. The adaptive mechanism breaks down and the body is no longer able to resist.

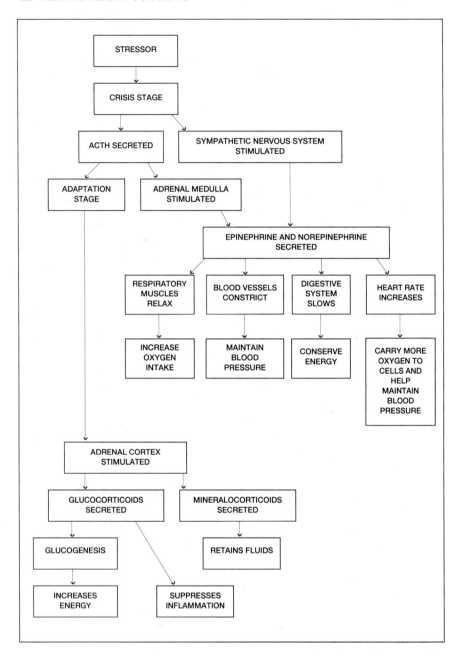

Fig. 2-1   Physiological effects of the General Adaptation Syndrome

## Coping Mechanisms

Stress is an automatic response and cannot be avoided. However, people can learn to conserve their adaptive energy. This is important because the energy supply is limited. How much is used for coping depends on conditioning. *Conditioning* occurs when one is continuously taught a behavior until it becomes automatic. Because of conditioning, same people handle a great deal of stress while others find a minimum of stress intolerable. Other factors which affect a person's ability to cope with stress include the degree of perceived danger, the immediate needs of the individual, the amount of support received from others, the person's beliefs about his or her ability to handle the stressful event, previous successes and failures in coping, and the amount of cumulative or concurrent stresses that must be handled.

Coping measures that use a minimal amount of energy are called *adaptive measures*. Coping measures that require a great amount of energy are called *maladaptive measures*. Generally, measures which deal directly with the stressful event or its symptoms are adaptive. Measures used to avoid conflict are considered less effective and some are maladaptive, Table 2-1. Adaptive measures which may be used when stressful events are confronted include:

- Utilizing support people
- Relaxing to alleviate tense muscles
- Problem solving
- Changing behavior
- Developing more realistic goals

**TABLE 2-1   Levels of Adaptation to the Stress Response**

| ADAPTIVE COPING MEASURES | LESS ADAPTIVE MEASURES | MALADAPTIVE MEASURES |
|---|---|---|
| Relaxation<br>Problem solving<br>Behavioral change<br><br>Developing more<br>  realistic goals | Some defense mechanisms<br>Avoidance<br>Denial<br><br>Sleepiness<br>Pointless activity<br>Physical withdrawal | Neurosis<br>Somatic disorders<br>Excessive use of alcohol<br>  or drugs<br>Some mental mechanisms<br>Excessive eating<br>Fantasy<br>Ritualistic behavior |

Measures used to avoid stress may include utilizing some defense mechanisms, extreme sleepiness, or depression. People who try to avoid stress may rely on rituals such as constant handwashing, or they may simply deny the stressful experience. Some people tend to transfer stress to an organ and develop physiological disorders such as asthma, heart failure, rheumatoid arthritis, ulcers, and perhaps even cancer. Still others may withdraw from their stressors through the excessive use of alcohol, drugs, or promiscuous sexual behavior.

The psychotic person has a lack of sufficient adaptive energy. This person finds stress so overwhelming that he or she withdraws from reality into a private world where there is comfort and little stress.

## STRESS AND THE NURSING PROCESS

The nursing process is a method of achieving patient care through deliberate systematic and individualized procedures. It serves as a guide in determining and organizing needs, setting priorities, and implementing and evaluating nursing intervention. It provides a systematic approach to the utilization of the stress theory. The nursing process consists of four subprocesses: assessment, planning, intervention, and evaluation.

### Assessment

Assessment is the analyzing of needs in terms of problems. According to the stress framework, a problem is any stressor with which the patient is unable to cope or of which the patient is unaware. Assessment is an ongoing process that begins with the initial contact, usually when the patient is admitted to the hospital. Determining the patient's stress level and coping mechanisms is part of the nurse's assessment of the patient. In order to assess effectively, the nurse observes and communicates with the patient and the patient's family. She then shares this information with the professional nurse and other health team members. Through observation, the nurse may be able to determine the following about the patient:

- Self-image
- Level of anxiety
- Level of coping
- Degree of contact with and orientation to the outside world
- Reaction to unfamiliar sights and sounds in the environment

Through communication, the nurse may learn the patient's:

- Knowledge of agency or hospital routines
- Interpretation of his health status
- Prior health habits
- Distressful symptoms
- Duration of the presenting problem
- Interpersonal relationships, especially with family members
- Degree of contact with reality
- Usual coping mechanisms

The information obtained through observation and communication is then used to determine possible causes of stress. Note the following examples.

Example 1:

> Mr. Jones is admitted to the hospital for a cholecystectomy. He appears very distressed. His wife tells the nurse that they have no insurance. They have been saving to buy a house, but now the money will be needed to pay the hospital bill.

**Cause of Stress.** Surgery is itself a stressor. Also, studies have shown that financial worries rank high as stressors for people being admitted to the hospital. People are able to cope with a certain amount of stress. However, when stressors accumulate, physical and psychological symptoms may appear. In this case, it is manifested as depression.

Example 2:

> Judy Ann, aged two, is admitted to the hospital with diarrhea and vomiting. Her mother states that Judy Ann has not used a bottle for about a year. Judy Ann sucks her thumb and cries for a bottle when her mother is gone.

**Cause of Stress.** In addition to stress caused by internal or external trauma, loss of usual coping resources can cause stress. Judy Ann may insist on her bottle because of the stress created by being separated from her mother, whom Judy Ann feels protects her from distressful events.

Example 3:

> Mrs. Thomas tells the nurse that she is frightened about impending labor. She asks if it is really as painful as everyone says. She states that she doesn't know how she will cope if it is painful because she cannot stand pain.

**Cause of Stress.** Mrs. Thomas is conditioned to maladaption. Conditioning can turn an otherwise tolerable stress into a *pathogenic* (disease-causing) stress.

Determining the underlying cause of stress is an important part of assessment. When the problem and possible causes of stress have been determined, the next step is to plan care to meet the needs of the patient.

## Planning

Planning involves determining goals, priorities, and nursing actions to help the patient. Nursing goals are desired changes that meet the needs of the patient. They are objectives that nursing actions achieve, but are not necessarily as specific as objectives. After goals are set, their order of priority is considered. The action that would best achieve the desired results is then determined.

Helping Mr. Jones obtain his home or pay his hospital bill would be beyond the scope of nursing and should not appear in the nursing care plan as a goal. In some instances, however, a referral to the social service department might be appropriate. An example of a nursing goal for Mr. Jones would be to enhance his usual adapting/coping mechanisms in order to enable him to handle the added stress of surgery.

Providing support is one way of enhancing coping mechanisms. Considering the resources available, the nurse could provide the needed support, or she could encourage Mrs. Jones to provide it. Since Mrs. Jones is also having difficulty coping, the action most likely to succeed is for the nurse to provide the care and support directly.

## Intervention

Intervention is the actual nursing measures used to help the patient. All interventions have a rationale based on sound nursing knowledge and theory. Interventions help the patient meet basic needs and include all actions taken to relieve stress and restore the patient's homeostasis. Supervision of activities of daily living is one way the nurse intervenes to help relieve the patient's stress. Other ways are encouraging patient participation in diversional activities, administration of medications, and manipulation of the patient's environment. Patients sometimes require controls on their activities. Other times, tasks are specifically assigned to them. Encouraging patients to socialize is an important intervention.

People who are able to socialize usually adapt better than those who are not able to socialize.

The nurse may also be involved in supportive counseling, either individually or as a co-therapist in a group. Teaching new coping mechanisms, following the prescribed course of treatment, and helping patients achieve homeostasis are other responsibilities which may be assigned to the nurse.

For Mr. Jones, appropriate nursing interventions might be to spend time with him, to encourage him to talk about his anxieties, and to demonstrate an understanding and empathetic attitude toward him.

## Evaluation

Evaluation involves determining whether or not the nursing intervention has been successful. It also includes the patient's response to the intervention. Mr. Jones appeared depressed when he was admitted. The success of the nursing intervention would be evaluated by observing Mr. Jones' subsequent behavior. For example, if he talked more, smiled, exhibited increased energy, and/or appeared more hopeful of the future, the nurse could assume that the intervention was successful.

Evaluation of patient progress is the responsibility of all members of the health team. In the nursing process, the licensed practical nurse (LPN) functions under the direction of the registered nurse. The responsibilities of the LPN involve direct patient care, so they will vary according to the situation and the patient's needs. Being in direct contact with the patients puts her in a position to see the day-to-day changes that determine the effectiveness of the plan, but the registered nurse is responsible for the overall assessment and plan of care.

The nurse can have a profound effect on patient progress because of her involvement and interaction. It is through the professionals and para-professionals around him that the patient gains support and learns to see himself as important. Knowledge that others genuinely care and expect improvement encourages the patient's recovery.

## STRESS AND THE NURSE

Constant contact with patients overwhelmed by stress is a stressor for the nurse. It may eventually cause the nurse to become overwhelmed.

This phenomenon is termed *burnout*. At best, it results in ineffective relationships. The nurse may become angry, display an attitude that the patients deserve their problems, or she may emotionally withdraw from the patients. To avoid burnout, the nurse may need to physically withdraw from the stressful situation and engage in other activities, Figure 2-2.

Even a well-adjusted person may have trouble thinking clearly or making constructive decisions during a crisis. Depending on the degree of stress perceived, there may be a heightened awareness of self, tension, and a feeling of ineffectiveness. There may also be depression and a lack of energy. Well-adjusted people use internal and external resources to conserve energy by making a realistic assessment of the problem. They also recognize and accept situations that cannot be changed and find alternative actions for those that can be changed.

**Fig. 2-2 Nurses enjoying a pleasant diversional activity.**

The nurse owes it to herself and her patients to follow rules of good health in order to prevent physical illness. A physically ill person has less ability to cope. A nurse who in unable to handle her own stressors adequately is unable to help others. The nurse should get adequate rest, proper nutrition, plenty of exercise, and engage in wholesome, enjoyable activities. She should work on strengthening her own adaptive methods.

## SUMMARY

There is little agreement on a definition for mental health. There is also little agreement on what may be termed a healthy personality. Most authorities believe that mental health is a positive quality—more than the absence of disease. The two factors influencing the way an individual functions are heredity, nurturing or potential, and the psychosocial environment.

Mental health problems are a major social difficulty. Mental illness is classified for ease in study.

According to Hans Seyle, stress is a nonspecific response to any stimulus. Symptoms that occur are the result of the body's attempt to adapt to stress. The body's attempt to adapt to stress is called the General Adaptation Syndrome (G.A.S.). Stress response is automatic, but people can learn to conserve energy. Factors that affect a person's ability to cope include: conditioning, degree of perceived danger, immediate needs, support received from others, beliefs about one's ability to handle the stressful situation, previous successes and failures, and the degree of accumulated or concurrent stress. Coping measures that the person uses to confront the stressful event are generally adaptive. Coping measures that avoid stress are loss adaptive, or maladaptive.

The nursing process is a method of achieving patient care through deliberate, systematic, and individualized procedures. It serves as a guide in determining and organizing care to lessen stress and enhance the patient's ability to cope with stress.

## SUGGESTED ACTIVITIES

- Visit a local mental health center or acute care facility and talk to a nurse about her duties.
- Discuss the meaning of mental health with a group of students.

- Have a class discussion about current attitudes toward the mentally ill.
- Recall the last time you experienced stress. Make a list of the coping mechanisms you used to deal with the situation.
- Read one or more of the following books:

*The Myth of Mental Illness: Foundations of a Theory of Personal Conduct* by Thomas S. Szasz (New York: Harper & Row, 1974).

*Reality Therapy: A New Approach to Psychiatry* by William Glasser (New York: Harper & Row, 1975).

*The Stress of Life* by Hans Seyle (New York: McGraw-Hill Book Co., 1978).

## REVIEW

A. Multiple choice. Select the best answer.
1. The mentally healthy person
   a. has no problems.
   b. is simply free from mental illness.
   c. sets realistic limits.
   d. is unchanging.

2. Symptoms associated with the stress response are the result of the body's attempt to
   a. run from the impending threat.
   b. conserve energy.
   c. identify the impending danger.
   d. shield the person from unpleasant experiences.

3. The purpose of the first stage of the G.A.S. is to
   a. alert the individual to danger.
   b. determine the extent of the danger.
   c. mobilize energy needed for adaptation.
   d. shield the individual from unpleasant experiences.

4. The physiological changes during the second G.A.S. stage are caused by hormones from the
   a. thyroid.
   b. thymus.
   c. pituitary.
   d. adrenals.

5. Coping mechanisms used to deal directly with stress are considered
   a. adaptive measures.
   b. less adaptive measures.
   c. nonadaptive measures.
   d. maladaptive measures.

6. It is important to use coping mechanisms that require a small amount of energy because
   a. excessive energy causes psychosis.
   b. adaptive energy is limited.
   c. sleep is impossible during stress.
   d. the appetite is decreased during stress.

7. The term *burnout* refers to
   a. a physical exhaustion because of overwork.
   b. making decisions during a crisis.
   c. the nurse who acts in a forgetful, hostile manner.
   d. being overwhelmed by stress.

B. Match the subtype listed in column II with the new classification if mental illness in column I.

| Column I | Column II |
|---|---|
| 1. Disorders Usually First Evident in Infancy, Childhood, or Adolescence | a. Antisocial |
| 2. Organic Mental Disorders | b. Mental Retardation |
| 3. Personality Disorders | c. Alcoholism |
| 4. Substance Use Disorders | d. Organic Brain Syndromes, Resulting from Unknown Causes |
| | e. Malingering |

C. Briefly answer the following.

1. List four characteristics of the healthy personality.

2. Name the three stages of the General Adaptation Syndrome.

3. List four factors that affect a person's ability to cope with stress.

4. Name four rules of good health the nurse needs to follow in order to maintain coping ability.

# CHAPTER 3
# UNDERSTANDING SELF
# AND OTHERS

## OBJECTIVES

After studying this chapter, the student should be able to:

- Define self-concept.
- Name the two important factors in personality development.
- State the significant contributions made to the study of growth and development by Erikson, Maslow, Sullivan, and Havinghurst.
- Identify development tasks for each stage of the life cycle as proposed by Erikson.
- List the needs of people as developed by Maslow.
- Identify the common mental mechanisms.
- List three advantages of increased self-awareness.

The nurse-patient relationship is the basis of nursing. It is through this relationship that the nurse assesses the patient's needs, assists in determining the care to be given, and evaluates this care. For the patient, this relationship depends, in part, on the nurse's knowledge of people. An understanding of how personality develops and the ability to recognize behavior and motives as they actually exist are essential to developing a helping relationship.

## PERSONALITY DEVELOPMENT

An individual's personality continues to develop throughout the life cycle. It is dependent on two interacting factors, the *hereditary base or potential* and the *psychosocial environment*. Each individual has a unique makeup that is contained within the genes from conception. This makeup sets the direction and ultimate potential, or ceiling for the individual's achievements. Whether or not an individual fulfills his or her potential is dependent on the nurturing, support, and opportunities available in the environment and the type and number of stressors encountered throughout the life cycle.

There are many theories of personality development, and none has the answer to all aspects of the subject. This chapter is based on the combined work of Erikson, Havinghurst, Maslow, and Sullivan, Table 3-1. These men were selected because their theories better fit the framework for this book. For other theories, refer to Chapter 5.

**TABLE 3-1**
**Selected Theories of Personality Development**

| THEORISTS | IDEAS ON PERSONALITY DEVELOPMENT |
|---|---|
| Erik Erikson | 1. Develops over the life span.<br>2. Affected by the environment.<br>3. Divided into stages.<br>4. Each stage has a specific task to be accomplished.<br>5. Goal is task accomplishment. |
| Abraham Maslow | 1. Develops over the life span.<br>2. Affected by the environment.<br>3. Divided into needs, which are used as motivators.<br>4. Goal is self-actualization. |
| Robert Havinghurst | 1. Develops over the life span.<br>2. Influenced by Erikson.<br>3. Developed set of tasks within each of Erikson's stages.<br>4. Goal is to learn increasingly higher level skills. |
| Harry Stack Sullivan | 1. Develops over the life span.<br>2. Maternal relationships very significant.<br>3. Satisfying interpersonal relationships important to growth.<br>4. Anxiety stimulates growth.<br>5. Overwhelming stress retards growth.<br>6. The goal is security. |

Erik Erikson's work was done in the early 1900s. Until that time, Freud had been the leading theorist. Unlike Freud, Erikson looked at growth potential rather than pathology. Where Freud thought personality developed by the age of five, Erikson carried his theory throughout the life cycle. He recognized stages and named certain developmental tasks that must be accomplished during each of the stages. The stages are infancy, toddler, preschool, school age, adolescence, adult, and old age.

Abraham Maslow is recognized as the founder of humanistic psychology. He stresses the need to provide nurturance, acceptance, love, a feeling of belonging, and a sense of self-worth. He developed a hierarchy of needs to serve in motivating behavior. Like Erikson, he viewed personality development as a lifelong process and believed that it was affected by the environmental conditions under which the person lived.

Robert Havinghurst was an educator who developed a set of tasks to be mastered during each stage of the life cycle. These tasks were based on the work of Erikson, Table 3-2. Accomplishment of the tasks in each stage set the foundation for the learning of the higher level skills of the next stage.

### TABLE 3-2
### Developmental Tasks in the Life Cycle

| Age | Erikson's Developmental Tasks | Specific Developmental Tasks Based on the Work of Havinghurst |
|---|---|---|
| **Infancy** (Birth to 18 months | Trust versus mistrust | Differentiate self from the environment<br>Begin to develop a self-concept<br>Develop trust<br>Develop a relationship with a caring person or persons<br>Learn to sit, stand and walk<br>Learn to feed self |
| **Toddler** (18 months to 3 years | Autonomy versus shame and doubt | Develop autonomy<br>Begin to develop an identity<br>Develop motor skills<br>Learn to control bowel movements<br>Learn to talk |
| **Preschool** (3 to 6 years | Initiative versus guilt | Develop a conscience<br>Develop initiative<br>Begin to relate to others socially<br>Learn sexual role identity<br>Begin to fantasize about the future<br>Adjust to prolonged absence from parent (if the child goes to nursery school) |

## TABLE 3-2 (continued)

| Age | Erikson's Developmental Tasks | Specific Developmental Tasks Based on the Work of Havinghurst |
|---|---|---|
| **School Age** (6 to 12 years) | Industry versus inferiority | Develop pleasure in work completed<br>Learn and validate social role<br>Learn to relate to age mates<br>Develop musculature for sports and school activities<br>Adjust to prolonged absence from home<br>Adjust to a structured schedule<br>Achieve independence in personal care<br>Increase learning skills |
| **Adolescence** (12 to 18 years) | Identity versus role diffusion | Acquire a sense of identity<br>Establish a new role<br>Achieve more mature relationships with friends<br>Accept changed body image<br>Accept new sexual feelings<br>Achieve emotional independence<br>Develop intellectual skills<br>Clarify values |
| **Young Adult** (18 to 35 years) | Intimacy versus isolation | Adjust to college or employment<br>Select a life-style<br>Accept adult responsibility<br>Achieve economic independence<br>Establish an intimate relationship<br>Select a mate<br>Establish a home<br>Accept a new social role as parent or mate |
| **Middle Adult** (35 to 65 years) | Generativity versus stagnation | Achieve economic security<br>Help children to become responsible citizens<br>Assess accomplishments<br>Adjust to children leaving the home<br>Adjust to new life-style<br>Accept the physical changes of middle age<br>Develop leisure time activities |
| **Senescence** (65 years to death)` | Integrity versus despair | Adjust to decreased health<br>Accept a new identity<br>Get life in order<br>Accept dependence as needed<br>Accept reality of own death<br>Adjust to death of spouse and/or friends<br>Adjust to retirement<br>Review life<br>Establish relationships with peers<br>Adjust to new life-style, if necessary |

Harry Stack Sullivan was a neo-Freudian. Like Freud, he believed in the significance of the maternal relationship in personality development. He felt security was the major goal in life, and it was achieved through satisfying interpersonal relationships. He felt anxiety stimulated growth, but overwhelming stress was to be avoided.

## Infancy (Birth to Eighteen Months)

The newborn is well aware of his environment. He can see within seven to ten inches as well as hear and discriminate between sounds. He also has a preference for particular visual and auditory stimuli. He likes complex patterns, curved lines, and the human face. He follows brightly colored objects with his eyes and pays more attention to the high-pitched female voice. Music seems to have a soothing effect on him. The infant requires stimuli for his continued growth. As he grows older, the stimuli must become more varied and complex, Figure 3-1. The newborn infant is particularly sensitive to tactile stimuli and cannot by spoiled by attention. Cuddling, stroking, rocking, and talking to him are essential to his optimal growth. Neglecting an infant who is wet, hungry, or otherwise unhappy causes added stress and inhibits development.

**Fig. 3-1  Stimuli must become more varied and complex as the baby grows.**

The newborn is almost totally dependent on his environment and does not see himself as separate and distinct from it. He responds to his environment in a general manner rather than a specific way. When the newborn is hungry, hot, hurt, or otherwise uncomfortable, he experiences stress. He reacts by crying and vigorously moving his arms or legs. His reaction to all uncomfortable stimuli is the same.

The infant's crying and moving behavior cues the caring person, usually the parent, to act. If the action relieves stress, the infant begins to associate that person with relief and to see that person as good. Because the infant cannot separate himself from his environment, he also sees himself as good. This is the beginning of the self-concept.

*Self-concept* refers to the way in which a person feels, views, or thinks of himself. The self-concept is strong but not static. It continues to develop as the child interacts with others. What significant others tell the child, as well as all of the child's experiences, successes, and failures, helps to mold and change the self-concept. The infant is extremely sensitive to the attitudes of those around him. He feels good when he senses satisfaction, but he experiences bad feelings about himself when he experiences anxiety. Mild anxiety is a motivator for action. The baby learns that crying will bring relief for stress. Frequent feelings of anxiety, however, lead the infant to see himself as bad. If the child is told he is good, he believes it; but if he is constantly criticized or ignored, his self-concept is poor, Table 3-3.

At one time it was thought that the infant was totally dependent. He was simply a receiver of stimuli. Now it is known that children are born with certain temperaments. These temperaments influence the infant's environment. Research has shown that an infant can and does effect child-parent relationships. Dr. Berry Brazelton was the pioneer in recognizing the individuality of infants and the infant's ability to influence his or her environment. The infant's reaction to parental attention may actually help to generate inadequate or inconsistent parenting patterns. A temperament leading to poor parenting can quickly initiate a cycle of maladaptive behaviors on the part of the parent and child. This may lead to a poor self-concept and a mistrust of the environment.

The developmental task identified for the infant by Erikson is the learning of trust. As mentioned previously, experience with the caring person is the basis for developing trust. As the child grows and learns to differentiate himself from the environment and meets new challenges, trust becomes very important. The child must trust enough to feel comfortable in new situations, and he must still trust others to meet his needs.

**TABLE 3-3**
**Statements Made by Significant Others May Have an Effect**
**on the Child's Developing Self-concept**

| Statements that may have a positive effect on the child's self-concept | Statements that may have a negative effect on the child's self-concept |
|---|---|
| "Something is troubling you. Would you like to talk about it?"<br><br>"Right now I really need to finish this job, but I will be glad to listen to you in a few minutes. Would that be all right?" | "Don't bother me. Can't you see I am busy?" |
| "You may find it works better if you do it this way."<br><br>"You seem to be having a problem with that. Can I help?" | "That's not the way to do it. Can't you do anything right?" |
| "What would you think about adding this scarf to that dress?"<br><br>"Have you thought about wearing your blue dress tonight? It looks so pretty on you." | "You're not going out dressed like that are you? You never did have any fashion sense." |
| "What you did was very wrong."<br>"I am really upset with your behavior." | "You're a bad boy." |
| "This is one way I have found that seems to be more efficient. May I show you?"<br><br>"I found if I do it this way I get the job done thoroughly. It helps me remember all the details so I don't have to do it again." | "Every time you do something, I have to do it over again." |
| "Thank you for helping me."<br>"I love you."<br>"You're very special." | "Did you get that done yet?"<br>"Sometimes you make me so angry." |

The developmental tasks developed by Havinghurst are also based on trust as shown in Table 3-2.

**Failure to Thrive.** Anxiety is manifested in the infant by sleep and feeding problems and excessive crying. Extreme stress may develop into a condition called *failure to thrive* in which the infant fails to gain weight. There are some physical reasons for infant's not gaining weight, and these should be ruled out first by the physician. The term *failure to thrive*, however, is usually used to identify infants who fail to grow and develop when there is no physical cause. If not reversed, this condition can lead to death. It is estimated that 50 percent of infants who fail to thrive do so because of poor family relationships. Parents may feel inadequate. They may not react to the infant because the infant's responses do not meet with parent expectations, or they may simply lack knowledge of the child's psychosocial needs. Nurses may find it necessary to make the parents aware of the need to hold and talk to their infants. The necessity of promptly and consistently meeting the infant's needs cannot be overemphasized.

**Separation Anxiety.** Separation anxiety is the feeling the child has when separated from a familiar face. It usually occurs around the sixth month and extends into the toddler years. The child experiences feelings of distress and responds by screaming. He may withdraw and/or refuse to eat. There may be sleep disturbances. If the separation is short, no permanent damage results, but if separation continues, the child may become depressed. He may regress to an earlier stage of development or may even fail to thrive.

When parent and child are reunited, the child may act as if the parent were a stranger. The child seems not to trust any longer. It is for this reason that parents are encouraged to remain with their hospitalized infants. Separation anxiety seems to occur less in infants who have had several care givers.

## Toddler (Eighteen Months to Three Years)

The young toddler has a long trunk and short legs. Because his brain is three-quarters the size of the adult brain, he is top heavy and his weak abdominal muscles give him a potbellied look. As each year passes, the child's legs grow longer. His muscles grow stronger, and he begins to take on the trimmer, childlike appearance.

The toddler is self-centered and possessive. He cannot share a toy with which he is playing, but the older toddler may, primarily to please a parent, pick out another toy and offer it. Children in this group have short attention spans, and everything they want they want now. They are easily frustrated if they do not get their way.

Erikson calls this period the *stage of autonomy versus shame and doubt.* A sense of identity is gradually emerging during this time. The toddler sees himself as an independent individual. As motor skills develop, he begins to realize he can function with some autonomy. Though the toddler enjoys his independence, he couples the enjoyment with a fear of giving up dependence. The child is constantly struggling with when to let go and when to hold on. He often dawdles because he wants to please his parents, but at the same time he wants to assert himself. Sometimes this dependence is transferred to objects like pillows, blankets, or dolls. Because these objects are movable and can be carried around by the child, they fit better into his growing world, Figure 3-2.

**Fig. 3-2 This toddler clings to a doll as she learns to gain some independence in her widening world.**

Autonomy is characterized by independence in some activities of daily living such as moving, feeding self, and partially dressing and undressing. The establishment of bowel control is also a measure of autonomy. The child's frequent use of the word *no* is another measure of autonomy. As he learns that he has some control over his environment, his negativism is his way of challenging authority and determining his own limits. The toddler also engages in rituals that must be strictly adhered to. This ritualistic behavior provides some predictability and security to his changing life.

As mobility and curiosity increase, the child needs new stimuli to prevent boredom. For this reason, toddlers often got into dangerous situations. It is important that parents give toddlers some freedom, but it is also important that consistent and realistic restrictions be placed on the child. It is through these restrictions that the child learns the boundaries of safety and acceptable behavior. Self-doubt is more apt to occur when the child does not have these parental controls. Frequent criticism and constant disapproval, however, often lead to shame.

**Fears.** As the child grows, he is confronted with increasing challenges, and new challenges lead to fears. Each age group has its particular fears. For the toddler, darkness is frightening. Parental support and understanding, along with a security blanket, are needed. Night-lights can also help alleviate this fear.

Stranger anxiety is a continuation of separation anxiety seen in the younger child. The toddler usually reacts in a more subtle way by clinging to the parent and refusing to cooperate. When parents are going away, they need to provide a consistent substitute or nurse who will use supportive behaviors with the child. The parent substitute or nurse who is a stranger needs to recognize this fear and approach the child slowly, smiling and speaking softly. The use of toys also helps to alleviate some of the anxiety. In fact, play therapy is the best way of communicating with the child. It is advantageous to have the parent remain as long as possible.

Sibling rivalry also creates anxiety in the toddler. The child is not accustomed to sharing his parents with anyone else; therefore, he may feel he has lost their love, that the new child is taking his place. He may regress to the infant's level of behavior in an attempt to regain his parents' love. He may also react with anger and aggression toward the "intruder." The toddler is capable of real harm if the situation is not recognized and dealt with.

A new infant can easily take all of the parents' time, and the toddler just seems to get in the way. The stress the toddler feels at being pushed aside can be diminished if the parents find some special time just for him. There are things the young child can do to help with the infant's care, and he should be encouraged to participate according to his ability. Frequent references to "our baby" may also help in making the toddler feel that he is still a part of the family.

## Preschool (Three to Six Years)

Erikson terms this period *initiative versus guilt.* Since the preschooler has achieved some autonomy and has mastered the ability to ambulate, he is ready to meet the new challenges in his ever-widening sphere. Initiative is needed for further exploration of the environment. The preschooler has a consuming curiosity and questions everything incessantly. He runs, jumps, and climbs, always exploring the limits of his world. The restrictions that the parent or caring person places on the child, however, continue to be important. Without restrictions, the child is unable to develop a sense of values. At first, the child does what is expected because of fear of punishment. The rules are eventually internalized and become values. The values then develop into what is commonly called a *conscience.* Too much restriction, though, may result in the child's fear of further exploration and of trying new experiences. This child is unable to successfully accomplish the developmental task of initiative and experiences guilt in normal activities and interpersonal relationships. For this reason, it is important that the child be allowed to explore within limits of safety. It is also important that initiative be encouraged and questions answered simply and truthfully so that growth will continue.

At the age of three, the child begins to socialize. At first the child plays next to other children and later with them. Play is important to the preschooler. It relieves anxiety, stimulates cognition and imagination, and increases motor skills.

Aggressive behavior is common. This child enjoys roughhouse play with a parent or a friend, and he may be destructive to his own toys. With consistent and firm limits, along with parental support and understanding, the child will learn to control his behavior.

Sometime during this stage, the child begins to fantasize about the future, Figure 3-3. These daydreams may eventually lead to the choice of an adult role. The preschooler may also have frightening nightmares because his imagination is so vivid. During periods of semisleep, before he wakes completely, the child may see monsters in his dreams. He then needs reassurance and comforting from his parents. A night-light may also help. The preschooler enjoys participating in adult activities and should be given simple responsibilities. He also enjoys mimicking adults and may be seem dressing up or talking like his parents, Figure 3-4. Some significant relationships with other adults may develop.

**Fig. 3-3 This preschool child enjoys dressing up as a cowboy and pretending he is riding his horse.**

Fig. 3-4  This preschooler enjoys dressing up as her mother.

**Enuresis.** Enuresis is the involuntary wetting of the bed or clothes after the child has been toilet trained. It is a condition seem in the preschooler and young school-age child. There are physical reasons, but sometimes bed-wetting can be attributed solely to stress. The exact cause needs to be determined, but often the condition is caused by poor interpersonal relationships. If this is found to be the case, the preferred treatment is behavior modification.

## School Age (Six to Twelve Years)

School is important for the cognitive processes of thought, reasoning, comprehension, and memory development. Because of the length of time the child spends in school, it has a great impact on his personality as well. It is in school that the child continues growth toward independence and relies more on teachers and peers rather than parents. Through his teachers and primarily his friends, the child has an opportunity to test and modify his ideas, feelings, and behaviors. Relating to friends helps the child learn to cooperate, compromise, and complete.

At first, friendship associations are informal and loosely structured; eventually, they become more organized. Same-sex clubs and secret societies evolve, and some very good and lasting friendships develop, Figure 3-5. Same-sex friends discuss parental relationships and problems with siblings, thus providing support to each other. They also validate each other's goals and desires.

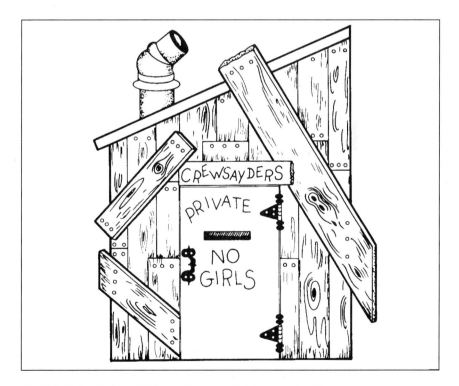

Fig. 3-5 School-aged children enjoy secret clubs involving the same sex.

According to Erikson, this is the stage of *industry versus inferiority*. If the child receives recognition for work well done and is accepted by his peers, the child's self-concept is enhanced. If he fails, the child begins to feel inferior.

Normally young school-age children enjoy learning. They apply themselves to the accomplishment of intellectual and motor skills and receive satisfaction from their successes. If the child fails to achieve a sense of industry, resulting in feelings of inferiority, he may then continue to be reluctant to try new tasks as he grows to adulthood.

Parents need to encourage their child's intellectual pursuits and praise his accomplishments. Because the school-aged child will try to meet them, parental expectations need to be realistic. Assigning the child to do simple chores around the house not only teaches skill but it also helps the child develop a sense of responsibility as a family member. By giving their child an allowance, parents help their child learn judgment and money management.

The child continues to need limits set by the parents as well as discipline for infractions of the rules. Discipline needs to be consistent and appropriate to the situation and age of the child. There also needs to be follow-through. For example, a child is given five minutes of time out, a behavior modification technique in which the child is removed from the possibility of getting attention. This action will be effective only if the child actually stays the entire five minutes. School-aged children often try to escape discipline.

Sibling rivalry may still exist, especially in the young school-aged child. Normally it becomes less intense as the child grows and it eventually disappears. Although siblings fight among themselves, they will often join together against an outside threat. Sometimes sibling rivalry does remain unresolved. It can then continue throughout the life cycle, resulting in increased stress.

For the child who has not attended nursery school, entry into school can represent the first prolonged absence from the security of the family. Children who have not developed trust, autonomy, and initiative in earlier stages can become fearful about attending school.

**School Phobia.** Children show some distinctive fears at all ages. The infant reacts to loud noises or fear of falling with the Moro reflex. The young child cries in the presence of strangers and clings to mother. The toddler fears animals and the preschooler dreads the dark.

A fear becomes important when it is severe and persistent and when it interferes with the child's ability to function effectively. School phobia is a fairly common problem in the school-aged child. The child who suffers from this phobia is often intelligent and achievement oriented, but refuses to go to school. The child may give many excuses, present various physical complaints, and display anxiety.

School phobia occurs more often in the first five grades, but it also is seen in the adolescent. The phobia may result from traumatic experiences at school, a long illness, or academic failure, but the most frequent cause is thought to be separation anxiety. Many phobic children are immature and excessively dependent. They frequently have overprotective parents.

**Encopresis.** Encopresis is the inability to control bowel movements in a child who has previously gained control. Involuntary stooling may be due to chronic constipation, but most often it has an emotional cause. Generally the child is reacting to some type of stress such as felt rejection by a parent. The condition causes further stress because the child is unable to hide the problem from friends and classmates. He will certainly be ridiculed and teased unmercifully. The problem must be recognized and dealt with immediately. Because the child's inability to control his bowels causes embarrassment to the parents as well, they may not seek professional help. They may verbally chastise the child or even beat him as a punishment. This only adds to his stress and increases the problem. The treatment of choice is behavior modification (see Chapter 4).

## Adolescence (Twelve to Eighteen Years)

The goal of adolescence is the attainment of adult stature, privileges, and responsibilities. This means that the adolescent must learn to give up his dependence and accept a more independent role. He has to provide for his own basic needs, select and prepare for a career, decide on a permanent life-style, and establish his own identity.

Adolescence is a period of vast changes. The teenager must forge new biological and social roles while coping with strange new feelings and a widening cognitive sphere. The fact that everything seems to be changing at once increases the child's chances of experiencing stress. The growth spurt, coupled with secondary sex characteristics, often makes the child feel awkward and self-conscious. His body looks, acts, and feels differently. Moods change rapidly. One minute the child is up and the very next he is down. Boredom is prevalent. The young adolescent can be seen wandering aimlessly with his same-sex friends because he can think of nothing exciting to do. Because he is bored, because it represents a challenge, or simply to test his limits, the teenager may damage property, steal, or break other community rules. It is estimated that 95 percent of adolescents do something for which they would be arrested if caught.

Teens, especially young teens, are introspective and spend much time daydreaming. Their thoughts and ideas are then shared with friends. Because the teenager is trying to break away from dependence on the family, peers are used to clarify the child's worth, his relationship with others, and his place in the world. Parental values that the child has internalized and previously followed are challenged. Values are individual rules that govern behavior. They form the basis for making life's decisions. Personal values are developed by comparing parental and social standards with one's own beliefs. Value clarification is a developmental task of the adolescent. The child tests his beliefs and parental standards by screening them through peers.

The peer group is extremely important to the young adolescent. Being different is the predominant fear. The child will dress, talk, and behave like his friends. Both boys and girls spend hours in front of the mirror to make their appearance acceptable. They are very choosey about clothing. Skin problems such as acne are a major embarrassment. Under the influence of peers, some teens may give up family religious beliefs, while others change church affiliations. Others may choose a life-style objectionable to parents. In late adolescence, the identity emerges. The child is clearer about his beliefs. He no longer is quite as dependent on the peer group as he was and has established his own individuality. Although parental values are questioned and even temporarily discarded, most children eventually incorporate many of the old values into their adult life.

Erikson has assigned the task of *establishing identity* to this age group. Part of identity development centers around the child's learning to relate to the opposite sex, Figure 3-6. If the teenager is unable to establish an identity, he will feel self-conscious and have doubts about himself and his role. Although the shift away from the family is accelerated during this time, the adolescent still needs parental controls. They provide some security to his otherwise unstable world. Too much parental control, however, can stifle identity formation.

Adolescence is a stormy time for parents as well as for children. The teenager may resent demands made by his parents and refuse to accept their advice. At the same time, he still expects the parents to pay the bills, feed him, and do his laundry. He wants the privileges of adulthood, but not the responsibilities.

Adolescents coin new words unfamiliar to the parents. This tends to interfere with the effectiveness of communication (see Chapter 8).

**Fig. 3-6 Part of an adolescent's search for identity.**

Parents may fear the dangers and temptations the child may face such as accidents, alcohol, drugs, and early pregnancy. They are fearful of entrusting adolescents to their own judgment and want to protect them. The parent may be frightened because he or she sees this as a test on the effectiveness of parenting. If the child succumbs to one of the temptations, it may be interpreted by the parent to mean that he or she has failed. Parents may also see this time as the last chance to influence their child's life. In desperation, they push more demands and insist upon obedience. The child, feeling overwhelmed, may retaliate. Rather than changing the child's behavior, parental demands tend to increase the rift.

Contrary to popular opinion, the rift only *seems* to be great. As the child grows to adulthood, it becomes evident that the distance between parent and child was, in most families, only superficial. Parents and children do have disagreements, but they primarily disagree over such things as the use of the telephone and the car, curfews, appearance, and loud music.

Teens enjoy music and, in fact, do not seem to be able to get along without it. They usually have the stereo blaring continuously. When out of the house, many teens can be seen with portable stereos or Walkmans. Television, movies, and the VCR are popular forms of entertainment. Teens particularly like adventure stories and stories of conflicts between generations.

Teens have a need for intimacy, which involves sharing confidences with friends. This sharing is often done on the telephone, with the child actually tying up the phone for hours, Figure 3-7. This is one of the points of contention between parent and child, but the parent must realize that the telephone is an important part of the child's growth process. This is true for three reasons: (1) Talking on the phone takes up time and so lessens boredom; (2) things are constantly changing in the teen's life, and the need to share with friends is felt as urgent; and (3) the adolescent finds talking on the phone easier because the distance between the parties provides some safety when sharing intimacies.

**Early and Late Maturing.** Early and late maturing can cause stress for the teen. The child whose body changes occur much earlier or much later than those of his peers is placed in the position of being different at the very time when differences are intolerable. Early maturing girls may be given prestige by their classmates, but they also experience some difficulties. They usually associate with older teens who share their physical matura-

Figure 3-7  Teens often find it easier to talk on the telephone.

tion. Unfortunately, they do not share the same interests or the same level of judgment as do their older friends. Adults seem to expect the early maturing girl to act more mature, which may frustrate her. She feels awkward dating prepubescent boys her own age, but she may find herself over her head if she dates older ones.

Early maturing boys seem to have the easiest time. They tend to be good at athletics; therefore, they have the respect of both boys and girls. They tend to take leadership roles and retain them. Adults give them more freedom and responsibility.

Late maturing girls may be anxious about when their body changes will occur, but they do not feel the stress that early maturing girls do. When puberty occurs, late maturing girls are more intellectually and emotionally ready for it.

The child that seems to suffer the most is the late maturing boy. He has to watch his classmates, both male and female, pass him by in height and maturation. His small stature and high-pitched voice can become the object of ridicule and teasing. Because of his size, he is unable to successfully compete in contact sports with his larger age mates. Undressing in the locker room is often a source of great embarrassment for him. Many young boys are acutely concerned about their failure to develop and worry that something is drastically wrong with themselves.

Both boys and girls need knowledge concerning puberty. They need to know that the time the changes occur has little effect on the degree of maturation. They also need to know that the normal age range for puberty is wide.

**Teen Suicide.** Teen suicide is an ever-increasing problem. The depressed adolescent is of growing concern to the community. It is important that the child be identified as quickly as possible so that proper treatment can be started. Usually a child thinking of suicide gives one or more of the following clues. He expresses his intentions and/or feelings to someone. He withdraws to an abnormal degree. Grades usually drop drastically, and he pays less attention to appearances. The child sometimes overindulges in alcohol or drugs, and his driving becomes more reckless. It is suspected that many deaths attributed to accidents are, in reality, suicides.

Why this problem exists is not readily known, but there are several possible factors that contribute to the child's decision to end his life. The many stressors the child must face in his transition to adulthood are often overwhelming. He may be unable to cope with a loss such as rejection by a girlfriend or the actual death of a friend. He may fear he cannot meet his life's expectations that have been set by himself or his parents, or he may simply be lonely and bored.

There seems to be an increase in teen suicide when there is little or no adult guidance or support, where drugs and alcohol are abused, in teens who are pregnant, or where a friend or classmate had committed suicide. The adolescent most apt to take his own life feels that he has no purpose. He feels he is of little value because he contributes nothing worthwhile to society. His self-esteem is low. Because he has no control over his life, he cannot change things.

If the nurse suspects that a child may be thinking of suicide, she should verify her suspicions. Not only is it proper to ask the child about his intentions, but it is a responsibility. The child is usually very willing to talk about his intentions. The nurse can say, "Have you had any thoughts of suicide?" or "Are you planning on hurting yourself?"

The teenager contemplating suicide needs to be placed in a protective environment. Certainly, if the causative stressor is one that can be changed, it should be taken care of immediately. If it cannot be changed, the child needs to be watched very carefully. Sometimes a contract is used to prevent him from making an attempt while treatment is in progress. The child is asked to promise in writing that he will not try to harm himself for a specific period of time. At the end of each time period, the contract is renewed. Even though teens may use the threat of suicide to gain attention, it is more often a cry for help. A threat, whether expressed or intimated, should never be ignored. If the child gets the opportunity, he will probably attempt the suicide and may be successful.

The nurse can help the suicidal child by encouraging activities that will improve his self-image and by showing the child that she cares about him personally. The child needs adult guidance in developing goals and support in adjusting to his changing status. He needs to develop better coping mechanisms and to learn problem-solving methods. Most basically, he needs to know that someone is listening to him and really hearing him. For more information on depression and suicide, see Chapters 9 and 12.

**Anorexia Nervosa and Bulimia.** There has been an increased awareness of and interest in all types of eating disorders in the past few years. The two conditions that primarily affect teenagers and young adults, anorexia nervosa and bulimia, are now reaching epidemic proportions. The incidence of anorexia alone has been estimated at 0.24 to 1.6 persons annually per 100,000 population. Mortality rates caused by these disorders range from 3 to 5 percent.

Although much work is being done in this area, the cause or causes of anorexia and bulimia are still unknown and treatment methods remain controversial. It used to be thought that the cause of these eating disorders was developmental, that the starvation syndrome simplifies the anorexic's life. The body that retains a prepubescent figure can help the victim avoid the conflicts of autonomous growth, competition, sexual identity, and social independence. Other authorities, however, lay responsibility on the effects of the media's emphasis on thinness on the adolescent's normal concern about body image. Another group blames faulty family relationships. Patients with eating disorders appear to have difficulty separating and individuating themselves from their families. They manifest much ambivalence and unexpressed anger towards their families. When taking a family history, the professional may note that the family has continuously used food to express love or gain control. A fourth group says the cause is physiological or, at least, there is a physiological tendency to the disorder.

Whatever the cause, the teenagers most likely to have one of these disorders are from middle-class or upper-class white families. They are usually described as being intelligent and well behaved. Eating disorder patients often have restricted their own personal feelings. Many are shy and, being distrustful, do not easily communicate verbally. They are perfectionistic and self-sacrificing. They have probably been overprotected in some areas and given unrealistic expectations in others. Many have experienced a super togetherness in their family life with overprotectiveness, conflict avoidance, and rigidity. This family experience has been described as *enmeshment*. The family input fails to verify the developing child as a competent person who can function in an independent way. These children have unrealistic views of their body images along with feelings of inadequacy. Physical development is retarded and amenorrhea may occur. Normal hunger urges are repressed.

Anorexia nervosa is a disorder characterized by a loss of at least 25 percent of the body weight without a physical cause. There is an intense preoccupation with weight gain to the point of obsession. These children are constantly dieting and exercising to lose weight even to the point of starvation and hyperactivity. They have an intense fear of becoming fat and tend to see themselves as fat even after they become emaciated.

Bulimia is an episodic condition in which large quantities of food are consumed in a short period of time. For example, 50,000 calories may be eaten in only one or two hours. This is called *binge eating*. These children then consciously take measures to clear their digestive tract of the unwanted food and excess calories. They may take diuretics, laxatives, and/or emetics or they may physically force themselves to vomit. This is called *purging*. These children often plan for these binge-purge episodes in advance by storing food and supplies that will be needed. These children may have hunger attacks at any time, so they resist eating with friends or family. During the hunger attacks they lose control of their behavior and become unaware of people around them. They have been known to do things that would otherwise embarrass them. The binges are so strong that bulimics sometimes eat from garbage cans, off the floor, or even from the dog's dish. The bulimic may have self-deprecating thoughts when the binge is over and become very depressed. They are a suicide risk.

There is a question as to whether these conditions are distinct or if they are simply stages in the same disorder. The question arises because most anorexics do indulge in binge eating. There is a difference in their characteristics, though. The anorexic will play with food, often complain that it is not cooked right, and will be easily distracted. The bulimics, on the other hand, are intent on the task of eating. They are not easily distracted and can become angry if their concentration is interrupted.

There are serious physical complications to eating disorders. Complications include the following:

- electrolyte imbalance (potassium, chloride, and sodium)
- cardiac irregularities
- kidney disfunction or kidney failure
- neurological disturbances
- edema and dehydration
- gastrointestinal disturbances

Bulimics can experience painless swelling of the salivary glands. It is speculated that the swelling is caused by a combination of nutritional deficiencies, electrolyte imbalance, and trauma due to excessive vomiting. Also, the gastric acid from the self-induced vomiting can cause gum and teeth deterioration.

Many deaths in anorexics and bulimics result from compromised cardiac functioning. With the profound depletion of the electrolytes, serious heart beat irregularities (arrhythmias) and sudden death can occur.

Usually persons suffering from one of these eating disorders does not come to the attention of health care professionals until they are quite malnourished. It is essential that the first efforts be geared toward helping them attain and maintain adequate nutrition. They need to be admitted as inpatients so that they can be closely evaluated and stabilized metabolically. These children often resist any attempts to help them.

Behavior modification is often the means used to change the child's eating behaviors; with appropriate rewards being given for weight gain and/or adequate food intake. There are many schools of thought as to effective treatment; however, whichever method is used, it is imperative that all health care workers involved be consistent. The nurse can help by being supportive, by establishing a caring environment, and by encouraging activities to increase the child's self-esteem. The child also needs to learn about good nutrition and effective problem solving. She needs help in establishing improved interpersonal relationships and in the making of independent decisions. Support groups are effective in the treatment process, and the treatment of bulimia, in particular, seems to progress well with group therapy.

## Young Adult (Eighteen to Thirty-Five Years)

The young child continues the tasks of the adolescent. He further clarifies his values, continues to establish his identity, and chooses a lifestyle.

Intimacy is the main developmental task of this age group. If the person fails to establish close and sharing relationships, isolation results. Singles groups, computer dating services, and personal advertisements in newspapers attest to the fact that intimacy is not an easy task to accomplish.

Many young adults postpone marriage and other responsibilities by continuing their schooling. Others combine college and marriage or a committed relationship. Still others enter the world of work following high school. Each has its own stressors.

The college student copes with studying for long hours, writing papers, meeting assignment deadlines, and passing exams, Figure 3-8. There is often little time or money to pursue special interests.

Fig. 3-8 The college student copes with long hours of study.

Marriage means a change in ideals, behaviors, and aspirations. Working requires finding a satisfactory job that provides status and economic security, Figure 3-9. This is often a difficult task that requires much effort on the part of the young adult. He may change his mind several times and take many jobs before he actually decides on a career. If the child has accomplished the developmental tasks of earlier stages, has gained self-awareness and a good self-image, if he has learned problem-solving techniques, has established good interpersonal relationships, and takes the time to explore, he will find a rewarding career. It is sad that some adults spend their entire working lives in jobs that provide little satisfaction.

**Fig. 3-9 Working requires finding a satisfactory job that provides status and ecoomic security.**

Young adulthood is a time for establishing intimacy and for making many important decisions. Unfortunately, little research has been done in this area, and the young adult receives little help and recognition for the many choices he must make.

## Middle Adult (Thirty-Five to Sixty-Five Years)

Erikson calls this stage of *generativity versus stagnation*. Society puts the greatest demands on middle-aged adults. They are expected to be highly productive and financially secure. Many people at this age take time to assess their accomplishments. If they see them as worthwhile and productive and if they see themselves as having improved life for future generations, they have successfully accomplished the developmental task. The task includes having a positive influence on children. Because of a rapidly changing society, more middle-aged adults are finding their lives not worthwhile and have the feeling that they are stagnating. As a result, they find it necessary to alter their life-styles, marriage partners, and/or occupations.

It is during this period that many physical changes occur. Receding and/or greying hair begins to appear and eyesight becomes defective. Metabolism slows, which results in overweight if the diet remains the same. Menopause is another change with which the middle-aged adult must cope. The change in hormonal levels sometimes results in hot and cold sensations, insomnia, mood swings, and anxiety symptoms.

This is also generally the time when children leave the home. Parents who have devoted themselves almost entirely to the children may find themselves alone and feeling useless. This can, however, be a time of freedom and creativity—a time to do things of interest that could not be done before because of family responsibilities, Figure 3-10.

## Senescence (Sixty-Five Years to Death)

Old age is arbitrarily set at sixty-five, the age of retirement. The people in this group are far less homogeneous than they were at any other time. Development depends on how well the individual has accomplished the tasks in earlier ages. There is also a vast difference between the young old (65-75) and the old old. They young old are more aligned with the middle adult, while the old old experience most of the losses attributed to this group.

**Fig. 3-10 Many middle-aged adults use their newly found free time to return to school.**

In the past, older people were revered. They were the holders of vast amounts of knowledge and the teachers of the young. Their advice was sought after and used by younger generations. In recent society, however, technological changes occur so rapidly that the older person's knowledge and skills quickly become obsolete. Their values are no longer appreciated, and the computer has proven to be a more effective holder of information than the human brain. Although this is beginning to change, once a person has retired, he is seen by society as nonproductive and dependent.

Recently, though, there has been an increased interest in the feelings and needs of the aged. The term *senior citizen* was coined in an attempt to afford some status to them. In reality, it had little immediate effect. Nevertheless, things are *now* changing in both the society in general and in the health care field. There are several lay and professional journals on the subject of aging. More books are appearing in the library, and senior citizen groups are visibly campaigning for their rights. Although psychiatrists continue to shy away from the subject, there is an increased interest in geriatrics as a special field in both nursing and in general medicine.

Some people do reach their prime in old age and enjoy this period of life. This is especially true if they have prepared for it by developing hobbies or special interests in earlier years. They then look forward to taking it easy. They no longer have to compete or engage in the day-to-day drudgery of some jobs. They are free to pursue their special interests, to think and to take stock. Erikson says this is the time when people review their lives, accept their successes and failures, arrange matters, and get their lives in order.

Each age group has its stressors, but few suffer losses to the degree seen in old age. These losses make it more difficult to attain integrity and despair may result. There is a drop in income, loss of useful employment, death of friends and family, and, because of chronic illness, there may be mental or physical impairment. There is also a change in the body image and a loss of independence to some degree.

The older person may experience a loss of hearing and/or vision. Muscles become weaker and reaction time is slower. Even if the person does not have a chronic illness, it may still be more difficult to climb stairs, dress, maneuver on icy streets, get in and out of the tub, or drive a car. Even those who do not have a debilitating chronic disease may not be totally independent.

Retired people, including those capable of working, commonly find obstacles to obtaining employment. Although there are some older people who are rich and others who have adequate retirement incomes, some of the aged still live on incomes lower than poverty level. These people find themselves dependent on charity or on their families for financial support.

Often the individual's identity is tied to his occupation. Retirement can then lead to a loss of identity. Retirement also can mean a loss of friends and associations, which leads to loneliness. Grief is another stress with which the older person must deal. The danger of death exists at any age, but the time element makes it more relevant for the older person. The death of a spouse and/or friends can lead to further isolation and loneliness.

Despite the obstacles, many aged are able to complete the developmental tasks identified by Erikson and to enjoy this period in life. They keep busy by volunteering for community service, Figure 3-11, by becoming foster grandparents, or offering their services as retired consultants. Many just enjoy relaxing and engaging in activities of special interest, Figure 3-12. Such places or groups as retirement villages, senior citizen centers, day care for the aged, home-delivered meals, and homemaker home health aide services have helped the aged to overcome many stressors and to live the remaining years of their lives in comfort and dignity.

**Fig. 3-11 This senior citizen volunteers his time in a charitable thrift store.**

Fig. 3-12 The older person may find some relaxing and enjoyable activity.

## HIERARCHY OF NEEDS

The ability to see things as they really are is probably the most difficult aspect of understanding others. Needs, beliefs, knowledge, and anxiety affect perception.

Stimuli in the environment are constantly bombarding the body. Since the brain cannot handle all of the stimuli, perception is a selective process. Only the strongest stimuli reach the brain. The stimuli that do reach the brain are interpreted in terms of past experiences, immediate needs, knowledge, and the self-concept. Perception is the process of awareness which occurs between stimulus intake and thought. The way we perceive influences the impact of the stressors.

Immediate needs are probably the most significant influence on perception. Abraham Maslow developed a theory of motivation based on needs, Figure 3-13. Maslow arranged needs in a hierarchy from basic physiological needs to self-actualizing needs. Satisfying the basic physical needs is necessary for survival. These basic needs include oxygen, fluids, food, and rest. Society does a fairly good job of helping people to meet basic needs, so their power as motivators is lessened.

Safety and security needs relate to protection. These needs include shelter, stability, and freedom from undue anxiety. If these needs are not met, the person experiences fear, panic, and physical danger. According to Maslow these lower needs must be met at least in part before the person can progress to the next higher level.

Loneliness and isolation are the result if the third need, that of love and belonging, is not met. This need is extremely important for mental health and seems to be more difficult to meet in a technological society. The need for esteem is dependent upon feelings of being worthwhile. Meeting this need improves the self-concept. Failure to meet it leads to a lack of self-confidence.

The highest level of the hierarchy is that of self-actualization. Besides having the characteristics of the mentally healthy person, the self-actualizing person is confident, feels self-fulfilled, and sees beauty and harmony in even small things.

According to Maslow, the individual must meet the dominant lower needs, called *deficiency* needs, before attention can be paid to the higher, or *becoming*, needs. Progression does not occur at a steady rate. People may remain at one level for varying lengths of time, they may revert to a lower level, or they may simply remain at a particular level and never progress further.

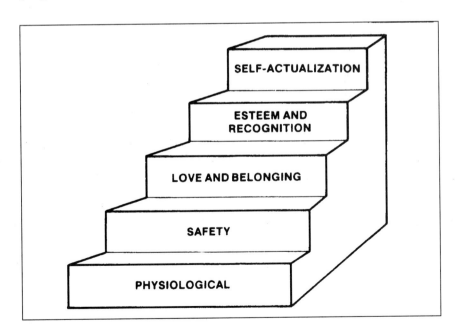

**Fig. 3-13  Maslow's hierarchy of needs.**

## MENTAL MECHANISMS

Mental mechanisms are learned patterns of behavior. Freud believed they were used by all people to a certain extent. The mental mechanisms basically identified by Freud were once thought to be healthy ways of relieving stress. They were considered to be ways of avoiding failure and salvaging self-respect.

Although mental mechanisms are used by most people, humanistic psychologists do not believe they are essential to mental health. In fact, they are now seen as actually inhibiting personality growth. Since they interfere with awareness, mental mechanisms are a means of avoiding, rather than solving, problems. They help to temporarily avoid, but do not change, threatening conditions. Many mechanisms are costly in terms of adaptive energy. They may lead to less-than-desirable behavioral patterns, such as becoming class clown to gain recognition.

Mental mechanisms are either subconscious or unconscious. They are difficult to categorize because they are not clear-cut. It is not the behavior but the motive behind the behavior which distinguishes one mechanism from another, Table 3-4. Common mental mechanisms include rationalization, repression, compensation, displacement, projection, conversion, regression, sublimation, identification, and reaction formation.

### TABLE 3-4
### Common Mental Mechanisms

| MENTAL MECHANISMS | EXAMPLE | POSSIBLE MEANING |
|---|---|---|
| Rationalization | I'm going to die of something anyway, so why quit smoking? | I am addicted to smoking and am unable to quit. |
| Compensation | I don't have time for dates. I'm too busy with my ceramics. | No one likes me enough to ask me out, but I can still feel important by excelling in art. |
| Displacement | How many times have I told you to keep that bike out of the driveway! | The boss was really upset with me today. |
| Projection | It's all your fault that I did not win the contest. | I cannot accept that I am not the best, so my loss must be your fault. |
| Repression | I can't seem to remember my supervisor's name. | I find my supervisor attractive. This feeling is unacceptable to me so my supervisor is blocked from my conscious level of thought. |

**TABLE 3-4 (Continued)**

| MENTAL MECHANISMS | EXAMPLE | POSSIBLE MEANING |
|---|---|---|
| Conversion Reaction | I am blind. I just suddenly went blind The doctors can't find out why. | No one will know why, either. What I saw is so horrible I cannot even think about it. |
| Regression | Since Jenny has been sick, she constantly cries for her mother. | When Jenny was younger, things were more secure. She had her parents to take care of her and help when things went wrong. |
| Identification | I have decided which shirt I want you to buy me. It's that one. | That shirt is just like Uncle Joe's. I really admire Uncle Joe and I want to be just like him. |
| Suppression | I'm really sorry I forgot. Now that you mention it, I do recall. | I wish she hadn't reminded me. I really didn't want to remember that. |
| Sublimation | I really love children, but I'm not ready for marriage. I will get a job working with chidren in a day-care center. | Working with children in a day-care center proteects my ego because it is a more acceptable way for me to fulfill my desire of working with children than having my own children without being married. |
| Reaction Formation | Bill, I am going to pay your way to college. After all, you're my brother and I love you. | You had everything, Mom and Dad loved you most. I got blamed for everything you did. I really hate you, but you're my brother, so I can't hate you. |

## Rationalization

In rationalization, the individual denies his real thoughts and excuses his actions by presenting false but seemingly more acceptable reasons for behavior. Rationalization helps to save face when one feels guilty about an action or behavior. It is much easier to say, "No one could get along with that patient," than to accept responsibility by saying, "I am not able to get along with that patient." After failing a course, a student finds it more acceptable to say, "I didn't want to be a nurse anyway," rather than saying, "I didn't study and now I have given up my chance to be a nurse." Rationalization is not lying. The truth is repressed and the real motive is unconscious.

## Repression

Repression is an involuntary exclusion of experiences or desires from awareness. The experience is forgotten, but it remains at the unconscious level and influences behavior. The repressed experience usually causes anxiety, but it may also result in physical defects and obsessions. Repression is different from suppression in that repression is on the unconscious level. Suppressed experiences are at the subconscious level and are more readily available to awareness.

## Compensation

When a person uses extra energy to overcome a real or imagined defect, the person is compensating. For example, the student who feels unpopular may devote more time to achieving good grades. The neighborhood bully may be compensating for feelings of inferiority.

## Displacement

Releasing pent-up feelings on a person or object that is less threatening than the person or object that caused the feeling is known as *displacement*. For example, a student may fear punishment if anger is displayed toward an instructor. To avoid a lower grade or some other form of discipline, the student vents the anger on an aide. The student has unconsciously substituted the aide for the teacher.

## Projection

Blaming personal shortcomings on someone else is called *projection*. The student who is late explains that "Mary wasn't ready." The truth is that the student started late. A student misses a question on a test and explains the mistake with "It was a trick question." Projection is transferring responsibility for unacceptable ideas, wishes, or thoughts to another. Projection is used more often by the mentally ill than the healthy person.

## Conversion Reaction

The term *conversion reaction* is used when an emotional conflict is repressed and appears as a physical symptom that has no physical cause. A person who has seen something overwhelming may repress it and then develop blindness. Another person may be unable to talk, while still another may become paralyzed. The internal conflict often relates to the physical disability, but not always.

## Regression

When a person returns to an earlier pattern of behavior, he is regressing. It occurs when the person's usual means of coping have not been successful. The earlier behavior represents a time that was more secure.

## Reaction Formation

Reaction formation is a defense mechanism through which a person acts in a way opposite of how he feels. He is unable to cope with his real feelings because they are socially unacceptable.

## Sublimation

Substituting a socially acceptable behavior for behavior which is not socially acceptable is called *sublimation*. A person who is unmarried but desires to be a mother (or father) may sublimate by becoming a worker in a day-care center.

## Identification

Consciously or unconsciously imitating the characteristics of another person is called *identification*. Identification is thought by psychoanalysts to be an important mechanism. They believe it is part of the personality development of children. It is also a way for adults to obtain satisfaction by participating in the success of people with whom they identify. Consciously internalizing the values and behaviors of an admired person is more growth producing than using identification as a mental mechanism.

## SELF-AWARENESS

Self-awareness involves noticing how the self feels, thinks, behaves, and senses at any given time. It is only through awareness of how the self blocks messages and uses mental mechanisms that people can achieve self-understanding. Self-awareness differs from introspection in that awareness is simply observation of the way the self reacts. Introspection usually involves evaluation, or determining why the self reacts as it does. Awareness is a constant process, while introspection is an intermittent one.

Awareness is a way of focusing attention on the present, thereby strengthening the impact of life experiences. It is always available and, with practice, can be used successfully to enrich life. Awareness is not only the key to self-understanding, it is also the key to fullness of living. It is the first step in coping with stress. Fullness of living comes from the richness of experience. The more aware one is, the deeper one can experience feelings such as joy and pleasure.

People function at various levels of self-awareness. Those at low levels are not fully experiencing life. Awareness focuses on the present. It is only in the present that changes can be made and actions modified. Individuals without awareness are more apt to be governed by fears, anxieties, and poor self-concepts. The nurse who is unaware is likely to make decisions in response to her own needs rather that the needs of her patients. With self-awareness, behavior can be accepted or modified. For instance, many students are anxious about taking examinations. Anxiety is a vague feeling of impending danger. As long as the anxiety remains vague, little can be done to control it. With awareness, the anxiety becomes more concrete. Instead of vague feelings, the student is aware of tense muscles, a squeaky voice, and mild nausea. These are symptoms that are concrete and can be controlled. The student owes it to herself and her patients to increase her self-awareness. She will find a fuller life in the process.

## Improving Self-Awareness

Improving self-awareness requires concentration and practice. The following suggested guidelines can be used to develop self-awareness. Awareness should never be forced; it should simply be allowed to flow. Instant results should not be expected, as growth requires time.

1. Periodically stop and concentrate on what your body is feeling at the moment. At first, concentrate only on what the body senses. Later, include environmental awareness as well. Tell yourself what you are aware of.
2. Ask yourself, "What am I aware of when I am anxious, happy, joyous, frustrated?" Concentrating on the bodily sensations that accom-

pany these feelings will make them more concrete and, therefore, manageable.

3. Listen to what you say and how you speak. Persons often phrase sentences to avoid awareness, particularly awareness of responsibility. When responsibility for behavior is excluded from awareness, a person loses control over that behavior and is then unable to change it.

   - A sentence such as "It is scary" is an attempt to give up ownership of an emotion. Changing the ownership from "it" to "I" helps to increase awareness that it is really "I" who is scared, not "it" that is scary. Ownership is accepted and the emotion becomes controllable.
   - "You make me angry" is another example of giving up ownership of an emotion. Changing ownership from "you" to "I" increases awareness of who is responsible for the anger, e.g. "I am angry with you." When an individual accepts responsibility for her own anger, she becomes aware that no one else can cause it. Only she has control. Only she owns the emotion and only she can accept it or change it.
   - People often explain their own feelings by using the second or third person (you or they). For example, a person may say, "You feel as if you're all alone and no one really cares." This is again giving up ownership.
   - Saying "can't" is another way of eliminating responsibility for an action. There are some legitimate "can'ts" but the majority are really "won'ts." Saying "I won't" helps the individual become aware of the fact that she also has rights.

4. Clarify vague feelings of dislike by a process called *exaggeration*. If you do not like something and do not really know why, you may be able to determine what it is you do not like through exaggeration. Pretend the disliked object (whether it be a dress, a classmate, or a piece of furniture) is directly in front of you. Tell it how you feel as if it were really there. Each time you repeat the statement, exaggerate. Allow yourself to say whatever comes to mind. At the same time, try to concentrate on the feelings.

5. Another way of increasing awareness is to handle disturbing experiences of the past by bringing them into the present. Relate the experience as if it were happening in the present. At the same time, try to sense the experiences and the sensations. This procedure can be

used when past experiences continue to disturb you and you do not know why. (For more information, see Chapter 5.)

## SELF-ACCEPTANCE

Self-acceptance is a regard for oneself with a realistic concept of strengths and weaknesses. Behaviors of the self-accepting person include the following:

- Persevering
- Minimizing weaknesses
- Seeing reality
- Trusting and accepting others
- Continuing growth toward self-actualization
- Recognizing and accepting one's own behavior
- Reaching out to others
- Increasing strengths
- Learning from mistakes

The person who is self-accepting accepts others more easily. Therefore, it is important that the nurse work toward self-acceptance. The self-rejecting person is critical of others, more anxious, insecure, and depressed.

Whether or not a person is self-accepting depends on the self-concept. Self-concept depends on how a person thinks he or she is viewed by others. Since all experiences are filtered through the self-concept, people tend to behave in ways which reinforce the self-concept. People respond to other people in terms of their behavior. This reinforces the self-concept, thereby creating a vicious circle. This is called a *self-fulfilling prophecy*. Since the self-concept really depends on others, individuals must interact with others to improve it. However, the individual must first be self-aware. Without self-awareness, there is no improvement.

Even though self-concept depends to a great extent on others, there are some things individuals can do to improve their own self-concept. Simply focusing awareness on personal strengths increases them and thus enhances the self-concept. A good self-concept leads to self-acceptance. Practicing potential strengths develops them into actual strengths. A *strength* is any interest, ability, talent, or characteristic that enhances worth.

# SUMMARY

Understanding how personality develops and the ability to recognize behavior and motives as they exist in reality are essential to the helping relationship. Personality depends on heredity, nurturing, and environment. Personality continues to change throughout life as it is affected by stressors or developmental tasks at each stage of the life cycle. Needs, beliefs, knowledge, and anxiety affect reality perception.

Abraham Maslow developed a theory of motivation based on need. He arranged needs into a hierarchy. The lower needs of the hierarchy must be met before the individual can meet the higher needs.

Many people use mental mechanisms to avoid stress. Freud thought mental mechanisms were normal ways of saving the self. However, humanistic psychologists now believe they interfere with personality growth.

Self-awareness involves noting how the self behaves, feels, thinks, and senses at any given time. Self-awareness is the first step to self-understanding. Self-awareness can be learned. The nurse owes it to herself and her patients to increase her self-awareness.

## SUGGESTED ACTIVITIES

- Visit a day-care center and observe the actions of the children at various age levels.
- List at least five things you like about yourself.
- Identify two personal weaknesses and develop a plan for strengthening them.
- Observe people around you. Try to detect mental mechanisms they may be using.
- Which mental mechanisms do you use most frequently? Under what circumstances do you use them?
- Practice the self-awareness exercises described in this chapter.
- Think about the self-actualizing people you have met. Discuss with classmates why you think they are self-actualizing.

## REVIEW

A.   Multiple choice. Select the best answer.

1.   The way in which needs are met during the infant stage
     a. determines subsequent steps in personality development.
     b. has no effect on personality development.
     c. is the total responsibility of the mother.
     d. is of no consequence as the infant cannot differentiate between emotional and physical needs.

2.   The self-concept is defined as
     a. how others see an individual.
     b. being aware of one's feelings.
     c. the true self.
     d. how people see themselves.

3.   According to Erikson, the developmental task of the infant is the acquiring of
     a. integrity.
     b. identity.
     c. initiative.
     d. trust.

4.   Personality is the result of
     a. temperament and heredity.
     b. heredity and environment.
     c. self-understanding.
     d. environment and nurturing.

5.   The development task identified by Erikson for the toddler is the acquiring of
     a. trust.
     b. autonomy.
     c. initiative.
     d. integrity.

6.   Another developmental task of the toddler is
     a. developing a conscience.
     b. relating to peer groups.
     c. beginning to develop a self-concept.
     d. controlling bowel movements.

7. One developmental task of the young adult is
   a. establishing an intimate relationship.
   b. achieving economic security.
   c. clarifying values.
   d. adjusting to decreased health.

8. The stage of industry involves which age group?
   a. Middle adult
   b. School-aged child
   c. Adolescent
   d. Young adult

9. If adolescents do not accomplish the development task identified by Erikson, they suffer
   a. despair.
   b. role diffusion.
   c. loneliness.
   d. inferiority.

10. Daydreams of superheros are common to
    a. adolescents.
    b. preschoolers.
    c. school-aged children.
    d. toddlers.

11. The adolescent who has the most difficulty adjusting is the
    a. early developing girl.
    b. early developing boy.
    c. late developing girl.
    d. late developing boy.

12. The peer group is most important to the
    a. young adult.
    b. adolescent.
    c. middle adult.
    d. school-aged child.

13. A suicide attempt on the part of a teenager is usually a
    a. means of getting attention.
    b. psychotic behavior.
    c. result of a dare.
    d. call for help.

14. The person who first did research that recognized the individual differences in infants was
    a. Havinghurst.
    b. Brazelton.
    c. Sullivan.
    d. Maslow.

15. If an infant cries incessantly, fails to gain weight, and has sleeping and eating problems, he is probably suffering from
    a. failure to thrive.
    b. malnutrition.
    c. infectious illness.
    d. separation anxiety.

16. Regression in an infant is most likely a result of
    a. failure to thrive.
    b. infectious disease.
    c. separation anxiety.
    d. ineffective parenting.

17. Rituals are characteristic of which age group?
    a. Toddler
    b. Infant
    c. Preschooler
    d. Adolescent

18. The toddler's frequent use of the word "no" means the child
    a. will continue to be disobedient.
    b. needs discipline.
    c. needs encouragement.
    d. is attempting to gain control over his environment.

19. The most common fear of the toddler is
    a. animals.
    b. darkness.
    c. monsters.
    d. separation.

20. The most common fear of the preschooler is
    a. animals.
    b. darkness.
    c. monsters.
    d. separation.

B.  Match the theorist in column I with his theoretical goal in column II.

| Column I | Column II |
|---|---|
| 1. Erikson | a. Security |
| 2. Maslow | b. Self-actualization |
| 3. Havinghurst | c. Task accomplishment |
| 4. Sullivan | d. Learning increasingly more difficult skills |

C.  Briefly answer the following:

1.  Give three reasons for ineffective parenting.

2.  Differentiate the characteristics of the child with anorexia and the characteristics of the child with bulimia.

3.  Name three things the adolescent is probably missing in his development if he develops a mental health problem.

# CHAPTER 4
# RELIEVING
# ANXIETY

## OBJECTIVES

After studying this chapter, the student should be able to:

- Define anxiety, fear, panic, aggression, and crisis.
- List seven symptoms of severe anxiety.
- State four ways of reducing anxiety.
- Explain modeling, role playing, confrontation, and behavior modification.
- List the three elements of assertive behavior.
- Name four factors that contribute to aggression.

Stress is a nonspecific response to any demand made on the body. These demands are called *stressors*. People are constantly affected by physical and psychological stressors. Adaptation usually goes unnoticed unless the stressors are severe or prolonged. How stress is perceived by the person determines whether or not the stress produces anxiety in that individual. It also determines the degree of anxiety produced.

## ANXIETY

Anxiety is a vague, uneasy feeling of discomfort. It is a term used to describe reaction to stress when the source is believed to be threatening but is not obvious. The source of anxiety is usually within the person's internal environment. Anxiety is different from fear in that fear is the reaction to a known and usually external threat. Everyone experiences anxiety at some point in their lives. In fact, some anxiety is necessary. Without it, people would be apathetic and disinterested in their surroundings.

Anxiety may occur at any time during the life cycle. It may be the result of a developmental or situational stressor. Situational stressors are disruptive changes in one's life such as divorce or serious illness, the death of a loved one, or loss of a job. Although anxiety is often acute and of short duration, there are people who consistently live with a certain level of anxiety. This is called chronic, or long-term, anxiety. People with chronic anxiety may additionally experience acute episodes of anxiety.

Anxiety can be mild, moderate, or severe. Mild anxiety warns the body to mobilize its forces to handle an impending threat. It increases the energy level and alertness. The individual is then better able to think, analyze, draw conclusions, and solve problems, Table 4-1.

Moderate anxiety decreases perception. The person focuses attention on the particular task or problem. This is called selective inattention. Other voices or events within the room may not be noticed. Physiological changes such as perspiration, muscle tension, and increased heart and respiratory rate may occur. Moderate anxiety, if not prolonged, may be useful for learning difficult tasks and for developing one's capabilities. If the anxiety is prolonged, discomfort such as fatigue, nausea, and diarrhea may result.

**TABLE 4-1**
**Characteristics of Mild, Moderate, and Severe Anxiety**

| ANXIETY | PERCEPTION | PHYSIOLOGICAL CHANGES | BEHAVIOR |
|---------|-----------|----------------------|----------|
| Mild | increased | increased adrenal activity<br>increased energy | alert<br>energetic |
| Moderate | decreased;<br>concentration<br>on a single<br>event | perspiration<br>muscle tension<br>increased heart and respiratory<br>  rate<br>gastric distress | concentration<br>  on particular<br>  problem<br>irritability<br>pacing |
| Severe | focuses<br>attention on<br>only part of<br>an experience | dry mouth<br>profuse sweating<br>rapid, shallow pulse and<br>  respirations<br>rise in blood pressure<br>speech impairment<br>increased muscle tension<br>rigid posture<br>tremors or shivering<br>headache | purposeless move-<br>  ments<br>concrete directions<br>  may be followed,<br>  but learning does<br>  not take place<br>crying<br>confused com-<br>  munication<br>inability to think<br>  abstractly |
| Panic | single detail<br>blown out<br>of proportion | same as in severe anxiety<br>  but to an increased<br>  degree | same as in severe<br>  anxiety but to an<br>  increased degree |

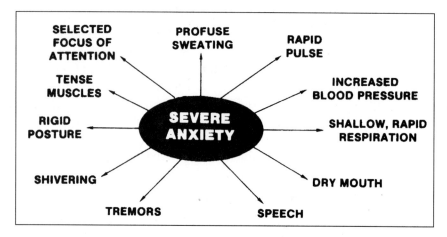

Fig. 4-1 Physical and mental responses to severe anxiety.

Severe anxiety decreases perception to an even greater extent. The person selects only part of an experience and focuses all attention on it. Abstract thinking is lost. Some concrete directions may be followed, but learning generally does not take place. Communication may be confused and the individual's speech may be difficult to understand. Physiological changes include profuse sweating; rapid, shallow pulse and respirations; a rise in blood pressure; dry mouth; speech impairments; increased muscle tension; rigid posture; and tremors or shivering, Figure 4-1.

Panic is a very high level of anxiety in which the person experiences intolerable stress. The physiological changes caused by anxiety are increased. Attention is focused on a minute detail which is often blown out of proportion. Speech is usually incoherent and communication ineffective. A prolonged state of panic can cause serious consequences. Death may even result.

Like stress, the degree of anxiety experienced depends on the individual's perception of the event and the degree of danger perceived. The level of anxiety also depends on the individual's immediate needs, his belief about his ability to handle the situation, the amount and quality of support available, and the degree of accumulated and concurrent stress experienced.

## ANXIETY-PRODUCING SITUATIONS

Anxiety-producing situations are not the same for all people. A situation that is unimportant to one person may cause anxiety in another, Figure 4-2. A situation that is seen as a challenge to one person may cause panic in another person. The following are examples of anxiety-producing situations:

Joyce was brought up in a family that considered time very important. She was continually admonished to hurry and was punished for
being late. She internalized this value of being on time and continued to function under its stress. Joyce coped with this stress by being
fully aware of time, by organizing her activities by the clock, and by
allowing added time for possible delays.

One morning Joyce overslept. She handled this added stressor by
hurrying. At the last minute, she discovered her car keys were missing. She felt overwhelmed and no longer able to rely on her usual
coping mechanisms, Figure 4-2. Her muscles became tense, her
thinking was disorganized, and she felt helpless. Having excess energy and not knowing what to do, she moved from place to place,
becoming less aware of her environment. She felt like screaming or
crying. She looked at her keys several times but did not see them. As
her anxiety grew, there was a greater disruption in processing stimuli
from her senses. When someone else found the keys and handed
them to her, the severe anxiety ended. By this time, Joyce had already spent a great deal of adaptive energy.

---

Karen, a straight *A* student, was know as a "brain." Her classmates
believed studies were easy for her. They did not realize the high
price Karen paid for her achievement. Karen came from a family
that prized success. Her father was a pathologist and her mother was
a college professor. When other children were praised for good
work, she was criticized for not doing more. Nothing less than the
best was tolerated. She began to feel inferior to others but was still
under the stress of constantly having to achieve. Karen discovered
she could make good grades by reading lessons over and over.
Consequently, she spent many extra hours in study and many anxi-
ety-filled days before each examination. Without time for friends
and other activities, Karen was left alone. In order to protect her
self-esteem and compensate for her lack of friends, Karen achieved
high grades.

---

John, too, functioned under stress. Because of his background, he
viewed all mentally ill patients not as they were but as he expected
them to be. He reacted to the expectations that had been established
in his youth. From the time John could remember, his family frequently talked about "crazy Aunt Suzy": "She should be locked up.
She can't be trusted. You never know what she is going to do." Even
though John never met his Aunt Suzy or any other mentally ill person, he formed opinions about them. These opinions laid dormant

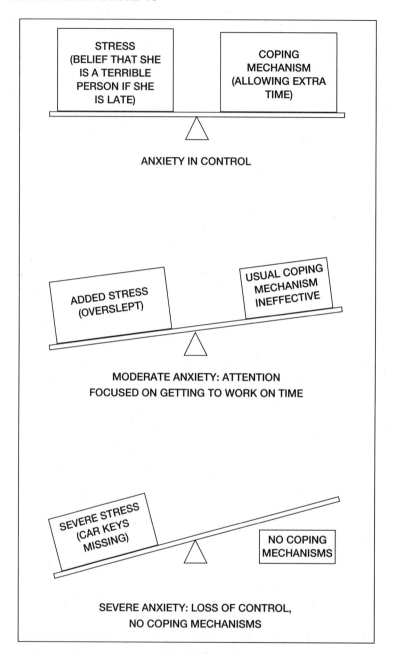

Fig. 4-2  A seemingly insignificant situation can lead to severe anxiety if the person views the situation as a severe threat.

beneath his awareness. John went into nursing from high school. He was well liked by his classmates and faculty.

During the first semester, John achieved scholastic success without difficulty. During the second semester, he was scheduled to take a class on the care of the mentally ill. His conditioned opinions were forced to awareness; he could no longer suppress them. As a result, he frequently argued with his classmates about what the instructor had said. He did not realize it, but he was filtering the instructor's words through his previously formed opinion. He heard only what he wanted to hear and what he was prepared to hear. When assigned to care for a psychotic patient, John's anxiety turned into physical symptoms. He felt uneasy, had headaches, and became sick to his stomach. He dropped out of school because the anxiety of facing one of those "crazy, distrustful lunatics" was overwhelming.

---

One evening, Jack was driving his car along a dangerous mountain road. His eight-year-old son was sitting next to him. Traffic was heavy in the opposite direction and most of the drivers failed to dim their headlights. Jack was driving slowly, but the drivers behind him seemed to be in a hurry. They followed closely behind and honked their horns. Jack began calling the other drivers names. He purposefully turned on his bright lights whenever a car approached. When his young son remarked that his dad seemed awfully tense, the father responded by shouting, "Don't you dare say a word. If it wasn't for you, I wouldn't be on this road, so you just keep quiet."

Common ways in which people tend to handle a stressful situation and lessen anxiety include dependence, domination, withdrawal, and aggression. Joyce was dependent on time. More commonly, one depends on other people. In a time of stress this is helpful, but it becomes a problem when the dependence persists and is extreme. The dependent person is insecure and cannot accept the fact that he has capabilities. He is highly sensitive to criticism, neglect, or anything that may be viewed as rejection. For this reason, the dependent person generally follows the demands of others, even if those demands conflict with his own wishes.

Karen is an example of domination. Many times domination is a facade; the person using it is often insecure. The dominant person must project an image of strength and competence. Karen dominated in the classroom, but others may project dominance in general. The dominant person must make all of the rules. Dependency causes anxiety because trust in others has never developed. Forced into a dependency position, the dominant person may defy the rules, complain about incompetence, and discredit others in order to remain superior.

Withdrawal is the way John coped. He ran away from something he wanted. When withdrawal is temporary, it can be helpful. It removes the person from the stressful event, allowing time to resolve a problem. If carried to extremes or if it interferes with the person's goals, withdrawal is detrimental. The person who uses withdrawal excessively has not learned to trust others and is threatened by the world around him. He progressively moves away from people and becomes indifferent to them. This leads to loneliness and isolation, as shown in the following poem.

## ISOLATION

I keep my real self
   deep inside somewhere
Hidden from a threatening world.
   I feel protected there.
I learned quite early not to trust
   life to treat me well,
And so I formed within myself
   a safer place to dwell.
What I think and what I feel,
   these things cannot be shared.
Too often I'm beset by fears
   and turn from those who've cared.
Unable to reach out, to touch,
   I'll always be alone.
Isolation precludes love.
   I reap what has been sown.

—L.F.E.

Anxiety may also be handled by aggression, as demonstrated by Jack. Aggression can be defined as a forceful or attacking behavior that is verbal, physical, or symbolic. It may be aimed at others or at the self. When a person feels threatened, the body produces extra energy and prepares the body to fight or to run away from the danger. This is called the *fight-or-flight* concept. When a person is experiencing anxiety, there is nothing known to fight. Therefore, there is no way for the body to use up this excess energy. Becoming angry and aggressive is one way to use up excess energy and cope with uncomfortable feelings of anxiety.

| | |
|---|---|
| • EMOTIONAL HURT | • LIVING WITH VIOLENCE |
| • EXCESSIVE NOISE | • VIOLENT FILMS AND TELEVISION PROGRAMS |
| • NOXIOUS SMELLS | |
| | • EXCESSIVE HEAT |
| • FRUSTRATION | |
| • OVERCROWDED AREAS | |

Fig 4-3  Some factors that may contribute to aggression.

Many factors contribute to aggressive behavior, Figure 4-3. Excessive noise and noxious smells seem to result in increased aggression. Aggression is seen more often in overcrowded areas and in persons who are accustomed to violence. Frustrated attempts to solve problems may also contribute to aggression.

Studies show that people tend to be more aggressive if they believe violence is socially acceptable. Studies also have shown that children who view violent films and television programs tend to be hostile in their actions. They seem especially affected by certain cartoons that make violence not only acceptable but fun.

Joyce, John, and Jack were in a crisis. A *crisis* occurs when the problem that produced the anxiety is overwhelming and the usual coping mechanisms are not effective. Helping a person resolve a crisis means helping the person solve problems. For problem solving to occur, anxiety must be lowered to a level at which learning can take place. Attempting to help Joyce, John, or Jack problem solve in their state of severe anxiety would have been fruitless.

## RELIEVING ANXIETY

### Systematic Relaxation

*Systematic relaxation* is one method developed by behavioral psychologists to relieve anxiety. It is based on the fact that anxiety and relaxation cannot coexist. Relaxation exercises stem from the idea that awareness of a tense muscle enables one to relax that muscle. This is not easy to do and conscious effort must be used. Although the level of anxiety may begin to lower immediately, total relaxation may take several weeks.

A comfortable position, either sitting or lying down, is assumed. Muscles are consecutively tightened and relaxed. To begin, the fists are tightened slowly. It might be helpful to count slowly to six while the muscles are being tensed. Concentrating on the tension is essential. The fists are then relaxed just as slowly, to concentrate on how the muscle feels when it is relaxed. This process is continued with other muscle groups: arms, feet, shoulders, legs, chest, pelvis, and face.

Each muscle group is tightened and relaxed separately while concentrating on how it feels. Practice sessions last for twenty to thirty minutes a day. It may be found that some muscle groups—such as those across the back of the shoulders—are more difficult to relax. Once muscle relaxation is learned, it can be used to relieve anxiety at any time.

## Desensitization

Another method to relieve anxiety used by therapists is called desensitization. *Desensitization* is a way of conditioning a patient to be nonresponsive to a stimulus. This technique is usually done by counselors, nurse clinicians, and psychologists, but other health care workers should be familiar with the method. The patient is first trained in muscle relaxation. He is then asked to identify: (1) the anxiety producing situation; (2) a place (usually home) in which he feels safe and secure; and (3) another place or situation which is relaxing, such as lying on the beach. The patient is then asked to imagine the anxiety-producing situation while the therapist describes it in some detail. When the patient feels the first sign of anxiety, he gives a prearranged signal, such as moving a finger. The description of the stressful event is stopped and the therapist begins describing the safe haven. When the patient feels secure, he is taken, through imagination, to the relaxing situation. When the patient is fully relaxed, the entire process is repeated.

Suppose Karen undergoes desensitization. The therapist might ask Karen to imagine herself in a specific situation as he talks. He might begin by saying, "You are now sitting in the classroom. Your desk is cleared. Your pencil is out. You are ready to take the exam. The professor walks in the room. He has papers under his arm. He asks everyone to clear their desks. The test papers are passed out. You receive your paper and look it over. There are some questions you don't remember ever discussing. You are trying to think of the answer but it won't come."

Karen might raise her finger at this point. The therapist immediately responds with, "O.K., you are now out of the classroom. You are at home with your family. You are sitting at the piano. Your mother is sewing and your father is smoking his favorite pipe. The dog lies nearby. There is a fire in the fireplace and the warmth from it feels good. Your father smiles as he listens to you play."

When Karen appears more relaxed, the therapist might continue with, "Now you are lying on the beach. The white sand is warm against your skin. You can hear the quiet splashing of the waves against the shore. The sun is warm. You can feel your muscles relaxing as the sun's rays warm each part. . . ."

The therapist then takes Karen back to the classroom when she appears relaxed. "You have now handed in the test paper. You have to wait for the grade. You have no idea how you did, but you are worried about the questions you didn't recognize. . . ."

The entire process is repeated over and over, until Karen no longer experiences anxiety while thinking about the stressful event.

### Implosive Therapy

Implosive therapy is in direct contrast to desensitization. *Implosive therapy* attempts to arouse as much anxiety in the individual as possible. Relaxation is sometimes used, but when it is, it is used only at the very end of the session. Caution: This technique requires a professionally trained therapist.

Relaxation and desensitization are not the only means of reducing anxiety. In working with others, the nurse will find that a calm attitude and quiet music can have a soothing effect. Warm baths or hot drinks sometimes help. Diversional activities have also been used successfully to relieve anxiety. Once anxiety is lowered to a manageable level, the problem which caused the anxiety must be solved.

## PROBLEM SOLVING

Solving a problem may involve selecting other options, changing beliefs about an event, changing behavior, or finding a more effective coping mechanism. Problem solving involves a change. Before a problem can be solved, the person must have a clear set of values. He must recognize the need for change and know that he has the ability to change.

Very few problems have clear-cut solutions. In making a decision, it is necessary to weigh possible satisfactions against possible risks and costs. Since all things that affect an action cannot be controlled, it is impossible to know if the chosen decision will actually produce the planned result.

However, a decision must be made. It will be a more effective solution if the entire health team, as well as the patient, is involved in the process.

The first step in problem solving is to clarify the problem and assess the situation. This is not easy. Often the real problem is hidden from awareness. Time is wasted on superficial difficulties while the real problem goes unsolved. If Joyce were asked what her problem was, she probably would answer, "I can't find my keys" or "If I could find my keys, I wouldn't have a problem." Karen would no doubt say, "I have to make an *A* on this test," even if she could not explain why. John could be expected to complain of physical distress. Even if Joyce finds her keys, Karen gets her *A*, and John's abdominal discomfort is relieved, the underlying problems—the ones that cause the anxiety in the first place—are still there. These underlying problems need to be identified.

The following information about Karen might help the team identify the problem and assess the situation.

- How does Karen view the problem?
- Has Karen ever received less than an *A* in an exam? What coping mechanisms did she use at that time? Were they effective?
- Has Karen ever felt overwhelmed by anything before? If she did, what was the situation? What coping mechanisms did she use then? Were they effective?
- What are Karen's future goals?
- What is her relationship with her family?
- On whom does she call for help? Did she ask this person's help at the time of the problem? Did the person respond?
- In whom does Karen confide?
- What is Karen's developmental level?

Answers to these questions will help the team reach some conclusions about Karen. Some of the conclusions they might reach are:

- Karen has a poor self-concept.
- She is unable to function effectively when things do not go as she planned.
- She has poor problem-solving skills.
- She does not use adaptive coping mechanisms.
- Her present situation is making excessive demands on her.
- She does not utilize her family as a support system.
- She has not clarified her goals for the future.

Once the problem or problems have been identified and the situation assessed, the team can prepare the plan. Planning involves setting goals

and determining possible actions to reach these goals. Goals are extremely important in this process, because they set priorities and give direction
to the nursing care Karen will receive. Possible goals for Karen might be:

- Help Karen become more aware of her situation.
- Teach Karen problem-solving skills.
- Teach her more adaptive coping measures.
- Assist her in setting more realistic goals for herself.
- Teach her assertive skills.
- Help Karen improve her relationship with her family.

## TECHNIQUES FOR CHANGING BEHAVIOR

Behavioral psychologists have developed several techniques designed to change behavior. One or more of these might be chosen to help
Karen reach her new goals. Some of these techniques are modeling, role
playing, confrontation, behavior modification, and assertive training.

### Modeling

Modeling is a method used to improve interpersonal communication
skills. The nurse, acting as the teacher, demonstrates how Karen might
handle a particular problem.

### Role Playing

Role playing is another technique useful in improving interpersonal
relations. Its primary purpose is to identify and understand the feelings
and attitudes of others. Karen might be asked to play the part of her
father as the therapist plays Karen. As Karen plays the part of her father,
she begins to get some feeling or understanding of her father's attitudes.
Usually, role playing is done in a group setting. It is a fairly structured
technique and is divided into several steps:

- **Preparation.** The participating group is made aware of the problem.
  Each character is described briefly and the group is helped to identify with each character. The players are given a few minutes to discuss the situation together. Questions are asked of the actors in an
  attempt to give them the feel of the role they are playing.
- **Enacting the Situation.** The players then act through the situation.
  There is no prepared script or specified length of time. The players
  act and speak as they feel.

- **Discussion.** Following the role playing episode, the group is asked to: (1) identify feelings demonstrated in each character and, (2) identify responses that seemed to elicit effective or ineffective responses in the other players. The actors are also asked how they felt in each instance.
- **Reenacting the Situation.** It may be helpful to reenact the situation a second time. In the reenactment, Karen may be asked to play herself or she may observe others in the role.
- **Drawing Conclusions.** Conclusions and suggestions for problem solving are then discussed by the entire group.

## Confrontation

Confrontation is a method of communication which forces the patient to look at inconsistencies in feelings and vocalizations. It is a means of helping the person validate reality. The nurse might confront Karen with, "You told me your father expects you to get all *A*'s. Can you relate one incidence in which your father told you this?" Another example might be, "Give me one good reason why you should always get *A*'s."

## Behavior Modification

Behavior modification is a technique based on the theory that behavior must be rewarded or reinforced to continue. This technique has been frequently used with children but is effective with all age groups. Behavior is determined by the reinforcement pattern the individual has learned throughout his life. This is known as *operant conditioning*. Rewarding an undesirable behavior is known as *negative conditioning*; reinforcing a desirable behavior is called *positive conditioning*. Behavior, Whether socially acceptable or not, is continued for a reason. The individual exhibiting the behavior sees this reason as good, no matter how distressing it may seem to others.

To change an undesirable behavior, the reward for the behavior is removed. To strengthen an acceptable behavior, the behavior is rewarded. It sounds simple, but in actual practice it is not easy. Not all behaviors are continued by the same reinforcement and not all people respond to the same reward.

If a behavior is to be changed, it must first be specifically identified. The behavior must be stated in concrete terms. A baseline is then established by observing the behavior to be changed and recording the number of times it occurs. This provides a basis for determining the effectiveness of modification attempts.

One of the most difficult aspects of behavior modification is to discover the reward the individual is receiving from the behavior. During the baseline observations, events before and after the behavior are recorded. This may give a clue to the reward the individual is receiving from the behavior. In the following example, it is evident that the reward an individual receives from a behavior is not always obvious.

On several occasions, Billy hit Annie while playing in the playroom. After each occurrence, the nurse reprimanded Billy and took him out to the nurses' station where she could watch him. Even though the nurse punished Billy by cutting short his playtime, the behavior continued. Although the nurse thought she was punishing Billy, she was actually rewarding him with her attention. Behavioral scientists have discovered that attention is a very powerful reward. When the nurse began ignoring Billy's action and taking Annie out to the desk with her, Billy's aggressive behavior stopped.

Sometimes a written contract is used in behavior modification. The patient and the nurse agree in writing on the desired behavior change and the reward to be received when the behavior is achieved. The contract is dated and signed by both the patient and the nurse, Figure 4-4.

---

August 28, 199__

During the week of September 7 through September 14, we, the undersigned, agree to the following:

1. Each mealtime that Jamie eats all her vegetables, she will be rewarded with a dish of ice cream.
2. If Jamie eats all her vegetables at each meal, she will receive an extra dessert of her choice on September 14.

Signed,

_____

_____

---

Fig. 4-4  An example of a contract used in behavior modification.

## Assertiveness Training

People may respond to situations in an aggressive, passive, or assertive manner. Aggression implies meeting one's own needs without regard for others. The passive person suppresses his own desires in favor of others. Assertive behavior implies meeting one's own needs, but unlike aggression, it also involves considering the other person's needs.

Traditionally, women were conditioned to be passive. This means they were taught to suppress their needs. The passive person is often taken advantage of. Passive people can be counted on to do what is asked of them, but they may resent it. They can become very angry, but seldom is the anger expressed openly. If they do express anger, they feel guilty and must make amends. Passive people have a great need to be liked. Their self-concept is vulnerable to the comments of others. Because of this, they are not self-directing and cannot feel good about themselves.

Males in our society have traditionally been taught to be openly aggressive. Females have been encouraged to be aggressive only in a passive sense. Passive aggression refers to a manipulative type of behavior. The manipulator attempts to get her way by inflicting guilt on the receiver. The following is an example of manipulative behavior.

> "It is all right if you want to go to your party and leave me all alone. Enjoy yourself and don't give a thought to your poor mother in this big house with nothing to do. I stayed home with you when you were small because I loved you, but I don't want you to feel obligated. You go to your party and have a good time."

This kind of statement is effective for getting what is desired by inflicting guilt feelings.

Assertive requests are made in a normal tone of voice. They are specific and reasonable and include three elements:

- Consideration of the other person's feelings
  (I understand how you feel.)
- A statement of one's own feelings
  (This is the way I feel.)
- The request itself
  (This is what I would like.)

The following example illustrates the difference between aggressive, passive, and assertive responses.

**Situation:** Jane is a nurse working in a twenty-bed complete care unit. There is a head nurse, a staff RN, and an aide. Jane has been assigned eight patients, the RN has five patients, and the aide has been assigned seven. Jane feels she cannot give adequate care to eight patients and that the assignment is unfair since she has taken the heaviest assignment all week. She decides to talk to the head nurse about the situation. The head nurse responds, "I am sorry. There is nothing I can do. The floor is understaffed and we all have to do the best we can."

AGGRESSIVE: (loud, stern, angry voice) "I have been given the majority of patients for a week now. It isn't fair. The RN could do more. Why am I the one who has to do all the work?"

PASSIVE: (low, calm, quiet tone) "It's all right. I understand. I'll do the best I can."

ASSERTIVE: (normal tone of voice)
(I understand) "I realize we're shorthanded and you're trying to do the best you can under the circumstances, but I don't
(This is how I feel) feel I can give the care these patients need when my assignment is so heavy. Since I have taken the heaviest assignment all week, I would like to have one or two
(This is what I want) of my patients reassigned."

Assertive requests may need to be repeated. Assertiveness is a skill and, like all skills, needs to be practiced. Assertiveness helps people cope with interpersonal conflicts. It enhances the self-concept and is necessary in overcoming passive behavior, Table 4-2.

When the chosen intervention has been carried out, the nurse evaluates the situation to determine whether or not the intervention has been successful in changing behavior. If it has not, the nurse goes back to step one in the problem-solving process.

## SUMMARY

Anxiety is a vague feeling of impending danger. It is a term used to describe reactions to stress when the source is believed to be threatening

**TABLE 4-2**
**Mental Health as Affected by Passive, Assertive, and Aggressive Behavior**

| PASSIVE BEHAVIOR | ASSERTIVE BEHAVIOR | AGGRESSIVE BEHAVIOR |
|---|---|---|
| Lowered self-esteem | Increased self-esteem | Lowered self-esteem |
| Lack of self-direction | Self-directing | Vulnerable to criticism |
| Resentment | Controls the situation | Easily exhausted because of |
| Vulnerable to criticism | Has own needs met | increased use of adaptive |
| Increased stress | Limits stressors | energy |
| Susceptible to colitis, | Meets needs of others | Guilt feelings |
| ulcers, and coronaries | | Increased stressors |
| Depression | | May be feared but not liked |

and when it is not obvious to the person involved. Anxiety is different from fear, which is a reaction to a known threat.

Everyone experiences anxiety at some point in their lives. Anxiety can be mild, moderate, or severe. Extreme anxiety is called panic. Some anxiety is necessary, but as anxiety increases, perception and the ability to learn and think lessen. Anxiety produces physical and emotional symptoms.

Anxiety-producing situations are individual. What is stressful for one person may be unimportant to another. When a person encounters anxiety, he attempts to lessen it with usual coping mechanisms. Common methods of lessening anxiety include dependence, domination, withdrawal, and aggression. Dependence and withdrawal can be helpful if not carried to extremes.

Aggression is defined as a forceful or attacking behavior that may be verbal, physical, or symbolic. Several environmental factors such as noise, heat, and overcrowding tend to contribute to aggression.

A crisis occurs when the problem producing the anxiety is overwhelming and the usual coping mechanisms are not effective. Helping a person resolve a crisis requires problem solving. Since anxiety interferes with problem solving, stress must be lowered before crisis resolution can begin. Some ways of relieving anxiety include relaxation, desensitization, and implosion.

Problem solving involves assessing the situation and defining the problem, deciding on an appropriate goal, implementing techniques to meet the goals, and evaluation. Modeling, role playing, confrontation, assertive training, and behavior modification are ways of changing behavior.

## SUGGESTED ACTIVITIES

- Consider the circumstances under which you become anxious. Do you usually respond by becoming dependent, withdrawn, aggressive, or dominant?

- Try to recall the feelings evoked in you when you are around someone who is experiencing moderate or severe anxiety.

- Practice the relaxation exercises described in this chapter for twenty to thirty minutes a day.

- Make a conscious effort to relax before your next examination. During the exam, try to detect your feelings. Were they different from your usual feelings during an examination?

- Make a list of behaviors you would like to change in yourself. Think about possible reinforcers that are sustaining each behavior.

- Plan a behavior modification project for someone in your family.

## REVIEW

A.   Multiple choice. Select the best answer.

1.   Anxiety is different from fear in that anxiety
   a. usually results from an external threat.
   b. only occurs in people with an unhealthy personality.
   c. is due to an obvious threat.
   d. is due to an unknown stimulus.

2.   When interpersonal skills are demonstrated for a patient, the nurse is using
   a. modeling.
   b. behavior modification.
   c. confrontation.
   d. assertive training.

3.   In order to change an undesirable behavior by behavior modification, the nurse
   a. confronts the patient.
   b. removes the reward for the behavior.
   c. sets limits.
   d. reprimands the patient.

4. Passive aggression is
   a. manipulative behavior.
   b. used by people with limited adaptive energy.
   c. used by dependent people.
   d. aimed at relieving guilt.

5. A crisis occurs when a person experiences
   a. stress.
   b. aggressive behavior.
   c. a need to depend on others.
   d. overwhelming anxiety and coping mechanisms are ineffective.

6. The ultimate aim of crisis resolution is
   a. relieving stress.
   b. teaching problem-solving skills to patients.
   c. solving problems for the patient.
   d. giving support during the crisis.

7. Behavior modification is based on the theory that
   a. tension and relaxation cannot coexist.
   b. behavior must be reinforced to continue.
   c. people create their own crisis.
   d. awareness of a behavior leads to its modification.

8. The behavior displayed by a hospitalized patient who constantly complains and defies rules is
   a. dependence.
   b. withdrawal.
   c. domination.
   d. aggression.

B. Define the following.
1. anxiety
2. panic
3. fear
4. aggression

C. Briefly answer the following.
1. List seven physiological indications of severe anxiety.

2. What are four ways to relieve anxiety?

3. Name four factors that may contribute to aggression.

# CHAPTER 5
# PSYCHOTHERAPIES

## OBJECTIVES

After studying this chapter, the student should be able to:

- Identify the theories of various psychotherapies.
- Identify techniques used by each type of psychotherapist.
- Define terms frequently used in psychotherapy.
- State the function and level of consciousness of the id, ego, and super-ego.
- Name three essential attributes of the client-centered therapist.
- Explain how self-awareness helps to solve mental problems.

There are many methods used to treat mental health problems. Methods used directly on the body are called *somatic therapies*. When the environment is changed or controlled, the treatment is referred to as *milieu therapy*. Psychotherapy uses verbal and expressive techniques in order to help patients resolve inner conflicts and modify behavior.

Freud, Rogers, and Perls are just a few of the people who have developed psychotherapies. Each of these men has contributed information useful in understanding and treating human behavior problems.

The nurse needs to have some knowledge of the techniques employed, the terminology used, and the basic beliefs underlying each psychotherapy, Table 5-1. Although she is not a psychotherapist, the nurse interacts with patients who are being treated by psychotherapy and, therefore, should understand the principles of the psychotherapy involved.

## TABLE 5-1   Psychotherapies

| THERAPY | CONCEPT | PURPOSE | TECHNIQUES |
|---|---|---|---|
| Behaviorism | Behaviorism is a result of conditioned reflexes caused by previous events; it can be unlearned and replaced by new, more appropriate behavior. | Determine stimulus for current behavior and then help person change that behavior by removing the stimulus. | behavior modification modeling desensitization muscle relaxation assertiveness training role playing |
| Client-centered Therapy | Every person wants to achieve self-actualization and this drive is the person's motive for action. | Help the person become self-aware so that he can change his own behavior and improve his self-concept. | reduce anxiety, tension, and defensiveness by providing a nonjudgmental environment reflect feelings accept person as is restate person's thoughts and feelings |
| Gestalt Therapy | The mind conceives experiences as a whole; when an experience is incomplete, a problem may result. | Help the person become more aware so he completes experiences, accepts responsibility for his life, and solves his problems. | dream experiences learning self-awareness relaxation presentizing fantasizing exaggeration |
| Psychoanalysis | Abnormal behavior is a result of experiences that have been repressed into the person's unconscious mind. | Bring repressed experiences to the conscious mind where they can be resolved. | therapist interpretation of statements free association catharsis hypnosis dream analysis |
| Rational Emotive Therapy | Behavior is due to what people believe about an event and not the event itself. | Help the person to achieve a more realistic belief system and to know that he has the ability to cope with events. | behavior modification desensitization muscle relaxation problem solving assigned readings and activities. |
| Reality Therapy | People have limited control over their feelings so only behavior can be changed. People must take responsibility for changing their behavior. | Help the person see himself accurately, face reality, and fulfill his own needs by becoming responsibie for his behavior | self evaluation of behavior decision making development of plan for change commitment to change. |
| Transactional Analysis | People act according to a script and counterscript based on parental influences and the decisions they make about themselves and others. | Help the person to analyze his transactions with others and have a positive feeling about himself and others. | analysis of transactions with others improving self-concept through positive feedback. |

# PSYCHOANALYSIS

Psychoanalysis is a commonly used form of therapy in which the therapist obtains information about past and present experiences that have been repressed to the patient's unconscious mind. By learning the source of the problem, the problem can be brought to the conscious mind and then changed or eliminated. Psychoanalysis is based on the work of Sigmund Freud.

The mind is divided into three levels—the conscious, the subconscious, and the unconscious. The conscious or upper level contains all the things of which a person is aware. Thoughts in the subconscious or second level are not in the person's present awareness. However, they can easily be moved to the conscious level at any time. The unconscious contains all thoughts, experiences, and beliefs which cannot be easily moved to the conscious level. The aim of psychotherapy is to move troublesome thoughts in the unconscious to the conscious level where they can be controlled.

The id, ego, and superego balance each other to check behavior. The *id* controls the physical needs and instincts of the individual. It is thought that the id is the first part of the personality to develop and that it is responsible for the survival instinct. Freud used the term *instincts*, whereas modern psychoanalysts use the term *drives*. Two major drives are aggression and sex. The id operates at the unconscious level and is ruled by the pleasure principle. There is no sense of right or wrong in the id—only the seeking or demanding of immediate satisfaction.

The *ego* is the conscious self. It is through the ego that thoughts, feelings, sensations, and compromises are formed. The ego serves to control the pleasure principle of the id by substituting the reality principle. This means that the ego seeks to delay the drives of the id until they can be released through appropriate behavior.

The ego serves to control and to guide the actions of an individual. It is a mediator between the instinctive drives of the id and the demands of society. It develops through interaction with the environment. Development of the ego begins during the first six to eight months of life. At about the age of two years, it is usually fairly well developed.

The superego develops later, usually around the age of three or four. It is usually fairly well developed at the age of ten years. The *superego* is the internalized parental value system called the conscience. It is concerned with the demands of society and, therefore, controls impulses that would endanger society. It is responsible for helping the individual to distinguish right from wrong. The superego works at both the conscious and unconscious levels, but primarily at the unconscious level.

*Libido* refers to the sexual drive. Freud proposed that the libido begins to develop at birth and goes through characteristic stages in the life of the individual, Table 5-2. The first stage of libido development is from birth to eighteen months. This is known as the oral stage because the infant receives all of its pleasure through the mouth. The second stage is the anal stage, which occurs between the ages of one and three. It is in this period that toilet training becomes very important. The third stage is the phallic stage. Here the child begins to develop a sexual identity and becomes aware of his or her body, especially genitalia.

During the third stage, the child develops strong feelings toward the parent of the opposite sex. The boy falls in love with his mother and becomes jealous of his father. The girl grows closer to her father and becomes jealous of her mother. This behavior, necessary for normal development, is called the Oedipus complex in males and the Electra complex in females. The Oedipus complex is named after the mythical king, Oedipus Rex, who killed his father and married his mother.

It should be noted that some experts do not believe that all children experience Freud's stages of libido development. Furthermore, these stages are not accepted by all authorities.

## TABLE 5-2
## Freud's Stages of Psychosexual Development

| | |
|---|---|
| Oral Stage | The chief source of need gratification is through the mouth in the form of sucking, eating, and chewing. |
| Anal Stage | Need gratification is obtained through ability to control elimination or retention of feces. |
| Phallic Stage | Sexual identity begins to develop. The pleasure zone is the genital area. The child develops intense feelings for the parent of the opposite sex and wants that person all to himself or herself. The stage ends when the child starts to identify with the parent of the same sex. |
| Latency Stage | Between the ages of six and eleven, sexual urgings are dormant. The child participates in more socially approved activities. Group interaction is very important. |
| Genital Stage | This is the final phase and is a reawakening of sexual urges. The stage begins with adolescence and moves toward sexual maturation and heterosexual relationships. |

According to Freud, psychological problems may occur because of arrested development of the libido. The therapist attempts to discover where the libido stopped developing and why. It is believed that this information is in the unconscious. Through psychoanalysis, this information is raised to the conscious level where it can be dealt with.

Free association, catharsis, hypnosis, and dream analysis are techniques used in psychoanalysis. *Free association* refers to a process of counseling in which the person says aloud whatever comes to mind. The therapist listens and interprets the person's statements. *Catharsis* is a method of recalling to memory an experience that is causing a problem and helping the person to express it. *Hypnosis* is an artificially induced state in which there is increased responsiveness to suggestion. In *dream analysis*, the therapist interprets the imagery that occurs during sleep.

Resistance and transference are also terms frequently used in psychoanalysis. *Resistance* occurs when the person tries to prevent the moving of information from the unconscious to the conscious level. Unless the person is able to work through this resistance, progress will not continue. Transference occurs when the person gives the therapist characteristics of significant others in the person's past life. This process is thought to be necessary for recovery.

Psychoanalysis is a very slow process. Recovery may require from one to many years of intensive treatment.

## CLIENT-CENTERED THERAPY

Client-centered or nondirective therapy was developed by Carl Rogers, a contemporary psychologist. According to Rogers, the actualizing tendency is the person's motive for action. He believes that under the proper conditions, people have a natural tendency to progress to self-actualization.

Rogers does not use terms such as subconscious or libido. He does not believe it is helpful to interpret past experiences. Instead he uses terms such as self-awareness and actualization tendencies. Rogers believes that attention should be centered on the person's personality and feelings at the present.

A poor self-concept can prevent self-actualization. When a person sees himself as something different that what he is actually experiencing, the person becomes *incongruent* (lacking internal harmony). He distorts and denies anything that is not consistent with his self-concept. Incongruence causes him to become anxious. The purpose of client-centered therapy is to help the person increase his self-awareness and thus improve his self-concept. By becoming self-aware, the person can view his problems more realistically. This enables him to begin to accept himself and his environment.

Techniques used by the therapist are based on the belief that the person has a strong drive for self-actualization. The therapist tries to help the person reduce the anxiety, tension, and defensiveness that block this drive by providing a nonjudgmental environment in which the person actually helps himself. A nonjudgmental environment helps the person to feel safe and understood. When defenses are relaxed, a more realistic concept of self and the environment can develop. The therapist accepts the person as he is and does not try to change him. The therapist promotes an environment in which the person can change himself. The client is encouraged to express his feelings. The therapist listens, tries to understand, and then restates the person's thoughts and feelings. In this way, the person is able to hear his own feelings expressed. This leads to increased self-awareness. Once a person is aware of how he feel and what makes him feel that way, he can begin to improve his behavior. Rogers' approach to psychology is humanistic and hopeful.

The attitude of the therapist is of primary concern to Rogers. Rogers believes that the therapist must have three basic qualities in order to bring about behavioral change: empathy, positive regard, and genuineness. The most important of these is empathy. *Empathy* is the quality of fully understanding the person, knowing his experiences, and trying to see the world as he sees it. Empathy is understanding the person's feelings; even those that are below awareness. The second quality, positive regard, means that the therapist must accept the person as he is. The therapist never judges, interprets, or probes. The patient is trusted to make the changes necessary for himself. Genuineness is the third quality. For change to occur, the therapist must communicate sincerity to the person.

## BEHAVIORISM

*Behaviorism* is a type of therapy that examines normal and abnormal behavior as a result of conditioned reflexes. It is primarily used for people in anxiety states or with affective disorders. It is seldom used with the psychotic. Joseph Wolpe has done much work in behaviorism.

Behaviorism is based on the belief that all action (*response*) is caused by a previous event (*stimulus*). Responses are learned during life processes. When a stimulus occurs, a person responds in a way that gives pleasure or prevents hurt. For example, each time a child goes near a glass vase, the mother says "no" with a threat of punishment. This is the stimulus. The child stops to save himself from hurt. This is the response. When the child learns that stopping is the safest behavior, this behavior continues each time the stimulus occurs. Eventually the response becomes automatic. The child is then said to be *conditioned*. All responses have both positive and negative aspects. The child's response saves him from punishment, but it denies him the pleasure of touching the vase. If a response has more positive than negative aspects, it is said to be *adaptive*.

The child may respond to the stimulus with a temper tantrum. If the tantrum results in his getting what he wants (in this case, handling the vase), he will continue using this behavior. However, a tantrum is costly in terms of energy, so it is considered a maladaptive response.

Once a behavior has been learned, it may result from a stimulus similar to or associated with the original one. This is called *generalization*. For example, a man develops a fear of plane trips because of an accident. Eventually, this fear may generalize to other things. The man may feel anxiety when he goes to the airport to meet a friend. The sight and sound of a plane may bring distress. Even tall buildings may cause him to feel uneasy.

Some terms common in behaviorism are extinction, displacement, reinforcement, and conflict. *Extinction* occurs when a conditioned response is stopped. To Freud, displacement meant taking out hostility on someone other than the one for whom it is intended. To behaviorists, *displacement* is the act of engaging in substitute behavior. *Reinforcement* is the satisfaction one gets from a particular response. It is why the behavior continues. *Conflict*, as used by the behaviorists, refers to a situation in which two conditioned responses oppose each other. For example, Jane's boyfriend has requested that she wear a particular dress on a special date. Unfortunately, Jane has gained weight and the dress no longer fits. Jane has been conditioned to please her boyfriend, so she goes on a diet. She also has been conditioned to satisfy frustration by eating. If Jane becomes frustrated while dieting, she is faced with conflict because she must give up one conditioned response in order to satisfy another.

Maladaptive responses result from earlier events, but the behavioral therapist is not interested in exploring the patient's past. It is the current behavior and its current stimulus that interests the therapist. Behavior continues only as long as it is reinforced. The stimulus and/or reinforcer must be determined and stopped, an aversive consequence added or a different behavior reinforced for change to occur.

During the first session, the therapist takes a detailed history. The history includes such items as the client's age, marital status, education, and occupation as well as his relationships with others. Usual behaviors, activities, and likes and dislikes also are discussed at this time. The focus is on the behavior the client wishes to change. The therapist may ask the client to keep a diary. The history and diary help the therapist determine the maladaptive behavior, the extent of the behavior, and the stimulus for and consequences of the behavior.

The behaviorist is primarily a teacher of new behaviors. Actions are oriented toward a goal that is stated in specific, measurable terms. Helping a person to improve his personality is not a measurable goal, as it is too vague. Success of the therapy cannot be determined by a vague goal. Goals must be specific. An example of a specific goal is : "Teach the patient muscle relaxation exercises he can use to relieve anxiety prior to examinations."

The technique used by the behaviorist depends on the situation and the consent of the client. Techniques may include:

- Modeling to demonstrate appropriate behavior
- Desensitization
- Muscle relaxation
- Assertiveness training
- Role playing
- Behavior modification

## RATIONAL EMOTIVE THERAPY

This approach, known as RET, is related to behaviorism. Rational refers to the person's ability to think; to *emote* is to express feelings. Its founder, Albert Ellis, was convinced that a person's behavior is due to his own thinking. Problems are not caused by specific events, but are a direct result of what the person believes about the events.

For example, Karen expects all *A*'s but receives a *B* on a test. As a result, Karen becomes depressed and leaves school. Superficially, it seem that the grade caused the depression. Ellis, however, would take the position that it was not the grade, but how Karen viewed the event that caused the depression. To Karen, the *B* meant failure. She tells herself that she is an awful person because she did not get an *A*. This makes the event a disaster that Karen cannot handle. If the grade had not been all-important, the depression would not have occurred. Ellis calls this type of thinking *musturbatory* and says it is the cause of all mental health problems.

In RET there are no "musts" or "shoulds." There is only the reality of the situation. One should not demand, but only desire. It is not rational to believe that one must get all *A*'s. It is irrational to demand that others respond in a certain way. There are some events that are important but none are all-important. Some events are undesirable or inconvenient, but none are disastrous.

To Ellis, when a person sees as event as awful or terrible, he is *awfulizing* or *catasrophizing*. Catastrophizing results in a loss of control over behavior. Without control, there is no problem solving. The consequences may be self-defeating or maladaptive. The philosophy of rational emotive therapy is expressed in the phrase, "If the world gives you a lemon, make lemonade." It is not what happens to a person but what the person does about the event that counts.

Since problems are a result of musturbatory thinking, the therapist verbally attacks the patient's thinking or belief system. Though other techniques are used, this confrontation or attack is the one true, basic RET technique. The therapist might say something such as, "Where is the law that says you must always get an *A*?" "Show me the proof that you are an awful student." Through this technique, the therapist teaches the person to think realistically. Realistic thinking leads to problem solving or to the ability to cope with situations that cannot be changed. Many RET therapists encourage their clients to live by the following prayer:

"God grant me the serenity to accept the things I cannot change, the courage to change the things I can, and the wisdom to know the difference."

## GESTALT THERAPY

Gestalt therapy was developed by Fritz Perls. It is a very complex system based on the theory that the mind conceives experiences as a whole. When an experience is incomplete, a problem may result. The goal of the Gestalt therapist is to help the person complete the experience and increase awareness. A completed experience is called a *gestalt*.

To the Gestalt therapist, homeostatic balance between the person and his environment is important to health. The healthy person is in balance with the environment and is motivated by an awareness of needs, resources, and restrictions. This awareness makes choices available and allows the person to take control of his life. Problems result from a disturbance in homeostasis. Symptoms arise as a result of the body's attempt to maintain the status quo.

Experience and awareness are the two most important aspects of Gestalt therapy. Only the present exists because only the present can be experienced. Gestalts which were incompleted in the past must be brought to the present in order to be completed. Each person has the ability to complete his experience and relieve the problem. The therapist acts as a guide in helping the person become more aware.

Gestalt therapy is used to treat people in anxiety states and those with somatic and affective disorders. It can also be used to enhance living for the mentally healthy person. Three common techniques in Gestalt therapy are exaggeration, fantasizing, and presentizing.

*Exaggeration* is a technique used to help the person become aware of his body language, verbal language, and/or feelings. For example, the student just bought herself a new dress. She spent a great deal of money on it, but now she doesn't like it. The problem is that she doesn't know why. The student is told to look at the dress and tell the dress she doesn't like it. She may be asked to repeat the words several times, each time saying them louder and more forcefully. Soon awareness will occur if the student is listening to her feelings instead of just her words.

Exaggeration is also used when a person is unaware of his body language. If the patient waves his hand while talking, the therapist might ask him to exaggerate the movement by waving his arm in an ever-widening arc. Since the movement is exaggerated, awareness of the movement increases. When a person is aware of behavior, he can control it.

When *fantasizing*, the patient is asked to bring the future to the here and now. The student wants to buy a new car, and she has to choose between two possibilities. One is a brightly colored sporty car and the other is a much less expensive compact. She continually vacillates between the two and just cannot make up her mind. To help her, the therapist will ask the student to fantasize that she has each of the cars, one at a time. She is asked to pretend that she is sitting in them, driving them, and meeting her friends. When she tries on each situation, she is asked to concentrate on how each feels.

*Presentizing* is a means of bringing a past event into the present as shown in the following example.

A student comes to the therapist because she feel guilty. She had been invited to visit her great aunt, but went out with her friends instead. The aunt died suddenly and the student cannot forgive herself. The therapist encourages a dialogue between the aunt and the student. An empty chair is placed in front of the student. The student pretends the aunt is seated in the chair. She is then asked to converse with the aunt. The student alternately takes the part of her aunt and herself, changing chairs when appropriate. She is encouraged to say whatever comes to her mind while playing each part. She is also encouraged to be aware of her feelings while playing each part. This dialogue is a fantasy, but it helps to increase awareness. Through the experience, she is able to become aware of her feelings toward her great aunt. Awareness is usually sudden, as if a light has been turned on. With awareness comes control. The student is then able to rid herself of her guilt feelings.

For Gestalt therapy to be effective, the person is not to think during presentizing, fantasizing, or exaggeration; he is just to experience feelings. Feelings are the major concern. For the person to experience feelings, it is necessary for him to be self-aware. A great deal of time may be spent by the therapist in helping the patient increase his self-awareness. The therapist may draw attention to the patient's posture or tone of voice. The therapist's own feelings, doubts, faults, and strengths may also be expressed.

Dreams are a dramatization of an incomplete experience. Unlike Freud, the Gestaltist does not attempt to understand or analyze dreams. The therapist helps the patient experience the dream and increase awareness. Experiences are taken at face value. The Gestalt therapist feels that meanings emerge by themselves with time. The therapist uses varied and personalized techniques. All techniques are geared to help the person increase his self-awareness, experience feelings, and complete incomplete experiences.

## REALITY THERAPY

William Glasser's reality therapy is one of the newest psychotherapies. Its purpose is to help the person see himself accurately, to face reality, and to fulfill his own needs. Glasser believes that each person has a responsibility for his own behavior. A person's present behavior cannot be blamed on what occurred in the past. Reality therapy has been used extensively in the rehabilitation of juvenile delinquents and with children who have failed in school. It has also be successfully used to enhance the life of people during marital conflicts or crises. Reality therapy has been successfully applied by parents, teachers, and other laymen.

The reality therapist must be a warm, concerned person who is real and genuine. When appropriate, therapists discuss their own experiences, admit personal faults, and are willing to have their views challenged. Most importantly, the therapist truly cares about the person.

The reality therapist is concerned about behavior, not feelings or thoughts. Glasser believes that people have limited control over their feelings and that only behavior can be changed. If the person complains of guilt feelings, the therapist might ask what the person is doing to make himself feel guilty. This changes the complaint from a feeling to a behavior. It also focuses responsibility for the guilt on the person. Only the present is important; the past is gone and cannot be changed. If the past is discussed at all, it is to discover the person's strengths. The strengths are then related to current behavior.

Each person has a responsibility to evaluate his own behavior. This evaluation is essential because behavior cannot be changed unless the person is convinced the behavior is harmful to him. The therapist may express personal values, but does not attempt to impose them on the other person.

After behavior is evaluated and a decision is made to change a specific behavior, a plan is made for changing that behavior. Much of the therapist's time is spent in helping the person make plans for this change. The next step is for the person to commit himself to carrying out his plan. This is essential to reality therapy. The commitment may be verbal or in the form of a written contract. It is usually made to someone other than himself. Glasser believes people fail because they cannot make commitments to themselves.

If a plan fails, no excuse is accepted. Sometimes the person is asked whether or not he intended to fulfill his commitment. Sometimes he may be asked when he intends to do what he has promised. At other times, the plan may require revision. Absolutely no excuse is acceptable, not even a disaster. This is extremely important to reality therapy. An excuse takes responsibility from the person and emphasizes failure. Reality therapy aims at providing success.

Verbal or physical punishment is never used by the reality therapist. Glasser does employ what he terms the *natural consequences* of an act. For example, a child may commit himself to practice the drum every day in exchange for playtime. If he fails to practice, he does not get to play.

This is the natural consequence because it was mutually agreed upon before the act. Reality therapists believe that responsibility is the same as mental health. If people act in a responsible way, they attain growth, happiness, and success.

## TRANSACTIONAL ANALYSIS

Transactional analysis was developed by Eric Berne in the 1950s. The aim of transactional analysis is to help people improve their lives. It has been successful with mentally healthy people as well as those in anxiety states and with affective disorders. Unlike the other therapies, transactional analysis is primarily concerned with groups.

Berne believes that each person acts according to a script or a counterscript. The counterscript comes from parental influences. The script is written by the individual at a very early age. The script is based on a decision the individual makes about himself and others. According to transactional analysis, a person can make one of four decisions:

- "I'm O.K., you're O.K."
- "I'm O.K., you're not O.K."
- "I'm not O.K., you're O.K."
- "I'm not O.K., you're not O.K."

The actual script is patterned on the life of a significant other. At first, it is an outline, but gradually it is modified and detailed. Eventually, it becomes the script which influences the person's life.

A person ensures the outcome of his script through game playing. A *game* is a series of interpersonal relationships which leads to the desired results for each game player. A script based on "I'm not O.K." may call for the individual to get hurt. If people do not automatically hurt him, the person engages in behavior which will force them to do so. This behavior is what Berne calls *game playing*. The end result of a game is the reinforcement of the person's feelings about himself.

Transactional analysis recognized three ego states: the parent, the child, and the adult. These three ego states exist simultaneously in all people; however, only one is dominant at a time. Behaviors belonging to the three ego states are learned by the child from his significant others. The parent contains all the rules and admonitions the child has heard; the looks of love and the disapproval seen on the mother's face; the tender hugs and the severe spankings the child has received. Parents can be either nurturing or critical.

The child holds all the feelings and may be natural or adaptive, joyful, sad, or mischievous. The natural child behaves by laughing, smiling, playing, and crying. He is impulsive and spontaneous. He feels joy, sorrow, guilt, and fear. The natural child is creative, while the adaptive child is involved with rituals and conformity.

The adult is the computer, processing and analyzing stimuli. It is the adult who asks questions, reasons, plans, and makes decisions, Table 5-3.

People respond in any interaction through one of these ego states. A husband comes home from work and asks in his "adult," "When will dinner be ready?" His wife may respond by saying, "Is that all you think I have to do? You could do some things around here to help. Then maybe you'd have your dinner on time." She would be responding in her "critical parent." Had she replied, "It will be ready in a few minutes. You just sit down there and put your feet up. Gee, honey, you look so tired," she would be

### TABLE 5-3  Various Ego States

| EGO STATE | CHARACTERISTICS | EXAMPLE |
|---|---|---|
| Critical parent | — critical<br>— holds all rules and admonitions | "What do you have to do all day? I would think you could at least have my dinner ready on time."<br>"Your hands are dirty. You'd better go wash them."<br>"I do not approve of that kind of behavior." |
| Nurturing parent | — sympathetic<br>— caring<br>— solicitous | "You look tired. You just sit down and I'll take care of everything."<br>"Oh you poor darling, you fell down. Does it hurt much?"<br>"So you didn't get that job. You need something better than that, anyway." |
| Adult | — information keeper<br>— computer | "Dinner will be ready in an hour."<br>"It looks like rain today."<br>"The price of beef is rising." |
| Adaptive child | — conformity<br>— rituals | "I can't do this. My mom said no."<br>"That's not right. It has to be this way." |
| Natural child | — spontaneous<br>— creative<br>— impulsive | "I have a great idea. Let's go out to dinner tonight."<br>"Oh, come on. It'll be great fun."<br>"I just love surprises." |

responding in her "nurturing parent." Her "child ego" might have said, "Let's go out and eat tonight" or "Is that all you expect from me?" Her "adult" would have simply said, "Dinner will be ready in a half hour."

In any transaction, one cannot predict the ego state in which another person will respond. If the response is in the same ego state as addressed, a simple uncrossed transaction occurs and communication continues freely, Figure 5-1. A crossed transaction occurs when the response comes from an ego state that was not addressed. When transactions become crossed, communication ceases or becomes destructive. Often, one or both parties are hurt, Figure 5-2. Transactional therapy helps the person to:

- Analyze his transactions with others
- Keep his "adult" in control at all times
- Allow the other ego states to be used in constructive ways

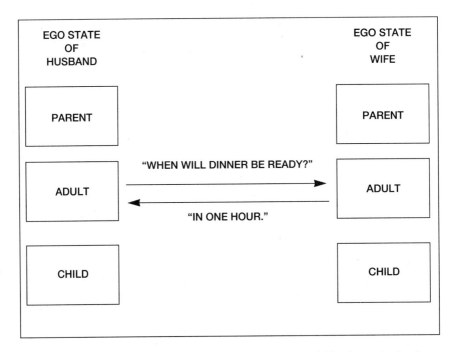

Fig. 5-1 A simple uncrossed transaction. Three ego states exist in all people simultaneously. People respond in any interaction through one of these ego states. If the response is in the same ego state as addressed, a simple uncrossed transaction occurs and communication continues.

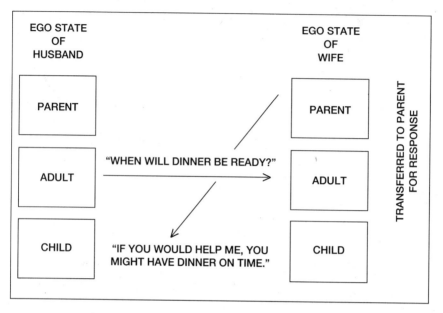

Fig. 5.2 Crossed transaction. The husband asks a question in his adult ego state, but the wife responds in her critical parent. The critical parent directs her statement to the child; thus, the transaction is crossed. Crossed transactions are often destructive.

The patient is helped to recognize the games he plays and is guided to the conclusion of "I'm O.K., you're O.K.." Berne believes that if a person is aware of transactional principles, he can make a decision to be mentally healthy and to rewrite his script.

Many therapists do follow a specific school of psychology. That is, they are Freudians, Gestaltists, Transactional Analysts, Rational Emotive therapists, or Behaviorists, etc. They use exclusively the techniques of their chosen philosophy.

Others, though, feel that the various schools of psychology have something to offer, but none has the entire answer. These therapists are known as eclectics. They pick and choose techniques from any school that seems to fit the situation. They might analyze relationships with one client and use fantasy with another. They may confront one client and use word association with another. Many times these therapists have two or three favorite therapies that they use most often, but they use none exclusively.

# SUMMARY

Psychotherapy is a method of treating mental illness in which verbal and expressive techniques are used to help the person resolve inner conflicts and modify behavior. Many techniques are used, including psychoanalysis, client-centered therapy, behaviorism, rational emotive therapy, Gestalt therapy, reality therapy, and transactional analysis.

Psychoanalysis is based on the work of Sigmund Freud. The therapist obtains information about past and present experiences that have been repressed in the person's subconscious mind. By learning the source of the problem, the problem can be brought to the conscious mind where it can be dealt with. The id, ego, and superego balance each other to check behavior. Psychoanalysis is a very long process, sometimes taking many years.

Client-centered therapy is based on the belief that people naturally grow toward self-actualization under the right conditions. It is the purpose of the therapist to provide these conditions. The therapist provides an accepting, nonjudgmental environment aimed at reducing the patient's anxiety and defenses that block this drive. The patient is encouraged to express his feelings and increase his self-awareness. When a person is aware of how he feels and what makes him feel that way, he can work on improving behavior. Empathy, positive regard, and genuineness are characteristics that the client-oriented therapist must show the patient.

Behaviorism is a school of therapy that believes actions are caused by past events. Behaviors continue only if they are accompanied by a reward. When a learned response becomes automatic, the person is said to be conditioned to the response. The therapist is primarily a teacher of new behaviors. He uses a variety of techniques to eliminate rewards for undesirable behavior or increase rewards for desirable behavior.

Rational emotive therapy is related to behaviorism. Its founder, Albert Ellis, was convinced that a person's behavior is due to his own thinking. Problems are not caused by events that happen, but are a direct result of what the person believes about the events. Therapy is aimed at changing the person's belief system and teaching the person that he has the ability to cope with any event.

Gestalt therapy is based on the theory that the mind conceives experiences as a whole. When an experience in incomplete, a problem may result. The goal of the Gestalt therapist is to help the person complete the experience through awareness. Experiencing and awareness are the two most important aspects of therapy. With awareness, the person can change his own behavior. The therapist spends much time helping people become more aware.

Reality therapy aims to assist a person to see himself accurately, to face reality, and to fulfill personal needs. The individual is responsible for his own behavior; present behavior cannot be blamed on past events. The reality therapist is concerned with behavior, not feelings. The person is encouraged to evaluate his behavior and to make a commitment to change maladaptive behavior. The therapist helps the patient to make plans for that change. Reality therapists believe that responsibility is the same as mental health.

Transactional analysis is a group therapy method. It helps people to analyze their transactions with others and guides them to the conclusion, "I'm O.K., you're O.K."

The Eclectic therapist uses techniques from more than one school of psychology.

The nurse is not a psychotherapist. However, since she works with patients under treatment, she needs to understand the basis of the therapy the patient may be receiving. She should be familiar with the terms commonly used and the goals of the therapies she might encounter.

## SUGGESTED ACTIVITIES

- With a small group, make and play word bingo. Make several bingo cards with definitions of psychotherapy terms. A caller calls out the terms. Each player tries to find the definition on her card. The first play to cover the definitions correctly wins.
- Make a card file for the various psychotherapies. List the psychotherapy, its intended goal, and the techniques used to accomplish this goal.

## REVIEW

A.  Multiple choice. Select the best answer.
1.  Conditioning is a term associated with
    a. behaviorism.
    b. Gestalt psychology.
    c. client-centered therapy.
    d. reality therapy.

2. According to Freud, the element that controls and guides the actions of a person is the
   a. ego.
   b. id.
   c. libido.
   d. superego.

3. Bringing the past into the present is called
   a. fantasizing.
   b. presentizing.
   c. resistance.
   d. awareness

4. The Oedipus complex represents
   a. abnormal behavior.
   b. a feeling of inferiority.
   c. a strong feeling of closeness a child has for the parent of the opposite sex.
   d. a strong feeling of closeness a child has for the parent of the same sex.

5. Libido is the
   a. conscience.
   b. self-concept.
   c. available sex energy.
   d. conditioned response.

6. Transference is
   a. moving unconscious thoughts to the conscious level.
   b. attributing characteristics of a significant other to the therapist.
   c. substituting one behavior for another.
   d. verbalizing feelings.

7. Incongruence occurs when a patient
   a. sees himself as different from what he is experiencing
   b. is playing a game.
   c. uses an irrational belief system.
   d. changes his behavior.

8. Desensitization and relaxation techniques are used by the
   a. behaviorist.
   b. client-centered therapist.
   c. psychoanalyst.
   d. reality therapist.

9. Presentizing and fantasizing are techniques used by the
   a. client-centered therapist.
   b. Gestalt therapist.
   c. transactional analyst.
   d. behaviorist.

10. Asking the person to evaluate his own behavior is a technique used by the
    a. Gestalt therapist.
    b. client-centered therapist.
    c. reality therapist.
    d. rational emotive therapist.

B. Match the psychotherapy in column II with the correct statement in column I.

|  Column 1 | Column II |
|---|---|
| 1. bringing experiences repressed in the unconscious to the conscious level | a. behaviorism<br>b. client-centered therapy<br>c. Gestalt therapy |
| 2. providing an accepting, non-judgmental environment aimed at reducing the patient's anxiety and defenses that block self-actualization tendencies | d. psychoanalysis<br>e. rational emotive therapy<br>f. reality therapy<br>g. transactional analysis |
| 3. removing or increasing a reward to change conditioned responses | |
| 4. therapy based on the belief that problems are caused by what a person believes about an event and not the event itself | |
| 5. helping the patient to complete an incomplete experience | |
| 6. helping the patient to see himself accurately, to face reality, and to make plans to change maladaptive behavior | |

7. group therapy in which patients are
helped to analyze their transactions
with others

C. Briefly answer the following.

1. Define psychotherapy.

2. State the function of the id, ego, and superego. Indicate the level of
consciousness at which each operates.

3. Name three essential attributes of the client-centered therapist.

4. How does becoming self-aware help a person to solve a mental
problem?

# CHAPTER 6
# GROUP PROCESS

## OBJECTIVES

After studying this chapter, the student should be able to:

- Define group and group work.
- Differentiate between explicit and implicit group norms.
- Differentiate between group content and group process.
- Discuss the role of the group leader.
- Identify task versus maintenance group functions.
- Compare and contrast at least two stages of the group.
- List three curative group factors.
- Describe group psychotherapy.

People have a need for social interaction. Human needs can be provided within a group. Belonging, acceptance, and validation are some of the needs that a group has the potential to provide. A group can offer an opportunity to work with others on common tasks or to share common experiences with one another. Some groups form and have a particular, clearly spoken objective that is set within a specific time frame; other groups form with a more diffuse goal but have other supportive, enduring elements. In a group, boundaries can be tested and experiences can be taken from the group and generalized to other relationships outside of the group. The quality of one's life can be improved through cooperation and coordination learned within a group. A group member can begin to explore and understand why he does what he does and learn to accept help willingly and wait patiently. Group participation can increase communication and observational skills, increase problem-solving abilities and emotional expressiveness. Nurses work in both formal and informal groups throughout their nursing experiences: ward conferences, staff meetings, family meetings, and the psychiatric unit's community meetings.

## GROUP WORK

The primary work of a group is to build trust. As people become more trusting and accepting, the effectiveness and productivity of the group increase. Group members are able to listen to others and recognize the importance of developing openness. Group learning occurs, and the following accomplishments are seen:

- Improved eye contact
- Increased listening skills
- Increased use of open-ended questions
- Giving and receiving of feedback
- Self-disclosure

In contrast, the development of fear in a group member can lead to extreme politeness, horsing-around behavior, or resistance. Resistance occurs when a group member works against the group's goals or purposes or the member deliberately withholds active participation in the group. Sometimes a person fears being a part of a group and worries that the group will reject him if he speaks out.

As the group progresses to a more mature group, the following characteristics are observed:

- Cohesion—a mode of sticking or hanging together
- Clear communication
- Goals accepted by group members
- Feedback mechanism
- Decision-making method

*Norms* are standards or ground rules adhered to by the group. Assumptions or expectations held by the group members can be helpful to the group or create group barriers. For instance, a person's beliefs may be that she is to speak only when spoken to; therefore, as a group member she remains silent, waiting to be singled out by the group leader for her comments.

All people have beliefs concerning what kind of behavior fits into the following categories:

|       |       |
| ----- | ----- |
| right | wrong |
| good  | bad   |

allowed        not allowed
appropriate    inappropriate

Key sources of norms are our past experiences. Norms can be explicit or implicit. *Explicit norms* are overt and are openly verbalized and clearly stated. *Implicit norms* are covert and unspoken. They are sensed but are not immediately obvious and are below the individual's level of awareness. Implicit norms can lead to hidden agendas by group members. The group cannot resolve a problem until the problem is brought forward by the group, recognized, and discussed.

## PROCESS VERSUS CONTENT

Two major components of an interaction are content and process. *Content* is the subject matter on which the group is working. It is the group's basic material or what the group is talking about. However, the major dynamic of the group is called *group process*. Group process is what is happening to the group (i.e., morale, feeling tone, atmosphere) and what is happening between the group members (i.e., influence, participation, cooperation, competition, and styles of leadership). If one pays attention to group process, one gains the ability to access group problems, look at the norms developing in the group, and determine major causes of ineffective group action.

## ROLES

Group participation gives one an opportunity to look at personal communication styles and behavioral patterns. A role is the position one undertakes in the group. Four components of one's role are:

- Expectation—what others desire
- Conception—what others think his job is
- Acceptance—what you are willing to do
- Behavior—what you actually do

Many roles may be observed in a group, Table 6-1.

### Role of the Group Leader

The group leader can be considered as a facilitator, trainer, or therapist. The leader models effective communication and assists the group

**TABLE 6-1**
**Group Participation Roles**

| GROUP BEHAVIOR | DESCRIPTION | STATEMENT |
|---|---|---|
| Harmonizer | agrees, understands, accepts | "O.K., that's understandable." |
| Clarifier | restates an issue | "Sally, when you said _____, did you mean _____?" |
| Dominator | interrupts | "I would just like to add that I believe the way we used to do things was better, and furthermore _____." |
| Self-discloser | shares a personal feeling or experience with others | "I experienced something similar when I got divorced." |
| Gatekeeper | invites other group members to talk; looks at nonverbal cues | "John, did you have something to add to that _____?" |
| Summarizer | restates discussion | "Today this group has been _____." |
| Compromiser | yields his/her position | "After what you just said, Jane, I'll change my mind about _____." |
| Consensus validator | determines if group is reaching an agreement | "Does everyone agree with Mary's statement?" |

members in achieving their goals. Behaviors of the leader include the following: understanding, flexibility, tolerance, encouragement, sensitivity, and caring.

Yalom states that the leader demonstrates liking, valuing, noticing, and reinforcing of a member's strengths. It has been noted that group members pattern their behaviors after the leaders. The group leader observes, assesses, and analyzes the group while encouraging interaction, exploring problems, focusing, and offering support to all members on group progress. Yalom states that the group member's trust and understanding is enhanced by the leader's self-disclosure. Self-disclosure is the exposing of one's feelings or point of view on a particular subject matter or personal experience. The group leader needs to be attuned to verbal and nonverbal communication. The group leader may have to facilitate improved communication.

- "I believe we have gotten off the subject."
- "Maggie, I'm not sure you heard John correctly."
- "John, could you restate what you just said?"

Cotherapy or coleadership of a group can occur. Cotherapy consists of two or more designated leaders. This style allows for peer feedback and personal growth. Time needs to be scheduled for cotherapists to share feelings and opinions so that the therapists can feel comfortable with each other's leadership styles.

The leader can appoint a group observer. The observer does not actively participate in the group but observes the group for some of the following behaviors:

- Was the group purpose attended to?
- Was clear communication established?
- Did the group stay with the topic or get tangential?
  (Tangential—going off the subject being discussed and talking about another topic.)
- Did all group members talk?
- Was conflict open or hidden?
- What was the general atmosphere and morale?

## GROUP STRUCTURE

Structural patterns are networks that develop and come forth as group members work together. Argyle divided structure into four pattern areas: task, power, communication, and sociometric.

*Task* structure refers to the patterns of individual role performance in the group. Look at interactions as they relate to the talk or work of the group—who suggests, initiates, summarizes, or pushes for group decision making.

*Power* structure refers to the identification of patterns of influence. Influence is the power to indirectly effect a person or events in the group. Look at who communicates to whom, who is listened to, and who makes decisions.

*Communication* structure refers to the exchange of thoughts and messages. Look at who talks to whom, who listens to whom, who responds to whom. Also be aware of who does not participate in the communication structure.

*Sociometric* structure refers to preference and interpersonal intimacy. Look at who refers to whom in the group, who sits next to whom, and carefully observe physical proximity, facial expression, tone of voice, and eye contact.

The environment influences the growth and development of the group. Group environment includes room size, physical location, type of furniture (i.e., comfortable chairs), seating arrangements, educational resources (i.e., blackboard, video). Observation of the group atmosphere is important. Is the group congenial and friendly? Are unpleasant feelings expressed? Do group members disagree? Are members spontaneous or withdrawn?

## FUNCTIONS OF GROUPS

There are two basic functions of groups: task and maintenance. The task function keeps the group on target and gets the job done. Some behaviors that occur during task are: initiating activity, seeking information, giving or asking for feedback, coordinating, summarizing, and evaluating. Task function can be slow moving, may be defined or may need to be defined, and pertains to content.

The maintenance function is to strengthen the group spirit and satisfy the needs of group members. Some behaviors during maintenance are: standard setting, consensus testing, encouraging, energizing, and expressing a group feeling. Maintenance functions create an effective group atmosphere among group members so they can attempt to work together in a smooth and effective manner. If maintenance functions are inadequate, nonfunctional behaviors such as the following usually occur:

- Blocking—resisting contributions of other group members or going off on a tangent with unrelated information
- Dominating—manipulating, controlling
- Clowning—horsing around, disrupting the group, mimicking another group member
- Self-confessing—tells all, uses the group as a sounding board
- Withdrawing—pulling away from the group although remaining physically in the group; sometimes whispers to others or wanders from the subject
- Scapegoating—someone bearing the blame for others

Silence, hostility, and humor can be considered as either functional or nonfunctional behaviors. Silence in the group can prove to be awkward, tense, and anxiety producing. Nonverbal cues need to be carefully observed, because sometimes silence can be reflective and the group members can be relaxed in posture. Group members verbalizing hostile feelings can actually contribute to the group's growth. Humor at any appropriate moment can be tension reducing; however, joking and horsing around can block group and personal growth experiences.

Another group function is to develop a basic operating agreement or group contract. A group contract includes the following: general expectations, purposes, goals, time for group meeting, rules (i.e., tardiness versus punctuality—we will begin promptly at 10 A.M.; no one can enter the group after the meeting has started), attendance (i.e., after three consecutive absences, you will no longer be considered a group member), and group confidentiality (i.e., what we talk about in these group meetings is not to be discussed outside the group).

## STAGES OF GROUP DEVELOPMENT

There are four stages of group development, Table 6-2. The stages are distinct but can overlap. Regression to an earlier stage can occur at any time during group development.

**TABLE 6-2**
**Stages of Group Development**

| STAGE | PERSONAL RELATIONS | BEHAVIOR | TASK |
|-------|--------------------|----------|------|
| 1 | Dependency | Insecurity<br>Lack of trust/support | Orientation |
| 2 | Conflict | Frustration<br>Resistance | Organization |
| 3 | Cohesion | Fitting into new roles<br>Group-ness | Group Work |
| 4 | Collaborating | Working together<br>Summarizing<br>Evaluating | Creative Problem Solving |

During the orientation task (stage 1), affirmation and emotional skills are being demonstrated and can provide valuable cues for the group and group leader. Affirmation skills can include: the awareness of each individual's rights, verbalizing appreciation, praising, showing interest per verbal reaching-out, or non-verbal affirming of an individual in the group through observable nodding in agreement or leaning forward to listen attentively. Assessing individual emotional skills is important during this orientation stage. How is a feeling expressed to another? Who is openly sarcastic or humorous? Do people disagree openly? Who continues to remain silent and on the fringe? How are conflict, anger, silence, and compliments handled?

During the organizational stage (stage 2) it becomes important to define the ground rules and time elements. Ground rules include expectations: all members will participate in each session, members will listen with openness, confidentiality will be maintained, and each member will give and receive positive feedback. Creating a colorful poster stating the rules is helpful so it can be visible at each session. Define how many sessions the group will have and the length of each session (i.e., 1 1/2 hours) and include information about a break (i.e., one 15 minute break will be provided). If applicable, there will be no break and everyone is expected to remain in the room during the session. Starting and finishing the session on time will contribute to an organized group style.

Reserve time at the end of the session for summarizing. At first, the group leader can summarize by clarifying the issue/problem discussed, focus on ideas that emerged from the group and any goals or actions decided on. Later, as the group's cohesiveness and collaborating spirit is in place, the group leader can ask for a group member to volunteer to summarize for the group "what happened here today at this session."

## GROUP PHASES

The group phases can be divided into the following categories: initial or orientation, working, termination, and evaluation. In the orientation phase, the group settles down to work. The members size up each other and look for approval, acceptance, and respect. Questions the group might ask are: Why are we here? What are we going to set as our goals and how are we going to get this done? There is usually a polite atmosphere with dependency needs being expressed toward the group leader. The group discusses its purpose, and group rules are discussed to arrive at a group contract. Conflict will surface as group members become preoccupied with control and power. During the conflict phase, the group may even insist that the leader "fix it" for them. Carl Rogers describes this first stage as milling around, with group members demonstrating a resistance to expressing past personal experiences. Finally, a cohesive state emerges. The suspicious, guarded behavior of the group members decreases and trust and self-disclosure increase.

During the working phase, group identification increases, and the group begins to realize that conflict can be useful. One need not hide feelings or remain silent in a group. Similarities and differences in the group members are recognized, and mutual acceptance begins. Cooperation, compromise, and collaboration are key words that describe this working phase. Feedback is given and requested by the group members. The group begins to look forward to the completion of the task.

The termination phase usually occurs when goals have been met. This phase can be difficult because the group will be ending and the individual members will lose the group support. Separation anxiety may be evident. The work of this phase is putting the group into perspective, evaluating what has been significant/important for each group member, and sharing feelings. The increased awareness that coping strategies learned in the group must be applied to other situations.

During the evaluation phase, the group takes time to observe and comment on the changes that are observable in each group member. The effectiveness of the group in meeting its goals and abiding by the group contract can be discussed.

To visualize a group data base, see Figure 6-1.

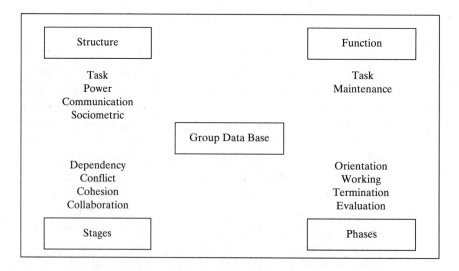

**Fig. 6-1  Group data base.**

Yalom has described curative factors that occur in the group. Some of Yalom's curative factors include the following:

- Installation and maintenance of hope
  "Others have the same problems as I do."
- Universality
  "We are people—all in the same boat."
- Altruism
  "I'm now putting the needs of others above myself."
- Self-understanding
  "I'm learning why I think and feel the way I do.
  I have some hang-ups from long ago."
- Group cohesiveness
  "I belong to a group now, and I'm being accepted by others."
- Catharsis
  "I'm beginning to express my positive and negative feelings toward other group members. I like being able to say what bothers me."

## TYPES OF GROUPS

There are many types of groups that the nurse may encounter. The primary purpose of a group is to be therapeutic to the group members through supporting, educating, motivating, and/or problem solving with them. Following are some sample groups:

### Teaching Group

This group presents specific information. Active participation by the members is encouraged (i.e., a four-week nutritional group led by the dietician for cardiac patients, a medication group co-led by a nurse and pharmacist for in-patient psychiatric patients).

### Discussion Group

This group encourages communication and the building of the individual's self-esteem. It usually has an educational and motivational component (i.e., a discharge planning group on a psychiatric unit, a "Coping with Diabetes" for a newly diagnosed group of diabetic patients, an assertiveness training group). It creates a friendly, informal atmosphere. Understanding the purpose of the discussion group helps the members stay focused and increases participation in the group. At each session, summarize and arrive at a decision. What have we said here today? How does all of this relate to your individual problems? Specific assignments or homework can be appropriate group enhancement.

## Self-help Group

This group meets to share mutual concerns and goals and to offer supportive help (i.e., Weight Watchers, Ostomy Club, Alcoholics Anonymous). Since group members are coping with a common problem, important curative group factors can occur: instillation of hope, universality, catharsis, and group cohesiveness.

## FOCUSED TASK GROUPS

Group dynamics occur in a wide variety of situations in our work environment: task groups, team meetings, committees. We are assigned themes or problems to solve through working with others. If a committee is not functioning at an optimum level, observe low work behaviors: socializing, playfulness, casual conversing, attitude (boring, not interested, wasting my time), leadership style (no direction). A group task must look at the time available and what decisions need to be made. Allocating 5 minutes to agenda setting can save time and make certain that each member understands the problems to be discussed and the resources needed. Setting priorities and time limits allows the group to be flexible, yet have a sense of organization. List problems on a chalkboard or flipchart and then number according to importance per group consensus—Why are we here? What are we supposed to do? How are we going to get it done? What is our time frame? What are our goals? (i.e. a protocol for the suicide patient, documentation guidelines for a mental status exam, a standard of care that meets JCAHO criteria). Task groups whose goals are clear, concise, and accomplished provide consistency and continuity for the patient care and increase team-unit efficiency and overall satisfaction.

## Psychotherapy Groups

Another type of group is a psychotherapy group led by a therapist. Group therapists can be a psychiatrist, psychologist, social worker, or nurse. It is important that the group therapist has expert knowledge and experience in the dynamics of human behavior and psychopathology. The group is approached from the therapist's theory base. A theory is a systematic, organized knowledge base that helps one analyze, predict, or explain a phenomenon (i.e., what is happening: in the group, to the group members). This theory base serves as a guide for the therapist when he is leading the group interactions; therefore, utilizing a theory base is quite different from experimenting, practicing, or "doing therapy by the seat of your pants."

The following are examples of theoretical approaches:

**Gestalt.** The group focus is on the individual within the group. Role playing is used to help the individual group member explore his feelings. Some therapists use the "hot seat" approach. A person concentrates on his problems as the group observes.

**Transactional Analysis.** Group members' behaviors and communication patterns are observed and analyzed according to the adult-child-parent transaction model.

**Communication Theory.** The group is observed for ineffective communication patterns. Patterns are identified and problems solved through the establishment of feedback channels. The therapist models good communication styles in order to diminish dysfunctional communication by the group members.

In psychotherapy groups, the group members are selected for a group through an interviewing process, and personalities and behaviors are considered. The group experience will facilitate behavioral changes and allow for reality testing and risk taking in a safe environment. The goal is that the group members will experience an increase in caring and belonging and a decrease in loneliness and isolation.

## SOCIAL SKILLS GROUP

With a chronic mental illness, the patient is frequently isolated and needs to develop/assess their social skills. The main goal of this group is to decrease the amount of anxiety experienced by the patient in social interactions and provide a safe environment where they can be social and friendly. For a group of elderly, a reminiscing group may be appropriate. Young schizophrenics may enjoy planning a barbecue with outdoor games and activities. Day hospital patients may enjoy a shopping excursion for food for their designated menu, and then returning to their facility and participating in the meal preparation. Gatherings with holiday themes and decorations can be enjoyable for patients and staff.

## SUMMARY

Groups provide people with the basic human need of social interaction. The primary work of a group is to build trust. All groups adhere to certain explicit and implicit norms. Two major components of an interaction are the content and the process. Each group member undertakes a role in the group. The group leader models communication and assists the group members in achieving their goals. Group structural patterns can be divided into task, power, communication, and sociometric. Two basic functions of groups are concerned with task and maintenance. Functional and nonfunctional behaviors can occur. There are four stages that groups experience: dependency, conflict, cohesion, and interdependence. Group phases can be categorized as the initial or orientation, working, termination, and evaluation phases. Many curative factors emerge during the group process. Groups can support, educate, motivate, or assist with problem solving. Group work can be growth promoting as the group leader and group members have an opportunity to explore their interpersonal styles and behavior patterns within a group

### Suggested Activities

1. Select one of your leadership qualities that you can identify and would like to improve. Focus on specific ways of improving this quality.

2. Identify one area of communication is a group (listening, clarifying, asserting, etc.) for which you are *not* assuming responsibility, and state how you are going to change this behavior.

3. Assess a group of which you are a member for individual roles in relation to:
   a. Task structure—how does the work get done?
   b. Power structure—who influences whom?
   c. Communication structure—who talks to whom?
   d. Sociometric structure—who likes whom?

4. Draw up a sample group contract.

## REVIEW

A. Multiple choice. Select the best answer.

1. The *primary* work of a group is to
   a. increase listening skills.
   b. increase clear communication.
   c. build trust.
   d. improve eye contact.

2. A major component of a group interaction is the process. Process is defined as
   a. what the group desires to do.
   b. the group subject matter.
   c. what the group is talking about.
   d. what is happening between group members.

3. The group structural patterns that refer to personal preference and interpersonal intimacy are called
   a. sociometric.
   b. communication.
   c. power.
   d. task.

4. Exposing one's feelings or point of view on a particular subject matter or personal experience is called
   a. clarifying.
   b. gate keeping.
   c. self-disclosing.
   d. dominating.

5. The "milling around" phase of group work is called
   a. orientation.
   b. working.
   c. evaluation.
   d. termination.

6. Universality can be described as
   a. "I belong to the group now."
   b. "I'm beginning to express my positive feelings."
   c. "I'm now putting the needs of others above myself."
   d. "We are people—all in the same boat."

B.   Define the following.

1.   content

2.   harmonizer

3.   power structure

4.   group contract

5.   catharsis

C.   Briefly answer the following.

1.   Define norm as it pertains to group, and give examples of an explicit and implicit norm.

2.   List and define the two functions of a group.

3.   Differentiate between two functional and nonfunctional aspects of silence in a group.

4.   Describe three of Yalom's curative factors that occur in group therapy.

D.   Formulate a problem in patient care that needs to be solved. Role play a focus-task group—set an agenda, time frame, assignments, and goals. Designate a participant observer and place feedback on a chalkboard or flipchart.

## ARTICLES

Burnard, P. Group discussion. *Nursing Times* 86(37): 36-137, Sept. 12–18, 1990.

Byers, P.H., et al. Psychiatric nurses' and patients' perceptions of discussion topics in therapeutic groups. *Issues Mental Health Nursing* 11(2): 185–191, Apr.–June, 1990.

Emerick, R.E. Self help groups for former patients: relations with mental health professionals. *Hospital & Community Psychiatry* 41(4): 401–407, April, 1990.

Puskar, K.R., et al. The role of the psychiatric/mental health nurse clinical specialist in an adolescent coping skills group. *Journal Child Adolescent Psychiatric Mental Health Nursing* 3(3): 103–105, July–Sept. 1990.

# CHAPTER 7
# EFFECTIVE
# COMMUNICATION

## OBJECTIVES

After completing this chapter, the student should be able to:

- List three goals of therapeutic communication.
- Give three reasons why communication can be ineffective.
- Explain three ways to improve listening skills.
- Identify responses that block communication.
- Identify at least five effective communication statements according to category.
- Name five ways to show caring.
- Pair at least ten verbal responses with caring behaviors.
- Name at least two ways of developing trust.
- Use effective communication techniques.

Effective communication adds to the patient's psychological comfort; therefore, it is as necessary to recovery as diet, medication, or other treatments. Patients who experience psychological discomfort are often noncompliant, use poor coping mechanisms, and have less effective problem-solving skills. This results in actions that increase physical distress and complications, and slow recovery.

Communication is usually thought as of an exchange of words. In reality, it includes all methods used to relay messages to another person, including gestures, body movements, and tone of voice. Communication that does not involve the spoken work is referred to as nonverbal.

A sender and a receiver are necessary for communication to occur. To be effective, the message must be understood by the receiver in the way that the sender intended. Unfortunately, ineffective communication does occur, Table 7-1.

## TABLE 7-1
### Some Reasons for Ineffective Communication

- The sender may not send the message he though he was sending.
- The receiver may not hear the message the sender intended.
- Verbal and nonverbal messages may conflict.
- The message may be disguised by the sender.
- Many English words have multiple meanings.
- The message may be abstract and therefore confusing.
- The receiver may be prepared to hear another message.

## INEFFECTIVE COMMUNICATION

**Disguised Messages.** Because the patient may not trust the nurse's reactions to his feelings, he may disguise his message before sending it. A patient who says "No one is doing anything for me" may really be saying "I'm afraid because I feel weaker and I don't think anything is going to help."

**Conflicting Messages.** Verbal messages have a nonverbal message attached to them. The tone of voice, the posture, and so forth can give the receiver a message that conflicts with the stated message. For example, a patient who is sitting slumped over with his head in his hands says in a low, dull voice, "There is nothing wrong, I'm just fine." Although the patient may be thinking , dozing, or meditating, his posture tends to communicate that things are not fine; thus, the nonverbal message is different from the verbal message. When this happens, the receiver tends to believe the nonverbal message.

**Unclear Meanings.** Some English words have many meanings, and meanings change with use over the years. For this reason, statements may have one meaning for the sender and another for the receiver. "Gross" is an adjective that can be used to describe something terrible, something big, or something very noticeable. It can also refer to the amount, like twelve dozen, or the total amount, as in gross salary. A "bat" is a flying rodent, a stick for hitting balls, and a mean, old woman. "Gay" used to mean a state of happiness; now the word refers to a homosexual. "Bad" means one thing to a senior citizen and just the opposite to the modern teenager. If the young adult says, "It's cool," the older person would probably expect him to be talking about the weather.

**Abstractions.** There is even a greater chance for misunderstanding when the terms used are abstract. Young children have not developed the ability to think abstractly, and people under stress lose it. "The grass is always greener on the other side of the fence" and "a rolling stone gathers no moss" are common abstract proverbs that are difficult for some to interpret.

**Perception.** Perception is the means by which the receiver processes and interprets information and can be another source of misunderstanding. Each message is screened through past experiences, expectations, and self-concept. The receiver selectively tunes out messages that do not fit in with preconceived ideas. People hear what they are prepared to hear. Because the nurse is often the receiver, it is most important that she increase her self awareness. It is her responsibility to listen to messages and clarify possible misunderstandings. Communication is only effective if the message gets to the receiver the way the sender intended it to.

## PURPOSE OF COMMUNICATION

**Getting Information.** Effective communication is purposeful. The message is intended to accomplish a goal. As seen in Table 7-2, there are many purposes for which the nurse can use communication. One is to obtain useful information about the patient. Information is useful if it aids in developing nursing care plans. Before the patient gives information to the nurse, he has to feel secure with her. He has to trust her. Communication is also used to help develop that trust.

## TABLE 7-2
### Goals of Communication

- Obtain useful information
- Develop trust
- Show caring
- Help the patient understand himself
- Relieve stress
- Provide information
- Teach problem-solving skills
- Encourage acceptance of responsibility
- Encourage activities of daily living

**To Show Caring.** Trust is developed much more quickly if the patient knows that the nurse cares for him and accepts him as a person. All of the little things a nurse does for a patient, like rearranging a pillow or giving him a drink of water, show caring. The idea of caring, though, is reinforced if the behavior is paired with verbal responses. This will be explained later in the chapter.

**Provide Information.** Patients often need information from the nurse. She provides this information when she answers questions, when she teaches, and when she encourages. Vivid details of one's personal life need not be shared with the patient.

Help patients understand themselves. Restating what the nurse hears the patient saying sometimes makes the meaning clearer to the patient. Sometimes the patient's ventilating feelings to someone who accepts them is sufficient to relieve stress. This makes listening and understanding therapeutic.

If the goal is to be met, communication must not be blocked. Certain responses tend to close communication. When the receiver hears one of these messages, he usually stops sending and further communication is stopped. The nurse needs to be aware of responses that block communication and must work toward more effective responses. Table 7-3 lists some statements that block communication.

**TABLE 7-3**
**Blocks to Communication**

| TECHNIQUE | EXPLANATION | EXAMPLE | |
|---|---|---|---|
| Belittling | statement which tends to make light of the patient's beliefs or fears | Patient: | "I won't leave here alive." |
| | | Nurse: | "That's ridiculous. You shouldn't even think that way." |
| Disagreeing | response which indicates that the nurse believes the patient to be incorrect. It generally relates to the cognitive rather than the affective message. | Patient: | "Why am I here? Nothing is being done for me and I'm not getting any better." |
| | | Nurse: | "You are getting better." |
| Defending | statement used to repel a verbal attack | Patient: | "I had my light on for fifteen minutes." |
| | | Nurse: | "I am doing the best I can. You are not the only patient I have." |
| Stereotyped statement | common statement made without sincerity | Patient: | "I am really worried about the children. I came to the hospital so quickly and I didn't get to see them. They just won't understand. I wish I could have talked to them." |
| | | Nurse: | "I know exactly what you are going through." |
| Changing the subject | different subject introduced to prevent talking about a topic that causes anxiety | Patient: | "They are doing a biopsy tomorrow. I hope it isn't cancer." |
| | | Nurse: | "Are these your children? That's such a nice looking family." |
| Reassuring cliché | reassuring statement which is not sincere | Patient: | "What will I do if it is malignant?" |
| | | Nurse: | "Don't you worry. Everything will be all right." |
| Giving advice | statement which tells the patient what the nurse thinks the patient should do | Patient: | "I broke my arm when I fell off a skateboard." |
| | | Nurse: | "At your age, I would suggest you give up skateboards." |
| Agreeing | statement which shows that the nurse believes the patient's cognitive message is correct. It may not be the patient's real concern. | Patient: | "I am afraid the doctor won't discharge me tomorrow." |
| | | Nurse: | "I am sure you are correct. I doubt he will let you go home so soon." |

# BLOCKS TO COMMUNICATION

**Belittling.** A patient says, "I have been looking forward to going to the senior prom since I was a freshman. Now with this broken leg, I won't be able to go." The nurse responds, "If you had been more careful, this would not have happened," or "Don't get so upset over a silly prom. It isn't that important." This communication does nothing to enhance the nurse-patient relationship. It makes light of the patient's feelings. She is effectively telling him that he is silly. Because the patient sees that the nurse thinks so little of his problem, he will probably be afraid to talk further. The nurse will never know how the patient really feels.

**Disagreeing.** A response such as "You don't have to stay home just because of a cast" may be just what the patient wants to hear. However, the nurse does not know this, because she has not taken the time to find out. She is responding to the patient's verbal message only.

**Defending.** "We're doing the best we can to heal your leg" is a response that defends the nurse's ego, but it puts the patient on the defensive. He is placed in a position of having to apologize for the nurse's misperception of his statement.

**Stereotyped Statements.** Nurses often use stereotyped comments like "I know just how you feel" or "I understand." The nurse does not really understand because she has not taken the time to do so. The patient recognizes this and feels there is no point in responding to such a comment.

**Changing the Subject.** If the nurse feels threatened by the patient's statement or does not know how to respond, she may change the subject. "These are beautiful flowers. Did they come from your husband?" This is an effective way of telling the patient "I don't want to hear about your problems." Changing the subject temporarily can be helpful if the patient is having difficulty coping with the present topic, but it should be temporary and done to meet the patient's need.

**Reassuring Clichés.** "Everything will be all right, you'll see" is a reassuring cliché. Reassurance is important if it is real. False reassurance is easily detected and makes the receiver distrustful of the sender. The receiver may feel the statement means that his leg will be healed in time to go to the prom. The sender may mean that he will probably get over not going to the prom. Even if believed, reassuring clichés are ambiguous.

**Giving Advice.** "Now this is what you should do. Call your girlfriend and tell her about the accident. She'll understand." or "If I were you, I would forget all about the dance." This is giving advice, which is seldom effective. The patient will accept it only when he is ready to accept it. Even if the patient wants the nurse's advice, she must take time to determine this before offering it.

**Agreeing.** A statement like "That's right, you won't be able to go to the prom" closes communication. What is there left for the receiver to say? So it belittles the patient's concern. "That's the way it is, so accept it" shows no understanding of the patient's strong feelings about the prom. Something that seems trivial to the nurse can be of extreme importance to the patient.

## ATTITUDES THAT AFFECT COMMUNICATION

Certain attitudes do affect a nurse's ability to communicate effectively, Table 7-4.

**Self-disclosure.** Whenever the nurse interacts with another person, she makes an impression. She causes some sort of reaction. It may be the reaction she intended or it may be just the opposite. The more the nurse lets people know her, the more likely she is to make the right impression. The process of letting people get to know one is called self-disclosure. To be effective, self-disclosure must be appropriate to the situation.

**TABLE 7-4**
**Attitudes Affecting Communication**

| | |
|---|---|
| Self-disclosure | the process of letting people get to know one |
| Caring | feeling that the patient is important and caring for him is not just a job |
| Genuineness | being oneself and not acting a role; being open and truthful |
| Warmth | feeling of affection |
| Attentiveness | demonstrating a concentration of time and attention on the patient |
| Empathy | understanding the patient's feelings; seeing things as he sees them |

Self-disclosure means talking about oneself. It means opening up to another, discussing things like feelings, expectations, and ideas. It does not mean letting skeletons out of the closet, and it does not mean discussing one's date last night. It means letting the real self be known. In order to self-disclose, the nurse must trust in herself, in her feelings, and in others. She must see the worth of her feelings, ideas, and goals. She must also trust that the receiver will see their worth. Developing trust means taking risks. Unless the nurse is willing to take a chance, communication will be ineffective. If, on the other hand, the nurse is willing to risk opening herself, the rewards can be great. Risking shows trust in the patient. The more the patient feels trusted, the more he will trust the nurse. The more the patient trusts the nurse, the more apt he is to disclose his fears, hopes, and expectations to her.

Risking is easier if the nurse thinks positively about herself and the person with whom she is attempting to communicate. Thinking positively about a person and accepting him as he is is known as *positive regard*. In order for the nurse to self-disclose, she must trust the patient. In order for the patient to reveal himself to the nurse, he must trust her. The development of mutual trust is called *establishing rapport*. It is fundamental to effective communication. Sometimes trust can be established quickly, but sometimes it can take days, weeks, or even months to develop. If the patient sees by her verbal and non-verbal behavior that the nurse really cares, if he sees by her self-disclosure that she really trusts him, rapport will be established.

**Caring.** The nurse performs caring behaviors every day, Figure 7-1. In fact, all of her daily contacts with the patient can show caring. Taking the time to do extra things for the patient definitely shows caring, Figure 7-2. The idea of caring is even more effectively conveyed to the patient if it is reinforced with verbal messages. For example, the nurse can say, "Here is some nice fresh water for you," when she offers a drink. "Now that should feel better" can be paired with rearranging a pillow, Table 7-5. It does not really matter what the nurse says as long as her message communicates the idea that she is acting because she cares and not just because it is her job.

Another way the nurse can show caring is to notice the patient. First, she should make it a point to always greet the patient by name. The patient has to feel a little less worthwhile if the nurse who has been caring for him walks by without even a glance. Knocking on the door before entering shows respect, and a greeting each time the nurse enters the room can only help to make the patient feel good. When talking to a co-worker in the patient's room, the nurse should:

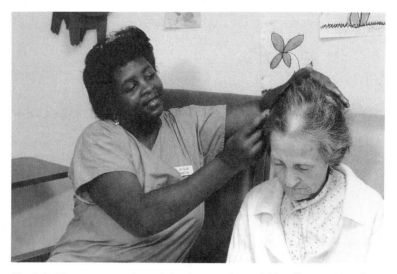

Fig. 7-1 The nurse can show caring in everyday activities, like combing the patient's hair.

- Include the patient in the conversation
- Avoid colloquialisms that the patient would not understand
- Refrain from topics that would not interest the patient
- Speak in the patient's native tongue if at all possible.

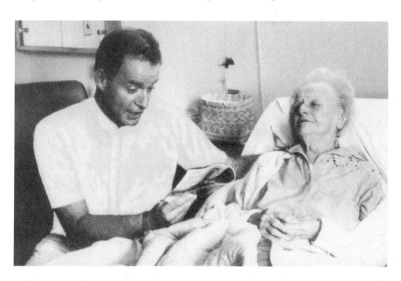

Fig. 7-2 Reading a story to a patient who cannot see well enough to do so herself shows you care.

**TABLE 7-5**
**Statements That Show Caring**

| ACTIVITY | EXAMPLES OF STATEMENTS TO PAIR WITH ACTIVITY |
|---|---|
| Bringing something for the patient | "I brought you a book to read. It's one I thought you'd like." |
| Covering the patient with a blanket | "It feels chilly in here. Perhaps this blanket will help." |
| Assisting the patient to dress | "I really like that robe. It brings out your color," or "I noticed you're having a little trouble getting your robe on. Perhaps I can help." |
| Feeding the patient or serving a tray to the patient | "It's time to eat. I hope you're hungry because it really looks good." |
| Giving the patient a drink of water | "Here's some nice fresh water for you," or "I bet some nice cool water would taste good right now." |
| Offering the patient a chair | "You look tired. Why don't you sit down?" |
| Offering the patient assistance | "Here, let me help you. Perhaps together we can arrange these flowers." |
| Leaving a room | "Is there anything more I can do for you before I go?" or "I'm leaving now, but I'll be back in twenty minutes." |
| Moving the patient up in bed | 'You look so uncomfortable. Let me move you up in bed." |
| Making the patient's bed | "There is nothing like a nice fresh bed, is there?" or "Now you have a nice fresh bed." |
| Regulating the temperature of the environment | "It seems very warm in here. Perhaps if I turn the air conditioner up, it will help." |
| Rubbing the patient's back | "A back rub always feels so good, doesn't it?" |
| Turning the patient in bed | "Changing position really makes a difference, doesn't it?" |
| Straightening a pillow | "Let me straighten your pillow for you," or "That ought to feel better now." |

The nurse can also choose something unique about the patient and comment on it. For example, the nurse can say, "That's a lovely robe you're wearing. It is the right color for you," or "I really like the way you fixed your hair today."

**Genuineness.** No communication is effective unless it is genuine. The nurse should not try to play a role. She must be herself. Being genuine implies self-disclosure and means being honest with one's feelings and sharing them with patients.

A student has taken care of Mrs. Jones for several days and has become attached to her. The student is in the room when the doctor tells Mrs. Jones that he has found a tumor and has scheduled a biopsy for the morning. All Mrs. Jones hears is "tumor," and to her, this is a death sentence. The student and the patient are both very upset. Both want to cry, but neither does. The student can no longer control herself and leaves the room after a few minutes. The instructor visits Mrs. Jones later. Mrs. Jones reveals to the instructor that she had a very difficult time controlling herself, but she knew that if she cried, the student would cry, too. She knew the student had been trying hard not to cry.

Crying together would have allowed the patient the needed release and would have demonstrated the care the student felt. It might have given Mrs. Jones the opportunity to talk about her fears, but instead she was forced to control herself.

Genuineness also means being truthful. The nurse should never attempt to answer a question when she does not know the answer. Patients ask some very difficult questions. If the nurse does not know the answer, she should say so. If the patient asks a personal question and the nurse does not want to answer, again, she should be truthful. If the nurse does not know how to respond, she should admit it.

Mrs. Jamison had just attended the funeral of her two-year-old daughter when she was admitted to the labor room. The nurse who had cared for Mrs. Jamison two years before when her first child was born was on duty at the time of the second admission, so she knew the situation. She was anxious about meeting Mrs. Jamison this time because she did not know how to relate to the patient. When Mrs. Jamison arrived, the nurse greeted her. During the examination, she simply said, "I'm really sorry about your daughter, but I honestly don't know how to handle the situation." Mrs. Jamison then told her that it was all right. Her daughter had been ill for a year. She had watched her suffer, and she was thankful that her child did not have to suffer any longer. They were then able to talk.

Another patient might have said, "I am not ready to talk about it." The nurse takes her cues from the patient's response to her disclosure.

Genuineness also means taking responsibility for one's own feelings rather than placing blame on someone else. "You make me angry" is not as helpful as "I am angry." The nurse should also direct feelings toward an object, behavior, or situation rather than a person. "I am upset with your behavior" is more effective and more genuine than "I am upset with you."

**Warmth.** Warmth is communicated primarily by nonverbal means. When appropriate, the nurse should smile. Smiling shows that the nurse cares and demonstrates that she is paying attention to the patient. Closely associated with smiling is a sense of humor. This does not mean that the nurse must be a stand-up comedian. It does mean that she should be able to see the humor in everyday situations. Humor can give the patient just the reprieve he needs to cope with more serious news. Using humor to block unpleasant messages is inappropriate. As in everything else, the nurse must take her cue from the patient.

Touch is another way of showing warmth, Figure 7-3. Touch is important to people of all ages, but it is extremely important for the very young, the old, and others who are vulnerable because of physical or emotional problems. Touch is an extremely valuable tool, but it, too, must be used appropriately. Society generally dictates what touching action is proper in a particular situation. Holding or shaking a hand, stroking or touching an extremity, patting a shoulder, or even giving a hug can be therapeutic. The nurse may find the more intimate modes of touch helpful when caring for her more distressed or vulnerable patients.

Fig. 7-3  Touch is another way of showing warmth.

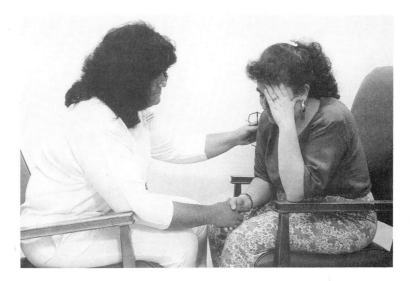

Fig. 7-4  Attentiveness is necessary for therapeutic communication.

**Attentiveness.** Posture and position indicate attention and showing attention is necessary for effective communication, Figure 7-4. Leaning forward toward the patient is better than leaning back or sitting up straight. Although tables and desks can give the nurse some security, they do not help the communication process and should be avoided. There are exceptions, but generally it is best if the nurse sits in front of the patient as close as possible without violating the patient's personal space, Figure 7-5. Personal space refers to the area that surrounds people or exists between them. Each person claims a specific territory around himself as his own personal space. The amount of territory varies with individuals, but anxiety results if an unwanted person intrudes. When the nurse sits so that she has eye contact, she not only communicates attention but she is also in a better position to observe for nonverbal cues.

Listening is another way of showing attention. It is a very important aspect of communication. Unless the nurse truly listens, she cannot hope to understand what the patient is saying. The patient needs to know that he has the nurses's undivided attention. The nurse should look at the patient with whom she is communicating. Eye contact is essential.

Listening involves both verbal and nonverbal areas. It is an art and requires concentration. The following exchange demonstrates a lack of listening that results in ineffective communication.

Fig. 7-5  The patient's positive response to the nurse's friendly touch shows that she feels her personal space has not been violated.

Daughter: "Mom, I made an appointment to see a marriage counselor."
Mother: "That's nice, dear. Would you hold this for me?"
Daughter: "John and I are having problems. We just don't seem to understand each other."
Mother: "John is such a nice boy. I liked him the first time you brought him home to meet us."
Daughter: "Mom, you're not listening to me."
Mother: "Of course I am, dear. I heard every word you said."

Many times people are so concerned about what they are going to say when the other party stops talking that they fail to listen to the entire message. People often have difficulty avoiding distractions. They pay more attention to what is going on around them and therefore only partially listen. Listening is interrupted when the receiver starts judging what the sender is saying. Once a person starts judging, she is no longer listening attentively. Instead, she is focusing on her own judgment. Often nurses have their own concerns with which they are preoccupied. Listening totally to the patient is impossible while the nurse is thinking of all the work she has to do, the patient down the hall, or the argument she had with a co-worker.

Listening takes total concentration. Fortunately, concentration is a skill that can be learned. The nurse should continuously practice giving the patient her total attention. She can begin by practicing with a classmate.

Ask a classmate to say a few words or a phrase. Concentrate on the content of her message. Try to repeat it word for word. When this can be done, have her gradually lengthen it to a sentence, then two sentences, and so on. Keep going until an entire paragraph can be repeated verbatim.

**Empathy.** The ability to know and appreciate another is called *empathy*. It means seeing things in the way others do. It means putting away one's own values and taking on the values of another. It means literally walking in another's footsteps. It means really knowing what the other person feels and thinks.

Most messages have two parts: content and feeling. Paying attention and actively listening allow the nurse to recognize each component. Effective communication requires that the nurse respond to both parts.

> I was really worried about that anatomy test. I never did well in school. I always had to work very hard. Anatomy is a difficult subject, too. I really needed to pass this test. I studied hard and I guess it paid off. I got an *A*. Imagine me getting an *A*. I still can't believe it. Now I feel as if I can do anything.

The content of the message includes all the facts, "not expecting to do well," "anatomy is difficult," "had to work hard," "study paid off," and "I got an *A*." Besides the content message, there is a feeling message. He is amazed and thrilled. He has developed a great deal of confidence in his ability to learn. These feelings are revealed in the statements, "imagine me getting an *A*," "I can't believe it," and "I feel as if I could do anything."

The full meaning of the message cannot be understood without recognizing both parts. The full meaning of the message is that the sender is proud of himself and he has increased confidence in his ability to succeed. To get that meaning, the receiver must understand both the content and feeling messages. When the receiver understands the real message, she has empathy.

Acquiring empathy can seem like an impossible task, but the nurse can learn to use it if she concentrates on listening, uses caring responses, and is warm and genuine. All of the attitudes and behaviors previously mentioned help the nurse to develop empathy. Empathy sets the stage for effective and helping communication.

# EFFECTIVE HELPING COMMUNICATION

Empathy lays the foundation for effective communication. Only after the patient feels close to the nurse can she begin to assist with more helpful responses. Unless the nurse has first acquired the attitudes and mastered the behaviors previously mentioned, her attempts at helpful responses will be, at best, ineffective. The importance of building a firm foundation cannot be overemphasized.

## Techniques of Helpful Communication

**Reflecting.** Although both feelings and content give meaning to a message, either one can be more important at any given time. Some messages are predominantly content messages with very weak feelings. Others have strong feelings attached to them. To determine which kind of message is being sent, the nurse must be able to recognize both so that she can determine which is prominent.

Reflecting is a response that lets the patient know the nurse understands both content and feeling messages. The nurse puts into other words what the sender has communicated. She does not interpret the message in the Freudian sense. She restates the patient's message and brings out both the content and feeling portions. She adds nothing to it except her empathy. She does not assume the patient's feelings, but if she has established rapport, listened attentively, and developed empathetic understanding, she will have a good idea of what the person is experiencing.

Reflective responses usually start with such phrases as "you feel like," "sounds like you," "you mean," or "it seems like you." The beginning phrases can be implied or stated. If stated, phrases should be varied so they sound less mechanical. It is a better idea if the nurse uses her own words and phrases, ones that feel more comfortable to her. Phrases such as "you feel guilty" or "you're depressed" should be avoided. Even if they are true, words like "guilt," "depressed," "hostile," and so on, will probably be denied by the sender because of their strength.

> I just took over as head nurse and I am going through a lot of stress. It seems all the decisions are mine now. I worry that I have forgotten something or that I have made the wrong decision. I keep wondering if the patients are alright. I can't eat and I can't sleep. I'm losing weight and I'm tired and cranky all the time.

The content message includes taking a new job, experiencing a lot of stress, thinks too much about the job, losing weight, and not sleeping. The feeling message is more implied but includes being worried, overwhelmed, and depressed. The following are some possible reflective responses:

- "It seems to me that you are overwhelmed with your new responsibilities."
- "You feel like you have more responsibility that you might be ready for."
- "You're saying that the new position is really getting you down."

Reflective responses act like mirrors, allowing the sender to review the message. By restating the spoken message, including both content and feelings, the real meaning can be made clearer to the sender. This is the purpose of reflecting.

**Clarification.** It is easy for the nurse to have some difficulty in following what someone is saying, even if she is paying attention. As stated at the beginning of the chapter, there are several ways communication can be misunderstood. Regardless of the reason, the nurse should never pretend she understands when she does not. This only leads to more misunderstanding. Nurses sometimes think they probably understand and that things will become clearer as the patient goes on. This is generally not true. The misunderstood part needs to be clarified or it will lead to more misunderstanding.

The nurse asks the patient for clarification using several phrases. Such statements as "Let me see if I have this right," "If I am hearing you correctly," "I seem to have missed something," or "Do you mind going over it again?" are examples of good opening phrases, Table 7-6. The receiver's understanding of the sender's message follows the opening statement. The receiver's understanding is then matched by the sender to the actual message. The sender can then verify whether or not the receiver's understanding is correct.

> I don't want to go to therapy now. I'm really tired and, besides, it isn't helping anyway.

This statement can mean that the patient does not want to go to therapy until after he has a nap; he does not want to go today; or, because he says it doesn't help anyway, he may be completely discouraged. Only through asking will the nurse be able to clear up any doubt and determine just what the patient has said.

## TABLE 7-6
## Techniques of Helpful Communication

| TECHNIQUE | EXPLANATION | EXAMPLE |
|---|---|---|
| Validation | a statement which attempts to verify the nurse's perception of the patient's message in both content and feeling areas | "You really look distressed. Something must be wrong." |
| Clarification | a statement used to clear up possible misunderstandings or to seek information necessary to understanding | "If I understand you correctly, you are upset because your daughter has just told you she is getting married." |
| Reflection | stating the nurse's perception of the patient's message in both content and feeling areas | "You are afraid you won't be needed after your daughter marries." |
| Broad questions | questions used to encourage the patient to talk | "Would you like to tell me about it?" |
| Confrontation | attack on the patient's belief in an attempt to get the patient to rethink his ideas | "What proof do you have that your daughter is making a mistake?" |

**Validation.** Validation is the process used to determine the meaning of nonverbal communication. Actions, posture, tone of voice, facial expressions, and so on always communicate a message, Figure 7-6. It can be different from the verbal message that is being communicated at the same time. The nonverbal message must be interpreted by the receiver and is often misinterpreted.

Specific gestures, postures, etc. are often interpreted by the receiver in specific ways. For example, a gentle touch usually says, "I care." A vigorous handshake conveys enthusiasm or confidence while a limp one denotes shyness or a lack of interest. With a smile, one sends the message that everything is good, but a frown says something is wrong.

Raised eyebrows may indicate surprise, while lowered ones say, "I'm sorry" or "I'm ashamed." Fear can be shown by hesitancy. Leaning or turning away says, "I don't care," but leaning toward says, "I'm interested." Outstretched arms mean "come" but arms crossed on the chest means "stay away" or "I don't want to talk." Facial expression can show boredom, disinterest, anger, irritation, fear, love, compassion, or hate, etc. These nonverbal cues are generally associated with the stated feelings, though they may not always be. As was stated before, nonverbal messages are often misinterpreted.

Fig. 7-6  Posture can be a nonverbal cue.

Perception of observations is based on past experiences, learning, and the self concept. Nonverbal messages have different meanings for different people. For example, a patient is sitting on the edge of the chair, shaking. This action may indicate that the patient is anxious, cold, excited, angry, or ill. The nurse cannot make the determination by herself; she must check with the patient. The process of checking with the patient to determine if her perceptions are right is called *validation*.

First, the nurse makes a judgment, an educated guess, as to the meaning of the nonverbal message. In order to do this she must know what the behavior could mean. She must listen carefully to the verbal message. Then she uses her knowledge of people in general and her knowledge of her patient in particular to arrive at an appropriate assumption. She can then ask the patient if she is correct by using validating statements.

Validating statements start with phrases such as "you look like" or "I see you are." "You appear to be" or "I get the feeling you are" are other examples. The validating phrase can appear at the beginning of the statement or at the end; for example, "You say everything is fine, but you appear to be very tense." As with reflective and clarifying statements, validating phrases can be implied. Instead of saying, "You look lonely," the nurse can say, "Being new around here is hard isn't it?"

**Confrontation.** Confrontation is a useful tool when used under the proper circumstances. First, the nurse should be certain that she has acquired the fundamental attitudes and mastered the caring behaviors before attempting this technique. Confrontation must be done in a calm voice. Without caring, it is more likely to turn into an argument.

With this technique, the nurse can point out a discrepancy between the patient's verbal message and the nonverbal message; for instance, "You say you are happy, but you look like you've lost your last friend."

Confrontation is also useful in helping the patient when it is necessary for a patient to realize that his beliefs are unfounded. This time the nurse actually attacks the patient's belief system. "Where is the law that says you must get an *A* on that test?"

Confrontation can also be used to help clarify two conflicting verbal messages. "You said that you did not mind losing the class election, but here you are still complaining about your opponent."

Confrontation must be done in an assertive manner. The tone of voice must be calm. The nurse has to be careful that she does not communicate disgust, anger, or pity.

**Questioning.** Generally, questions should be avoided if possible. A constant barrage makes people feel like they are being interrogated. Probing just increases anxiety. The person under more than mild stress does not have the ability to think of answers to anything more complex than a simple concrete question. When questions are used, they should be interspersed with other types of responses.

Mrs. Smith is admitted to the orthopedic floor because of a fractured hip. The nurse goes in with the interview form to get information.

Nurse: Mrs. Jones, I'm Miss Goodheart and I'll be taking care of you today. Now I need to ask you some questions.
Patient: All right.
Nurse: Who is your doctor?
Patient: Dr. Rafman.
Nurse: Does he know you are here?
Patient: Yes.
Nurse: How did you break your hip?
Patient: I fell.
Nurse: Do you have pain?
Patient: Yes
Nurse: Where is it?
Patient: Right here.
Nurse: Are you taking anything for it?
Patient: No.
Nurse: Are you allergic to anything?

This type of interrogation is cold and does not demonstrate caring. Questions that can be answered with a yes or no tend to close communication. They provide little information. When questions are interspersed with other communication techniques, however, the conversation is warmer. For example, instead of the running barrage of questions, the nurse can say:

Nurse: Good morning, Mrs. Jones. I am Miss Goodheart and I will be taking care of you today.
Patient: Good morning.
Nurse: You're a patient of Dr. Rafman's right?
Patient: That's right. Do you know if he'll be in today?
Nurse: He usually comes in during the afternoon. Does he know you're here?
Patient: Yes, my daughter called him right after I fell, and after they looked at the X-rays in the emergency room, they called again.
Nurse: I'm sure that breaking your hip and coming to the hospital today were not on your priority list. Can you tell me what happened?
Patient: Well, it was kind of dumb. I was working in my garden and stopped to admire my roses. I decided to pick some for the table and I stumbled over a rock. No one was home, so I laid outside for two hours before I could get help.
Nurse: That was quite an ordeal. Can you tell me more?

This conversation is warmer and demonstrates caring. It also tends to produce more information. Questions should be stated clearly and concisely, and only one question should be asked at a time. If the answer can be obtained from some other source, the patient should not be asked. For instance, the doctor's name can be easily obtained from the admission records. Give patients time to answer. Do not rush them.

Open-ended or broad questions are the most effective kind of questions. They are the questions that cannot be answered with one or two words. Open questions allow the patient to interpret and respond as he sees fit. These questions are good for getting the patient to discuss feelings, fear, expectations, and so forth. "What do you think about. . .?" "Would you explain further?" or simply "Will you go on?" are examples of open-ended questions.

Questions can be stated directly or indirectly. Indirect questions are statements that imply that the nurse is seeking information: "You look worried about something." "You must have a lot of questions on your mind." "You must be tired after your long trip."

Although broad, open-ended questions are most effective, there are exceptions. Questions that start with the word *why* are broad, but they tend to put the receiver on the defensive and should be avoided. Questions such as "Why didn't you take your medicine?" "Why didn't you keep your appointment?" or "Why did you get out of bed?" are examples of this type of question. They tend to close communication. A better way for the nurse to state her concern would be, "I noticed you didn't keep your appointment. Is there some reason?"

## COMMUNICATING WITH DISTRESSED PATIENTS

It is difficult to establish rapport with distressed patients because they do not trust easily; therefore, the attitudes and caring behaviors become even more important. The nurse needs to be patient but persistent. This does not mean that she should push her distressed patients to talk. It does mean that she should not get discouraged. She should continue to show that she cares. Sometimes just sitting quietly with a silent person is enough to help. Eventually, enough trust can be established for the patient to feel he can communicate.

Probing and interrogating are to be avoided because these techniques add to the patient's anxiety. Arguing and trying to reason with him are futile. The patient under stress is less able to concentrate; therefore, he cannot be expected to remember. Directions may have to be repeated, or the nurse may have to take the patient by the hand and guide him.

The patient under stress cannot process information well and more than one-step directions can overwhelm him. For instance, the nurse should never say such things as, "I'm going to get you up now, Charlie," "Turn over, I'm going to change your bed," or "I'm going to lay out your clothes and I want you to get dressed." With statements like these, there are just too many things for the patient to think about. Because of this, he is unable to process the message and becomes confused. He may then retaliate with aggression.

Statements spoken to these patients need to be broken down into single steps. For example,

- "Sit up. That's right."
- "Bring your legs over. Good."
- "Now, turn toward me."

If this is done and the patient is given time to process each step, he will be more cooperative. The more distressed the patient is, the clearer and simpler the steps must be.

The nurse must always remain calm, even if the patient becomes agitated. She must accept his anger and allow him to vent it. Some patients try to engage the nurse in a power struggle. She needs to recognize this and avoid getting caught up in it.

## Dealing with Aggression

There are two types of patients who may exhibit aggressive behavior. The first type has a distorted view of reality because of acute or recent stress. This type of person becomes aggressive when he cannot verbally let needs be known. The actions are spontaneous and a response to a situation. There is no warning other than the person's increasing frustration. The other type of person is one who has never learned how to handle anger. There is resentment, although the reason why has long since been forgotten. The aggressive acts of this person are deliberate and thought out. Usually, it is a reaction to something real or imagined. There is often some warning before the attack.

When a patient threatens that he will harm himself or others, the threats should not be ignored. Many times they are a call for help. If the threats are not heeded, aggression will most surely occur. If the nurse can intervene in time, she may be able to calm the person sufficiently. When she intervenes, the nurse approaches the patient calmly and carefully. She verbally talks to him and reassures him that everything is under control. Talking is important because silence is seen as approval of the aggressive behavior. Calm talking seems to diffuse the anger. The nurse should not attempt to touch the patient, however, or make any sudden moves. These actions can be interpreted as counteraggression and cause more anxiety.

Other patients need to be moved away from the aggressor for their own protection and so they don't unwittingly encourage the aggression. Time is the most important weapon in calming aggression. If the nurse's intervention is ineffective, leaving the patient in a safe place for a few minutes can be enough to lessen the tension.

## Confusion

Reality orientation is the most useful tool for helping confused patients (see Chapter 9). With this technique, patients are directed back to reality. "This is Wednesday and you are in Atlanta." The nurse should never argue with the patient. If the situation tends to get out of hand, the nurse can use distraction therapy—change the subject and get the confused person's mind on something else.

As with the aggressive patient, all tasks need to be broken down into simple steps. The directions for each step are given one at a time. The patient then needs time to respond. His concentration is limited and his memory for recent events is poor, so it is a good idea to call a confused patient by his first name. Generally, the earlier something is learned, the longer it is retained.

It is important that the nurse get the patient's attention before she starts to speak and that she maintains that attention with eye contact. This way the patient is not confused about who the nurse is talking to. The conversation needs to be concrete, and the nurse needs to remain calm and relaxed. Touch is essential to keeping this patient in reality, Table 7-7.

**TABLE 7-7**
**Techniques for Communicating with Distressed Patients**

| |
|---|
| • Use caring behaviors. |
| • Exercise patience and persistence. |
| • Limit questions. |
| • Use simple, concrete statements. |
| • Talk calmly. |
| • Approach the patient calmly. |
| • Give one-step directions. |
| • Get the patient's attention first. |

## COMMUNICATING WITH THE DEPRESSED PATIENT

Communication is the major nursing tool for the depressed or withdrawn person. The focus of this tool is to improve the patient's feelings of self-worth. First, trust must be established. This can entail sitting silently with the patient. This lets him know that it is all right to be silent and puts no pressure on him to talk. It also lets him know that the nurse cares enough to take the time.

After sitting silently for a time, the nurse can begin to talk about nonthreatening things. She can begin to build the patient's self-esteem by pointing out his positive aspects. If the patient voices feelings, they should be acknowledged and then reflected. The patient should be allowed to talk about past unhappy experiences, because venting feelings lessens stress. Repeatedly voicing frustrations, though, reinforces them. It is important that the patient be allowed to tell his story, but there needs to be a limit on the number of times an incident can be repeated.

As with all other distressed patients, the nurse needs to remain calm. She uses simple, concrete sentences. She does not attempt to argue, probe, or interrogate. She accepts the patient's anger, but, above all, she continually stresses reality. Once rapport is established, confrontation is an extremely effective method of helping the patient see the discrepancy between his feelings and reality.

## SUMMARY

Effective communication adds to the patient's psychological comfort, so it is necessary to physical and emotional recovery. Communication is not just an exchange of words. It includes all methods used to relay messages to another person, including body movements, posture, and tone of voice.

Communication can be ineffective if the sender sends disguised messages, when there are conflicting verbal and nonverbal messages, or when the receiver fails to listen. It can also occur if words with multiple meanings are used, if abstract messages are sent, or if the receiver's conditioning prepares her to misperceive the message.

Effective communication is purposeful. Gathering information, showing caring, and developing trust are some of the goals. Many times, the nurse needs to provide information as well when encouraging or teaching good health habits.

Communication must remain open until the goal is reached. Certain responses tend to close communication and include: belittling, disagreeing, defending, making stereotyped statements, changing the subject, falsely reassuring, giving advice, and agreeing.

Whenever the nurse interacts with another person, she makes an impression. She causes some sort of reaction. The more the nurse allows herself to be known, the more apt she is to make the right impression. Allowing oneself to be known is called self-disclosure. In order to self-disclose, the nurse must trust and work toward developing trust in the patient. The development of mutual trust is called *establishing rapport*, and it is fundamental to the communication process.

The nurse must demonstrate certain attitudes if she is to effectively communicate. These include caring, genuiness, warmth, attentiveness, and empathy. Effective helping techniques include reflecting, clarifying, validating, questioning, and confronting.

Communication with distressed patients requires all of the nurse's skills. It is difficult to establish rapport because distressed patients do not trust easily. These patients need a clam, accepting atmosphere. Probing and interrogating should be avoided. Arguing and trying to reason with him is futile. The nurse should establish eye contact so the patient knows she is talking to him. Statements are simple and concrete. Directions are broken down and given one step at a time.

## SUGGESTED ACTIVITIES

- With a group, take turns communicating with nonverbal cues. See how many messages the group can correctly identify.
- Practice effective responses with classmates.
- Read *Nursing 85*, October 1985, p.53.
- Do a process recording and evaluate your responses.
- Make a list of all the things you do for patients that show caring. Pair these with statements that reinforce your behavior.

## REVIEW

A. Multiple choice. Select the best answer.
1. Communication is
   a. an exchange of words.
   b. a nonverbal message.
   c. the spoken and written word.
   d. all methods used to convey messages.

2. All of the following block effective communication except
   a. disagreeing.
   b. humorous statements.
   c. agreeing.
   d. reassuring clichés.

3. The means by which the receiver processes or interprets information is
   a. empathy.
   b. perception.
   c. reflection.
   d. validation.

4. Responding with what the nurse perceives as the patient's message is
   a. confrontation.
   b. clarification.
   c. genuineness.
   d. reflection.

5. If a nurse feels like crying with a patient, she should
   a. leave the room.
   b. cry.
   c. control herself.
   d. change the subject.

6. When the nurse says, "I don't know how to answer that," she is being
   a. genuine.
   b. empathetic.
   c. evasive.
   d. inattentive.

7. The patient states, "Look how healthy I am. This tumor can't possibly be malignant." The nurse responds, "I'm sure everything will be all right. You just try to get a good night's sleep and don't worry." What will happen here?
   a. The patient will feel reassured.
   b. The conversation will stop.
   c. The patient will think his hospitalization is unnecessary.
   d. Communication will stay open.

8. A technique that should be used with distressed patients is
   a. probing.
   b. trusting.
   c. reality orientation.
   d. reasoning.

9. If the nurse tells a distressed patient to get out of bed and get
   dressed, the patient will probably
   a. get out of bed and get dressed.
   b. tell her he can't do it.
   c. scream.
   d. feel anxious.

10. When a patient threatens to harm himself, the nurse should
    a. intervene.
    b. forget it.
    c. ignore it unless it persists.
    d. confront the patient.

11. The most effective tool for helping the confused patient is
    a. reality therapy.
    b. argumentation.
    c. reality orientation.
    d. confrontation.

12. When talking to a patient, the nurse should sit facing him because
    that position is better for
    a. listening.
    b. restraining.
    c. intimidating.
    d. observing.

B. Briefly answer the following.

1. List three goals of therapeutic communication.

2. Name three reasons for ineffective communication.

3. Name three attitudes essential for therapeutic communication.

4. List three techniques for effective listening.

5. Name the block to communication in each of the following responses:

   a. Patient to the nurse: "I'm so fat I don't have any friends."
      Responses:
      • "Since you know what it is, why don't you do something
        about it?"
      • "Oh, you're not so fat."

   b. One nurse talking to another nurse: "That Mrs. Jones is the most
      ungrateful patient I have ever met."

Responses:
- "You should be more patient with her."
- "Boy, I know exactly what you mean."

c. Disturbed patient to the nurse: "Get out of my room. Next time you show your face, I'll throw something at you."

Responses:
- "O.K., but if you don't get well, don't blame me."
- "My, what pretty flowers."
- "There now, you'll feel better tomorrow."

## BOOKS

Chunn, J. *Mental Health and People of Color*, Howard Press: Wash., D.C., 1983.

Janosik, E., & Davies, J. *Psychiatric Mental Health Nursing.* Jones & Bartlett, Pub.: Boston, MA., 1989.

Norris, J., & Kunes-Connell, M., et al. *Psychiatric Nursing: A Continuum of Care.* Delmar Pub.: Albany, N.Y., 1989.

## ARTICLES

Burgess, A.C., et al. Partners in care: patients as consumers of health care *American Journal of Nursing*, 90(6): 73–75, 1990.

Davis, A.J., et al. The competency quagmire: clarification of the nursing perspective concerning the issues of competence and informed consent. *International Journal of Nursing Studies*, 26(3): 271–279, 1989.

McBride, A.B. Psychiatric nursing in the 1990's *Archives Psychiatric Nursing*, 4(1): 21–28, Feb. 1990.

McKeon, K.L. Introduction: a future perspective on psychiatric mental health nursing. *Archives Psychiatric Nursing*, 4(1): 19–20, Feb. 1990.

Siantz, M.L., et al. Issues facing child psychiatric nursing in the 1990's. *Journal Child Adolescent Psychiatric Mental Health Nursing*, 3(3): 79–84, July–Sept., 1990.

Slavinsky, A.T. Psychiatric in the year 2000—from a nonsystem of care to a caring system. *Image* 16(1): 17–20, 1984.

# CHAPTER 8
# EMOTIONAL ASPECTS OF
# MATERNAL AND
# CHILD CARE

## OBJECTIVES

After studying this chapter, the student should be able to:

- Compare the normal developmental stressors of pregnancy with the stressors faced by the pregnant teenager.
- Briefly explain the nursing care needs of the pregnant teenager.
- List three ways in which primary bonding is enhanced.
- Explain the effects of bonding on the infant.
- Describe the mechanisms used by parents to cope with a malformed child.
- List the needs of the mother with a malformed infant.
- List five behaviors of the abused child.
- List six characteristics of the abusing parent.
- Describe conditions in which child abuse should be suspected.
- Contrast the reactions of children of each age level to hospitalization.
- Describe the general nursing needs of hospitalized children.

Emotional care in maternal and child health is a vast subject. Though every pregnant woman and every child has emotional needs to be met by the nurse, this chapter is limited to the teenaged unwed mother; fostering the bonding process; assisting parents to cope with a malformed or stillborn infant; child abuse; and the general emotional needs of the hospitalized child.

# PREGNANCY AS A DEVELOPMENTAL STRESSOR

Too often, nurses caring for pregnant women concern themselves primarily with physical care. Testing urine, checking vital signs, and making relevant observations are important to a safe delivery and a healthy child. However, it is also important to recognize that psychological factors affect physical status.

Pregnancy is a developmental stressor. Many of the emotional manifestations in pregnancy are thought to be due to normal physiological changes. Child-bearing women often become progressively more introspective. They become primarly concerned with themselves and their infants as thinking turns inward. Pregnant woman experience frequent and exaggerated mood swings which may disturb them and their families. They often become more passive and dependent. This may result in increased sensitivity to anything that might be interpreted as inattention or lack of concern.

Pregnancy is often thought of as being joyous, but all families may not be happy about it. A child means extra expenses, added responsiblity, and a change in life-style for the couple. A baby may interfere with future educational or career plans, Figure 8-1. Parents may fear the pain of labor or birth of a malformed infant. Even in families that are pleased, practically every woman encounters anxiety to some extent at some point during her pregnancy. Most women, even those who sincerely desire a child, experience some negative feelings.

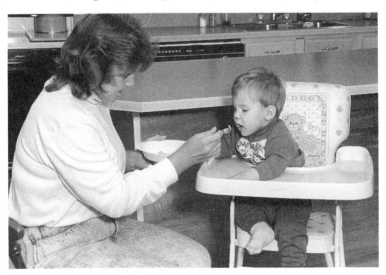

Figure 8-1 This young mother's education has been put on hold until her son is old enough for school.

Certain women are better able to cope with the stressors of pregnancy. These include women who have accomplished previous developmental tasks; women who have their physiological, safety, love and belonging needs met; and women who have the support of their husbands. The unwed teenager may have her physiological, safety, and love and belonging needs threatened, and may also be missing the support of a husband.

## PREGNANCY AND THE UNWED TEENAGER

The pregnant teenager has a more difficult time adapting to the stressors of pregnancy, Table 8-1. She must face the normal hormonal, physical, and matabolic changes of pregnancy before she has had time to adjust to the changes of adolescence. She must adapt to the role of parenthood while still facing the role change to adulthood. She must accomplish Erikson's stage of identity and at the same time accomplish the stage of generativity. She must discover who she is as a mother before she discovers who she is as a person. Her search for independence is often blocked

**TABLE 8-1**
**Stressors in Adult and Teenage Pregnancy**

| ADULT PREGNANCY | TEENAGE PREGNANCY |
|---|---|
| • Cope with hormonal changes brought on by pregnancy | • Cope with hormonal changes brought on by adolescence and hormonal changes brought on by pregnancy |
| • Adjust to the role of parent | • Adjust to the role of adult and adjust to the role of parent |
| • Accomplish the stage of intimacy and cope with the stage of generativity | • Accomplish the stage of identity and the stage of intimacy while coping with the stage of generativity |
| | • Develop independence while increasing dependency caused by pregnancy |
| | • Develop cognitive abilities while often being forced to quit school |
| • Take on responsibility for another person | • Clarify own values and take on responsibility for a child |
| | • Improve the self-concept in spite of a pregnancy which tends to lessen it |

by the financial and emotional demands of pregnancy. Even in this sophisticated society, teenagers have a lack of knowledge about pregnancy and parenthood. This lack of knowledge gives rise to exaggerated and unrealisitc fears. The young teenager's reasoning skill is still developing and she has not yet acquired the ability to look at things apart from the particular instance. Without this ability, she has difficulty recognizing the future consequences of her actions.

While she has more stressors to face, the adolescent has less coping ability. She is still growing, clarifying her values, and developing her self-concept. If her sexual partner refuses to acknowledge responsibility for the pregnancy, the girl's self-concept is lowered. Her family may also reject her, which further lowers her self-worth as well as giving her added financial burdens.

Teenagers are categorized according to young, middle, and late adolescence. Pregnancy has been increasing in the youngest group. This young adolescent thinks in the present. She gives little thought to the possible effects of coitus. Knowledge of her body, pregnancy, and contraception is limited and what knowledge she does have is often incorrect. There is usually no lasting relationship between the young teen and her boyfriend. She often becomes pregnant following the first sexual experience. Denial is a common mental mechanism and she may deny the pregnancy even when it is evident to others. If she does accept the pregnancy, she often denies responsibility. This blame is placed on her sexual partner who is then despised. Adoption is seldom considered. More often, the baby is turned over to the grandparents to raise as the mother's sibling.

The middle adolescent is a little more sophisticated in her knowledge. She is aware of the possible effects of coitus. She knows about contraceptives, but many times fails to use them. There are many theories to explain this. If the girl uses contraceptives, she is obviously planning on having sexual relationships, which goes against her parentally instilled values and makes her a "bad" girl. If coitus is not planned, she can save her self-concept by blaming "the moment" or "passion." Pregnancy is actually sought by some middle teens because it means maturity and independence to them. It may also be a rebellious act against her parents. In some groups, it is simply the "in thing" to do. Whatever the reason, the middle adolescent usually denies responsibility for the pregnancy. She often blames her parents.

The middle teen rarely has a desire to marry her boyfriend, but she does need his support. Without his support, she experiences increased anxiety. Even though she may have consciously or unconsciously sought the pregnancy, she often has unrealistic fantasies and ambivalent feelings about motherhood. The pregnant teen demonstrates her extreme anxiety through rebellion, anger, disinterest, and boredom, as well as numerous somatic complaints. She is usually very frightened of medical care and seeks care late, if at all. Because of anxiety and distrust of authority, she may be uncooperative during examinations and may not follow through on directions. The baby may be raised by the grandmother. In other cases, the teen is forced to assume complete care to the detriment of her educational and social life.

The late adolescent girl frequently views her relationship with her sexual partner as meaningful and often has planned to marry him at some time in the future. Even if marriage is not sought when pregnancy is discovered, recognition and support from the sexual partner seems to be important. Although older adolescent males tend to accept responsibility for paternity more often than younger adolescents, the vast majority still reject the girl. Unfortunately, the older adolescent is also the one most often rejected by the family. This girl is able to recognize the financial, social, and emotional problems to be faced as a single mother. Without the needed support, she is apt to become depressed and to feel that no one cares. Although schools are now more lenient, the older adolescent is often forced to quit school because of financial and time constraints. Most pregnant adolescents keep their infants, but abortion and adoption are becoming more acceptable alternatives.

## Nursing Care of the Unwed Pregnant Teenager

It is easy to stereotype all unwed adolescents, but unwed adolescents do not fit neatly into one category. Although there are many problems, some teenagers are proud of the pregnancy and look forward to the experience of motherhood. As with any other patient, it is important that the nurse get to know the teenager.

Mary Ann is fifteen years old. She presents herself at the clinic because she has missed some periods. She isn't certain how many. She sits quietly while her blood pressure is taken and submits reluctantly to a weight check. She rebels at the vaginal examination, pushing the doctor away and screaming, "Don't do that."

Mary Ann acted as she did because she was frightened of certain things that she did not understand. She was embarrassed, self-conscious, and distrustful of all the new people around her.

Before the nurse can effectively help Mary Ann, she must develop a trusting relationship. Trust takes time; several visits may be needed. It would be ideal if one nurse saw Mary Ann each time she came to the clinic. To develop trust, the nurse needs to explain all procedures before they are done and explain them in terms that the teenager understands. Mary Ann is still developing her ability to think in general rather than specific terms. Since she is experiencing stress, explanations should be in simple terms, using visual materials whenever possible. Developing trust also involves continuity, accepting Mary Ann without criticism, and providing understanding and concern.

Communicating with the adolescent is not easy. The nurse should not expect to discuss Mary Ann's needs on the first visit. Mary Ann, as other teenagers, is more apt to talk to a person with whom she has established trust. The average teenager communicates more with nonverbal methods. Therefore, the nurse can often be more effective with a smile or a look, Table 8-2. Generally something that bothers the teenager will surface nonverbally. However, few adolescents will offer information without direct questioning. Young and middle teenagers think in specific terms and respond literally to questions. If the nurse asks, "Can you tell me about it," the answer is liable to be simply, "Yeh." To get the right answer, the nurse should say, "Tell me about it." Teens also use the language differently.

Nurse: "I hear you have a new motorbike."
Patient: "Oh yeh, it's cosmo."
Nurse: "It's cosmo! What does that mean?"
Patient: "You're really a squid. It's qual, real bad."
Nurse: "You mean it's cool?"
Patient: "Right. It's a b-a-a-d bike."

**TABLE 8-2**
**Characteristics of the Adolescent Communication Pattern**

Uses more nonverbal communications.

Responds literally to questions.

May have different meaning for words or use neologisms.

May not be aware of feelings or have words to express feelings.

Frequently repeats because of fear of being misunderstood.

To express confusion, a teen may say, "I don't have my head on straight" or "I'm hung over." A "bummer" means things are not too good.

Young and middle adolescents may not be aware of their feelings or they may not have the words to express their feelings. When an adolescent describes an experience, she may start over several times because she has a fear of not being understood. It takes good observation and timing to initiate therapeutic communication with the adolescent.

> Nurse: "You look like you've lost your last friend. Bad news, Mary Ann?"
> Patient: "Nah, piece of cake."
> Nurse: "Then why the long face? What did the doctor tell you?"
> Patient: "Oh, nothing."
> Nurse: "He confirmed the pregnancy, didn't he?"
> Patient: "It's a real bummer."

Sometimes the nurse must take the initiative, such as "Mary Ann, there are some things we need to discuss." This is less effective because the adolescent may or may not comply.

To determine Mary Ann's needs, the nurse should access

- What pregnancy and parenthood mean to her.
- Her level of anxiety.
- What effect the pregnancy has on her relationship with her family and her boyfriend.
- With what other developmental stressors she is dealing.
- The level of her need for fulfillment according to Maslow. (Are her physiological needs, safety needs, and love and belonging needs being met?)
- How she sees her situation.
- What plans she has for herself and her baby.
- What she feels she needs from the nurse.

From the assesment, the nurse or nursing team may determine that she has the following strengths and weaknesses:

| Strengths | Weaknesses |
| --- | --- |
| - She accepts responsibility for the pregnancy. | - She has not told her family and fears rejection. |
| - She has continued support from her boyfriend. | - Her future plans are vague. |

- The school has a program for pregnant teens.

- She feels she needs preparation for labor and delivery and parenthood.

- She has the support of her boyfriend's parents.

- She has an unrealistic view of pregnancy and parenthood.

- Her physical, safety, and love and belonging needs are threatened.

Mary Ann, like all teenagers, needs the support of her family. She may need help in gaining it. A referral to social service or a visiting nurse mght provide support while she tells her parents. Mary Ann also may benefit from modeling. Modeling would demonstrate how she might talk to her family. If the family does reject her, she will need a referral for financial assistance and shelter.

Since Mary Ann expressed the need for education, this should be given priority. This need can be met in a group with other teenagers or individually during her clinic visits. Preparation for labor should include relaxation exercises and some type of breathing techniques to lessen anxiety during labor. Probably the most important thing the nurse can do for Mary Ann, and teenagers like her, is to provide support and be there when she needs someone.

During labor, Mary Ann has the same needs as any other mother: Relief of pain, information, and emotional support. She needs to have the person she trusts, whether it be her mother, her boyfriend, or both, with her.

To help the young mother after birth, the nurse should manipulate the environment to provide success experiences for her. She should provide compliments and gently correct mistakes. If the girl decides to keep her baby, rooming-in should be encouraged so that the mother can learn to care for her infant with the nurse's help. If she is planning on putting the baby up for adoption, she may want to see the child and care for it while the baby is in the hospital. When the baby is adopted, she will face separation anxiety, but not seeing the baby often causes lasting anxiety. Since the young mother is in the hospital for such a short time, referral to the Visiting Nurses Association is usually indicated.

## PRIMARY BONDING

Primary bonding is the process of establishing an intimate interdependent attachment among mother, father, and infant, Figure 8-2. Re-

Figure 8-2  Some bonding behaviors are eye-to-eye contact and holding the baby no more than seventeen inches from their face.

search on bonding, which began to surface in the 1960s, indicates that bonding is important to the child's future interpersonal relationships. It also shows that infants not bonded to their mothers in the critical immediate postpartum period were more apt to be abused and neglected. Children who were not bonded experienced more anxiety and were less able to cope with stress. The bonded person is the child's primary support.

Bonding normally begins in the prenatal period when the mother feels *quickening* (the first movements of the baby). The mother then can be seen massaging her growing abdomen, delighting in fetal movements, and talking to the fetus. The immediate postpartum period seems to be most crucial. Mothers who have had negative feelings about being pregnant during their pregnancies have effectively bonded to the infant during the time just after birth. Although bonding may occur later, it seems to be more difficult and intervention is usually essential.

Natural bonding is initiated by either the parent or the infant through behavior to which the other person responds. The baby cries and the mother picks him up and cuddles him. The baby stops crying and molds itself to the mother's body. The mother further responds by smiling. Eye contact, skin-to-skin contact, and touching seem to be essential to the process, Table 8-3. If not interfered with, bonding occurs automatically. The process can be enhanced prenatally and postnatally.

**TABLE 8-3**
**Factors That Enhance Bonding**

Eye-to-eye contact at no more than seventeen inches distance

Skin-to-skin contact

Touching and stroking

Speech in high-pitched voice

Cuddling

Baby Care

Bonding is encouraged prenatally by allowing parents to listen to fetal heart tones, teaching them to massage the mother's abdomen, and showing them how to feel and recognize fetal parts. In the postnatal period, the parent is taught to hold the infant no more than seventeen inches from the face. The infant cannot see clearly beyond seventeen inches. Eye-to-eye contact is important. Talking to the infant should be encouraged. Some mothers feel uncomfortable talking to an infant. They may feel as if they are talking to a doll or a wall. The nurse can help by pointing out the baby's responses.

Allowing the mother to care for the baby, including feeding, changing diapers, and bathing, are also ways of encouraging bonding. The young mother in particular should be encouraged to provide physical care for her infant. Rooming-in helps the bonding process. The nurse supervising the infant's care should compliment the mother and minimize corrections. If the mother is having difficulty with the baby's care and becomes upset, it is important that the nurse not take over. The mother sometimes believes the baby evaluates her against the more skilled nurse and her self-concept is lowered. Of course this is not true, but it is nonetheless a real concern to the mother. Instead of taking over, the nurse should help the mother to relax and then assist her with suggestions. If the environment is manipulated to give the mother success, her self-concept is enhanced.

The unwed teenager sometimes opts to turn her baby over to her mother to raise, hoping to later assume the mothering role. This may be impossible. The infant who has bonded to the grandmother may refuse to relate to her as a mother.

# COPING WITH A STILLBORN OR MALFORMED INFANT

Whenever a problem in delivery occurs or is anticipated, the father is usually banned or banished from the scene. The infant's then taken quickly to the nursery and bonding with either parent is interrupted. If the mother is awake, she quickly becomes aware that something is wrong and anxiety results. If she is anesthetized, anxiety is only delayed.

Parents dream of having a perfect child. When a malformed or seriously ill infant is born, the parents must grieve for the loss of the dream child before they can even begin to accept the real child. Denial is often the mechanism used. Denial is manifested by a refusal to name the baby, by refusing to see or touch the baby or talk to it. The parents may withdraw. They may accuse the hospital of changing babies or of not doing what they could to save the infant. The parents often feel guilty about malformations and wonder what they have done to cause it. They are embarrassed and feel inadequate as people. Having a malformed child can be a blow to the self-concept.

Sometimes the mother is given a tranquilizer to help calm her. She may be transferred off the maternity floor. This is seldom helpful because the parent must cope with the grief at some time. Rather than delay the grief process, it is better to handle it with the support of the nursing staff. Denial may lessen anxiety, but the problem still remains. The parents should see the child as early as possible. No matter how deformed the child is, reality is usually less disturbing than the parent's imagination.

The mother should be the one to make the choice of moving to a private room or off the floor. If she decides to leave the maternity floor, she should be allowed to return whenever desired. The maternity nurse should, at least, visit her and keep her informed of the baby's progress.

Parents have the right to truthful information. Though it is generally the doctor's responsibility to keep them informed, the nurse should be prepared to answer questions. The parents need to be encouraged to talk together and share their feelings. Though talking may seem difficult and the parents may cry or become angry, it must be remembered that it is the event that is disturbing, not the talking about it. Talking brings out the hurt, but is also allows the event to be faced. Denial only delays problem solving.

Nurses often neglect the mother with a malformed child because they experience anxiety themselves and they do not know what to say. The nurse's withdrawal only adds to the mother's anxiety. The nurse can best help by letting the mother know it is all right to talk about her feelings if she desires, Table 8-4. Many times mothers feel they must maintain a facade for nurses and visitors. The nurse can give the mother permission to talk by saying, "Would you like to talk about it," or "I'll be here if you would like to talk," or "Getting it out sometimes helps." She can then take cues from the mother. "What can I do to help you?" "Would it help if I called your minister?" "Would you like to see the baby?" "Would you feel better if I limited your visitors?" False reassurances such as "You're baby is going to be all right" are never helpful. The parent is not ready to hear statements such as "At least you have a healthy child at home" or "You're still young, you may have other children."

### TABLE 8-4
### Needs of the Mother of a Malformed Infant

- To be given continuous and truthful information about the baby's progress
- To be encouraged to discuss feelings with spouse
- To have nonjudgmental acceptance of behavior
- To be given the chance to ventilate feelings if desired
- To be given emotional support
- To have periodic visits from the nursing staff if transferred off the maternity floor
- To see and touch the baby
- To be able to withdraw, if necessary, without being labeled a rejecting parent

The nurse should point out the baby's healthy aspects. If the child has a name, it should be used and the child should always be referred to by the correct sex. As she cares for the child, the nurse should be alert for signs of anxiety in the mother and allow her to withdraw from the child if the mother feels the need.

If the infant dies or was born dead, allowing the parents to see the child prevents denial. The infant may have been severely deformed and the death anticipated, but the event is still stressful. This parent, too, needs to have time with the baby in order to complete the grief process. Crying should be encouraged. Nurses may also feel like crying. By doing so, they share the sadness with the parents.

## POSTPARTUM DEPRESSION

Mild depression is thought to occur in a large proportion of postpartum women. It usually begins two or three days after delivery and disappears within a week or two. Approximately 40% of women with mild depression have symptoms that persist for a year. Medical treatment is not necessary, but nursing care is important.

Symptoms include a feeling of let down, irritability, loss of appetite, insomnia, and anxiety. The mother cries easily and she may complain of discomfort and an inability to concentrate.

This mother needs to know that her depression is normal and that the symptoms will disappear. She must be able to verbalize her feelings. The family should be aware of what is happening, because the mother needs their support and understanding as well. Rest and nutrition should be encouraged and it is essential that any new mother have help in the home for the first few days at least.

The cause of postpartum depression is not known, but it is thought to be due to hormonal changes and perhaps, partly, to the mother's reaction to her changing role.

About 1–2% of new mothers have severe depression which does require intervention. Severe depression affects the relationship between the mother and her infant. She may be overprotective or reject the child. She may have delusions and she may endanger the child's life. Severe depression has many times gone undetected until the infant has been harmed. Early detection is essential, so that the mother may be hospitalized and treatment begun. Treatment includes medications, behavioral management, or, at times, ECT.

## CHILD ABUSE

Child abuse is defined as maltreatment of a child by the child's caretaker. It is not a new phenomenon. Children from birth through adolescence have been victims of physical and sexual mistreatment and neglect throughout history. If the nurse works with children, she will at some time become involved with a child who has been abused. In most states, nurses are part of the group that is required to report suspected cases of child abuse.

Abuse can be suspected when the parent's story does not explain the injury or when the parents frequently change doctors or clinics. Abuse also may be suspected when there are many unexplained old injuries or when there are multiple scars in various stages of healing. An abused child may be aggressive or apathetic and unresponsive. There may be an unrealistic fear of adults or an overattachment to the parents. In some instances, the child may become the caretaker of the parent. Most abused children protect their parents because of fear of abandonment or fear of reprisal.

The majority of abusing parents are not psychotic. They care about their children and have no desire to seriously hurt them. The abusing parent comes from all economic and educational levels. The average abusing parent has a low self-concept and poor coping ability, Table 8-5. He or she lacks parenting skills and often was abused as a child. This parent has unrealistic expectations of the child and employs physical means of discipline almost exclusively. He or she is usually dependent and has a spouse that it too passive to meet dependency needs. The average abusing parent relates poorly to others and has marriage difficulties. As a result, he or she is often lonely.

There is apt to be a lack of bonding. The child who is abused is often seen as different from others in appearance and/or behavior. Most severe damage is done to small children. Two-year-olds and those between thirteen and fifteen years of age are often abused because they are difficult to care for and place added stress on the parent.

**TABLE 8-5**
**Characteristics of the Abusing Parent**

All economic and educational levels
Has low self-concept
Has poor coping ability
Lacks parenting skills
Was abused as a child
Has unrealistic expectations of the child
Primarily uses physical means of discipline
Has a dependent personality
Has a passive spouse
Has poor interpersonal relationships
Is lonely
Has marriage difficulties
Has not bonded to the child
Cannot handle criticism well

It is not easy, but if the nurse is going to help prevent child abuse, she must look beyond the injured child. If abuse is to stop, it is the parent who must be helped.

The abusive parent may use abuse as a disciplinary technique. The twelve-month-old may be beaten because he is not yet able to walk. The toddler may be burned because he wouldn't stay away from the stove. A school-aged child may be whipped with a belt because that's the way the child's father was disciplined. The school-aged child may be shoved or thrown against a wall because he disturbs a parent. The thirteen-year-old may be beaten and confined to home indefinitely because of a rule infraction. The parent may expect complete obedience, which is impossible for the thirteen-year-old.

Abusing parents, like all dependent people, cannot handle criticism well. The person who is trying to help must be nonjudgmental and nonauthoritarian. The helper must develop a trusting relationship with the parent, which may take weeks or months, and must also supply the nuturing and support the parent is lacking. The helper needs to allow the parent to be dependent while guiding the parent toward growth and independence.

Since stress is a factor, the nurse needs to determine where the parent is on Maslow's hierarchy of needs. If physical needs such as food, shelter, and employment are not being met, the parent should be referred for help in these areas. Marital and/or personal counseling by a psychologist or professional nurse counselor may be needed. The parent may also benefit from assistance in budgeting, marketing, and child care. Growth and development of the normal child are often unclear to the abusing parent. The self-concept can be improved by providing success experiences for the parent and by realistic compliments.

Parents Anonymous is a self-help group of abusing parents who have joined together to help each other learn to handle stress and do problem solving. Homemaker home health aides are nonprofessionals trained to help abusing parents in their homes by providing assistance and support.

Child abuse is a widespread and complex problem that requires a multidisciplinary approach. The nurse can play an important role because she can represent a knowledgeable but nonauthoritarian figure to the parent.

## THE HOSPITALIZED CHILD

The child's response to hospitalization depends in part on the developmental stage of the child. Very young children do not understand why they must be hospitalized and often see it as punishment. If the child has any concept of illness, it is thought to be due to disobedience. Although regression is a mental mechanism observed in all age groups, it is most common in the very young child. One who has been drinking from a cup may seek comfort in a bottle during hospitalization.

When the hospitalized child is removed from all that is familiar, he looks to the bonded person for support. If that person is missing, anxiety increases. This is known as separation anxiety which is normally seen in children between seven months and three years of age. In the hospital, separation anxiety may be seen in children up to four or five years of age, and occasionally in older children. When the parent leaves, the child exhibiting separation anxiety responds with temper tantrums, crying, and attempts at clinging to the parent. It is important to the child that at least one parent remain and participate in his care if at all possible. If both parents must leave, they need to understand that separation anxiety is a normal reaction. The child who is old enough to understand should be told that the parent is leaving but will return. It is best that the parent not sneak away. The nurse should be sure that the child has his "security blanket" nearby as well.

Although preschoolers still see hospitalization as punishment, there is an increased awareness of the hospital experience. Fantasies are common; intrusive procedures can be made very frightening through fantasy. The preschooler knows the missing parent will return. However, he worries that the parent will not be able to find him, particularly if he is moved. Bleeding is extremely frightening; a small bandage often lessens anxiety as effectively as a kiss.

The school-aged child's hospitalization causes anxiety mainly because of immobility, a possibility of bodily harm, and a loss of friends and parents. This child may be embarrassed when forced to surrender privacy. Though hs is not expected to have separation anxiety, he sees the loss of parents as a stress and is relieved when the parent is around. This child's concept of illness is dependent in part on the parent's concept of illness. It is generally a simple concept; most children fear mutilation of the body.

If the school-aged child is not in pain, he may actually enjoy his stay in the hospital. It may mean a recess from schoolwork and added attention. It may represent a change in his routine and he may enjoy experimenting with the many push buttons in the unit.

The adolescent who is attempting to gain independence is thwarted by illness and hospitalization. He must submit to sometimes strict rules and regulations. The adolescent may be told what he can and cannot eat, when and how he can move, and activities in which he may and may not engage. Illness that affects the body image is more frightening to the young adolescent, but the increased attention of the medical and nursing staff may be welcome. The young teen often accepts the diagnosis but is optimistic about the prognosis.

The middle adolescent finds his independence threatened. Hospitalization limits association with friends, intrudes on his privacy, and makes him less attractive. The more visible the condition, the more distressing it is to the middle teen.

The older adolescent is more stable. He can understand illness and the effects it may have on his future life. He sees the more serious illness as being the most threatening. Friends primarily comprise his support system.

## Coping Methods of the Hospitalized Child

Other factors which affect the child's response to hospitalization are past experiences, the child's support system, and the child's coping methods. If the previous hospital experience has been good and the child has learned to trust the nursing staff, readmission is less traumatic. Almost all children benefit by the presence of the parent. Children seem to adapt to hospitalization better if they have a close relationship with their parents. Nurse may find some parents difficult, but they are important to the child. Therefore, the nurse needs to make the parents feel welcome. She should keep the parents informed about what is happening to their child and why.

Play is a major source of support. It relieves boredom and tension. Also, the child learns through play. The child can learn about hospital procedures and better ways of handling stress. Play helps the young child communicate. All children need age-related toys, Table 8-6. Infants like bright mobiles, busy boxes, and rattles. The adolescent wants a radio or telephone.

**TABLE 8-6**
**Examples of Age-related Toys**

| INFANT | TODDLER | PRESCHOOL | SCHOOL | ADOLESCENT |
|---|---|---|---|---|
| mobiles | push toys | blocks | action dolls | radio |
| busy boxes | stuffed animals | cars | models | telephone |
| rattles | dolls | trucks | books | puzzles |
| | | dolls | puzzles | books |
| | | stuffed animals | | |

The very young child copes by crying and clinging to the parent. The child who is able to use language may ask questions to relieve stress. "How" and "why" are common words in the preschool-aged group. At other times, children display dependence by saying, "Will you stay with me?" or hostility with, "I'll hit you." Regression to a more secure stage of development is most common in this age group.

Denial is the most common mechanism seen in children and adolescents, but the denial is usually temporary. The child who uses denial does not accept the extent of his illness. He may be uncooperative, overly complaint, or even stoic about painful procedures. Another mechanism is intellectualization. The child who uses this method disassociates himself from the illness and views it objectively. This child displays an interest in factual aspects; it is as if he were discussing someone else.

Some children cope by acting out. Children who act out exhibit aggression and uncooperativeness. These children may disconnect an IV from their arms, hide their medications, or refuse to stay in bed. Children who are depressed often act out. Almost all children use manipulation which effectively lessens anxiety.

Children need to know what procedures are to be done and forewarned about discomfort. The information needs to be presented in a way the child understands. Puppets, storytelling, games, and handling equipment are ways of preparing children for procedures. Preschool children need to follow their usual routine. The school-aged child needs to know that his things at home will not be disturbed while he is away. All children need to have their life routines changed as little as possible.

## SUMMARY

Pregnancy is a developmental stressor for every woman, but for the pregnant teenager stress is increased. She must cope with the stressors of adolescence as well as the stressors of pregnancy. Her basic needs may be threatened and she may be missing the support of her sexual partner.

Teenagers are categorized into young, middle, and late adolescence. The young adolescent often becomes pregnant following the first sexual experience. Denial is the mechanism commonly used. Blame is usually placed on the sexual partner. The baby is generally turned over to the grandmother to be raised as the mother's sibling.

The middle adolescent may choose pregnancy for various reasons. It may mean maturity and independence, or it may be an act of rebellion against her parents. In some groups it is simply the "in thing" to do. Denial of responsibility is often seen in this age group. The middle adolescent needs the support of her sexual partner. She often has unrealistic and ambivalent feelings toward motherhood. The middle teen is usually an anxious and frightened child. She may be rebellious, angry, disinterested, or bored. She may offer numerous somatic complaints in exhibiting her anxiety.

The late adolescent often intends to marry her sexual partner. The support of her sexual partner is important. Although many older adolescent males accept responsibility for paternity, the vast majority still reject the girl. The older adolescent is able to recognize the many problems of being a single parent. Abortion and adoption are becoming more acceptable alternatives.

Teenagers cannot be stereotyped; it is important for the nurse to get to know the adolescent parent. Trust is an essential component of the helping relationship. Developing trust may require several visits. The nurse needs to listen, assist with meeting the needs identified by the teenager, and offer support. Education for labor and parenthood is the most common need expressed.

Communicating with a teenager may be difficult because the adolescent uses language differently and responds literally to questions. Teenagers may not be aware of their feelings or they may not have words to express their feelings.

Nursing care should be based on an assessment of the mother's strengths and weaknesses. Since the young mother is in the hospital for such a short time, referral to a visiting nurse service is usually indicated.

Bonding is the process of establishing an intimate attachment among the infant, mother, and father. Bonding is very important to the child's future interpersonal relationships and ability to handle stress. The immediate postnatal period seems to be a critical time for bonding. Skin-to-skin contact, touching, and eye contact are essential to the bonding process. The nurse can help to enhance the bonding process by encouraging these activities.

When a malformed or stillborn infant is born, the parents must grieve for the dream child before they can begin to accept the real child. Denial is a mechanism often used. Denial is often fostered by the health care professionals who provide tranquilizers and move the mother off the maternity floor. The mother should be the one to make the choice of moving to a private room or to another department. If the mother does decide to move, she should be visited by the nursing staff so she does not feel forgotten.

Parents need to have truthful information about their child's condition. Parents need to be encouraged to talk together regarding their feelings. The nurse can best help by letting the mother know it is all right for her to talk about the event and by following the mother's cues. The nurse can point out the baby's healthy aspects. The child's name and sex should be used. The nurse needs to be alert to signs of anxiety in the mother.

Mild depression occurs in a large percentage of postpartum patients. It lasts only one to two weeks and requires no treatment. The mother, however, does need support, understanding, rest, and nutrition. Severe depression occurs in 1–2% of postpartum patients and requires immediate detection and treatment.

Child abuse is defined as maltreatment of a child by the child's caretaker. Children of all ages are abused, though the very young are usually the most seriously injured. Nurses are required to report suspected cases of child abuse. Abuse can be suspected when the parent's story does not explain the injury or when parents frequently change doctors or clinics. It may also be suspected when there are many unexplained old injuries and when there are multiple scars in various stages of healing. The behavior of an abused child may range from aggression to apathy. The abused child usually protects the parent.

Abusing parents come from all economic and educational levels. Stress seems to be an important factor. The child that is abused is often seen as different in appearance or behavior.

If the nurse is to help prevent child abuse, she must look beyond the injured child and assist the parent. Abusing parents need help handling stress; in learning new ways to discipline; in getting information on normal growth and development; and in providing child care. They may need professional counseling to aid in personality growth. Child abuse is a widespread problem that requires a multidisciplinary approach.

The child's response to hospitalization depends on the developmental level of the child and the parent's concept of illness. Other factors are previous hospitalizations, the child's support system, and the child's coping methods.

The hospitalized child has been removed from all that is familiar. He is sometimes subjected to embarrassing procedures and strict rules. There is often an interruption in his developmental needs.

The hospitalized child should have a parent near and be told what is going to happen to him and why. His routine should be changed as little as possible. Children cope with stress in different ways. The very young child cries, has tantrums, and clings to the parent. Older children may use denial, intellectualization, acting out, and manipulation.

## SUGGESTED ACTIVITIES

- Volunteer time at a child abuse center, if one is available in your area.
- Attend a prenatal class in which preparation for labor and delivery is discussed.
- Volunteer time in a home for unwed mothers, if one is available in your area.
- Spend a day with a play therapist. Observe the therapist's responses to and effects on children.
- Plan an age-appropriate activity for a pediatric patient.
- Make a list of bonding behaviors observed while visiting or caring for a mother and her newborn.
- With a small group of classmates, discuss feelings toward the abusing parent.
- With a small group of classmates, discuss feelings toward the birth of a malformed child.

## REVIEW

A.  Multiple choice. Select the best answer.

1.  Emotional manifestations of pregnancy are thought to be due to:
    a. psychotic disorders.
    b. somatic disorders.
    c. neurotic disorders.
    d. normal physiological changes.

2.  The pregnant teen must accomplish the stages of
    a. autonomy and generativity.
    b. trust and initiative.
    c. identity and generativity.
    d. autonomy and identity.

3. The middle adolescent often becomes pregnant out of
   a. ignorance.
   b. failure of birth control methods.
   c. overwhelming passion.
   d. rebellion against her parents.

4. Bonding should be encouraged because it
   a. assures that the child will not be abused.
   b. prevents postnatal complications.
   c. aids in involution.
   d. is important in the child's future interpersonal relationships.

5. Parents should be encouraged to hold their infants
   a. no more than seventeen inches from the face.
   b. only when the child is wrapped securely.
   c. in the football hold for ease in handling.
   d. away from the face to avoid germs.

6. The mental mechanisms most often used by parents of a malformed child is
   a. rationalization.
   b. intellectualization.
   c. denial.
   d. reaction formation.

7. The mother of a malformed child can best be helped by
   a. giving a tranquilizer to calm her.
   b. being transferred from the stressful maternity department.
   c. making her face reality and forcing her to see and touch
   the infant.
   d. allowing her to talk about her feelings if she desires.

8. The parent who abuses a child should
   a. be understood and counseled.
   b. be locked away in jail.
   c. be admitted to a psychiatric hospital.
   d. none of the above.

9. A major factor in child abuse seems to be
   a. the parent's economic level.
   b. the parent's age.
   c. stress.
   d. the number of children in the home.

10. The mental mechanism most commonly seen in the very young hospitalized child is
    a. denial.
    b. regression.
    c. fantasy.
    d. identification.

11. The most common mental mechanism seen in the young, pregnant adolescent is
    a. denial.
    b. regression.
    c. fantasy.
    d. identification.

12. One of the most important stresses the school-aged child faces in the hospital is
    a. immobility.
    b. lack of opportunity for creativity.
    c. missing school.
    d. increased attention.

B.   Briefly answer the following.

1. Name four stressors of pregnancy that the teenager must face.

2. Name three actions essential to the bonding process.

3. List five behaviors that might be exhibited by an abused child.

4. List six characteristics of the abusing parent.

# CHAPTER 9
# GERIATRIC
# MENTAL HEALTH

## OBJECTIVES

After studying this chapter, the student should be able to:

- List five causes of reversible confusion.
- List five ways to prevent reversible confusion in the elderly.
- Name the three categories of confusion.
- Name three things the nurse does to assess confusion in a patient.
- List four things the nurse can do to help prevent confusion in her patients.
- Explain how prevalent attitudes affect the care of patients with irreversible confusion.
- List the theories explaining the cause of Alzheimer's disease.
- Describe the different types of depression.
- Explain the pathology found in patients with Alzheimer's disease.
- Differentiate between pseudodementia and true dementia.
- Briefly explain the nursing needs of the patient with dementia.
- Briefly explain the nursing needs of the patient with depression.
- List the signs and symptoms of depression.

Old age is arbitrarily defined as sixty-five years and older. This group contains a very diverse population physically, mentally, economically, and so on. Unfortunately, many people still believe the stereotyped picture of the aged as debilitated, poverty stricken, cranky, and confused.

Chronic diseases are more prevalent in the aged, but the percentage that are disabled is very small. Personality does not radically change as one becomes older. It gradually develops throughout the life cycle. If the individual is able to meet the developmental tasks of each age level and cope with the stressors encountered, the older person will not suddenly become cranky on his sixty-fifth birthday. Confusion is not a part of normal aging, but a symptom of disease. Although there are certainly elderly poor, most have adequate incomes and assets to live comfortably.

The number of elderly has greatly increased in the past few years and it is expected to continue to rise steadily. This is primarily due to the vast improvements in maternal and child health. More infants are now living to reach old age.

There is a big difference between the old old and the young old. Those who are turning sixty-five today are healthier, better educated, more affluent, and more outspoken than their older peers. They are speaking up and letting their needs be known. They are using political power to push through improvements in their lives and particularly in health care. As a result, there has been a surge of interest in the problems of the aged.

The care of the aged with mental health problems has unfortunately lagged behind. Deinstitutionalization had the effect of moving the mentally distressed elderly into nursing homes, where the facilities and preparation of the personnel are generally inadequate to care for them. Although the situation is improving, most of the health care disciplines find little challenge in working with the elderly. The more common mental health problems of the aged, namely confusion, dementia, and depression, are considered to be within the realm of the general practitioner.

Although the mentally distressed elderly are more concentrated in nursing homes, many are being taken care of by their families. Nurses working in hospitals, doctor's offices, and in the community are more apt to be the first to see these patients. If the nurse is able to recognize the different types of problems, she may be able to save some patients great expense in terms of time, money, stress, self-esteem, and independence. More than a few elderly whose problems are reversible find themselves in institutions rather than living independently at home simply because the confusion was not treated.

# CONFUSION

Confusion is not clearly defined. It means different things to different people. Patients can be termed confused if they do not know where they are or the day's date. If the answer to a question is inappropriate or behavior does not meet acceptable standards, the older person will be labeled confused. If they appear to have a blank stare or ignore simple directions, older people will most certainly be considered confused.

Confusion is one of the most common problems in old age and is extremely detrimental to the quality of life in later years. Confusion is not a normal part of aging, but can result from the internal and external stressors on any of the older person's body systems. Confusion is divided into three main categories: (1) confusion resulting from acute illness, drugs, emotional stress, or environmental factors (this is the most common type of confusion seen in this age group and it is generally reversible if treated early); (2) confusion resulting from brain damage, commonly referred to as dementia; and (3) confusion associated with affective disorders and psychosis, Table 9-1.

### TABLE 9-1
### Categories of Confusion

- Reversible confusion associated with external factors such as drugs, acute illness, environment
- Dementia, or irreversible confusion
- Confusion associated with affective disorders or psychosis

## Reversible Confusion

Before labeling a patient as confused, the nurse must be certain that the problem is not a result of factors that mimic confusion, Table 9-2. It is assumed that everyone living in the same area shares the same culture and speaks the same language. It is hard for most young people to realize that the culture of the elderly is quite different from the culture today. The customs and manners learned in youth are carried into old age. The elderly person's own culture continues to influence his behavior even though the world around him is changing. For example,

## TABLE 9-2
### Conditions That Mimic Confusion

- Different cultural norms
- Poor eyesight
- Poor hearing
- Lack of orienting devices
- New surroundings

Mrs. Jones, age seventy, was admitted to the hospital two days ago. Her nurses had labeled her confused. While growing up in the old country, her family ate lunch at noon and dinner at 10:00 P.M., a custom she continued to date. When her dinner tray was served at 5:00 P.M., she refused to eat because it was not her dinnertime. At 10:00 P.M., after everyone was in bed, she demanded her dinner, stating that she had had nothing to eat since noon. Although her nurses did not understand this, Mrs. Jones was simply following accepted behavior for the only culture she knew, her family pattern.

Normal hearing loss limits the older person to the lower pitched tones, so that parts of a question can easily be missed. Rather than admit to a hearing loss, the older person often answers the question he thought he heard. Visual hallucinations may be nothing more than a misperception of the environment, particularly when the older person is not wearing his glasses.

Sensory losses due to the normal aging process can result in an incorrect diagnosis of confusion in yet another way. The changes have the effect of lessening sensitivity to stimuli, resulting in sensory deprivation. Because the normal loss of hearing and sight is within a given range, there is also the possibility of sensory overload. When the individual turns on his favorite program, he has to turn up the volume in order to hear the higher pitched tones. The lower tones are also turned up. Because he can hear these within normal range, the increased volume bombards the brain and thus results in sensory overload.

When the elderly person is admitted to the hospital, the new environment is strange. When one day is like the next, it is easy to lose track. With no large clocks or calendars around, it is easy for anyone to forget the date and/or the time. Unfortunately, when the older person does this, he is termed confused.

When first admitted to the hospital, the elderly person may wake up in the middle of the night and wonder where he is. He may get out of bed and wander in an attempt to orient himself. He may be trying to figure things out, resulting in a blank, lost look on his face. He will no doubt be considered confused, and in all probability, he will be put back to bed and restrained. As a result, he will remain lost, and the nursing staff will have unwittingly added to the misdiagnosis.

**Causes of Reversible Confusion.** Reversible confusion is the most common type of confusion in the aged. Until definitely proven otherwise, all confusion should be considered reversible so that attempts will be made to find and eliminate the causes, Table 9-3.

*Hypoxia* is a lack of oxygen in the brain. Approximately 20 percent of the total oxygen consumption is used by the brain. Nerve cells cannot live for more than a few minutes without it. Because there is no storage area, the brain must get a continuous supply. Such conditions as respiratory disease, cardiac problems, hypothyroidism, hypotension, and anemia affect the oxygen supply to the body and, thus, to the brain.

*Hypothermia* is a lowering of the body temperature. The elderly are very sensitive to this condition. They do not sense cold as easily as younger people do, and their temperature can drop to dangerous levels very quickly. A temperature over 102° F is considered hyperthermia, and it, too, can present as confusion in the elderly.

**TABLE 9-3**
**Causes of Reversible Confusion**

| CONDITION | EFFECT |
|---|---|
| Hypothermia | slows  brain cell functioning |
| Hypoxia | diminishes cell functioning and can kill brain cells if prolonged |
| Dehydration | ineffective brain cell functioning because of a lack of electrolytes |
| Drugs | adversely affect brain environment |
| Constipation | diminishes brain cell functioning |
| Sensory deprivation | changes brain environment |
| Depression | slows brain cell functioning |
| Malnutrition | diminishes brain cell functioning by changing the brain's environment |
| Pain | diminishes brain cell functioning as a result of stress effects |

Thirst is often ignored by the older person. They may not be aware of water's importance to them, it may be too much trouble to get a drink, or water may be inaccessible to them. Dehydration is a very dangerous condition for the aged, and the only symptom may be confusion. This is especially true when electrolytes are involved. *Electrolytes* are chemicals necessary for the functioning of the nerve cell. Unless they are in balance with each other, confusion results.

The elderly take many drugs and some of them can lead to confusion, Figure 9-1. Tranquilizers and sedatives lessen stimuli to the brain, a condition that can be sufficient to cause a deprivation. Drugs such as diuretics, hormones, and alcohol affect the fluid and electrolyte level of the brain. Medications, such as digitalis, that are used to treat hypertension and cardiac problems, can cause a lessened blood supply.

Some narcotics depress the respiratory center of the brain and, thus, cause a lessening of oxygen. Besides oxygen, the brain requires a constant supply of glucose to function effectively. Hypoglycemics used to treat senile diabetes lessen the amount available. Anticholinergics, which dry secretions, and antidepressants, which alter the chemicals in the brain, can also affect the brain's environment adversely. Antibiotics, so necessary to treating infections, have also caused confusion. Drug-induced confusion is more common than previously thought, Table 9-4.

Fig. 9-1 Elderly patients take many medications, some of which can cause confusion.

**TABLE 9-4**
**Drugs That Can Cause Confusion in the Elderly Patient**

| DRUG | EFFECT |
|------|--------|
| Tranquilizers and sedatives | lessen stimuli to the brain, resulting in sensory deprivation |
| Diuretics | affect fluid and electrolyte balance |
| Alcohol | affects fluid and electrolyte balance |
| Hormones | affect fluid and electrolyte balance |
| Digitalis | lessens oxygen to the brain by slowing heartbeat |
| Narcotics | lessen oxygen to the brain by depressing respirations |
| Hypoglycemics | lessen glucose available for the brain |
| Anticholinergics | dry secretions, thus changing the environment of the brain |
| Antidepressants | affect the brain's environment |
| Antibiotics | affect the brain's environment |

Sometimes the confusion can be totally due to the drug. Sometimes a person with dementia also has confusion as a result of drug therapy. In other words, a reversible confusion can be superimposed on an irreversible one. People with this problem have increased confusion and part of it is treatable. If drug-induced confusion is recognized, another drug can be substituted that increases clarity in the patient's mind. Too often confusion is attributed to old age and is not treated at all.

Mrs. Stevens, age eighty-five, was visiting her daughter. The daughter noticed that her mother seemed confused. She set her suitcase down and the next minute couldn't find it. She turned the faucet on, saying she wanted a drink of water, but then quickly forgot and left the water running.

She never did get her drink. Even though she had been in the house many times, she could not seem to remember where the bathroom was. The daughter took Mrs. Stevens to see the doctor, who admitted her to the hospital.

Mrs. Stevens had been on a maintenance dose of digitalis following a heart attack several years ago. She told the nurses that she did not want her heart pill anymore. Because it was believed that she needed the drug, it was given to her by injection. As time went on, she became more confused.

Finally, the doctor told Mrs. Stevens' daughter that she must consider nursing home placement for her mother. "After all, your mother is eighty-five. It is time." he reasoned. The daughter reluctantly did as directed. She then sold her mother's house and disposed of most of her furniture, clothes and household goods. After all, her mother had no use for them anymore, and besides, she needed the money to pay the expensive nursing home bills.

In the nursing home, Mrs. Stevens told the new nurses that she did not want her "little yellow pill," the digitalis. When it was brought to her, she clenched her teeth and steadfastly refused to take it. This time, no injections were given. The drug was offered to her when it was due, but if she refused, no attempt was made to force her to take it. Mrs. Stevens' confusion, having been caused by the digitalis, began to clear up, and, eventually, she was discharged. Unfortunately, by that time she had no home to go to and no belongings to call her own. This happened because the confusion was wrongly assumed to be irreversible.

Mr. Roberts fared a little better. He, too, was diagnosed as having Alzheimer's disease. He was confused, presented bizarre behavior, and was hostile toward his wife. When the diagnosis was made, his wife got him to sign a power of attorney and then admitted him to a nursing home. Because the nursing home was in another town, the patient had to have another doctor. The new doctor saw no reason why Dilantin had been ordered and began to wean the patient from it. As the Dilantin level fell, Mr. Roberts's confusion began to clear up.

The nursing staff noticed the change in his behavior and soon questioned his diagnosis. They asked the doctor to order a Dilantin level, which was done. Although Mr. Roberts was improving, his Dilantin level was still dangerously high. With the problem recognized and treated, however, he continued to improve.

He went to senior citizen's centers and to church socials. He made many friends and one lady friend in particular. First, he got his power of attorney back and then decided to divorce his wife in order to be with his new friend. He was able to leave the nursing home and move in with his lady friend for a happier ending.

In addition, simple things like constipation, pain, immobility, and other forms of emotional and physical stress can also cause confusion in the elderly.

## Assessment

The first part of the nursing process is assessment. Before doing any assessment for confusion, the nurse must see that the patient has his glasses and his hearing aid, if needed. She also must be certain that she knows the answers to the questions she intends to ask. For instance, to test long-term memory, the nurse can ask, "What is your birthdate?" The patient may be confused and have no idea, but he may know enough to realize that the nurse is asking for a date and give one. In order to recognize a change, the nurse must be aware of the patient's history and past behaviors. This information should be contained in a good psychosocial history.

A psychosocial history is the first step in assessing confusion or any of the other problems of the aged. If there is reason to believe that the patient is confused, information should be obtained from the family or at least verified by them. It is best to obtain the history in an informal setting (see Chapter 7 for questioning techniques).

The family and/or the patient must first be aware of the reason for the history. Time should be taken to establish some rapport. This can be done by talking about some noncontroversial subject like the weather. The basic identifying information can be collected easily after that. Patient's name, address, marital status, number of children, religious preference, type of work done, and educational level are examples of basic identifying information, Figure 9-2A.

Figure 9-2B is the Minimum Date Set or MDS. This form or another approved form containing the same information is required to be used by all nursing homes having certified medicare beds. It is a comprehensive assessment tool, but it is a minimum data set and other information may be needed. This assessment must be started on admission and completed within 14 calendar days. The assessment along with its accompanying protocols and trigger rap sheets help the nurse determine needs and transfer these needs to the care plan. Protocols (see Figure 9-2C), help the nurse understand the problem she has assessed and help her think about other problems that might be related. The rap sheet, Figure 9-2D, gives the nurse guidelines in care planning. The MDS must be coordinated by a nurse, but other disciplines may complete aspects of the MDS.

The psychosocial history provides a baseline to which present behavior can be compared. It provides information on the patient's strengths and support system available to him. The history can help determine whether or not the confusion is reversible and provide clues as to the cause and treatment of the condition. The history can be taken at a formal setting, but more often the information is obtained through informal conversations, section A, Figure 9-3.

**Arizona Elks Major Projects, Inc.**
**LONG TERM CARE UNIT**      Date:_____
**SOCIAL HISTORY**           Hospital No.:_____

The information on this form will be used solely to aid in the adjustment of your relative and you to the nursing home life. You are not obligated to answer any questions that you deem intrusive or unnecessary, but all information given will be considered confidential.

Patient's name: _____     Date admitted: _____
Age:_____ Date of birth:_____     How long in Tucson:_____
Marital status: M ( )W ( )D ( )S ( )   Previous area:_____
Religion:_____             Clergyman's name:_____
Responsible person: _____  and address: _____
Diagnosis:_____            Relationship:_____

I.  PRIOR TO ILLNESS

   A.  Tell me about _____
       before he became ill.            _____
       (What type of person was he?)    _____
       (How would you describe him?)    _____

   B.  How would you describe his      Relative's Name:      Relationship:
       relationship with his family?    _____
       (Are they able to visit?)        _____

   C.  How would you describe his       _____
       relationship with friends?       _____
       (Are they able to visit?)        _____

   D.  Was religion an important       Yes ( ) No ( ) Comment:
       factor in his life?              _____

   E.  What kind of work did he do?     _____
       (Educational level?)             _____
       (How long unemployed? retired?)  _____

   F.  How did he usually handle        _____
       problems or difficulties?        _____

II. AFTER ILLNESS

   A.  Date of onset.                   _____

   B.  Which of the changes that you    _____
       have noticed concerned you       _____
       the most?

   C.  What factors did you consider    _____
       before deciding on nursing       _____
       home placement?

III. LIKES AND DISLIKES

   A.  Does he have any talents?        _____
       (singing, dancing, painting,     _____
       writing, etc.)

Fig. 9-2A  Psychosocial history and assessment samples.

B.  What things does he
    particularly like? (Food,
    objects, attitudes, actions,
    activities)
C.  What things does he
    particularly dislike?
    (Objects, attitudes, actions,
    activities)
D.  Describe his daily routine prior
    to coming to the Elks.
E.  What possessions are most
    important to him?

## LONG TERM CARE UNIT
## PSYCHOSOCIAL EVALUATION

Name:_____          Hospital No.:_____
Marital status: M (  )W (  )D (  )S (  )    Age: _____
Admitted from:_____          Admitted from:_____

I.  PATIENT'S STRENGTHS
    AND WEAKNESSES
    A.  Family support              Yes (  )  No (  )
        1. Who visits?              Comment: _____
        2. Frequency
        3. Patient's reaction to visits
        4. Family reaction to patient
    B.  Adjustment to illness
        1. Knowledge of illness     (  ) unaware   (  ) limited
                                    (  ) moderate   (  ) well aware
        2. Stage of loss            (  ) denial   (  ) anger
                                    (  ) bargain   (  ) acceptance
        3. Independent as much as   Yes (  )  No (  )
           possible?                Comment: _____
    C.  Adjustment to the institution
        1. Accepts therapeutic      Yes (  )  No (  )
           program                  Comment: _____
        2. Accepts need to be in    Yes (  )  No (  )
           nursing home             Comment: _____
        3. Occupies time            Yes (  )  No (  )
           constructively           Comment: _____
    D.  Socialization
        1. Relates well to other    Yes (  )  No (  )
           patients                 Comment: _____

Fig. 9-2A (Continued)

    2. Participates in activities    Yes ( )  No ( )
                                  Comment: _____

  E.  Mental Capacity
    1. Alert                    Yes ( )  No ( )
    2. Oriented               Time ( )  Person ( )  Place ( )
    3. Appropriate reactions    Yes ( )  No ( )
                                    Comment: _____
    4. Memory               Past events ( )  Present events ( )

  F.  Personal Characteristics

| | | | | | | |
|---|---|---|---|---|---|---|
| 1. Outgoing | Yes ( ) | No ( ) | 7. Mature | Yes ( ) | No ( ) |
| 2. Intelligent | Yes ( ) | No ( ) | 8. Sensitive | Yes ( ) | No ( ) |
| 3. Quiet | Yes ( ) | No ( ) | 9. Happy | Yes ( ) | No ( ) |
| 4. Aggressive | Yes ( ) | No ( ) | 10. Demanding | Yes ( ) | No ( ) |
| 5. Altruistic | Yes ( ) | No ( ) | 11. Coping | | |
| 6. Selfish | Yes ( ) | No ( ) | Mechanism _____ | | |

II.  LIKES AND DISLIKES

  A.  Activities: _____
  B.  Food: _____
  C.  Objects: _____
  D.  Attitudes: _____

III.  FAMILY

  A.  Stage of loss    Denial ( )  Anger ( )  Bargain ( )
                          Depression ( )  Resignation ( )
  B.  Relationship with patient: _____

IV.  POTENTIAL PROBLEMS

  A.  Lack of stimulation            ( )
  B.  Disorientation                ( )
  C.  Lack of family support        ( )
  D.  Adjusting to institution or illness  ( )
  E.  Family needs                 ( )
  F.  Lack of strength              ( )
  G.  Poor coping mechanism        ( )
  H.  Memory loss                  ( )
  I.  Tension                       ( )
  J.  Dependence on staff           ( )
  K.  Other comments             ( )

COMMENTS:

_____
_____
_____

Fig. 9-2A (Continued)

# MINIMUM DATA SET

### FOR NURSING FACILITY RESIDENT ASSESSMENT AND CARE SCREENING (MDS)
(Status in last 7 days, unless other time frame indicated)

▭ = Write in the appropriate alpha or numeric response

▢ = Check (✓) if response is applicable

UPON COMPLETION OF THIS FORM, GO TO RAP TRIGGER LEGEND

## SECTION A. IDENTIFICATION AND BACKGROUND INFORMATION

1. **ASSESSMENT DATE**
   Month — Day — Year

2. **RESIDENT NAME & I.D.#**
   (First) (Middle Initial) (Last)
   ID#

3. **SOCIAL SECURITY NO.**

4. **MEDICAID NO. (If applicable)**

5. **MEDICAL RECORD NO.**

6. **REASON FOR ASSESS-MENT**
   1. Initial admission assess.
   2. Hosp/Medicare reassess.
   3. Readmission assessment
   4. Annual assessment
   5. Significant change in status
   6. Other (e.g., UR)

7. **CURRENT PAYMENT SOURCE(S) FOR N.H. STAY**
   (Billing Office to indicate; check all that apply)
   a. Medicaid   [a.]
   b. Medicare   [b.]
   c. CHAMPUS   [c.]
   d. VA   [d.]
   e. Self pay/Private insurance   [e.]
   f. Other   [f.]

8. **RESPONSI-BILITY/ LEGAL GUARDIAN**
   (Check that apply)
   a. Legal guardian   [a.]
   b. Other legal oversight   [b.]
   c. Durable power attrny./health care proxy   [c.]
   d. Family member responsible   [d.]
   e. Resident responsible   [e.]
   f. NONE OF ABOVE   [f.]

9. **ADVANCED DIRECTIVES**
   (For those items with supporting documentation in the medical record, check all that apply)
   a. Living will   [a.]
   b. Do not resuscitate   [b.]
   c. Do not hospitalize   [c.]
   d. Organ donation   [d.]
   e. Autopsy request   [e.]
   f. Feeding restrictions   [f.]
   g. Medication restrictions   [g.]
   h. Other treatment restrictions   [h.]
   i. NONE OF ABOVE   [i.]

10. **DISCHARGE PLANNED WITHIN 3 MOS.**
    (Does not include discharge due to death)
    0. No   1. Yes   2. Unknown/uncertain

11. **PARTICIPATE IN ASSESS-MENT**
    a. Resident
    0.No
    1.Yes
    b. Family
    0.No
    1.Yes
    2.No family

12. **SIGNATURES**
    Signature & Date of RN Assessment Coordinator
    
    Signatures & Dates of Others Who Completed Part of the Assessment

3. **MEMORY/ RECALL ABILITY**
   (Check all that resident normally able to recall during last 7 days) Fewer than 3 ✓ = ▲²
   a. Current season   [a.]
   b. Location of own room   [b.]
   c. Staff names/faces   [c.]
   d. That he/she is in a nursing home   [d.]
   e. NONE OF ABOVE are recalled   [e.]

4. **COGNITIVE SKILLS FOR DAILY DECISION-MAKING**
   (Made decisions regarding tasks of daily life)
   0. Independent—decisions consistent/reasonable ▲⁴
   1. Modified independence—some difficulty in new situations only ▲⁴ ▲²
   2. Moderately impaired—decisions poor; cues/supervision required ▲⁴ ▲²
   3. Severely impaired—never/rarely made decisions ▲²

5. **INDICATORS OF DELIRIUM —PERIODIC DISORDERED THINKING/ AWARENESS**
   (Check if condition over last 7 days appears different from usual functioning)
   a. Less alert, easily distracted ●¹   [a.]
   b. Changing awareness of environment ●¹   [b.]
   c. Episodes of incoherent speech ●¹   [c.]
   d. Periods of motor restlessness or lethargy ●¹   [d.]
   e. Cognitive ability varies over course of day ●¹   [e.]
   f. NONE OF ABOVE   [f.]

6. **CHANGE IN COGNITIVE STATUS**
   Change in resident's cognitive status, skills, or abilities in last 90 days
   0. No change   1. Improved   2. Deteriorated ●¹ ▲¹⁴

## SECTION C. COMMUNICATION/HEARING PATTERNS

1. **HEARING**
   (With hearing appliance, if used)
   0. Hears adequately—normal talk, TV, phone
   1. Minimal difficulty when not in quiet setting
   2. Hears in special situation only—speaker has to adjust tonal quality and speak distinctly
   3. Highly impaired/absence of useful hearing

2. **COMMUNI-CATION DEVICES/ TECHNIQUES**
   (Check all that apply during last 7 days)
   a. Hearing aid, present and used   [a.]
   b. Hearing aid, present and not used   [b.]
   c. Other receptive comm. technique used (e.g., lip read)   [c.]
   d. NONE OF ABOVE   [d.]

3. **MODES OF EXPRESSION**
   (Check all used by resident to make needs known)
   a. Speech   [a.]
   b. Writing messages to express or clarify needs   [b.]
   c. Signs/gestures/sounds   [c.]
   d. Communication board   [d.]
   e. Other   [e.]
   f. NONE OF ABOVE   [f.]

4. **MAKING SELF UN-DERSTOOD**
   (Express information content—however able)
   0. Understood
   1. Usually Understood-difficulty finding words or finishing thoughts
   2. Sometimes Understood-ability is limited to making concrete requests ▲⁴
   3. Rarely/Never Understood ▲⁴

5. **ABILITY TO UNDER-STAND OTHERS**
   (Understanding verbal information content-however able)
   0. Understands
   1. Usually Understands-may miss some part/intent of message ▲²
   2. Sometimes Understands-responds adequately to simple, direct communication ▲² ▲⁴ ▲⁵
   3. Rarely/Never Understands ▲² ▲⁴ ▲⁵

6. **CHANGE IN COMMUNI-CATION/ HEARING**
   Resident's ability to express, understand or hear information has changed over last 90 days
   0. No change   1. Improved   2. Deteriorated ●¹

## SECTION B. COGNITIVE PATTERNS

1. **COMATOSE**
   (Persistent vegetative state/no discernible consciousness)
   0. No   1. Yes (Skip to SECTION E)

2. **MEMORY**
   (Recall of what was learned or known)
   a. Short-term memory OK—seems/appears to recall after 5 minutes
   0. Memory OK   1. Memory problem ▲²   [a.]
   b. Long-term memory OK—seems/appears to recall long past
   0. Memory OK   1. Memory problem ▲²   [b.]

## SECTION D. VISION PATTERNS

1. **VISION**
   (Ability to see in adequate light and with glasses if used)
   0. Adequate—sees fine detail, including regular print in newspapers/books
   1. Impaired—sees large print, but not regular print in newspapers/books ●³
   2. Highly Impaired—limited vision, not able to see newspaper headlines, appears to follow objects with eyes ●³
   3. Severely Impaired—no vision or appears to see only light, colors, or shapes ●³

● = Automatic Trigger     ▲ = Potential Trigger

| | | |
|---|---|---|
| 1 - Delirium | 5 - ADL Functional/Rehabilitation Potential | 9 - Behavior Problems |
| 2 - Cognitive Loss/Dementia | 6 - Urinary Incontinence and Indwelling Catheter | 10 - Activities |
| 3 - Visual Function | 7 - Psychosocial Well-Being | 11 - Falls |
| 4 - Communication | 8 - Mood State | 12 - Nutritional Status |

13 - Feeding Tubes
14 - Dehydration/Fluid Maintenance
15 - Dental Care
16 - Pressure Ulcers
17 - Psychotropic Drug Use
18 - Physical Restraints

**Form 1828HH**   BRIGGS, Des Moines, IA 50306 (800) 247-2343   PRINTED IN U.S.A.   1 of 4

Fig. 9-2B

Resident Name _____     I.D. Number _____

| 3. | STABILITY OF CONDITIONS | a. Conditions/diseases make resident's cognitive, ADL, or behavior status unstable—fluctuating, precarious, or deteriorating. | a. |
| | | b. Resident experiencing an acute episode or a flare-up of a recurrent/chronic problem. | b. |
| | | c. NONE OF THE ABOVE | c. |

### SECTION L.  ORAL/NUTRITIONAL STATUS

| 1. | ORAL PROBLEMS | a. Chewing problem | a. | c. Mouth pain ●15 | c. |
| | | b. Swallowing problem | b. | d. NONE OF ABOVE | d. |

| 2. | HEIGHT AND WEIGHT | *Record height (a) in inches and weight (b) in pounds. Weight based on most recent status in last 30 days; measure weight consistently in accord with standard facility practice— e.g., in a.m. after voiding, before meal, with shoes off, and in nightclothes.* HT (in.) [a.] WT (lb.) [b.] | |
| | | c. Weight loss (i.e., 5% + in last 30 days; or 10% in last 180 days) | |
| | | 0. No    1. Yes ●12 ▲14 | c. |

| 3. | NUTRITIONAL PROBLEMS | a. Complains about the taste of many foods ●12 | a. | d. Regular complaint of hunger ●12 | d. |
| | | b. Insufficient fluid; dehydrated ●14 | b. | e. Leaves 25%+ food uneaten at most meals ●12 ▲14 | e. |
| | | c. Did NOT consume all/almost all liquids provided during last 3 days ▲14 | c. | f. NONE OF ABOVE | f. |

| 4. | NUTRITIONAL APPROACHES | a. Parenteral/IV ▲14 ●12 | a. | e. Therapeutic diet ●12 | e. |
| | | b. Feeding tube ▲14 ●13 | b. | f. Dietary supplement between meals | f. |
| | | c. Mechanically altered diet ●12 | c. | g. Plate guard, stabilized built-up utensil, etc. | g. |
| | | d. Syringe (oral feeding) ●12 | d. | h. NONE OF ABOVE | h. |

### SECTION M.  ORAL/DENTAL STATUS

| 1. | ORAL STATUS AND DISEASE PREVENTION | a. Debris (soft, easily movable substances) present in mouth prior to going to bed at night ●15 | a. |
| | | b. Has dentures and/or removable bridge | b. |
| | | c. Some/all natural teeth lost—does not have or does not use dentures (or partial plates) ●15 | c. |
| | | d. Broken, loose, or carious teeth ●15 | d. |
| | | e. Inflamed gums (gingiva), oral abscesses, swollen or bleeding gums, ulcers, or rashes ●15 | e. |
| | | f. Daily cleaning of teeth/dentures    If not checked = ●15 | f. |
| | | g. NONE OF ABOVE | g. |

### SECTION N.  SKIN CONDITION

| 1. | STASIS ULCER | (i.e., open lesion caused by poor venous circulation to lower extremities) 0. No    1. Yes | |
| 2. | PRESSURE ULCERS | *(Code for highest stage of pressure ulcer)* | |
| | | 0. No pressure ulcers | |
| | | 1. Stage 1 A persistent area of skin redness (without a break in the skin) that does not disappear when pressure is relieved ●12 ●16 | |
| | | 2. Stage 2 A partial thickness loss of skin layers that presents clinically as an abrasion, blister, or shallow crater ●12 ●16 | |
| | | 3. Stage 3 A full thickness of skin is lost, exposing the subcutaneous tissues—presents as a deep crater with or without undermining adjacent tissue ●12 ●16 | |
| | | 4. Stage 4 A full thickness of skin and subcutaneous tissue is lost, exposing muscle and/or bone ●12 ●16 | |
| 3. | HISTORY OF RESOLVED/ CURED PRESSURE ULCERS | Resident has had a pressure ulcer that was resolved/cured in last 90 days 0. No    1. Yes | |

| 4. | SKIN PROBLEMS/ CARE | a. Open lesions other than stasis or pressure ulcers (e.g., cuts) | a. |
| | | b. Skin desensitized to pain/pressure/discomfort | b. |
| | | c. Protective/preventive skin care | c. |
| | Nothing Checked From C Thru G = ▲16 | d. Turning/repositioning program | d. |
| | | e. Pressure-relieving beds, bed/chair pads (e.g., egg crate pads) | e. |
| | | f. Wound care/treatment (e.g., pressure ulcer care, surgical wound) | f. |
| | | g. Other skin care/treatment | g. |
| | | h. NONE OF ABOVE | h. |

### SECTION O.  MEDICATION USE

| 1. | NUMBER OF MEDI-CATIONS | (Record the number of *different medications used in the last 7 days*; enter "0" if none used.) | |
| 2. | NEW MEDI-CATIONS | Resident has received new medications during the last 90 days 0. No    1. Yes | |
| 3. | INJECTIONS | *(Record the number of days injections of any type received during the last 7 days.)* | |
| 4. | DAYS RECEIVED THE FOLLOWING MEDICATION | (Record the number of days during last 7 days; Enter "0" if not used; enter "1" if long-acting meds. used less than weekly) | |
| | | a. Antipsychotics 1-7 = ▲9 ▲11 ▲17 | a. |
| | | b. Antianxiety/hypnotics  1-7 = ▲9 ▲11 ▲17 | b. |
| | | c. Antidepressants  1-7 = ▲9 ▲11 ▲17 | c. |
| 5. | PREVIOUS MEDICATION RESULTS | *(SKIP this question if resident currently receiving anti-psychotics, antidepressants, or antianxiety/hypnotics— otherwise code correct response for last 90 days)* | |
| | | Resident has previously received psychoactive medications for a mood or behavior problem, and these medications were effective (without undue adverse consequences). | |
| | | 0. No, drugs not used 1. Drugs were effective 2. Drugs were not effective 3. Drug effectiveness unknown | |

### SECTION P.  SPECIAL TREATMENTS AND PROCEDURES

| 1. | SPECIAL TREAT-MENTS AND PROCE-DURES | SPECIAL CARE—Check treatments received during *the last 14 days.* | | | |
| | | a. Chemotherapy | a. | f. IV meds | f. |
| | | b. Radiation | b. | g. Transfusions | g. |
| | | c. Dialysis | c. | h. O₂ | h. |
| | | d. Suctioning | d. | i. Other _____ | i. |
| | | e. Trach. care | e. | j. NONE OF ABOVE | j. |
| | | THERAPIES—*Record the number of days each of the following therapies was administered (for at least 10 minutes during a day) in the last 7 days:* | | | |
| | | k. Speech—language pathology and audiology services | | | k. |
| | | l. Occupational therapy | | | l. |
| | | m. Physical therapy | | | m. |
| | | n. Psychological therapy (any licensed professional) | | | n. |
| | | o. Respiratory therapy | | | o. |
| 2. | ABNORMAL LAB VALUES | Has the resident had any abnormal lab values during the last 90-day period? 0. No    1. Yes    2. No tests performed | | | |
| 3. | DEVICES AND RESTRAINTS | Use the following code for last 7 days: 0 Not used   1 Used less than daily   2 Used daily | | | |
| | | a. Bed rails | | | a. |
| | | b. Trunk restraint  1 or 2 = ▲9 ●18 | | | b. |
| | | c. Limb restraint  1 or 2 = ▲9 ●18 | | | c. |
| | | d. Chair prevents rising   1 or 2 = ▲9 ●18 | | | d. |

---

● = Automatic Trigger       ▲ = Potential Trigger

| | | | |
|---|---|---|---|
| 1 - Delirium | 5 - ADL Functional/Rehabilitation Potential | 9 - Behavior Problems | 13 - Feeding Tubes | 17 - Psychotropic Drug Use |
| 2 - Cognitive Loss/Dementia | 6 - Urinary Incontinence and Indwelling Catheter | 10 - Activities | 14 - Dehydration/Fluid Maintenance | 18 - Physical Restraints |
| 3 - Visual Function | 7 - Psychosocial Well-Being | 11 - Falls | 15 - Dental Care | |
| 4 - Communication | 8 - Mood State | 12 - Nutritional Status | 16 - Pressure Ulcers | 4 of 4 |

**Fig. 9-2B (Continued)**

Resident Name _____     I.D. Number _____

| 2. | VISUAL LIMITATIONS/ DIFFICULTIES | a. Side vision problems—decreased peripheral vision; (e.g., leaves food on one side of tray, difficulty traveling, bumps into people and objects, misjudges placement of chair when seating self) ●³ | | a. |
|---|---|---|---|---|
| | | b. Experiences any of the following: sees halos or rings around lights, sees flashes of light; sees "curtains" over eyes | | b. |
| | | c. NONE OF ABOVE | | c. |
| 3. | VISUAL APPLIANCES | Glasses; contact lenses; lens implant; magnifying glass      0. No      1. Yes | | |

| 5. | MOBILITY APPLIANCES/ DEVICES | (Check all that apply during last 7 days) | | |
|---|---|---|---|---|
| | | a. Cane/walker | a. | d. Other person wheeled | d. |
| | | b. Brace/prosthesis | b. | e. Lifted (manually/ mechanically) | e. |
| | | c. Wheeled self | c. | f. NONE OF ABOVE | f. |
| 6. | TASK SEG-MENTATION | Resident requires that some or all of ADL activities be broken into a series of subtasks so that resident can perform them.      0. No      1. Yes | | |
| 7. | ADL FUNC-TIONAL REHAB. POTENTIAL | a. Resident believes he/she capable of increased independence in at least some ADLs ▲⁵ | | a. |
| | | b. Direct care staff believe resident capable of increased independence in at least some ADLs ▲⁵ | | b. |
| | | c. Resident able to perform tasks/activity but is very slow | | c. |
| | | d. Major difference in ADL Self-Performance or ADL Support in mornings and evenings (at least a one category change in Self-Performance or Support in any ADL) | | d. |
| | | e. NONE OF ABOVE | | e. |
| 8. | CHANGE IN ADL FUNCTION | Change in ADL self-performance in last 90 days      0. No change      1. Improved      2. Deteriorated ▲¹⁴ | | |

### SECTION E. PHYSICAL FUNCTIONING AND STRUCTURAL PROBLEMS

1. **ADL SELF-PERFORMANCE** *(Code for resident's PERFORMANCE OVER ALL SHIFTS during last 7 days*—Not including setup)*

   0. *INDEPENDENT*—No help or oversight—OR—Help/oversight provided only 1 or 2 times during last 7 days.
   1. *SUPERVISION*—Oversight encouragement or cueing provided 3+ times during last 7 days—OR—Supervision plus physical assistance provided only 1 or 2 times during last 7 days.
   2. *LIMITED ASSISTANCE*—Resident highly involved in activity, received physical help in guided maneuvering of limbs, or other nonweight bearing assistance 3+ times—OR—More help provided only 1 or 2 times during last 7 days.
   3. *EXTENSIVE ASSISTANCE*—While resident performed part of activity, over last 7-day period, help of following type(s) provided 3 or more times:
      - Weight-bearing support
      - Full staff performance during part (but not all) of last 7 days.
   4. *TOTAL DEPENDENCE*—Full staff performance of activity during entire 7 days.

2. **ADL SUPPORT PROVIDED**—*(Code for MOST SUPPORT PROVIDED OVER ALL SHIFTS during last 7 days; code regardless of resident's self-performance classification)*

   0. **No setup** or physical help from staff   2. One-person physical assist
   1. Setup help only   3. Two+ persons physical assist

| | | | 1 | 2 | SELF-PERFORMANCE | SUPPORT |
|---|---|---|---|---|---|---|
| a. | BED MOBILITY | How resident moves to and from lying position, turns side to side, and positions body while in bed      3 or 4 for self-perf = ▲⁵ | | | | |
| b. | TRANSFER | How resident moves between surfaces—to/from: bed, chair, wheelchair, standing position (EXCLUDE to/from bath/toilet)      3 or 4 for self-perf = ▲⁵ | | | | |
| c. | LOCO-MOTION | How resident moves between locations in his/her room and adjacent corridor on same floor. If in wheelchair, self-sufficiency once in chair      3 or 4 for self-perf = ▲⁵ | | | | |
| d. | DRESSING | How resident puts on, fastens, and takes off all items of street clothing, including donning/removing prosthesis      3 or 4 for self-perf = ▲⁵ | | | | |
| e. | EATING | How resident eats and drinks (regardless of skill)      3 or 4 for self-perf = ▲⁵ | | | | |
| f. | TOILET USE | How resident uses the toilet room (or commode, bed-pan, urinal); transfers on/off toilet, cleanses, changes pad, manages ostomy or catheter, adjusts clothes      3 or 4 for self-perf = ▲⁵ | | | | |
| g. | PERSONAL HYGIENE | How resident maintains personal hygiene, including combing hair, brushing teeth, shaving, applying makeup, washing/drying face, hands, and perineum (EXCLUDE baths and showers) | | | | |

| 3. | BATHING | How resident takes full-body bath, sponge bath, and transfers in/out of tub/shower (EXCLUDE washing of back and hair. Code for most dependent in self-performance and support. Bathing Self-Performance codes appear below.) 3 or 4 for (a) = ▲⁵    0. Independent—No help provided    1. Supervision—Oversight help only    2. Physical help limited to transfer only    3. Physical help in part of bathing activity    4. Total dependence | | | a. | b. |
|---|---|---|---|---|---|---|

| 4. | BODY CONTROL PROBLEMS | (Check all that apply during last 7 days) | | | | |
|---|---|---|---|---|---|---|
| | | a. Balance—partial or total loss of ability to balance self while standing ▲¹¹ | a. | g. Hand—lack of dexterity (e.g., problem using toothbrush or adjusting hearing aid) | g. | |
| | | b. Bedfast all or most of the time ▲¹¹ | b. | h. Leg—partial or total loss of voluntary movement ▲¹¹ | h. | |
| | | c. Contracture to arms, legs, shoulders, or hands | c. | i. Leg—unsteady gait | i. | |
| | | d. Hemiplegia/ hemiparesis ▲¹¹ | d. | j. Trunk—partial or total loss of ability to position, balance, or turn body ▲¹¹ | j. | |
| | | e. Quadriplegia ▲¹¹ | e. | k. Amputation | k. | |
| | | f. Arm—partial or total loss of voluntary movement | f. | l. NONE OF ABOVE | l. | |

### SECTION F. CONTINENCE IN LAST 14 DAYS

1. **CONTINENCE SELF-CONTROL CATEGORIES**
   *(Code for resident performance over all shifts.)*

   0. **CONTINENT**—Complete control
   1. **USUALLY CONTINENT**—BLADDER, incontinent episodes once a week or less; BOWEL, less than weekly
   2. **OCCASIONALLY INCONTINENT**—BLADDER, 2+ times a week but not daily; BOWEL, once a week
   3. **FREQUENTLY INCONTINENT**—BLADDER, tended to be incontinent daily, but some control present (e.g., on day shift); BOWEL, 2-3 times a week
   4. **INCONTINENT**—Had inadequate control. BLADDER, multiple daily episodes; BOWEL, all (or almost all) of the time.

| a. | BOWEL CON-TINENCE | Control of bowel movement, with appliance or bowel continence programs if employed | | |
|---|---|---|---|---|
| b. | BLADDER CONTI-NENCE | Control of urinary bladder function (if dribbles, volume insufficient to soak through underpants), with appli-ances (e.g., foley) or continence programs, if employed      2, 3 or 4 = ▲⁶ | | |
| 2. | INCONTI-NENCE RELATED TESTING | (Skip if resident's bladder continence code equals 0 or 1 AND no catheter is used.) | | |
| | | a. Resident has been tested for a urinary tract infection | | a. |
| | | b. Resident has been checked for presence of a fecal impaction, or there is adequate bowel elimination | | b. |
| | | c. NONE OF ABOVE | | c. |
| 3. | APPLIANCES AND PROGRAMS | a. Any scheduled toilet-ing plan | a. | e. Did not use toilet room/ commode/urinal | e. |
| | | b. External (condom) catheter ▲⁶ | b. | f. Pads/briefs used ▲⁶ | f. |
| | | c. Indwelling catheter ▲⁶ | c. | g. Enemas/irrigation | g. |
| | | d. Intermittent catheter ▲⁶ | d. | h. Ostomy | h. |
| | | | | i. NONE OF ABOVE | i. |
| 4. | CHANGE IN URINARY CONTINENCE | Change in urinary continence/appliances and programs in last 90 days      0. No change      1. Improved      2. Deteriorated | | |

### SECTION G. PSYCHOSOCIAL WELL-BEING

| 1. | SENSE OF INITIATIVE/ INVOLVE-MENT | a. At ease interacting with others | | a. |
|---|---|---|---|---|
| | | b. At ease doing planned or structural activities | | b. |
| | | c. At ease doing self-initiated activities | | c. |
| | | d. Establishes own goals | | d. |
| | | e. Pursues involvement in life of facility (i.e., makes/keeps friends; involved in group activities; responds positively to new activities; assists at religious services) | | e. |
| | | f. Accepts invitations into most group activities | | f. |
| | | g. NONE OF ABOVE | | g. |
| 2. | UNSETTLED RELATION-SHIPS | a. Covert/open conflict with and/or repeated criticism of staff ●⁷ | | a. |
| | | b. Unhappy with roommate ●⁷ | | b. |
| | | c. Unhappy with residents other than roommate ●⁷ | | c. |
| | | d. Openly expresses conflict/anger with family or friends ●⁷ | | d. |
| | | e. Absence of personal contact with family/friends | | e. |
| | | f. Recent loss of close family member/friend | | f. |
| | | g. NONE OF ABOVE | | g. |

● = Automatic Trigger     ▲ = Potential Trigger

| | | |
|---|---|---|
| 1 - Delirium | 5 - ADL Functional/Rehabilitation Potential | 9 - Behavior Problems | 13 - Feeding Tubes | 17 - Psychotropic Drug Use |
| 2 - Cognitive Loss/Dementia | 6 - Urinary Incontinence and Indwelling Catheter | 10 - Activities | 14 - Dehydration/Fluid Maintenance | 18 - Physical Restraints |
| 3 - Visual Function | 7 - Psychosocial Well-Being | 11 - Falls | 15 - Dental Care | |
| 4 - Communication | 8 - Mood State | 12 - Nutritional Status | 16 - Pressure Ulcers | 2 of 4 |

**Fig. 9-2B (Continued)**

Resident Name _____     I.D. Number _____

| 3. | PAST ROLES | a. Strong identification with past roles and life status | a. |
|---|---|---|---|
| | | b. Expresses sadness/anger/empty feeling over lost roles/status ●² | b. |
| | | c. NONE OF ABOVE | c. |

### SECTION H. MOOD AND BEHAVIOR PATTERNS

| 1. | SAD OR ANXIOUS MOOD | (Check all that apply during last 30 days) | |
|---|---|---|---|
| | | a. VERBAL EXPRESSIONS of DISTRESS by resident (sadness, sense that nothing matters, hopelessness, worthlessness, unrealistic fears, vocal expressions of anxiety or grief) ●⁶ | a. |
| | | DEMONSTRATED (OBSERVABLE) SIGNS of mental DISTRESS | |
| | | b. Tearfulness, emotional groaning, sighing, breath-lessness ●⁶ | b. |
| | | c. Motor agitation such as pacing, handwringing or picking ●⁶ | c. |
| | | d. Failure to eat or take medications, withdrawal from self-care or leisure activities ●⁶ ▲¹⁴ | d. |
| | | e. Pervasive concern with health ●⁶ | e. |
| | | f. Recurrent thoughts of death—e.g., believes he/she is about to die, have a heart attack ●⁶ | f. |
| | | g. Suicidal thoughts/actions ●⁶ | g. |
| | | h. NONE OF ABOVE | h. |
| 2. | MOOD PERSISTENCE | Sad or anxious mood intrudes on daily life over last 7 days—not easily altered, doesn't "cheer up" | |
| | | 0. No        1. Yes ●⁶ | |
| 3. | PROBLEM BEHAVIOR | (Code for behavior in last 7 days) | |
| | | 0. Behavior not exhibited in last 7 days | |
| | | 1. Behavior of this type occurred less than daily | |
| | | 2. Behavior of this type occurred daily or more frequently | |
| | | a. WANDERING (moved with no rational purpose; seemingly oblivious to needs or safety)  1 or 2 = ●⁶ | a. |
| | | b. VERBALLY ABUSIVE (others were threatened, screamed at, cursed at)  1 or 2 = ●⁶ | b. |
| | | c. PHYSICALLY ABUSIVE (others were hit, shoved, scratched, sexually abused)   1 or 2 = ●⁶ | c. |
| | | d. SOCIALLY INAPPROPRIATE/DISRUPTIVE BEHAVIOR (made disrupting sounds, noisy, screams, self-abusive acts, sexual behavior or disrobing in public, smeared/threw food/feces, hoarding, rummaged through others' belongings)  1 or 2 = ●⁶ | d. |
| 4. | RESIDENT RESISTS CARE | (Check all types of resistance that occurred in the last 7 days) | |
| | | a. Resisted taking medications/injection | a. |
| | | b. Resisted ADL assistance | b. |
| | | c. NONE OF ABOVE | c. |
| 5. | BEHAVIOR MANAGEMENT PROGRAM | Behavior problem has been addressed by clinically developed behavior management program. (Note: Do not include programs that involve only physical restraints or psychotropic medications in this category.) | |
| | | 0. No behavior problem | |
| | | 1. Yes, addressed | |
| | | 2. No, not addressed | |
| 6. | CHANGE IN MOOD | Change in mood in last 90 days | |
| | | 0. No change     1. Improved     2. Deteriorated ▲¹ | |
| 7. | CHANGE IN PROBLEM BEHAVIOR | Change in problem behavioral signs in last 90 days | |
| | | 0. No change    1. Improved    2. Deteriorated ●¹ | |

### SECTION I. ACTIVITY PURSUIT PATTERNS

| 1. | TIME AWAKE | (Check appropriate time periods—last 7 days) Resident awake all or most of time (i.e., naps no more than one hour per time period) in the: | |
|---|---|---|---|
| | | a. Morning | a. |
| | | b. Afternoon | b. |
| | | c. Evening | c. |
| | | d. NONE OF ABOVE | d. |
| 2. | AVERAGE TIME INVOLVED IN ACTIVITIES | 0. Most—(more than 2/3 of time) ▲¹⁰       2. Little—(less than 1/3 of time) ▲¹⁰ | |
| | | 1. Some—(1/3 to 2/3 time) ▲¹⁰             3. None ▲¹⁰ | |
| 3. | PREFERRED ACTIVITY SETTINGS | (Check all settings in which activities are preferred) | |
| | | a. Own room | a. |
| | | b. Day/activity room | b. |
| | | c. Inside NH/off unit | c. |
| | | d. Outside facility | d. |
| | | e. NONE OF ABOVE | e. |

| 4. | GENERAL ACTIVITIES PREFERENCES (adapted to resident's current abilities) | (Check all specific preferences whether or not activity is currently available to resident) | |
|---|---|---|---|
| | | a. Cards/other games | a. |
| | | b. Crafts/arts | b. |
| | | c. Exercise/sports | c. |
| | | d. Music | d. |
| | | e. Read/write | e. |
| | | f. Spiritual/religious activ. | f. |
| | | g. Trips/shopping | g. |
| | | h. Walking/wheeling outdoors | h. |
| | | i. Watch TV | i. |
| | | j. NONE OF ABOVE | j. |
| 5. | PREFERS MORE OR DIFFERENT ACTIVITIES | Resident expresses/indicates preference for other activities/choices. | |
| | | 0. No      1. Yes ●¹⁰ | |

### SECTION J. DISEASE DIAGNOSES

Check only those diseases present that have a relationship to current ADL status, cognitive status, behavior status, medical treatments, or risk of death. (Do not list old/inactive diagnoses.) (If none apply, check the NONE OF ABOVE box)

| 1. | DISEASES | HEART/CIRCULATION | | | | |
|---|---|---|---|---|---|---|
| | | a. Arteriosclerotic heart disease (ASHD) | a. | r. Manic depressive (bipolar disease) | r. |
| | | b. Cardiac dysrhythmias | b. | **SENSORY** | |
| | | c. Congestive heart failure | c. | s. Cataracts | s. |
| | | d. Hypertension | d. | t. Glaucoma | t. |
| | | e. Hypotension | e. | **OTHER** | |
| | | f. Peripheral vascular disease | f. | u. Allergies | u. |
| | | g. Other cardiovascular disease | g. | v. Anemia | v. |
| | | **NEUROLOGICAL** | | w. Arthritis | w. |
| | | h. Alzheimer's | h. | x. Cancer | x. |
| | | i. Dementia other than Alzheimer's | i. | y. Diabetes mellitus | y. |
| | | j. Aphasia | j. | z. Explicit terminal prognosis | z. |
| | | k. Cerebrovascular accident (stroke) | k. | aa. Hypothyroidism | aa. |
| | | l. Multiple sclerosis | l. | bb. Osteoporosis | bb. |
| | | m. Parkinson's disease | m. | cc. Seizure disorder | cc. |
| | | **PULMONARY** | | dd. Septicemia | dd. |
| | | n. Emphysema/asthma/COPD | n. | ee. Urinary tract infection—in last 30 days ▲¹⁴ | ee. |
| | | o. Pneumonia | o. | ff. NONE OF ABOVE | ff. |
| | | **PSYCHIATRIC/MOOD** | | | |
| | | p. Anxiety disorder | p. | | |
| | | q. Depression | q. | | |
| 2. | OTHER CURRENT DIAGNOSES AND ICD-9 CODES | 260–263.9—●¹²   276.5—▲¹⁴   291.0—293.1—●¹ | | | |
| | | a. | | | |
| | | b. | | | |
| | | c. | | | |
| | | d. | | | |
| | | e. | | | |
| | | f. | | | |

### SECTION K. HEALTH CONDITIONS

| 1. | PROBLEM CONDITIONS | (Check all problems that are present in last 7 days unless other time frame indicated) | |
|---|---|---|---|
| | | a. Constipation | a. |
| | | b. Diarrhea ▲¹⁴ | b. |
| | | c. Dizziness/vertigo ▲¹⁴ | c. |
| | | d. Edema | d. |
| | | e. Fecal impaction | e. |
| | | f. Fever ▲¹⁴ | f. |
| | | g. Hallucinations/delusions | g. |
| | | h. Internal bleeding ▲¹⁴ | h. |
| | | i. Joint pain | i. |
| | | j. Pain—resident complains or shows evidence of pain daily or almost daily | j. |
| | | k. Recurrent lung aspirations in last 90 days | k. |
| | | l. Shortness of breath | l. |
| | | m. Syncope (fainting) | m. |
| | | n. Vomiting ▲¹⁴ | n. |
| | | o. NONE OF ABOVE | o. |
| 2. | ACCIDENTS | a. Fell—past 30 days ●¹¹ | a. |
| | | b. Fell—past 31–180 days ●¹¹ | b. |
| | | c. Hip fracture in last 180 days | c. |
| | | d. NONE OF ABOVE | d. |

Fig. 9-2B (Continued)

## RESIDENT ASSESSMENT PROTOCOL: COGNITIVE LOSS/DEMENTIA

### I.   PROBLEM

Approximately 60% of residents in nursing facilities exhibit signs and symptoms of decline in intellectual functioning. Recovery will be possible for less than 10% of these residents—those with a reversible condition such as an acute confusional state (delirium). For most residents, however, the syndrome of cognitive loss or dementia is chronic and progressive, and appropriate care focuses on enhancing quality of life, sustaining functional capacities, minimizing decline, and preserving dignity.

Confusion and/or behavioral disturbances present the primary complicating care factors. Identifying and treating acute confusion and behavior problems can facilitate assessment of how chronic cognitive deficits affect the life of the resident.

For residents with chronic cognitive deficits, a therapeutic environment is supportive rather than curative and is an environment in which licensed and nonlicensed care staff are encouraged (and trained) to comprehend a resident's <u>experience</u> of cognitive loss. With this insight, staff can develop care plans focused on three main goals: (1) to provide positive experiences for the resident (e.g., enjoyable activities) that do not involve overly demanding tasks and stress; (2) to define appropriate support roles for each staff member involved in a resident's care; and (3) to lay the foundation for reasonable staff and family expectations concerning a resident's capacities and needs.

### II.   TRIGGERS

A cognitive loss/dementia problem is suggested if two or more of the following deficits are present:

- Short-term Memory Problem [B2a = 1]
- Long-term Memory Problem [B2b = 1]
- Two or more Memory Recall Problems [B3a, B3b, B3c, B3d = fewer than three checked]
- Some Decision-making Problem [B4 = 1, 2 or 3]
- Problem Understanding Others [C5 = 1, 2 or 3]
- Diagnosis of Alzheimer's Disease [J1h = checked]; Dementia other than Alzheimer's [J1i = checked]; Mental Retardation [INTAKE I12 b-f = any checked]; Parkinson's Disease (J1m = checked); or Aphasia [J1j = checked]

### III.  GUIDELINES

Review the following MDS items to investigate possible links between these factors and the resident's cognitive loss and quality of life. The three triggers identify residents with differing levels of cognitive loss. Even for those who are most highly impaired, the RAP seeks to help identify areas in which staff intervention might be useful. Refer to the RAP KEY for specific MDS items and other specific issues to consider.

Cognitive Loss/dementia 1

Fig. 9-2C1

## NEUROLOGICAL

Fluctuating Cognitive Signs and Symptoms/Neurological Status. Co-existing delirium and progressive cognitive loss can result in erroneous impressions concerning the nature of the resident's chronic limitations. Only when acute confusion and behavioral disturbances are treated, or when the treatment effort is judged to be as effective as possible, can a true measure of chronic cognitive deficits be obtained.

Recent Changes in the Signs/Symptoms of the Dementia Process. Identifying these changes can heighten staff awareness of the nature of the resident's cognitive and functional limitations. This knowledge can assist staff in developing resasonable expectations of the resident's capabilities and in designing programs to enhance the resident's quality of life. This knowledge can also challenge staff to identify potentially reversible causes for recent losses in cognitive status.

Mental Retardation, Alzheimer's Disease and Other Adult-Onset Dementias. The most prevalent neurological diagnoses for cognitively impaired residents are Alzheimer's disease and multi-infarct dementia. But increasing numbers of mentally retarded residents are in nursing facilities, and many adults suffering from Down's syndrome appear to develop dementia as they age. The diagnostic distinctions among these groups can be useful in reminding staff of the types of long-term intellectual reserves that are available to these residents.

## MOOD/BEHAVIOR

Specific treatments for behavioral distress, as well as treatments for delirium, can lessen and even cure that behavioral problem. At the same time, however, some behavior problems will not be reversible, and staff should be prepared (and encouraged) to learn to live with their manifestations. In some situations where problem/distressed behavior continues, staff may feel that the behavior poses no threat to the resident's safety, health, or activity pattern and is not disruptive to other residents. For the resident with declining cognitive functions and a behavioral problem, you may wish to consider the following issues:

- Have cognitive skills declined subsequent to initiation of a behavior control program (e.g., psychotropic drugs or physical restraints)?
- Is decline due to the treatment program (e.g., drug toxicity or negative reaction to physical restraints)?
- Have cognitive skills improved subsequent to initiation of a behavior control program?
- Has staff assistance enhanced resident self-performance patterns?

## CONCURRENT MEDICAL PROBLEMS

Major Concurrent Medical Problems. Identifying and treating health problems can positively affect cognitive functioning and the resident's quality of life. Effective therapy for congestive heart failure, chronic obstructive pulmonary disease, and constipation can lead, for example, to functional and cognitive improvement. Comfort (pain avoidance) is a paramount goal in controlling both acute and chronic conditions for cognitively impaired residents. Verbal reports from residents should be one (but not the only ) source of information. Some residents wil be unable to communicate sufficiently to pinpoint their pain.

Cognitive Loss/dementia 2

Fig. 9-2C2

## COGNITIVE LOSS/DEMENTIA RAP KEY

### TRIGGERS

A cognitive loss/dementia problem deficit and retained abilities suggested if two or more of the following deficits are present:

- Short-term Memory Problem [B2a=1]
- Long-term Memory Problem [B2b=1]
- Two or More Memory Recall Problems [B3a, B3b, B3c, B3d = less than 3 checked]
- Some Decision-making Problem [B4 = 1, 2 or 3]
- Problem Understanding Others [C5 = 1, 2 or 3]
- Diagnosis of Alzheimer's (J1h = checked]; Dementia other than Alzheimer's [J1i = checked]; Mental Retardation [INTAKE I12b-f = any checked]; Parkinson's [J1m = checked]; or Aphasia [J1j = checked]

### GUIDELINES

Factors to review for relationship to cognitive loss:

1. Neurological. Delirium [B5], Cognitive decline [B6], Alzheimer's and other dementias [J1h, J1i], MR/DD status [INTAKE I12].

Confounding Problems that may require resolution or suggest reversible causes:

2. Mood/behavior. Sad mood or Mood decline [H1, H6], Behavior problem or behavior decline [H3, H7], Anxiety disorder [J1p], Depression [J1q], Manic depressive disorder [J1r], Other psychiatric disorders [J2].

3. Concurrent medical problems CHF [J1c], Other cardiovascular disease [J1g], CVA [J1k], Emphysema/Asthma/COPD [J1n], Cancer [J1x], Diabetes [J1y], Hypothyroidism [J1aa].

4. Functional limitations. ADL task segmentation [E6], Decline in ADL or continence [E8; F4].

5. Sensory impairment. Hearing/visual problems [C1; D1], Rarely/never understands [C5], Impaired tactile sense [N4b].

6. Medications. Antipsychotics, Antianxiety/hypnotics, Antidepressants [O4].

7. Involvement factors. New admission [INTAKE I2], Trunk or chair restraint [P3], Withdrawal from activities [H1d], Encouragement of small group programs [from record].

8. Failure to thrive. Terminal prognosis [J1z], Clinical complications [K1; L3, N2].

Fig. 9-2D1

## PSYCHOSOCIAL

After serious illness and drug toxicity are ruled out as causes of delirium, consider the possibility that the resident is experiencing psychosocial distress that may produce signs of delirium.

### Isolation

- Has the resident been away from people, objects and situations?
- Is resident confused about time, place and meaning?
- Has the resident been in bed or in an isolated area while recuperating from an illness or receiving a treatment?

**Recent loss of family/friend.** Loss of someone close can precipitate a grief reaction that presents as acute confusion, especially if the person provided safety and structure for a demented resident.

- Review the MDS to determine whether the resident has experienced a recent loss of a close family member/friend.

**Depression/sad or anxious mood.** Mood states can lead to confusional states that resolve with appropriate treatment.

- Review the MDS to determine whether the resident exhibits any signs or symptoms of sad or anxious mood or has a diagnosis of a psychiatric illness.

**Restraints.** Restraints often aggravate the conditions staff are trying to treat (e.g., confusion, agitation, wandering).

- Did the resident become more agitated and confused with their use?

**Recent relocation.**

- Has the resident recently been admitted to a new environment (new room, unit, facility)?
- Was there an orientation program that provided a calm, gentle approach with reminders and structure to help the new resident settle into the environment?

## SENSORY LOSSES

Sensory impairments often produce signs of confusion and disorientation, as well as behavior changes. This is especially true of residents with early signs of dementia. They can also aggravate a confusional state by impairing the resident's ability to accurately perceive or cope with environmental stimuli (e.g., loud noises; onset of evening). This can lead to the resident experiencing hallucinations/delusions and misinterpreting noises and images.

### Hearing.

- Is hearing deficit related to easily remedied situations—impacted ear wax or hearing aid dysfunction?
- Has sensory deprivation led to confusion?
- Has physician input been sought?

### Vision.

- Has vision loss created sensory deprivation resulting in confusion?
- Have major changes occurred in visual function without the resident's being referred to a physician?

Delirium 3

Fig. 9-2D2

Fig. 9-3  Taking a psychosocial history can be done in an informal setting.

After receiving the basic identifying information, the nurse can ask the family for the major problem, the behavior that led them to believe the patient needed help. How the family views the confusion and how they talk about their elderly relative will give the nurse an idea of the amount and type of family support available. The number of friends with whom the patient still has contact and the strength of religious beliefs are also indicators of support available to the patient.

To determine whether or not the present behavior is a change, the nurse needs to know what the patient was like previously. Was he outgoing or a loner? Was he fastidious or sloppy? Did he sleep well at night or wake often? Was he practical or a dreamer? Did he drink or abuse drugs? Did he keep busy or waste time? Did he hold his problems in or did he talk them out? What was a typical day like?

Concerning the confusion, the nurse should ask questions like, "When did the confused behavior start?" "Was the onset gradual or sudden?" "Can the family think of some stressful event that happened just before the confusion began?" "What kind of behavior does the patient exhibit now?" "Has the confusion gotten worse or better?"

Information about the patient's favorite belongings, his personal habits, his food likes and dislikes, and perhaps his long-time pet will give the nurse what she needs to help foster reality.

Following the psychosocial history, the nurse can determine the patient's mental status through observation and questioning. First, the nurse needs to know the patient's previous intellectual ability. This can be obtained, at least in part, by how far the patient went in school and the occupation in which he engaged.

Again, before starting the mental status exam, the patient should be given his glasses and his hearing aid, if needed. There are several areas in assessing mental status. The first three can act as a screening. If correct answers are given in these areas, the rest of the exam does not have to be given.

**Memory.** Memory loss can be either short term or long term. Some examples of questions to determine short-term memory, which is three to five minutes, are:

1. What is your age?
2. What is your address?
3. What did you do this morning?
4. Give the patient a series of numbers, an address, or a statement and ask him to repeat it for you in a few minutes.

For long-term memory, the nurse can ask:

1. When did you get married?
2. What kind of work did you do?
3. What date were you born?
4. Where were you born?

**Orientation.** Orientation is an awareness of time, place, and person. Questions that help assess orientation are:

1. What is your name?
2. What is this place?
3. What state are we in?
4. What is today's date?
5. What year is this?

It is possible for a person to make a mistake with the day's date without being confused. The year is another matter. If it is 1987 and the patient says it is 1945, confusion is present.

**Abstract Thinking.** This is the ability to generalize and categorize things. It is a higher cognitive power that is lost when confusion sets in. To test abstract thinking, the patient can be asked to interpret a proverb such as "The grass is always greener on the other side." Some other proverbs are

"A stitch in time saves nine" or "Don't count your chickens before they are hatched." If the patient is still able to think abstractly, he will be able to generalize the proverb. For instance, the confused person may interpret the first proverb as "The neighbor has greener grass." This is concrete. If the patient is able to generalize, he will say that it means that people often see others as having things better than themselves.

Another way to test for abstract thinking is to ask such questions as:

1. How are a cat and a bird alike?
2. How are an apple and an orange alike?
3. How are a bird and a plane alike?

It does not matter what the patient answers as long as he uses the words *they both*. He can say, "They both eat, they both have hair, or they both make good pets." What the nurse is looking for is the ability to generalize. "The cat has hair and the bird has feathers" is a concrete answer. The patient responding in this way would fail the test.

**Judgment.** The patient who loses judgment is unsafe. A person who is not confused will give answers to the following questions that reflect his understanding of safety. "What would you do if you saw someone drop a lighted cigarette on the carpet?" "How would you get something from a high shelf?"

**State of Consciousness.** This area is assessed through observation. Does the patient show an interest in things around him? Is he alert and aware of his environment? Does he remember his own belongings? Does he recognize himself in the mirror?

**Intellectual Functioning.** The patient's ability to communicate is an indication of his intellectual functioning. Can the patient carry on a logical conversation? Does he use words correctly? Is the conversation consistent? Are the answers relevant? A couple of other ways to assess intellectual functioning are to see if the patient can follow at least a three-step instruction. "Take this paper, fold it in half, and then fold it in half again, and then tear it along the folded lines" is an example of a multiple-step direction. The patient can also be asked to do a mathematical problem such as serial threes or sevens.

**Emotions.** The nurse must observe the patient's behavior. Does it seem inappropriate? If it does, she must then determine if it is a change in behavior. No matter how bizarre or inappropriate the behavior the patient exhibits, he cannot be considered confused unless the behavior is a change.

When Shirley Adams, age eighty-two, was admitted to the hospital, she was in need of a bath. Her hair was mussed and her clothes were dirty and torn. Shortly after admission, she had acquired a stack of paper cups, towels, pins, scratch pads, and pens. She had secreted them in her bedside table. This behavior does not meet acceptable standards so she would most certainly be considered confused. However, if a social history had been taken, it would have revealed that Shirley had been this way all her life. She was brought up in a very poor family. Water was a precious commodity and there was little for bathing and washing clothes. The family had very little, so they saved whatever items they could find. This was done in case there was a use found for them later. Shirley's actions were part of her lifelong pattern. She was not really confused.

Has the patient recently shown signs of depression, anxiety, or paranoia? These conditions, which are treatable, have been known to cause confusion.

**Physical Changes.** There are several physical indices that must be assessed to first rule out physiological causes, Table 9-5 and Figure 9-4.

**TABLE 9-5**
**Physical Assessment**

| | |
|---|---|
| Vital signs | temperature, pulse, respiration, and blood pressure<br>quality of the pulse and respiration |
| Hydration | skin turgor, intake and output<br>blood chemistry<br>urinalysis |
| Elimination habits | frequency<br>characteristics of stool<br>problems with constipation or diarrhea |
| Nutritional status | amount and type of food eaten<br>weight and height<br>appearance |
| Mobility and activity level | range of motion<br>ability to ambulate<br>amount of assistance needed |
| Heart and lung functioning | heart and lung sounds<br>color and condition of the skin<br>quality of the pulse and respiration |
| Vision | need for glasses<br>patient's ability to read a selected paragraph |
| Hearing | need for hearing aid<br>patient's ability to hear when voice comes from behind him |
| Pain | presence of pain<br>type, severity, duration<br>any relief measures taken |

Fig. 9-4 Physical assessment is necessary in care of the aged.

Areas to be assessed include the following:

1. Vital Signs. These are very sensitive indicators of change in the state of the elderly's health, Figure 9-5. They can indicate dehydration, poor circulation, and the presence of disease.
2. Hearing. The nurse must ask simple yes and no questions. She can also ask a patient to repeat what he heard from her.
3. Vision. The patient can be asked to read several sizes of print.
4. Hydration. Is the skin dry? Is there an adequate output? Are fluids available and easy to reach?
5. Nutritional Status. Is the patient gaining weight or at least maintaining it? Are there loose dentures and/or bad teeth? How good is the patient's appetite? What kinds of food is he eating?
6. Environment. Has there been a recent change in the patient's life? Does he have familiar things around him? Is there enough sensory stimulation without being too much? Are there orienting items around him like clocks, calendars, newspapers? Is there a window so the patient can see night and day? Is there a night-light turned on?

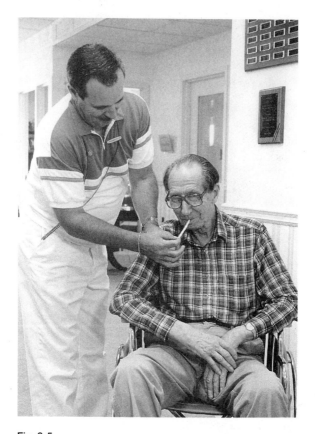

Fig. 9-5

7. Elimination. Is there a problem with constipation or diarrhea? Is the patient able to get to the bathroom? Is there embarrassment about using a bedpan? What does the patient usually take for constipation?

8. Pain. Is pain present? Where is it? When did it start? How severe is it? Is it constant or intermittent? Is there anything that triggers it? Does the ordered medication help?

9. Mobility. The nurse must determine if the patient is able to walk with or without assistance. Is he likely to fall? Is he able to turn himself in bed?

10. Chronic Disease. Has there been a change in any of the present chronic diseases? The nurse needs information about the diseases that affect the circulation or endocrine systems in particular because these are the ones most likely to cause confusion.

11. Medications. It is important to determine what medications the patient is taking. Is the patient taking any over-the-counter drugs? When it is determined that confusion results, the nurse should think about medications first. There are several that cause confusion in the elderly.
12. Activity. How much activity does the patient have? What kind of activity does he enjoy?

The nurse is only one of many who assist in determining whether or not confusion exists. If it is determined that it does exist, the confusion should always be thought of as reversible. The psychosocial history and the assessment should give clues as to the cause. The treatment is then simple. Treat the cause and the confusion will disappear. It is important to remember that there can be a reversible confusion superimposed on an irreversible one.

## Nursing Care of the Confused Patient

Reversible confusion can be prevented. The nurse has control over many of the aspects that can cause or contribute to the confusion. That means there is much she can do to prevent it. Whenever the nurse has an elderly patient admitted to her care, she should see that the patient has orienting items in the environment such as clocks, calendars, and a reality orientation board. She should encourage visits by family and friends who have familiar faces. It is important, too, that she makes sure her elderly patient has sufficient fluids. She must attend to other activities of daily living as well, such as adequate nutrition, good hygiene, and physical activity.

## Reality Orientation

Reality orientation is a process by which the confused person is reminded of orienting cues in the environment. He is taught to use these cues to reorient himself in time and place. Reality orientation goes on for twenty-four hours a day. Immediacy, simplicity, and consistency are the main factors. *Immediacy* means that the nurse must respond to the patient quickly. If she asks him a question, she must allow him time to answer, but not so much time that the patient loses interest. The patient's questions must be answered right away, and he should not be kept waiting to have his needs met. The attention span is short and that makes immediacy so important. *Consistency* means that all personnel treat the patient in the very same way. A written orientation plan is necessary to assure this.

Reality orientation is based on repetition, with everyone saying and doing the same things over and over again. This helps the confused person to relearn and lessens the extraneous stimuli with which he must cope. *Simplicity* demands that all responses to the patient be in simple, concrete terms. Pictures are more concrete than words; therefore, they should be used often when giving directions. Instead of telling a patient to go to the bathroom, the nurse can show him a picture or place a picture on the door of the bathroom. Only one-step directions should be given. The nurse does not tell a patient to comb his hair. He may not remember how. Besides breaking the task down to its simplest terms, she can also put a comb in the patient's hand and then move the hand through the motions. She can repeat this many times, but eventually the patient should learn to do it for himself again.

For some patients, reality orientation takes weeks to accomplish a simple change, and for others it takes months. Some patients do not benefit from it at all. The important thing is that the nurse does not become discouraged. Without consistency, the process will definitely not work.

Reality orientation goes on twenty-four hours a day. The patient is told where he is, the day, the date, and the nurse's name first thing in the morning and several times throughout the day. Other information that can be included is the time of the next meal, the weather, and/or upcoming events.

A reality orientation board is often posted in a prominent place, Figure 9-6. It serves to provide the same orienting information. The board should have a colorful background. It must be at eye level. It may be necessary to have two boards, one for ambulant patients and one for those in wheelchairs. Needless to say, all reality orientation boards should be current.

Many institutions also have a formal orientation class to supplement the twenty-four-hour program. The classes are held in a well-lighted, quiet place for fifteen to thirty minutes each day. Each class should be limited to five or six people. Besides encouraging reality, these sessions are used to help patients relearn a task such as telling time, tying a shoe, or writing with a pencil. Audiovisuals such as pictures, word and picture cards, large blocks and puzzles, felt boards, mirrors, and a record player, as well as mockups of clocks and calendars, are necessary to making the lesson concrete. Anyone wishing to start a formal program must begin by collecting all the audio and visual material available.

The class must be well planned. The leader should have a set goal and objectives in mind and should go slowly to allow each patient to

This is the Elk's Long Term Care Center

the day is:  Friday

the date is:  May 9, 1986

The City is Tucson

the state is Arizona

the next Holiday is:  Mother's Day

The weather outside is:

Fig. 9-6  Reality orientation board.

progress according to his capabilities. The leader should try to keep the class lively and avoid putting any patient on the spot. If she asks a patient a question and gets no response, she can reply with "I would like to help you identify this or read this or answer this," whatever the case may be. The idea is to prevent a loss of self-esteem. All correct answers or even attempts at answering should be praised. The importance of touch should never be forgotten.

A typical session may go like this:

Nurse: "Good morning, John Stevens." She would then proceed to greet each patient by name. Remembering the importance of touch, she would shake his hand. "This is our reality orientation class. It is planned to help improve memory and exercise the mind. It is eleven o'clock in the morning. The sun is shining and the temperature is eighty-five degrees.

"Sam, can you tell me what season this is?" If there is no answer, she would wait a minute and then say, "I would like to help you answer that question,

Sam. It is summer now. Do you like summer, Sam?" If Sam answers yes or no, his effort would be praised. "Of course summer is a great time, isn't it? George, can you think of some good things to do in the summertime?" If George says, "Go outside," the nurse might respond with, "That's right. That's a great idea. We could sit in the sun or take a walk. Andrew, do you enjoy going outside?"

Names are always mentioned first when a question is to be asked. This alerts the patient to the coming question. First names are used because they have more meaning to the patient. Generally the earlier something is learned, the longer it lasts in memory. This means that the person is more apt to remember a name given at birth than a nickname given in college. It is for this reason that confused patients should never be given a nickname by the caregiver, including "Pop," "Hon," or "Dear."

Not all patients will succeed to the same degree, and some will not succeed at all. It is essential that the personnel dealing with them do not become discouraged. Reality orientation takes time.

Reminiscing is an integral part of reality orientation and involves the discussion of life experiences within a group. Because the person with dementia will remember past events longer than current ones, the past events provide a topic for communication. Communication is the means by which people validate their worth. If a person feels accepted by a group, self-esteem will be improved. Most often the group becomes supportive. Their acceptance acts as a buffer against the many losses felt by the elderly.

Verbalizing about life experiences gives the patient an opportunity to rethink and reorganize his life. He can then see the meanings of some past events and find new meanings for others. These meanings help to validate the worth of the patient's life.

Reminiscing provides a means of effective interaction with the mentally impaired elderly. It also provides a tie to present-day reality. The nurse or therapist takes the person from where he is in memory and guides him to the present.

## IRREVERSIBLE CONFUSION

There is no sure way to tell if a patient has reversible or irreversible confusion; therefore, it is best to assume that confusion is reversible and rule out all possible causes. The nurse is only one of many who will participate in making this determination, but she is in a position to offer many clues.

Irreversible confusion is called dementia, organic brain syndrome (OBS), senile dementia, or, incorrectly, senility. Senility simply refers to old age. The term was popular when dementia was believed to be a normal part of aging, but unfortunately it remains in use.

The cause of irreversible confusion is brain damage. There are several causes of brain damage, but the most common is Alzheimer's disease. Other major causes are: multi-infarct, or several small strokes, which accounts for 20 to 25 percent; Alzheimer's with multi-infarct, which accounts for 5 to 20 percent; and all others, such as kuru, arteriosclerosis, Creutzfeld-Jakob's disease, and adult hydrocephalus, which account for 5 to 10 percent, Table 9-6.

Multi-infarct refers to a series of small vascular accidents commonly called *strokes*. The most common cause of strokes in the elderly is a blood clot in one of the brain vessels. The clot cuts off the oxygen and glucose supply behind it. The result is death to the part of the brain denied. Hemorrhages can also be a cause of brain damage, but are more apt to occur in a younger person.

## TABLE 9-6
### Irreversible Confusion

| DISEASE | CAUSE | SYMPTOMS |
|---|---|---|
| Multi-infarct | several small strokes | abrupt onset, stepwise progression, weakness and hemiplegia |
| Kuru | slow-acting virus | rapid progression, history of cannibalism |
| Arteriosclerosis | hardening of the arteries | hypertension, dizziness, orthostatic hypotension, headaches, sleepiness |
| Intracranial neoplasm | usually affects gliomas cause unknown | headache, convulsions, blurred vision, severe anxiety |
| Huntington's chorea | inherited | involuntary muscle movements |
| Hydrocephalus | blockage in the drainage of cerebrospinal fluid | progressive deterioration, crosses feet when walking |
| Creutzfeld-Jakob | slow-acting virus | rapid progression, muscle atrophy |
| Trauma | injury | immediate nonprogressive deterioration |
| Alzheimer's | unknown | may have been in coma, severe pain, insidious beginning, progressive deterioration |

When dementia results from small strokes, the onset is abrupt. Confusion starts as soon as the bloodflow to the brain is jeopardized, but it does not increase. Each time the patient has a small stroke, he becomes more confused. There can be some improvement as brain edema subsides, but the patient never fully recovers. Along with the mental symptoms, the patient will have the usual physical symptoms of stroke, like weakness, paralysis on one side, and/or a loss of speech.

Arteriosclerosis is hardening of the arteries. Because this results in less blood going through the vessels, blood supply to the brain cells is diminished. Arteriosclerosis is also accompanied by high blood pressure. If the pressure becomes high enough, brain hemorrhage can occur.

Kuru is a disease found in the women of a New Guinea native tribe. It is caused by a slow-growing virus found in the brain. It was the custom of the women to eat the brains of relatives. The men were generally not affected because they ate only the rest of the body.

Creutzfeld-Jakob's disease is also very rare. The cause is unknown, probably viral, and the course of the disease is rapid.

In adult hydrocephalus, there is a defect in the vessels that drain the cerebrospinal fluid. The fluid builds up and causes damage to the brain cells. The damage already done cannot be repaired, but future damage can be prevented by surgically placing a shunt in the brain. As long as the shunt remains open, it will drain off the excess fluid.

Alzheimer's is by far the most common cause of dementia, accounting for 50 to 60 percent. The onset is slow and gradual. It then progresses with increasing confusion until death occurs, usually from pneumonia. The family may recall some stressful event, such as surgery, that happened shortly before the confusion became apparent. Stress does not cause dementia, but it seems to speed up the progress of Alzheimer's disease. The confusion occurring before the surgery was so slight that the family paid little attention or passed it off as normal forgetting.

There are two major changes that occur in the central nervous system. Deposits of a starchlike protein in the brain are seen on autopsy. These plaques, as they are called, interfere with transmission of impulses through the nerve cells. The nearby neurons, Figure 9-7, undergo the second change. The neuron atrophies, and the axon and dendrites then wrap around the cells and entangle them in a mass of tissue. These are actually called *tangles*. They develop mostly in the cortex and cause forgetting of the higher cognitive functions first.

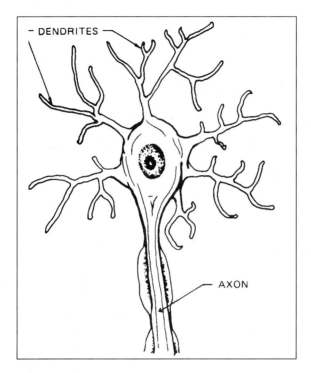

Fig. 9-7 The neuron. In Alzheimer's disease, the axon
and dendrites entangle themselves around the atrophied
body of the cell.

The cause of the disease is not known, but research is going on.
Several theories have been advanced, but neurotransmitters seem to be
the most promising at the moment. The possible causes are:

- Heredity. Some studies have shown a higher risk of the disease for
  people whose near relatives already have it. Another reason why it
  is thought there is some genetic reason lies in the fact that patients
  with Down's syndrome almost universally develop Alzheimer's if
  they live past thirty.
- Age. The incidence of Alzheimer's increases with age. As people get
  older, they seem to become more vulnerable to the disease.
- Increased aluminum concentration in the brain. There has been an
  increased aluminum concentration found the the brains of people

with Alzheimer's disease. For a time it was thought an increased ingestion of aluminum might be the culprit. Further studies have shown that it is probably a result rather than a cause of dementia.

- Slow-growing virus. Because symptoms of Kuru and Creutzfeld-Jakob are similar to Alzheimer's disease, some studies have looked at viruses as a cause. Thus far, this theory remains unproven.
- Neurotransmitters. A change in the amount of the neurotransmitter, acetylcholine, in a patient with a familiar tendency to the disease seems to be the most acceptable theory today.

There is no cure at present. The disease will continue to progress, with the patient living from two to twelve years. The disease does go through stages, although they are not always easy to detect. The stages are not clearly defined and even can overlap.

## Disease Progression

In the first stage, there is memory loss, Table 9-7. As was mentioned earlier, it is so slight that it can be overlooked or covered up. The patient is generally disoriented, particularly to time and place. He may not be able to find his way to the corner store where he had been going for years. His ability to think logically and his judgment are affected. There can also be emotional or behavioral changes.

**TABLE 9-7**
**Stages of Alzheimer's Disease**

| STAGE | CHARACTERISTICS |
|---|---|
| First | slight memory loss; some behavior changes; may wander and get lost; disoriented as to time and place |
| Second | further deterioration with increased memory loss; logic, reasoning, and judgment are diminished; neglects grooming and proper eating habits; exhibits antisocial behavior |
| Third | forgetting increases; may not recognize family and self; conversation is irrelevant; may scream incessantly; unsteady gait; may be incontinent |
| Fourth | not able to ambulate well or at all; incoherent speech; totally incontinent; seizures may occur |

There is further reduction in memory in the second stage. Logic, reasoning ability, and judgment are also further diminished. This person can forget social standards. He can neglect grooming and proper eating habits. He can undress in public or use profanity where he would not have used it before. In the third stage, forgetting increases. Perception changes and the patient may not recognize familiar faces or objects. He usually becomes incontinent of both bowel and bladder. Reading, writing, and the ability to problem solve are most likely gone. Although the patient can still pronounce some words, conversation is irrelevant and, at times, can be unrecognizable. The patient can scream and yell incessantly and not know why. Toward the end of this stage, there can be an unsteady gait and frequent falls may occur.

During the fourth or last stage, all symptoms become worse. The patient will probably be bedridden. He will have no control over his bowels or bladder. His speech is incoherent, and, if he speaks at all, it is usually only sounds. Seizures often occur.

## Nursing Care

There is no cure. Drugs can be used to control specific behaviors, but they may or may not be effective. Even though the confusion is irreversible, reality orientation should be employed. Many times these patients have a reversible confusion superimposed over the Alzheimer's, making the condition appear worse than it is. Research has shown that reality orientation can slow down the progress of the confusion, even when it is due to organic reasons.

Even though the patient may not answer or may answer with irrelevance, the nurse must continue to attempt to communicate with him (see section on reality orientation earlier in this chapter). The important points are summarized here:

1. Remain calm.
2. Don't argue or speak in a raised voice.
3. Break down all requests into the simplest form.
4. Speak in concrete terms.
5. Get patient's attention.
6. Give time to respond.
7. Refer to past life experiences that patient remembers.
8. Use touch frequently.

These patients need skilled nursing care. They require a regular, predictable routine. They need to be kept active, but not to be overwhelmed, Figure 9-8. The nurse must see that the environment is organized and safe. Because the patient is already confused, he does not need an untidy, cluttered room. Excess stimuli should be kept at a minimum. The patient's physical health must be monitored and his physical needs tended to promptly.

Caring for the Alzheimer's patient is a difficult and stressful job. The nurse needs imagination and a sense of humor. She must love these patients and look for enjoyment in the little things they accomplish.

Fig. 9-8 Patients with Alzheimer's disease must be kept active.

# DEPRESSION

Depression is a more clearly understood term than is confusion. Everyone has been sad because of a loss. However, sadness is not considered depression unless it is prolonged or interferes with one's life.

The elderly are more prone to depression because they sustain more losses, their adaptive energy has diminished, and they take more drugs that are apt to cause the condition. Chronic illness, more prevalent in the aged, decreases coping ability. There is also a decline in the production of hormones as people age. This reduction changes the chemical balance in the brain and predisposes the elderly to depression. The highest suicide rate of any group is found in the elderly male.

Depression is probably the most common problem of the elderly and the most easily treated, yet it is the most underdiagnosed and least treated of all. Other conditions mask the depression, and symptoms, if apparent, are often not taken seriously.

## Symptoms

The person who is depressed has prolonged or extreme sadness. It is a generalized sadness; that is, it is not connected to a particular loss. These patients are withdrawn and sometimes agitated and hostile. They can also be confused. Called *pseudodementia*, Table 9-8, depression involves a reduction in activity, obsessive worrying, and sleep disturbances. The patient's ability to reason and remember is diminished and he is more pessimistic.

**TABLE 9-8**
**Difference Between Pseudodementia and True Dementia**

| PSEUDODEMENTIA | TRUE DEMENTIA |
|---|---|
| depressed mood | mood fluctuates |
| impairment is inconsistent | impairment is consistent and progressive |
| onset is rapid | onset is slow and insidious |
| more likely to answer questions with "I don't know" | more likely to cover up by giving an answer that may be close to correct |
| more likely to give up easily | tries to stay independent as long as possible |

The elderly depressed person usually has more physical complaints. In fact, hypochondriasis is common. Physical complaints can even be the only symptom of depression. Elderly depressed patients are more apt to be constipated, and they can even be incontinent.

## Treatment

Treatment of depression depends on the cause. Depression can be the result of physical illness or drugs. It can be the result of changes in the chemicals of the brain, called *endogenous depression*. It can also be the result of abnormal grieving, called *reactive depression*.

Physical illness can act as a stress, making the person more vulnerable to depression. Illness can also cause a change in the oxygen or hormonal balance in the brain. Some diseases that do this are anemia, particularly pernicious anemia, brain tumors that cause pressure on the brain, and Parkinson's disease. A large percentage of people with Parkinson's are depressed. Parkinson's is due to a lack of a brain hormone, dopamine, which may directly cause the depression. Other illnesses associated with depression are cancer, particularly of the pancreas, and thyroid disease. Viral infections such as the flu are also associated with depression. Waste products circulating in the blood due to conditions like kidney and liver failure can lead to depression.

As a group, the elderly take many drugs. Unfortunately the drugs most often taken by them are the very ones most apt to cause depression. These drugs include analgesics and hypnotics that lessen stimuli to the brain, antihistamines, some antibiotics, anti-Parkinson's drugs, and cardiovascular drugs such as digitalis. Hypoglycemics lower the sugar level available to the brain, anticholinergics change the chemical balance in the brain, and antihypertensives lessen the amount of oxygen supply.

The group most apt to cause depression is the antihypertensive group, the drugs taken for high blood pressure. Estrogens and anti-anxiety drugs can also cause confusion. If a drug is found to be the culprit, the most logical treatment is to stop the drug.

Endogenous depression results from some chemical changes in the brain. There is no precipitating stressful event to which the patient can point. The depression just occurs. These people experience guilt and self-loathing. They do not have interest in anything because nothing is enjoyable. They generally are tired all the time, have no appetite, and lose weight. They will describe their feelings as different from when they experienced a loss in the past. The depression seems to be more severe in the morning and lessens as the day goes on. There is generally a family history of depression.

Reactive depression is the most common type of depression in the elderly. It is a result of a normal grieving process becoming abnormal. Normal grieving lasts no more than six to twelve months. If it is longer and more severe, grieving is abnormal. The person experiencing loss in a normal way begins to go through the normal grieving stages immediately (see Chapter 15). When the person experiencing the loss does not react emotionally immediately, the grieving will probably be abnormal. This person may instead complain of physical symptoms or exhibit disturbed behavior.

In the elderly, depression responds better to treatment than any other mental disorder. There may not be a complete freedom from any symptoms, but patients can be reasonably happy and return to a productive life. If the depression is a result of illness, it will disappear when the disease is treated. If the disease cannot be treated, drugs can be used. Reactive depression is often self-limiting. In time, the depression will diminish. Supportive care is always indicated. Psychotherapy may be needed. If the condition is very severe, drugs are prescribed.

The patient with endogenous depression is most likely to respond to treatment. This patient should be given supportive care. Drugs may be indicated. If the depression does not respond to supportive care and drugs, electroconvulsive therapy is used.

Supportive measures include encouraging the patient to talk about his feelings, giving information and encouragement, providing physical and mental activities, involving the patient with a social group like family or friends, providing good nutrition, and providing for adequate sleep.

**Electroconvulsive Therapy.** Electroconvulsive therapy, or ECT, is a viable but controversial treatment for depression. Some authorities believe it is safe and effective, particularly for people with endogenous depression and depressions that do not respond to supportive care or drugs. In these situations, ECT is considered the treatment of choice. According to other authorities, however, the treatment is not safe and should not be used under any circumstances. Still others say ECT is "preferable to suicide" and should be employed in the treatment of specific patients. Despite the controversy, ECT is still widely used in all parts of the country.

Treatments are generally given in 3–4 day intervals for the first few treatments, then the frequency is reduced to once a week. Each patient is scheduled for a set number of treatments prescribed by the doctor. Though still not widely available, there are newer machines that allow a drastic reduction in the number of treatments needed.

The policies and procedures governing ECT vary in different hospitals. Many time the procedure is carried out in the surgical unit or there may be a special ECT room with a specially trained ECT staff. The patient or guardian needs to sign an informed consent prior to the procedure. Though it is not the nurse's responsibility to initially inform the patient, it is usually up to him or her to obtain the signature. Therefore, the nurse needs to ascertain that the patient has been informed. The patient needs information regarding the steps in the procedure, the expected results, and the possible complications. Every attempt should be made to present the material so as to inform but not frighten the patient.

Besides the consent form, the nurse needs to see that certain other forms are on the chart and complete. These forms will vary in different institutions but, generally, the following are included.

- physical exam
- routine urinalysis
- routine blood work
- electrocardiogram
- brain scan
- surgical checklist

Prior to the procedure, the patient is given nothing by mouth, vital signs are taken and recorded, and the patient is asked to void. Pre-ECT medications are ordered by the anesthesiologist or psychiatrist. They include drugs to dry secretions in order to prevent the possibility of pneumonia and drugs to relax the muscles in order to relieve anxiety. Jerking spasms caused by the electrical currents may result in damaged muscle and bone if they are not controlled by the muscle relaxants given. Dentures, contact lenses, and all metallic objects are removed from the patient's body. The patient is dressed in a gown and transported to the surgical or ECT unit by cart or wheelchair.

There is some memory loss following the procedure that is usually temporary—at least in part. Sometimes oxygen is given before and during the treatment. Oxygen seems to lessen the possibility of complications such as memory loss. However, the memory loss is thought by some to be the reason why ECT is effective—the patient literally forgets to be sad. If this is true, the treatments have to be repeated periodically. On the other hand, staunch proponents of the treatment say that ECT actually changes the chemical and electrical environment of the brain, producing a more lasting effect.

Following the procedure, the patient continues to need support and reassurance, particularly regarding the memory loss. Vital signs need to be monitored until they are stable or according to the doctor's orders or the policy of the institution. When vital signs are stable and the patient has recovered from the effect of the medication, he or she is offered food and is encouraged to rest.

Working with the aged who have mental health problems is a stressful job. It can be frustrating and demands enormous patience. Mutual support among caregivers is one important ingredient in reducing job stress. A positive attitude is needed. Although this will not change the disease process, it can improve conditions and make good care more accessible to the elderly. Gerontologic nurse specialists are an excellent resource for support and for care plans. Their consultation should be sought when possible.

## ELDER ABUSE

It is estimated that approximately one million elderly are mistreated. Most abuse occurs in the home by family members, but abuse also happens in institutions. The elderly may be psychologically, physically, and financially mistreated. They may be abandoned, exploited, or neglected. Abuse does not have to result in fractures, malnutrition, or bruises. Not giving the elderly person glasses, hearing aides, or teeth could be considered abuse. Failure to bathe or shave a patient can be considered neglect. Speaking in a loud voice or disrespectfully is verbal abuse. Holding a resident too firmly causing bruising is physical abuse. These acts are abusive whether or not they are intentional.

Just as in child abuse, elders are more likely to be abused by someone who is frustrated, fatigued, and/or overstressed. Abusers are often elderly themselves. They tend to have unrealistic expectations of the older person's abilities. For instance a caregiver may be unable to accept incontinence in the elderly parent. The frustration the caregiver feels is translated into humiliation for the elderly and rough handling each time the elder person is found wet.

Abused elders are withdrawn, frightened, or aggressive, and may be unresponsive, particularly with strangers. They may complain of abuse, but usually they do not. They remain quiet because of a fear of retaliation.

The abused elder is most often female and dependent. The abuser is very similar in personality to the child abuser—he/she has a low self-concept, poor coping skills, unrealistic expectations; lacks interpersonal skills; and has a poor support system (see Chapter 8).

## SUMMARY

Old age is arbitrarily defined as sixty-five years or older. It is a very diverse group in terms of economics, intelligence, and health, both mental and physical. The stereotype of the elderly as poverty stricken, cranky, and confused is simply not true.

The common mental health problems in the aged include confusion, dementia, and depression. The elderly often do not receive treatment because of certain myths and attitudes that continue to persist. The following are some examples: "The problems of the disturbed elderly are inevitable, and there is no sense in bothering with them," "Working with the elderly is inferior to other forms of health care, and the people who work with them are either saints or stupid." Changing these myths will not improve the disease process, but it will improve conditions and make good health care more accessible to the elderly.

Confusion can be reversible or irreversible. Irreversible confusion is called *dementia*. All confusion should be considered reversible. The cause should be sought out and treated. Reversible confusion can result from acute illness, stressful events, drugs, and environmental factors.

Irreversible confusion, called dementia, is due to brain damage. A patient can have both reversible and irreversible confusion at the same time. The majority of people with dementia have the Alzheimer's type. This is a progressive disease for which there is no cure. The disease is not caused by stress, but stress does speed up the progress. Behavior modification techniques and drugs are used to control behavior, but there is no treatment for the disease itself. Reality orientation is used to help keep all confused patients in touch with reality.

Communication is the major tool used when working with the withdrawn patient. Once rapport has been established, confrontation is an excellent technique for this patient.

Working with all distressed patients requires some rules. Remain calm, speak in simple, concrete sentences, avoid questions, do not push the patient to answer. Be very attentive to his physical needs. Observe nonverbal cues carefully.

## SUGGESTED ACTIVITIES

- Volunteer to visit a patient in a nursing home.
- Attend a reality orientation class.
- Contact a local Alzheimer's support group and plan to attend the meeting.
- With a group, discuss the effect of commonly believed myths on the care the elderly receive.
- Examine your own feelings about aging.
- Find out the current legislation affecting nursing homes in your area. Are they helpful or restrictive?

## REVIEW

A.  Multiple choice. Select the best answers.

1.  The causes of reversible confusion include
    a. electrolyte imbalance, vascular accidents, and brain damage.
    b. dehydration, elevated temperature, and drugs.
    c. elevated temperature, a change in neurotransmitters, and drugs.
    d. dehydration, hypoxia, and cerebral infarcts.

2.  The three categories of confusion are
    a. reversible, irreversible, and combined.
    b. Alzheimer's, kuru, and multi-farct.
    c. affective disorders, dementia, and reversible.
    d. dementia, multi-farct, and reversible.

3.  The nurse assesses confusion in the patient through
    a. observation.
    b. a mental status exam.
    c. physical assessment.
    d. informal conversation.

4.  Reversible confusion can be prevented if the nurse sees that her aged patient has
    a. sufficient fluids.
    b. orienting items in the environment.
    c. visits from people with familiar faces.
    d. good hygiene.

5. The cause of Alzheimer's disease is unknown, but theories include
   a. a rapidly growing virus.
   b. diet.
   c. stress.
   d. a change in neurotransmitters.

6. The most common mental health problem in the elderly is
   a. depression.
   b. confusion.
   c. Alzheimer's disease.
   d. dementia.

7. Reactive depression is a result of
   a. some stressful event.
   b. a change in neurotransmitters.
   c. hypochondriasis.
   d. drugs.

8. If the elderly person is depressed without a precipitating cause, is self-loathing, and feels guilty, he probably has
   a. reactive depression.
   b. endogenous depression.
   c. reversible depression.
   d. pseudodepression.

9. A definite diagnosis of Alzheimer's can only be diagnosed by
   a. a CAT scan.
   b. blood chemistry.
   c. visual observation of the brain.
   d. a mental status exam with social history.

10. The pathology in Alzheimer's disease includes
    a. tangles and plaques.
    b. deterioration of the gray matter.
    c. destruction of the blood-brain barrier.
    d. increase in aluminum in the brain.

11. Patients who are confused need
    a. thorough directions.
    b. to be shown rather than told.
    c. simple directions.
    d. directions given in a loud, firm voice.

B.    Briefly answer the following.

1.    Name four things the nurse can do to help prevent confusion in her patients.

2.    List the nursing needs of the patient with dementia.

3.    Describe four things the nurse can do to prevent reversible confusion.

4.    Differentiate between dementia and pseudodementia.

C.    Discussion questions. Briefly discuss the following.

1.    The pros and cons of using electroshock therapy.

2.    The pros and cons of treating the elderly in nursing homes rather than mental health facilities.

3.    The ways in which prevalent attitudes toward aging affect the care of patients with reversible confusion.

# CHAPTER 10
# ALCOHOLISM

## OBJECTIVES

After studying this chapter, the student should be able to:

- Define alcoholism.
- List the four progressive stages of alcoholism.
- Describe the objectives of various community treatment programs for alcoholics.
- List six symptoms of alcohol withdrawal.
- State the treatment used for alcoholics on admission to a general hospital.
- List ten functions of the nurse in the care of the alcoholic.
- Identify various treatment approaches for alcoholism.

Alcoholism is one of the most neglected chronic health problems in the United States. Alcohol is a drug. Alcohol consumption can be both physically and mentally damaging. It is the third most common cause of death and is a major cause of traffic accidents. There are an estimated seven to nine million alcoholics in the United States.

Alcoholism is a progressive, complex disease. The alcoholic is unable, for physical and/or psychological reasons to refrain from frequent consumption of alcohol in amounts sufficient to produce intoxication. Ill health and social and vocational deterioration usually follow. There are a variety of definitions for alcoholism, but most definitions include the following four elements:

- Excessive consumption of alcohol
- Psychological disturbances due to alcohol
- Disturbances of social and economic functioning
- Loss of control over alcohol consumption

E. M. Jellinek, a pioneer in alcoholism research, defines alcoholism as any use of an alcoholic beverage that causes damage to the individual, society, or both.

The alcoholic is often thought of as a skid row bum. However, only 7 percent of the alcoholics are on skid row. The remaining 93 percent are found in every level of society and in every occupation. The number of women who are alcoholics is increasing.

There is no single cause of alcoholism. Researchers have found that societies that induce guilt and confusion regarding drinking behaviors are more likely to produce alcoholics. It also has been found that people who develop drinking problems are more likely to experience intense relief and relaxation from alcohol. The alcoholic usually gives a variety of reasons for drinking. The reasons may include the following:

- Relieving tension
- Helping unwind
- Drowning sorrow
- Making one feel free
- Helping one be sociable

Many people experience increased activity, laughter, and smooth-flowing speech with the consumption of alcoholic beverages, Figure 10-1. Alcohol can produce a temporary feeling of well-being, but it depresses the central nervous system. Alcohol abuse can have negative social and personal consequences. Arrest for DWI (driving while intoxicated) and PI (public intoxification) can occur with all the complicated legal involvements. Health problems (liver disease, gastrointestinal bleeding, esophogeal varices), automobile and occupational accidents, and impaired job functioning contribute to a disrupted lifestyle.

Alcohol dependence with an increased consumption and an inability to stop drinking until intoxicated. Thinking becomes confused and disorganized. Memory, concentration, judgment, and perception are dulled. Depression, frustration, and anxiety are some of the problems caused by alcohol.

## HISTORY OF ALCOHOL

The use, misuse, and abuse of alcohol dates back to primitive times. During the Stone Age, man found that chewing certain berries made his head light. This accidental discovery brought about the intentional manufacture of alcoholic beverages. By 3000 B.C., Egypt had perfected the art of manufacturing beer and wine. The making of wine also became popular in the Mediterranean countries. During the Middle Ages, grapes were cultivated throughout Europe, and monasteries began perfecting the manufacture of wines.

Distillation introduced a new and more potent alcoholic beverage. Instead of beers and wines containing 6 to 14 percent alcohol, beverages containing as much as 50 percent alcohol were made. The literature of this period reports drunkenness as a serious problem. Alcohol was available for religious and medical use when the colonists settled in America. Alcohol sometimes accompanied family meals. However, religion scorned the excessive use of alcohol. As young men went to war, family structure and religious influence diminished and alcohol intake increased.

Alcohol became a social concern toward the end of the eighteenth century. At this time the temperance movement began which stressed moderation in the use of intoxicating beverages. Strong support for the movement came from religious groups, legislators, farmers, businessmen, and schools. By 1919, twenty-five states participated in the Prohibition Amendment. The amendment made it unlawful to manufacture, distribute, or sell alcoholic beverages. Thirteen years later, it was repealed as a failure. Denying people access to alcoholic beverages was a simplistic way to deal with a complicated issue.

Fig. 10-1 Fun, friends, and lots of liquor. A good—or very dangerous trio.

Alcoholism is a problem among all ages. It can be seen in the newborn as a result of maternal alcoholism, and in the child, adolescent, and adult. Alcohol consumption is a way that some people cope with stress.

There is an increasing number of teenagers who drink on a regular basis. Liquors such as vodka and tequila have become popular among teenagers because they are difficult to detect on the breath. Parents do not always recognize alcohol as a drug. When told their child has a drinking problem, many parents are extremely thankful at least their child is not on drugs.

Parental influence can be a factor in teenage drinking. In many households, children see their parents enjoying daily cocktails before and after dinner. Peer pressure is another influence in teenage drinking. When people having equal standing within a group force or cajole another member of the group into doing something in order to gain respect of the group, it is referred to as *peer pressure*.

Advertisements show alcohol consumption coupled with glamorous and exciting activities. If the teenager already has emotional and psychological problems, drinking can be an escape from stressors. Partying and drinking can become a way of life.

The senior citizen may hide a drinking problem. Boredom and loneliness can make a day appear endless. Poor health and inadequate income can contribute to depression which, in turn, may lead to alcoholism. People entering old age with a well-established drinking problem should be observed for developing symptoms of alcoholism. Some families tolerate alcoholism or even supply the liquor in order to make the older member's life more tolerable. This misplaced affection can only lead to more loneliness and alienation.

## STAGES OF ALCOHOLISM

E. M. Jellinek conducted a study that revealed a series of stages for alcoholism. The stages do not always occur in the same order. The four progressive stages of alcoholism as described by Jellinek are:

PREALCOHOLIC

occasional drinking
constant relief drinking
increase in alcohol tolerance

PRODROMAL

onset of memory blackouts
secretive drinking
preoccupation with alcohol
gulping first drink
guilt feeling without drinking
inability to discuss problem
increase in memory blackouts

CRUCIAL

loss of control
rationalization of drinking behavior
failure in efforts to control drinking
grandiose and aggressive behavior
trouble with family and employer
self-pity
loss of outside interests
unreasonable resentment
neglect of food
tremors
morning drinking

CHRONIC

prolonged intoxication
physical and moral deterioration
impaired thinking
indefinable anxieties
obsession with drinking
constant alibis given

## PHYSIOLOGICAL EFFECTS OF ALCOHOL

The nurse should have an understanding of the physiological effects of alcohol. A small amount of alcohol may bring about skeletal muscle relaxation. An increased amount can impair the respiratory and cardiovascular systems. Alcohol physically depresses; tensions and fears appear to ease. With alcohol consumption, mental activity changes and judgment and self-concern are reduced. With increased levels of alcohol, a staggering gait is noted. Difficulty in standing follows. Finally the person falls and is unable to get up. A larger dose of alcohol can produce delirium. Delirium is a serious complication that usually follows a prolonged drinking spree. When alcohol is taken on an empty stomach, it is absorbed immediately. The effect on the central nervous system is felt in less than twenty minutes.

## THE ALCOHOLIC IN THE HOSPITAL

When the alcoholic arrives at the hospital, he is usually acutely ill. Even if his behavior is aggressive and abusive, the nurse's primary goal is quality care. It may be difficult to interview the alcoholic because his speech may be slurred and his thoughts confused. The nurse should not try to reason with the disruptive, uncooperative patient. However, she should allow the patient to verbalize his feelings. The nurse should speak slowly and softly. By her verbal responses, she shows the patient that she accepts his feelings and empathizes with his problems. The nurse should reinforce any of the patient's positive behavior.

Many alcoholics have neglected their health through poor hygiene and poor diet. Underlying physical problems should be observed. Respiratory infections are common. This must be considered in the planning of care. On admission to the hospital, treatment of the alcoholic usually consists of:

- Sedatives or tranquilizers
- Replacement of fluids
- Adequate diet (high-protein, high-vitamin diet for underweight and malnourished patients)
- Vitamin therapy (the alcoholic usually has a deficiency of thiamine, niacin, and folic acid)
- Antibiotics for infection

The alcoholic patient needs to be observed closely for convulsions.

## NURSING CARE

Many difficulties that occur with alcoholic patients are a result of withdrawal. Patients in mild withdrawal may suffer only trembling and agitation. A more severe withdrawal involves delirium tremens (DTs). In delirium tremens the patient has extreme restlessness and possible convulsive seizures. Delirium tremens may not occur until the second or third day of treatment. The patient must be carefully observed for any withdrawal symptoms. These may include:

- Tremors
- Profuse sweating
- Nausea
- Vomiting
- Confusion
- Convulsions
- Increased agitation
- Anorexia
- Hallucinations

The patient may struggle against attempts to feed or bathe him. The nurse must recognize the patient's need for care and be aware that his behavior is due to his illness. She must realize that the patient is reacting in fear, possible to hallucinations. He may see, hear, or feel things that are not there. Maintaining a relaxed environment and talking quietly to the patient are important aspects of care. The nurse's firm but gentle manner can be reassuring to the patient.

If possible, the nurse should stay with the patient to help keep him in touch with reality. The nurse should tell the patient what is being done to him and what is expected of him. If withdrawal occurs, an explanation that he is experiencing withdrawal from the alcohol should be given to the patient. The nurse should continue to speak slowly in a low, calm voice and use simple, understandable statements. Restraints may sometimes be necessary to prevent injury to the patient or to others. A doctor's order is needed before applying restraints. It is desirable to keep the room lighted at night to lessen the patient's fear and facilitate observation.

After the acute stage of withdrawal, the patient needs a non-stressful environment. He needs to learn social skills in a social setting with other patients. He may need to be encouraged to eat his meals and attend to personal hygiene. Because of dehydration, the patient may have a dry, sore mouth. Encouraging fluids is an important nursing measure. The nurse needs to inquire what nonalcoholic fluids the patient likes, and to order the fluids for him. A lemon and glycerine solution is soothing for the mouth and gums. Chewing gum may also be helpful.

The nurse needs to check the patient's knowledge of alcoholism. The subject should be dealt with realistically. The patient's family also needs support and an explanation of the facts of alcoholism.

The goal of nursing in regard to the alcoholic patient is to be non-judgmental and understanding and to help the patient to be responsible for his own behavior. The nurse should watch for such defense mechanisms as rationalization, denial, and projection. Compromise and manipulation are signs that also need to be observed. The compromising patient tries to get special privileges by presenting both sides of a situation and then coming up with his own workable middle line. The manipulative patient does not want to comply with demands. He tries to influence others in order to attain his needs or wants. He attempts to change his care plan to meet his own goals.

The alcoholic patient may show signs of final rejection of the world about him. He may withdraw from personal contact with others and not even attend to his needs of daily living. The alcoholic needs empathy and not misplaced sympathy. Innovative approaches for care are necessary for each patient. The nurse should demonstrate qualities of consistency, firmness, honesty, and patience. To do this, she must first determine her own prejudices concerning the alcoholic patient.

Prejudice is a prejudgment. Usually, it is an unfavorable judgment based on insufficient reasons. Nurses need to examine their own prejudices as prejudices can be reflected in nursing care. Nurses should think through their prejudices and recognize their fears and lack of information. Feelings of inferiority and insecurity need to be dealt with. Once prejudices are recognized, the nurse can take responsibility for her own behavior with others. Nurses particularly need to be understanding in their interactions with all patients. She renders care and does not pass judgment.

The majority of alcoholic patients in medical and surgical departments of a general hospital are admitted with a diagnosis other than alcoholism. The commonly seen diagnoses include:

- Pneumonia
- Bleeding ulcers
- Multiple trauma
- Neurological injuries
- Cirrhosis of the liver
- Malnutrition
- Orthopedic injuries

The physician may or may not be aware of the patient's drinking problem. The nurse may be faced with the undiagnosed alcoholic patient who is admitted for elective surgery. Many times, the alcoholic patient shows an exaggerated fear of procedures or surgery. If the patient's behavior appears nervous and high-strung, the nurse should ask questions concerning alcoholism. The word alcoholic need not be used. The nurse could say, "The amount of alcohol you drink may influence the choice of medication you receive. Could you estimate your average weekly or daily intake?" Often questions concerning drinking habits gain the necessary information.

## REHABILITATION OF THE ALCOHOLIC

In 1972, the Department of Health, Education, and Welfare established the National Institute of Alcohol Abuse and Alcoholism (NIAAA). Its purpose is to help the nation gain a better knowledge of the effects of alcohol and to become aware of the responsibilities associated with using alcohol. The Institute encourages public discussion of community drinking problems. Task forces were formed to study major drinking patterns of problem groups within the community. Prevention is now being recognized as essential in the battle to reduce alcohol abuse. To minimize alcohol abuse, attention should be given to the general population and not merely the problem drinker. It is important to act early in discouraging primary alcohol abuse patterns.

Rehabilitation of the alcoholic should begin when the problem is defined. This is when the alcoholic is more vulnerable and receptive to rehabilitation. However, it is usually impossible to convince the alcoholic that he is indeed an alcoholic and needs rehabilitation. This is reinforced by families who tend to protect the alcoholic and frequently deny the problem.

Tolerating stress is a problem for the alcoholic. Improved methods of coping must be learned. It is necessary to find a satisfactory substitute for alcohol as alcohol acts as a tension-reducing agent.

The values and customs of the community in which the individual lives influence his drinking behavior. The community's attitudes, concerns, and involvement with the problem of alcoholism need to be analyzed. Community resources such as family service agencies, mental health clinics, visiting nurse agencies, police, and judicial departments must be made available to help the alcoholic. It is interesting to note that recent studies have shown that the black population is disproportionately targeted for liquor advertisements. Billboards are crammed into poor areas and the pictures vividly connect alcohol with romance, power, and success. Cognac and malt liquor are two beverages frequently depicted. In some neighborhoods, community leaders are banning together and white-washing billboards as a show of defiance and to deliver a forceful message to change advertising approaches.

It is important that the community offers diversified rehabilitation programs. These programs might include emergency medical care, outpatient clinics, inpatient facilities, and halfway houses. Outreach workers can be helpful in visiting ethnic areas of communities to identify their particular needs. The nurse can play a role in case finding, referral, and coordination of community services.

The person with a psychiatric illness and a co-existing alcohol abuse problem is a major challenge. The goal is to monitor within communities seriously dysfunctional patients, attempt to stabilize their behavior, and improve their social functioning. Careful assessment of combined alcohol and drug abuse is needed as the dually-diagnosed or dual-disordered are difficult, noncompliant, and resistant to treatment. Dually-diagnosed patients will usually deny or minimize their substance use/abuse yet an astute mental health professional will note increased psychiatric hospitalizations and exacerbation of florid psychotic symptoms.

It is important to note that the incidence of alcoholism in women has risen and has contributed to a greater increase in suicide, death from accidents, and other alcohol-related diseases. The literature describes women as drinking in response to many stressful events; marital problems, poverty and single parenting, mid-life crisis, "empty nest syndrome," and unwanted pregnancy. A great concern with pregnant females is Fetal Alcohol Syndrome (FAS). It was estimated that in 1985, approximately 4,000 babies were born with FAS and another 36,000 were affected but to a lesser degree. FAS effects the central nervous system. Growth patterns are inhibited with low birth weights and small size infants. Unusual facial characteristics are present; i.e., eye slits, low placement of the ears, and a wide flat forehead with a flat nose.

Adolescents at younger and younger ages are being presented to alcohol rehabilitation centers. They are brought in by their parents, peers, or the juvenile judicial system.

The elderly are at risk for alcoholism. Many experience long periods of isolation and loneliness and drinking soothes these feelings. Family members can confuse their parent's depression and paranoia with growing old ("senility") and fail to recognize the need for alcohol treatment. The elderly frequently are excluded from intense alcohol programs. However, if alcohol use/abuse is suspected it can jeopardize their geriatric healthcare and possibility for residential placement.

Nurses can be alcoholics. Impaired by alcohol consumption, they will lack sufficient insight and judgment to practice their profession. It is a moral and legal responsibility to report the impaired nurse. Many areas provide intensive therapy programs either as an inpatient or outpatient and the person's job position remains intact during the rehabilitation period.

## TREATMENT

In contrast to the rapid response to treatment of many physical illnesses, response to treatment of alcoholism is generally very slow. Treatment methods for alcoholism vary. Many authorities believe that a multiapproach is best in meeting the needs of the alcoholic patient, Table 10-1.

**TABLE 10-1**
**A Multiapproach to Treating Alcoholism**

Alcoholics Anonymous
Rational Emotive Therapy
Industrial Alcohol Programs
Antabuse
Alcohol Program for the Aged
Halfway Houses
Hot Meal Programs
Detoxification Centers
Judicial Rehabilitation Programs
Transactional Analysis
Tranquilizers

### Alcoholics Anonymous

Alcoholics Anonymous (AA) is an organization run by former alcoholics whose personal experiences with alcohol enable them to under-

stand the alcoholic's problems. The alcoholic learns from direct observation of the many recovered alcoholics in the organization. The goal of
Alcoholics Anonymous is to abstain from drinking one day at a time.
Sobriety helps to provide the alcoholic with a growing sense of self-control, achievement, and mastery. This provides further motivation to
refrain from drinking. There is an increased awareness of self as the alcoholic begins to understand his problems and feelings. AA meetings use a
structured group approach with a well-defined 12-step program. Each
member has a sponsor and takes turns with a "lead." A lead is a presentation of a person's struggle with giving up alcohol and the devastating
effects of alcohol on their life. Each person defines his/her own spirituality
and their "higher power" and thereby increase their self-esteem and hope.
AA becomes a crucial part of their successful sobriety.

Co-dependency progresses until, in the late stages, depression,
lethargy, withdrawal, and isolation occur. Serious illness, i.e., alcohol/drug
addiction, eating disorders, and suicides, have been reported. Frequently,
these people are seen in inpatient medical units for physical problems.
However, a co-dependent can recognize their enabling behaviors and
begin to look inside themselves. Individual psychotherapy may be needed
to improve their own self-worth. Giving people permission to do for
themselves can be difficult to put into practice. Making personal choices
and developing the ability to say "no" firmly diminishes their symptoms.
In recovery, the co-dependent must be aware of sabotaging behaviors of
others and identify those people who consistently "suck them in."
Monitoring passive or aggressive behaviors will assist with increased numbers of assertive encounters with others in their personal and work-place
environments. Another helpful approach is the practice if daily personal
affirmations. Affirmation are "I" statements and chanted either silently or
out loud to one's self.

I deserve    satisfaction, contentment, a fulfilling relationship
I will       express my feelings today; act in an assertive manner today

Recovering co-dependents make their own choices and change their
belief/value systems through action-oriented daily new behaviors.

Al-Anon (family groups) and Alateen (teenagers) focus on the effects of alcoholism on family and children. ACOA (Adult Children of
Alcoholics) provides personal contact with others who grew up in a dysfunctional family network. This personal contact is therapeutic and provides emotional support.

Emerging from the literature on alcoholism is the concept of co-dependency. Co-dependency is an enabling behavior whereby someone assumes responsibility for someone else's behavior. This blocks change and personal growth in both people. Characteristics of the co-dependent include:

- caretaking          "I always give to others. Nobody gives to me."
- obsession           "I can't stop worrying about ____ problems."
- denial              "I pretend I don't have any problems."
- dependency          "Why doesn't ____ make me feel happy."
- poor communication  "No one understands what I mean to say."
- lack of trust       "I don't trust my feelings."
- anger               "I feel controlled and manipulated and I resent these feelings."

## Rational Emotive Therapy

Alcoholism is seen by proponents of rational emotive therapy as being a means of coping. The goal of this therapy is to help the alcoholic learn to tolerate the stressors that come with living and to use coping mechanisms that are less self-defeating. It teaches the alcoholic to recognize inaccuracies in his thinking. By changing his view of himself and his environment, the alcoholic can change his behavior. The rational emotive therapist believes that irrational thinking leads to irrational drinking.

## Transactional Analysis

Transactional analysis is another therapy approach to alcoholism that has found some success. The goal of transactional analysis is to help the alcoholic stop playing games and to rewrite his life script. Alcoholism involves several games and a variety of payoffs. With the cessation of game playing, the underlying problems emerge more clearly. The patient is then able to cope with his problems more directly.

## Psychoanalysis

Psychoanalysis involves the direct interaction of the patient with a therapist. The objective is to gain insight into behavior through talking. The therapist assists the patient to clarify and work through stressful areas in his life. The patient may be in therapy for a long period of time.

## Group Therapy

Group therapy involves meaningful interaction between members of a group. The group members relate their personal experiences to each other. The main objective is for each group member to examine his impact on others through increased understanding of his own behavior and relationships. The group can influence change.

## Antabuse

Antabuse is an optional drug therapy that reinforces abstinence. Antabuse (disulfiram) is taken daily after at least a twelve-hour abstinence from alcohol. Antabuse interferes with the metabolism of alcohol and produces a toxic reaction when combined with it. Patients know they will suffer very unpleasant reactions if they do not refrain from drinking. The drug is usually well tolerated, but there are sometimes side effects. These side effects usually disappear as the body adjusts to the drug. The most common side effects include drowsiness, fatigue, acne, and a metallic aftertaste.

If the patient takes a drink of alcohol while this drug is still in his system, he experiences dizziness, nausea, vomiting, and a severe headache. There may be a drop in blood pressure, a rapid pulse with heart palpitations, chest pain, and dyspnea (labored respiration). Within five to ten minutes after a drink, the face becomes flushed and the eyes red. This flushing quickly spreads over the rest of the body. All of this takes place after less than two teaspoons of alcohol is consumed. These effects may last from thirty minutes to several hours; death has sometimes occurred. During the reaction, the patient is in a life-threatening situation and should be observed closely. When the reaction is over, the patient is usually exhausted and goes to sleep.

No patient should be on Antabuse without his knowledge and consent. All patients should be thoroughly warned against consuming alcohol in any form. Over-the-counter medication such as paregoric, cough syrups, and some vitamins may contain alcohol. The patient should be advised to read labels carefully and be particularly watchful for foods prepared with beer or wine. Because of the severity of the reaction, Antabuse is not recommended for use by pregnant patients or patients with heart disease, diabetes, liver impairment, or mental illness. Success with Antabuse depends on a firm resolution by the alcoholic to abstain from drinking.

## Tranquilizers

Tranquilizers are drugs used in the management of alcoholism to facilitate psychotherapy and lessen anxiety. The drugs commonly used include Librium, Valium, Thorazine, and Sparine. However, substituting drugs for alcohol is not the solution to the problem.

# TREATMENT FACILITIES

Various treatment facilities are available to meet specific or general needs of the alcoholic. Detoxification centers are places where the alcoholic receives treatment and care during the withdrawal process. They comprise the first step in treatment. Later, the patient participates in a continuing care and rehabilitation program. Referrals are frequently made to long-term treatment programs. Other times, the patient is transferred to a residential treatment center. The halfway house is an intermediate residence for the patient before he re-enters the community, Figure 10-2. Frequently, the location of the house is in the patient's community. Individualized attention and a homelike atmosphere are just two advantages of the program. Most halfway houses are oriented to Alcoholics Anonymous and encourage future participation in that program.

Hot meals programs are usually run by paraprofessionals. They are particularly geared to the alcoholic with very inadequate nutrition and poor health. From these centers, referrals are made to physicians and visiting nurses. The hot meals program can be used as a detection center for disease and malnutrition. Diseases of the respiratory tract, chronic bronchitis, and tuberculosis are commonly seen in the alcoholic.

Each year, industry loses billions of dollars because of alcoholism. Between 6 and 10 percent of the employees in the United States have an alcohol problem. Employee alcoholism results in sporadic absenteeism and decreased quantity of work output. Unauthorized tardiness and faulty judgment are common. Some industries have begun employee assistance programs (see Chapter 16). The occupational environment is an excellent setting for early identification and treatment of problem drinkers.

For over 350 years, public intoxication was under the ruling of criminal law. The penniless drunk revolved through a process of arrest, jail, release, and rearrest. In the past five years, progress has been made toward transferring the problem drinker from the penal system to treatment programs. It is now recognized that the alcoholic needs appropriate

Fig. 10-2 A halfway house may look like any other home in the community.

treatment and rehabilitation. Legislation is providing the framework for this needed treatment.

School alcohol programs are a preventive measure. Teenagers need alcohol education programs in the schools. The romantic idea of alcohol as seen in the media must be challenged. The real facts and pertinent literature should be presented. Alcoholism is the most neglected health problem in America and needs to be presented to the adolescent in its true light.

Few treatment facilities care for the needs of the aged with a drinking problem. The aged need therapeutic programs geared to their underlying stressors. Treatment facilities should have an individualized approach that attempts to discover the particular problems of each aging person. Developing new friendships and a sense of well-being through group meetings helps alleviate loneliness.

If the drinking problem is due to a deep-seated, long-standing personality problem, the assistance of other agencies should be sought. Long-term goals of a program for the aged alcoholic are to make life worthwhile for the elderly person and to help him to see horizons, not dead-ends.

## SUMMARY

Alcoholism is defined as the use of alcoholic beverages that results in damage to the individual, society, or both. It is a progressive complex disease and a serious problem in the United States. Alcoholics are found in every level of society and in all occupations.

Alcohol depresses the central nervous system; makes thinking confused and disorganized; and dulls memory, concentration, judgment, and perception. Depression, frustration, and anxiety are some of the problems caused by alcohol. Alcoholism may be a way for some people to cope with environmental stress. Many alcoholics neglect their health through poor hygiene and poor diet.

Alcoholism is a problem among all age groups. Teenage drinking is on the rise. The aged may also be a high-risk group for alcoholism. The four progressive stages of alcoholism as classified by Jellinek are: prealcoholic, prodromal, crucial, and chronic. Most alcoholics are admitted to the hospital for reasons other than alcoholism. The nurse should have a knowledge of the physiological effects of alcohol so she may be aware of an undiagnosed alcoholic patient. Many difficulties that occur with alcoholic patients are a result of withdrawal. The goal of nursing in regard to the alcoholic patient is to be nonjudgmental and understanding and to assist the patient to be responsible for his own behavior.

Some treatment methods for alcoholics are: Alcoholics Anonymous, rational emotive therapy, transactional analysis, psychoanalysis, group therapy, Antabuse, and tranquilizers. Treatment facilities include detoxification centers and halfway houses. Legislation is providing changes in the framework for treatment and rehabilitation of the alcoholic. The psychosocial aspects of alcoholism such as family disruption and economic loss cannot be overlooked.

### SUGGESTED ACTIVITIES

- Investigate the problem of alcoholism in your community. Write a report on your findings.
- List the rehabilitation facilities available for the alcoholic in your community.
- Attend an AA or Alanon meeting.
- Organize a resource file on alcoholism. Obtain information by writing for literature concerning alcoholism from:

The National Council on Alcoholism, Inc.
2 Park Avenue
New York, New York 10016

The National Institute of Alcohol Abuse and Alcoholism
5600 Fischer Lane
Room 11 A 56
Rockville, Maryland 20852

## REVIEW

A. Multiple choice. Select the best answer.

1. The amendment forbidding the manufacture, distribution, and sale of alcoholic beverages was the
   a. Temperance Amendment.
   b. Prohibition Amendment.
   c. Distillation Amendment.
   d. Alcoholic Amendment.

2. The treatment method that focuses on changing behavior by changing the patient's view of himself and his environment is
   a. transactional analysis
   b. detoxification method.
   c. Alcoholics Anonymous.
   d. rational emotive therapy.

3. A treatment approach that tries to help the patient to stop game playing and rewrite his life script is
   a. rational emotive therapy.
   b. transactional analysis.
   c. drug therapy.
   d. Alcoholics Anonymous.

4. Alcoholism is a
   a. serious problem in the United States.
   b. progressive complex disease.
   c. way some people cope with stress.
   d. all of the above.

5. A small amount of alcohol can bring about
   a. muscle relaxation.
   b. muscle tension.

c. a staggering gait.

d. impairment of the respiratory system.

6. When mixed with alcohol, Antabuse may cause
a. very little effect.
b. mild unpleasant reactions.
c. hypertension and severe cramping.
d. life-threatening effects.

B. Briefly answer the following.

1. What is the purpose of the National Institute for Alcohol Abuse and Alcoholism?

2. List the four progressive stages of alcoholism as described by Jellinek.

3. State the treatment used for an alcoholic on admission to the general hospital.

4. List six symptoms of alcohol withdrawal.

5. List ten functions of the nurse in the care of the alcoholic.

6. Briefly describe the objectives of each of the following community programs.
a. Alcoholics Anonymous
b. detoxification centers
c. halfway houses
d. hot meals programs

## BOOKS

Beattie, M. *Codependent No More*. Harper & Row: N.Y., 1987.

Brisbane, E. & Womble, M. *Treatment of Black Alcoholics*. Hawoth Press: N.Y., 1986.

Hacker, G. *Marketing Booze to Blacks*. Center for Science in the Public Interest, Washington, D.C., 1987.

Nat'l. Institute of Alcohol Abuse & Alcoholism. *Alcohol & Health* (DHHS Pub. No. ADM 87-1519). U.S. Govt. Printing Office, Rockville, MD, 1987.

Task Force on Substance Abuse Nursing Practice: *The Care of Clients with Addictions, Dimensions of Nursing Practice*. American Nurse's Association, Kansas City, MO, 19 .

# ARTICLES

Allan, C.A. & Cooke, D.J. Stressful life events and alcohol misuse in women: a critical review. *Journal of Studies on Alcohol*, 46 147-53, 1985.

Creigs, B. Treatment issues for black, alcoholic clients. *Social Casework: The Journal of Contemporary Social Work*, June, 1989.

Drake, R. & Wallach, M. Substance abuse among the chronically mentally ill. *Hospital & Community Psychiatry*, 40: 1041-46, 1989.

Eells, M.A. Interventions with alcoholics and their families. *Nursing Clinics of North American*, 21: 493-503, 1986.

Gulino, C. & Kadin, M. Aging and reactive alcoholism. *Geriatric Nursing*, 7: 148-51, 1986.

Schneir, E.R. & Siris, S.G. A review of psychoactive substance use and abuse in schizophrenia: patterns of drug choice. *Journal of Nervous & Mental Disease,* 175: 641-52, 1987.

Tesson, B.M. Who are they? Identifying and treating adult children of alcoholics. *Journal of Psychiatric Nursing & Mental Services*, 28(9): 16-21, 36-37, Sept. 1990.

Vaccani, J. Borderline personality and alcohol abuse. *Archives of Psychiatric Nursing* - (2): 113-19, April 1989.

# CHAPTER 11
# DRUG DEPENDENCY

## OBJECTIVES

After studying this chapter, the student should be able to:

- Differentiate between drug use, misuse, and abuse.
- Describe the historical perspectives of drug use.
- List six symptoms of heroin withdrawal.
- State the factors that contribute to use of drugs.
- List the effects of commonly abused drugs.
- Describe nursing care for the drug-dependent person.
- Name the treatment approaches for rehabilitation of the drug-dependent person.

Most Americans use drugs at some time during their lives. A drug *user* is defined as a person who takes drugs according to directions for medical reasons. Drug *misuse* occurs when the directions are exceeded. When a person takes drugs for other than medical reasons, he is classified as a drug *abuser*. Any substance capable of altering the individual's mood or conscious state may be abused. Narcotics, depressants, tranquilizers, stimulants, and hallucinogens are the drugs most commonly abused.

*Tolerance* occurs after continued use of some drugs, when an increasing amount of the drug is needed to produce the desired effect. A person may be dependent on a drug either physically or psychologically. An addicting drug causes physical dependence and withdrawal symptoms if the drug is withheld. When physical dependence to a drug develops, the user is said to be *addicted*. *Habituation* is the term used for psychological dependency on a drug. A habitual drug user compulsively depends on the drug as a means for coping with conflicts of daily living. It is difficult to differentiate between habituation and addiction, so the preferred term for both is drug *dependence*. However, less emphasis is being placed on the question of addiction and more on psychological and social impairment. Occupational health has looked at substance abuse and the loss of job productivity and the increase of accidental injury and death.

A special population impaired by drug dependency use/abuse is the dually-diagnosed patient. This individual has a severe mental disorder and also a substance abuse. Who is to provide care and management to these patients? Behavioral characteristics of the dually-diagnosed include noncompliance and resistance. Consider that many drug centers discourage the use of medication, expel patients that are non-compliant, and base their group work on confrontation techniques. Studies have reported that the tension and monotony of daily existence for the chronically mentally ill can lead to drug use/abuse with the following drugs:

| | |
|---|---|
| amphetamines | "Helps me to feel more normal." |
| marijuana | "I can join in with my old friends." |
| cocaine | "People like me, they look for me, give me some thing, and borrow my money." |

It is important to note that many homeless people suffer from drug abuse.

The new DSM-IV proposes criteria for substance abuse and dependence with a presentation of the many different disorders related to substance abuse. They include: psychoactive substance use disorders dependence/abuse, psychoactive substance induced organic mental disorders, intoxification and withdrawal states (specific substance induced), organic disorder, and cocaine delusional disorder.

Another cogent point is that the trend nationally is to combine alcohol and drug abuse centers into one comprehensive treatment area entitled chemical dependency.

## HISTORICAL PERSPECTIVES

Drug abuse has existed for may centuries. Each era had its favorite drug. Opium was used in ancient Mesopotamia, Egypt, Greece, and Rome. The effects of cannabis were mentioned by the Arabians in the 1500s. Cocaine sniffing was popular in the 1700s. Hashish was the drug of choice in the 1800s.

China was the first country to attempt to control drug abuse. Opium was transported to that country from the Middle East by Arabian traders. During the nineteenth century, opium use was so widespread in China that the government banned it with an imperial edict. However, so much of the drug was smuggled in that the attempt to ban it was unsuccessful. Confiscation of large quantities of opium by the government led to the Opium War of 1839. The Chinese lost the war and as a result the British were able to force the Chinese government to legalize the opium trade. China eventually became the main source of opium and supplied the drug to the rest of the world. Since opium could be bought legally and inexpensively over the counter, its use increased among the civilian population. Opium was also the main ingredient in many patent medicines. It was given to women and children as cough syrup, diarrhea remedies, and pain-killers. Opium and its derivative, morphine, were the most frequently used drugs following the Civil War.

America's drug problems began with the Civil War in 1861. Wounded soldiers were given morphine by injection. Its use was uncontrolled; many soldiers were given their own supply. Cocaine, a refined product of the coca plant, became popular after World War I. In 1898, heroin (a derivative of morphine) was discovered in Germany and soon was imported to America. The new drug was approximately ten times more potent than morphine. Heroin became a popular drug during World War II. Methadone headed the list in popularity immediately following World War II. Marijuana was heavily used during the Vietnam War. Today, chemicals from opium to aspirin are misused and abused. Effects of drugs on society are very complex with medical, moral, legal, and economic consequences.

Drug controls began in 1906 when the Pure Food and Drug Act required accurate labeling of drugs. This forced many patent medicine makers to remove opium from their products. In 1909, Congress banned the importation of opium except for medicinal purposes. The Harrison Narcotic Act, passed in 1914, controlled the manufacture, importation, and sale of opium and coca leaves. Marijuana was banned in 1920. In 1930, the Federal Bureau of Narcotics imposed still more controls. By 1950, international responsibility for narcotics was given to the World Health Organization.

The 1950s brought the development of more synthetic drugs, including tranquilizers. Drugs were effectively used to treat a variety of physical and emotional problems. Successful use gave drugs the reputation of being good and beneficial. Society became conditioned to relying on drugs to alleviate distress. Drugs were thought of as an easy way to solve problems. This attitude often leads to misuse and abuse of drugs. ·

The Controlled Substance Act of 1970 gave authority to the Attorney General of the United States to place drugs in categories according to their effect, history, abuse potential, and scientific information gathered on them. There are approximately eleven categories. Each category carries a different penalty for violations.

## COMMON ADDICTING SUBSTANCES

Addicting substances have widespread use in our society. Frequently, these substances are used habitually and compulsively. People who chronically use addicting substances feel that they are unable to function satisfactorily without them. A physiological dependency is established. When the person refrains from the addicting substance, a problem exists as the body craves that substance.

### Caffeine and Nicotine

Two commonly used addicting substances are nicotine and caffeine. Caffeine is the least expensive and most abused drug in the United States. It is a central nervous system stimulant. Caffeine in large amounts causes insomnia. Over a long period of time, its use causes circulatory problems because caffeine constricts the blood vessels. People who habitually drink five to seven cups of coffee a day may suffer withdrawal symptoms if coffee is eliminated from their diet.

Nicotine, the addicting ingredient in tobacco, is also a stimulant. Nicotine narrows blood vessels, raises the blood pressure, and speeds the heart rate. Smoking during pregnancy can have adverse effects on the fetus. The harmful gases and poisonous substances from the smoke pass from the mother's blood through the placenta. There is a high correlation between smoking and retarded intrauterine growth, spontaneous abortions, and prematurity.

Coffee and cigarettes are socially acceptable and easy to obtain. Unfortunately, may people use these addicting substances regularly. Next to alcohol, nicotine is the most commonly used drug in the adolescent group. Adolescents often see smoking as an initiation into adulthood.

## Marijuana

Marijuana is a mixture of dried up leaves, stems, flowers, and seeds of the Indian hemp plant (cannabis sativa). Use of marijuana has become one of the biggest controversies since alcohol and prohibition. The main question is whether or not the drug is a sociological or an individual psychological problem. In August 1977, the decriminalization of marijuana was proposed. If marijuana is decriminalized, it would be legal to possess small amounts of marijuana for personal use.

Marijuana is known as grass, weed, maryjane, tea, and pot. The drug is usually crushed and rolled into cigarettes called reefers or joints. The smoke smells like burning rope. Users often burn incense to cover the odor. The effects of the drug are inconsistent and varied. They seem to depend on the user's mood and expectation and his interests and personality.

The effect of marijuana is immediate and lasts less that three hours. A small amount usually produces a sense of well-being, although some users experience anxiety. Light smokers appear talkative, relaxed, exhilarated, and happy. One of the most consistent effect of marijuana is an altered sense of time. Time passes very slowly for the marijuana user. Increased amounts of the drug seem to hinder memory recall. The sense of touch and hearing are enhanced and many marijuana smokers complain of hunger after use. Larger than moderate doses result in impaired coordination and moral judgment. The user is easily distracted and more suggestible.

Marijuana may be obtained in various strengths. The strength depends on the part of the plant used, where it is grown, the amount of the active ingredient, and whether or not it has been adulterated (weakened by the addition of other substances). Street marijuana is often adulterated. Marijuana may be adulterated with inactive tea, spices, grass, leaves, or parsley. It also may be adulterated with substances that are harmful to the body, such as angel dust (PCP). Many cities test street drugs and report their contents daily to prevent deaths from use of contaminated drugs.

True tolerance does not develop in the marijuana user. Abrupt withdrawal does not produce symptoms of addiction. However, chronic users can develop a psychological dependence on the drug. Although marijuana does not physically lead to hard drugs, users often experiment with other drugs. The adolescent and the young adult are frequent users. They are usually attracted to it out of curiosity and the belief that it is relatively harmless. The National Institute on Drug Abuse in 1985 reported a growing problem of marijuana use/abuse among the adolescent population.

When looking at substance use in the schizophrenic population, it was noted that marijuana was one of their drugs of choice.

Medical use of the drug is now being explored. The main active ingredient in marijuana is delta 9 tetrahydrocannabinol, or THC. In the 1800s, tincture of cannabis was used to relieve menstrual cramps. Marijuana has recently been found to be useful in the treatment of glaucoma and in reducing nausea and vomiting associated with chemotherapy.

Research on the effects of marijuana is still being conducted. Some researchers are studying the consequences of long-term use. Other researchers are examining marijuana's effects on mental and physical skills. Still others are trying to determine the drug's toxic level. Until there are more scientific facts, the debate over marijuana continues.

Hashish (hash) is a more potent form of marijuana. It is a resin from the top of the hemp plant. Because of its high concentration, it is often five or six times stronger than marijuana. Frequent use of hashish has been associated with physical, mental, and emotional deterioration.

## Inhalants

Inhalants include, glue, gasoline, spray paint, and aerosols which contain volatile hydrocarbons that are highly soluble in fats. The products usually contain a nonporous oily base which, when inhaled, causes the lungs to become coated, impairing air exchange. Using inhalants over a long period of time can cause brain damage. Use can also result in damage to the liver, heart, kidneys, and bone marrow. Occasionally, the use of inhalants can result in cardiac arrest. Sometimes the user places a plastic bag over his head to prolong the effect. This is a dangerous practice as death can occur from suffocating. Paint and gasoline contain lead which is a poison. When inhaled, lead accumulates in the body. If enough lead accumulates, death occurs.

Inhalants produce a state similar to alcohol intoxication. The user experiences a sense of floating or spinning. Tolerance may develop. Inhalants are a particular problem for children because of their availability. Preadolescent drug users often get started with inhalants, i.e. nail polish remover and hair spray.

## Tranquilizers

The tranquilizers most often misused are Librium, Valium, and Chlorpromazine. Tranquilizers can be effective in treating various medical problems, but they are often abused. Tranquilizers reduce agitation and produce a calming effect. The user thinks and behaves more rationally and frequently experiences a feeling of well-being. All tranquilizers appear to be addictive when taken in large amounts. The effect is made stronger in combination with alcohol and sedatives. This presents a serious potential for complications such as coma or death.

## Hallucinogens

A *hallucinogenic* or psychedelic drug is a drug capable of producing hallucinations. *Psychedelic* refers to distortion of perception. In reality, hallucinogenic drugs cause a heightened and distorted perception of things. Colors become more brilliant, flat objects are seen as three dimensional, stationary objects move, and faces are distorted. The senses are sharper and seem to merge together. The user may claim to be able to hear the grass grow. Hallucinogenic drugs include:

- LSD (lysergic acid diethylamide)
- Mescaline
- Peyote (the button of a small spineless cactus)
- Psilocybin (one of the two active substances isolated from the psilocybe mushroom)
- THC (the active ingredient in marijuana and hashish)
- MDA
- DMT (dimethyltriptamine)
- PCP (angel dust)

LSD has been controversial since its discovery in Switzerland in 1943. Some say it promotes a religious experience, while others say it only distorts reality. The true potential of LSD is unknown. It causes a loss of control over normal thought processes. Serious temporary or permanent mental changes may occur. Episodes of violence and self-destruction have resulted from use of LSD. There is evidence that it causes chromosomal damage. LSD has been used experimentally to treat psychic disorders, but its use in medicine has been limited. Even under close supervision, the behavior of users is highly unpredictable.

LSD is colorless, tasteless, and odorless. Most of it is synthetically made in illegal laboratories. LSD can be added to any food or drink. Some of the most popular items to which LSD is added are sugar cubes, chewing gum, hard candy, mints, and animal crackers. It is an extremely potent drug. An amount invisible to the eye can cause effects lasting eight to ten hours. On the street, LSD is known as 25, acid, sunshine, cubes, the big D, trips, the chief, the ghost, and the hawk. Like other street drugs, it is often adulterated. Tolerance to LSD develops quickly and is just as quickly lost, so the drug is usually taken intermittently rather than on a continuous basis.

The user's frame of mind and the environment are contributing factors to the drug's effects. A person with repressed desires, emotions, or fears may experience a *bad trip* (emotional experience that may result in panic reactions). Feelings of indestructibility or the feeling that one can fly have been reported. Serious injury and death have occurred from acting on these feelings. A *flashback* (re-experiencing of a trip) can occur months after the drug was last taken because LSD is stored in the fat tissue and released later.

Mescaline and psilocybin are related to LSD in action but they are somewhat weaker. Mescaline is an active chemical ingredient found in the peyote cactus. The American Indians have traditionally used the peyote cactus as a legitimate part of their religious ceremonies. Mescaline is now produced synthetically. Psilocybin is an extract of the Mexican grown psilocybe mushroom.

DMT is a hallucinogen prepared from the mimosa root. The active ingredient is N-cimethyltryptamine. DMT is found as either a liquid or a colorless crystal, which is usually mixed with other substances. Its effect comes on rapidly, producing a trip similar to LSD. The effect lasts one to two hours. Too much of this drug taken too fast can cause brain damage.

PCP or angel dust is an animal tranquilizer. It is important to be aware of its existence because it is often substituted for other hallucinogenic drugs on the street. PCP is an immobilizing and anesthetic agent for large animals. Its effect on humans is highly unpredictable. It may cause lapse of memory and difficulty in concentrating which can last for several days. Convulsions, partial paralysis, and death can occur.

MDA is an amphetamine-related drug. It makes the user feel very mellow. The MDA available on the street is often of low-grade quality and usually consists of less expensive substitutes. It may, in reality, contain more LSD or PCP than MDA.

Psychedelic drugs are again prevalent and in a dangerous form on tattoo paper, which small children may use to ornamentally tattoo on their hands or arms and subsequently absorb the drug. Schools are distributing information to parents and children to warn them of the danger.

## Cocaine

Cocaine use/abuse has reached epidemic proportions in all elements of society. Cocaine is a refined product of the coca plant found in South America. It comes in the form of a pure, white crystalline powder. Cocaine is also referred to as snow, coke, or a new change in form called freebase crack. Unfortunately, crack is inexpensive compared to cocaine, potent, and available. Previously, cocaine was thought to be the drug of the upper-middle class and used for recreation and as a status symbol. Cocaine can be used by several routes: nasal inhalation (sniffing or snorting), smoking, and intravenously. A language develops around the usage of cocaine:

| | |
|---|---|
| "wired" | hyper, high feelings |
| "coke run" | consecutive days of usage |
| "speedball" | high amount or pure given intravenously |
| "lightball" | approximately 1/8 oz. cocaine, with estimated cast $500 |
| "crashing" | a quick comedown physically, psychologically when drug is not obtainable |
| "dealing" | securing and selling drugs |
| "rush" | euphoric feelings |

Although we have developed a remarkable increased knowledge of cocaine use and its consequences, users/abusers possess great denial and large blinders that block their recognition of these consequences. Cocaine usage increases alertness, increases the heart rate, dilates pupils, and produces hyperactivity and decreased appetite.

With prolonged use malnutrition can occur. More serious side efects include schizophrenic-like symptoms with visual, auditory, and/or tactile hallucinations and in some cases cardiac irregularities and sudden death. Paranoid-like symptoms (fear, suspiciousness, jumpiness) can lead to impulsive or assaultive behaviors. Two serious problems that also emerge with cocaine use/abuse are: how do I get money to sustain a high? and if I can't, how can I counter the "crash"? Theft, prostitution, and "dealing drugs" to support the habit are common practices. To avoid "crashing," polydrug abuse (alcohol, sedatives) can be used to assist with the bringing-down process. Intravenous users are subject to abscesses, systemic infections, Hepatitis B, and AIDS. Contamination occurs from poor injection technique, dirty equipment, dirty environment, and sharing needles.

Although our national call is for a war on drugs, the yet-unborn are not escaping addiction to cocaine as women are using cocaine and/or crack pre-natally. The infant born addicted is of low birth weight with subsequent poor weight gain, withdrawal, hyperactivity, tremors, and a frantic sucking mechanism. These infants need special care and their mothers need an intervention for their drug abuse and assessment of their parenting skills.

## Amphetamines

Amphetamines are stimulants that cause the heart and other body systems to speed up. They are also known as dexies, pep pills, uppers, speed, drivers, bennies, footballs, whites, and white crosses. Amphetamines release stores of epinephrine into the body, which results in a high degree of sensitivity to stimuli and insomnia. Long-term heavy use can cause damage to vital organs. Chronic anorexia results in weight loss. Amphetamines can interfere with language control and decrease mental capability. The prolonged sleeplessness produced by the drug can promote an amphetamine psychosis. The user often called a speed freak, usually suffers from acute paranoia.

During the 1940s and 1950s, amphetamines were prescribed for a wide variety of reasons. They kept truck drivers awake and college students stimulated for study. Overweight people found their appetites depressed after taking the drug. Amphetamines are now used primarily to treat *narcoleptics* (those afflicted with brief attacks of deep sleep). They are sometimes given to hyperactive children, epileptics, and people with Parkinson's disease. Because of their dangers, medical use of amphetamines has been diminished.

An amphetamine user is a potential abuser. Since amphetamines cause insomnia, many users resort to a depressant drug to help them sleep, thus initiating a vicious cycle. Users take sleeping pills at night to sleep and amphetamines to get them going in the morning. Tolerance readily develops. After a period of time, amphetamines may produce an opposite effect. Users may find themselves becoming drowsy instead of alert. Large doses may lead to antisocial and aggressive behavior. Sudden withdrawal of amphetamines can cause depression and suicide.

In 1972, the Drug Enforcement Administration established guidelines for production of drugs. The amount of amphetamines legally manufactured was diminished. However, amphetamines are still readily available on the street. Street users run the risk of taking adulterated drugs; amphetamines have been known to be adulterated with strychnine. Caffeine tablets also are passed off as amphetamines at a premium cost.

## Depressants

Barbiturates are the best known and most abused of the depressant drugs. Barbiturates slow bodily functions and are used medically in the treatment of insomnia. All barbiturates are abused, but the most common are Amytal, Seconal, and Nembutal. The street names refer to the color of capsule such as reds, yellow jackets, or rainbows. They may also be called goof balls, downers, or barbs.

Barbiturates result in light-headedness, relieved inhibitions, drowsiness, slurred speech, and sleep. The drug produces a sense of well-being and relaxation. Tolerance is developed quickly and increasing amounts of the drug are needed to produce the desired effects. Large doses may cause restlessness, excitability, and delusions. The user has symptoms similar to the alcoholic.

There seems to be a correlation between barbiturate addiction and age. Younger adults are more susceptible to addiction than older adults. Emotional dependence can occur at any age. Withdrawal symptoms are very severe and can result in grand mal seizures. Withdrawal should be gradual and attempted only in a hospital environment under close medical supervision.

Barbiturates are one of the main causes of accidental deaths. Bodily functions can be slowed so much that breathing and heart action stop. Barbiturates are the most common method of suicide. The potential for overdose is especially high when mixed with alcohol.

Synthetic, nonbarbiturate sleeping pills are made to eliminate the dangers of addiction and habituation. Many are on the market but none have been proven to be completely safe. All are abused. One such drug is methaqualone, or quaaludes. Quaaludes are also known as ludes or soapers. This drug is addictive and has a sedative-hypnotic effect. Effects of the drug include motor incoordination, stupor, and difficulty in arousing. Severe respiratory depression can result. Quaaludes are addictive and extremely dangerous because of toxins which remain after the drug is synthesized. It is a restricted drug but reportedly available on the street as one of the current "in drugs."

## Narcotics

Narcotics are central nervous system depressants and are primarily painkilling drugs. Opium, its derivatives heroin and morphine, and synthetics such as Demerol and methadone are all classified as narcotics.

Opium is the dried milklike juice from the pod of the unripe opium poppy. It contains about 10 percent morphine. Heroin is similar to morphine, but four to ten times more potent. Neither opium nor heroin can be obtained legally in this country. Heroin is very addictive. However, heroin bought on the street has been cut many times and is usually only 2 to 10 percent pure. Heroin is also called smack, junk, horse, or skag. Its use is increasing and there appears to be more heroin available now than ever before.

Physical and psychological dependence rapidly develops from use of narcotics. The addict is "strung out" and may be dependent for the rest of his life. Heroin is usually taken intravenously. This is referred to as *mainlining*. The drug also can be snorted or smoked. Sometimes the addict *skin pops* (takes the drug subcutaneously). Users describe the initial dose of heroin as a *rush* (an intense feeling of well-being followed by warmth and peacefulness). The user then goes into a *nod*, which is a sleepy, drowsy state. There is no dysfunction in coordination and the addict can go about his regular business.

Heroin withdrawal symptoms occur four to forty-eight hours after the last dose and include:

- Allergic reactions
- Sore throat
- Watery eyes
- Sweating
- Elevated temperature
- Rhinorrhea (watery discharge from the nose)
- Diarrhea
- Nausea
- Vomiting
- Leg and abdominal cramps
- Extreme restlessness

More severe withdrawal symptoms include dilated pupils, muscular twitches, and elevated blood pressure.

Withdrawal without the aid of medication is called *cold turkey*. Symptoms are uncomfortable but not necessarily dangerous. A post-withdrawal syndrome of anxiety and depression frequently occurs. Stress in daily living may lead to the desire for heroin. If the addict takes the drug, the cycle of addiction begins again. Other health problems are created by the use of heroin. Dirty needles cause hepatitis and abscesses. Some addicts suffer from malnutrition. Death may result from an overdose, Table 11-1.

## TABLE 11-1
### Abused Drugs: Symptoms and Effects

| DRUG | STREET NAME | SYMPTOMS | ADVERSE EFFECTS |
|---|---|---|---|
| **Halluciogens**<br>marijuana | grass, weed, maryjane tea, pot, reefer, joint, hemp, hashish, hash, rope | sense of well-being; possible anxiety; talkative; relaxed; exhilarated, happy; altered time sense | reduced memory recall; impaired coordination and moral judgment; easily distracted, highly suggestible; long-term effect not known |
| LSD | 25, acid, cubes, sunshine, the big D, trips, the chief, the ghost, the hawk | heightened and distorted perceptions; euphoria; altered time perception; dreamy, floating state, enlarged pupils; bizarre sensations | chromosomal damage; loss of control over normal thought processes; violence, self-destructive feelings; highly unpredictable behavior,; slowed reaction and reflexes; personality changes; paranoid symptoms |
| PCP | angel dust | lapse of memory; difficulty concentrating; convulsions; partial paralysis | effects highly unpredictable |
| **Inhalants**<br>glue<br>gasoline<br>spray paint<br>aerosols | | similar to alcohol intoxication; sense of floating or spinning; blurred vision; confusion; staggering gait; slurred speech | brain damage; lead poisoning; damage to liver, heart, kidneys, and bone marrow; death |

# NURSING CARE

The nurse should familiarize herself with the street names of psychoactive drugs so that she can better communicate with the user. Nursing care includes the ability to feel confident and comfortable with the drug-dependent person. The nurse must have insight into her personal attitudes and value system. She must develop sensitivity to the feelings and reactions of others. She needs to have some understanding of the influences that led to the problem. Skill in assessing the mood and attitude of the patient is necessary. The drug addict is very persuasive and tends to manipulate the behavior of others. The nurse may have to limit visitors and mail and possibly do body searches. The nurse needs to deal with the addict in a straightforward, honest manner.

The nurse must watch for and report the danger signals of drug abuse. The symptoms and treatment vary with the type of drug. With heroin and barbiturate overdose, the symptoms are muscle flaccidity, respiratory depression, and coma. Time spent searching for needle marks or constricted pupils is wasted. Multiple drugs may have been taken.

The most important action for the nurse to take with an overdosed patient is to assure a patent airway. The mouth must be cleared of any obstructions and the neck hyperextended. The nurse should be sure that a flaccid tongue is not obstructing the airway. Mouth-to-mouth resuscitation or mechanical ventilation may be needed. If possible, assistance of another person should be obtained.

It must be remembered that barbiturate withdrawal is dangerous; abrupt withdrawal from barbiturates may be fatal. Withdrawal should be attempted only in a hospital situation and under close medical supervision. Researchers have found that misuse of barbiturates causes interference with the REM, or dream cycle of sleep. The user, being deprived of dreams, becomes less stable.

If the overdose is with amphetamines, the patient is irritable, hyperactive, and suspicious. He should be kept in a quiet environment and not touched. The user's feelings of persecution and suspicion may lead to violent behavior. Judgment is impaired due to the delusional state. No attempt should be made to administer injections as the needle may be misinterpreted as a knife.

Under the influence of LSD, the user is apprehensive and suspicious. He needs a quiet environment and calm reassurance. The room should be darkened and free from external stimuli. If a friend has accompanied the patient to the hospital, it is important to encourage the friend to remain quietly at the patient's bedside. The presence of an understanding friend can help establish a working relationship.

This patient needs to be talked down. *Talking down* is to softly and calmly help the patient to fully experience and complete his trip. It is very important that the trip not be interrupted. The patient should be told what is being done. He should be reassured that he is in a safe place with sympathetic people. He is very suggestible so his thoughts should be guided gently, keeping in mind the goal of a good trip.

Since many drugs are not pure, it may be difficult to identify the drug that has been taken. The patient withdrawing from drug use requires special nursing assessments. This includes the following:

- Vital signs; particularly respiratory function
- Level of consciousness (orientation and alertness)
- Reaction of pupils to light
- Patent airway
- Stage of withdrawal
- Nutritional needs
- Fluid intake
- Urinary output

If prn medications (medications that are ordered to be given as needed) are ordered for the patient, they should not be withheld. Withholding medications may cause the patient to convulse.

## Care of the Adolescent Drug Abuser

The National Institute on Drug Abuse in 1985 recognized the magnitude of the problem of drug dependence in the adolescent. The drug-dependent adolescent presents a special concern as adolescents at younger ages are moving through different treatment with their first appearance occurring in the justice system. Thus, a focus for the future needs to concentrate on the systems serving these minors and the ramifications.

The drug-dependent adolescent presents a special challenge for the nurse. Many adolescent drug users have a low self-esteem, which may have been the problem leading to the use of drugs. These patients are frequently hostile and negative. Accusations may be shouted at the nurse and tears of frustration may be seen. Coping mechanisms are often ineffective. The nurse must remain calm, supportive, and reassuring. As the adolescent's physical condition improves, the environment may need to be manipulated in order to increase external stimuli. The nurse should take time to talk to the patient about the issues that led to his drug in-volvement.

Schools have a great potential for preventive programs for the adolescent. Sound education can establish pathways in which students clarify values and improve their self-image. The school nurse can help by assessing the problem in her school. She may observe students for symptoms of drug misuse such as emotional instability, sluggishness, shakiness, and evasiveness. She also may watch for students who suddenly lose interest in school, sports, and other activities. The school nurse can provide students with factual information. She can be an understanding listener and an agent for referral to community agencies if needed.

## TREATMENT APPROACHES

Rehabilitation of a drug-dependent person is a long-term project. The drug user must be motivated and willing to cooperate. Treatment approaches include:

- Group therapy
- Methadone maintenance programs
- Narcotics Anonymous
- Psychotherapy
- Self-help programs

Live-in drug rehabilitation centers run by former drug addicts have proven effective in treatment of the drug addict. At the center, the addict withdraws without the support from any drugs. The addict must voluntarily decide to eliminate his drug habit. To be admitted to the homelike atmosphere, the addict must recognize that he has a commitment to himself and to the people at the center. The new resident is given the opportunity to relate to ex-addicts. Ex-addicts who have achieved success act as role models. The new member soon becomes involved in a sharing and caring familylike group. Group therapy and behavior modification are used. The members are rewarded for good behavior and punished for infractions.

One of the chief problems with a live-in drug rehabilitation center is follow-up care. When the former addict leaves the center, he no longer has the reinforcement of the center. The addict goes back to his old town, his old friends, and possibly his old drug habit.

Methadone is an opiate substitute that is taken orally and is used in the treatment of opiate addicts. It is classified as a synthetic narcotic and has painkilling properties. Methadone is legally dispensed by approved treatment centers. It is given once a day. An average dose lasts twenty-four to forty-eight hours. Randomized urine "drops" are done to secure drug screens. Methadone maintenance programs have specific guidelines to stringently follow for obtaining urines and maintaining active participation in the program.

Methadone relieves withdrawal symptoms and has no secondary effects. However, it is addicting. Many people are critical of treatment with methadone. They point out that the addict is only changing the drug on which he is dependent. When the heroin habit has become too expensive, the user may turn to methadone simply to lower his heroin tolerance. Some peddle methadone received at free clinics to purchase heroin for their own use. Methadone maintenance, however, has returned addicts to their community as functioning adult members. Methadone clinics should require some group therapy as part of their program.

Narcotics Anonymous holds group meetings similar in format to Alcoholics Anonymous. The meetings are held in the local community. Members include addicts and ex-addicts.

Many believe that psychotherapy and social therapy are very important treatment approaches to drug dependency. Since anxiety and depression are difficult to cope with during physical withdrawal, the patient is encouraged to participate in occupational therapy, recreational therapy, physical therapy, and social activities.

Some communities offer the drug-dependent person some help through drug hotlines, drug crisis centers, and drug treatment centers. These are considered self-help programs. Centers are located in target areas of the community where paraprofessionals assist the addict. The nurse may act as a liaison between the traditional hospital setting and the community.

The addict has a great deal of time on his hands. He needs to learn new patterns of living and to expand his interests. Some type of employment is advocated. Classes on current events or encouraging personal opinions are often successful. Vocational classes are a form of therapy. Members of the addict's family should be sought out for possible group meetings and discussions. The family members may also be in need of counseling or referrals.

Rehabilitation of the drug-dependent person requires long-term management, Figure 11-1. The addicted person must be motivated and willing to stop abusing drugs. Rehabilitation should include adequate follow-up care in the patient's own community and referrals as needed. Social skills training needs to be initiated and alternate means of coping need to be investigated. An open support line is necessary.

## SUMMARY

When a person takes drugs for other than medical reasons, he is classified as a drug abuser. Drug abuse dates from ancient times. In the United States, drug abuse began with the Civil War. Americans have become accustomed to taking medications to alleviate their problems; all drug users are potential abusers. People who are dependent on drugs are found in every level of society and in all age groups. The effects of drug abuse on society are complex with medical, moral, legal, and economic consequences. Legislation has been passed in an effort to control the drug problem.

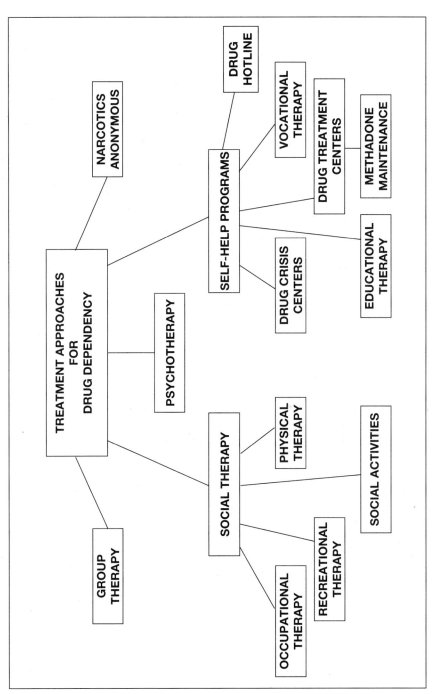

Fig. 11-1 Treatment approaches for drug dependency.

Coffee and cigarettes are two common sources of addicting substances. Frequently abused drugs include the hallucinogens (marijuana, LSD, mescaline, peyote, psilocybin, MDA, DMT, PCP); inhalants (glue, gasoline, spray paint, aerosols); tranquilizers; stimulants (cocaine, amphetamines); depressants (sedatives, barbiturates); and the narcotics (opium, morphine, heroin). Withdrawal symptoms range from uncomfortable to deadly. Physical and/or psychological dependency occurs with the use of most drugs.

Rehabilitation of the drug-dependent person requires long-term management. Treatment may include group therapy, social therapy, psychotherapy, Narcotics Anonymous, and self-help programs such as methadone maintenance programs. Rehabilitation centers have proven effective in helping the drug abuser give up drugs and return to a normal life. The nurse must be aware of the conditions to watch for and report concerning the drug-dependent patient.

## SUGGESTED ACTIVITIES

- Have a group discussion about current legislation regarding drug use and abuse.
- List your community resources available to the drug abuser.
- Write a report on your local hospital's method of treating the drug abuser.
- Role play a mental health professional nurse assisting a patient who has been admitted to the hospital while experiencing a bad trip from LSD.
- Obtain and review pamphlets from the National Clearinghouse for Drug Abuse Information, P.O. Box 1635, Rockville, Maryland 20850.

## REVIEW

A. Multiple choice. Select the best answer.

1. Drug problems in America began
   a. after World War II.
   b. during the Civil War.
   c. in the 1960s.
   d. after the Korean War.

2. Weakening a drug by adding other substances to it is called
   a. adulteration.
   b. drug abuse.
   c. tolerance.
   d. mainlining.

3. The addicting ingredient in tobacco is
   a. caffeine.
   b. cocaine.
   c. coca.
   d. nicotine.

4. An often abused substance that produces a state similar to alcohol intoxication is
   a. marijuana.
   b. an inhalant.
   c. LSD.
   d. heroin.

5. Drugs which cause heightened and distorted perception are called
   a. amphetamines.
   b. barbiturates.
   c. hallucinogens.
   d. tranquilizers.

6. Breathing difficulties due to a deviated septum may develop from the use of
   a. amphetamines.
   b. barbiturates.
   c. cocaine.
   d. heroin.

7. Speed is another name for
   a. amphetamines.
   b. barbiturates.
   c. cocaine.
   d. LSD.

8. The most abused stimulant in the United States is
   a. amphetamines.
   b. heroin.
   c. caffeine.
   d. nicotine.

9. Narcotics include
   1. heroin.
   2. opium.
   3. cocaine.
   4. morphine.
      a. all of these
      b. 1, 2, and 4
      c. 1 and 4
      d. 2

10. Heroin may be taken by
    1. intravenous injection
    2. snorting.
    3. smoking.
    4. skin popping.
       a. all of these
       b. 1
       c. 1 and 4
       d. 1, 2, and 4

B. Match the drugs in column II with the statement in column I.

| Column I | Column II |
|---|---|
| 1. produces a talkative, relaxed, exhilarated, happy feeling | a. barbiturates |
|  | b. caffeine |
| 2. associated with retarded intrauterine growth of the fetus | c. cocaine |
|  | d. heroin |
| 3. causes insomnia and circulatory problems | e. inhalants |
|  | f. LSD |
| 4. causes lungs to become coated, which impairs air exchange | g. marijuana |
|  | h. nicotine |
| 5. hallucinogen that produces highly unpredictable behavior | i. PCP |
| 6. animal tranquilizer that causes lapses of memory and difficulty in concentrating for several days | |
| 7. produces a sense of alertness and wakefulness | |
| 8. depressant drugs that are one of the main causes of accidental deaths | |
| 9. highly addictive narcotic that may cause lifelong dependence | |

C.  Define the following.

1.  drug abuse
2.  drug use
3.  drug misuse
4.  tolerance
5.  habituation
6.  addiction

D.  Briefly answer the following.

1.  List six symptoms of heroin withdrawal.
2.  List six nursing assessments required for the patient withdrawing from drug use.
3.  List three treatment approaches to rehabilitation of the drug-dependent person.
4.  What is the most important action of the nurse when a patient has taken an overdose of drugs?
5.  List four factors which contribute to the widespread use of drugs in American society.

## BOOKS

LaFountaine, W. *Setting Limits: Parents, Kids & Drugs*. Hazelden: MN, 1982

## ARTICLES

Ash, K.H., et al. Helping the teenage drug user. *Patient Care* 23(20): 58-62, 67-69, 72+, Dec. 15, 1989.

Bazzacco, V. Vulnerability and alcohol and substance abuse in the spinal cord injury. *Rehabilitation Nursing* 15(2): 70-72, Mar.-Apr., 1990.

Chuchula, N.M., et al. The cocaine epidemic: a comprehensive review of use, abuse and dependence. *Nurse Practitioner* 24(13): 129-32, 134, 136+, Aug. 15, 1990.

Drake, R. & Wallach, M. Substance abuse among the chronically mentally ill. *Hospital & Community Psychiatry* 40: 1041-46, 1989.

Holmstrom, C. Women and substance abuse. *Canadian Journal Psychiatric Nursing* 31(2): 6-10, Apr.-June, 1990.

Jefferson, L.V. & Ensor, B.E. Help for the helper: confronting a chemically impaired colleague. *American Journal of Nursing* 82: 574, 1982.

Kanwischer, R.W., et al. Screening for substance in hospitalized psychiatric patients. *Hospital & Community Psychiatry* 41(7): 795-97, July 1990.

Kircus, E., et al. Dealing with substance abuse among people with disabilities. *Rehabilitation Nursing* 15(5): 250-53, Sept.-Oct. 1990.

Kofoed, L. & Keys, A. Using group therapy to persuade dual-diagnosed patients to seek substance abuse treatment. *Hospital & Community Psychiatry* 39: 1209, 1211, 1988.

Lucas, G. Substance abuse in the workplace. *Occupational Health* 41(12): 355-56, Dec. 1989.

Oswald, L. Cocaine addiction: the hidden dimension. *Archives Psychiatric Nursing*, III(3): 131-41, June 1989.

Seilbert, J. Understanding chemical abuse and dependence in the elderly. *Journal of Home Health Care Practitioners* 2(3): 27-31, May 1990.

Slop, G. B. Substance abuse by adolescents. *Hospital Practitioner* 23(4A): 19–20, 23, 26–8+, Apr. 30, 1990.

Williams, A. Primary care of parental substance abuse. *Nurse Practitioner* 11(17): 29-33, 1986.

# CHAPTER 12
# MALADAPTIVE
# BEHAVIORS

## OBJECTIVES

After studying this chapter, the student should be able to:

- Define maladaptive behavior.
- Describe the characteristics of psychological, paranoid, schizophrenic, and personality disorders.
- State the four aspects of normal.
- Describe the type of care available at sustaining care centers and day treatment centers.

Maladaptive behavior is the inability to act or react to a particular condition or situation in an appropriate manner. Maladaptive behaviors are very complex. The person who is mentally ill is unable to adjust to the world in which he lives. During childhood, the person may have learned methods of coping which are costly in terms of adaptive energy and which may be considered abnormal by society. These coping methods may be ineffective, but also may be the only way the individual knows to manage his problems. Maladaptive behaviors can develop at any time from infancy through old age. Three critical stages are adolescence, menopause, and old age. Stress is experienced during every developmental stage and coping activity is required throughout the entire life cycle. Problems in any area can contribute to maladaptive behavior.

# THE MEANING OF NORMAL AND ABNORMAL

The word *normal* has a social, clinical, moral, and statistical aspect. It includes a wide range of acceptable behaviors. In the social sense, normal is concerned with actions that fit the social rules. The person who follows the rules of a particular society is considered normal. For example, self-sacrifice is considered normal in some cultures, but it is considered abnormal in other cultures. Social rules are important in any culture. People become disturbed if rules change too quickly.

Clinical normal is subjective. It is concerned with whether or not the individual sees himself as being normal; therefore, it is a personal consideration. The question is how well the person is satisfied with himself. Is he in control of his behavior? Is he happy?

Moralistic no rmal is an ideal. It concerns setting and attaining goals which may be set by society or by the person himself. An individual may become conditioned to a specific ideal. For example, he may continually tell himself he is not allowed to become irritable and must remain calm at all times. Setting unrealistic or impossible goals creates unnecessary stress.

The statistical concept of normal is based on the number of people engaging in specific behaviors. Statistics deal with numbers. If a behavior is practiced by the majority of people, it is statistically normal.

There are many misconceptions concerning the word *abnormal*. To many people, the word means weird or bizarre. Some people expect to see a sharp difference between normal and abnormal but there are many variations between the two. The disturbed person often exhibits normal behaviors. Behaviors which are found in the mentally ill also may be found in the normal individual under certain circumstances. Maladaptive behaviors are the reaction of an individual to stress, so there is no clear-cut line between normal and abnormal.

Psychiatry categorizes patterns of behavior. The nurse must realize that patients do not fit neatly into these categories because their patterns of behavior are individual reactions to stress. A diagnosis in psychiatry is not as clearly defined as a physical diagnosis. The nurse should be fully aware that the patient does not necessarily conform to a set standard of diagnosed behavior.

# PSYCHOLOGICAL DISORDERS

Psychological disorders are emotional disturbances characterized by maladaptive behavior aimed at avoiding anxiety. These disorders were formerly classified as psychoneuroses or neuroses. Since the psychological disorder represents a poor adaptation to stress, there is a crippling of personality growth. Suffering from a psychological disorder keeps a person from attaining full potential. A psychological disorder may occur at any time during the life cycle. Bedwetting, temper tantrums, extreme shyness, nail biting, excessive fear, and a poor school record may be early symptoms of a psychological disorder.

The individual with a psychological disorder maintains contact with his environment. He has the same view of reality as does the normal person. However, the person with a psychological disorder lacks awareness and so lacks control over his behavior. Anxiety disorders, somatoform disorders, affective disorders, and dissociative disorders are some common psychological disorders.

## Anxiety Disorder

Every individual experiences anxiety at some time during the life cycle. A situation such as a final exam can produce symptoms of anxiety. These symptoms include nausea, anorexia, dry mouth, diarrhea, tachycardia, difficulty in swallowing, and a nervous stomach. Anxiety may be classified as mild, moderate, or severe. During mild or moderate anxiety, there are usually manifestations of rapid speech patterns and irregular voice tones. There are attempts made to block communication, i.e., changing the subject of the conversation. When anxiety is so widespread that it is not associated with a specific object or situation, it is called *free-floating* anxiety. Severe, overwhelming anxiety is called panic. Panic causes the individual to feel helpless and immobilized.

An anxiety disorder is characterized by anxiety that is disproportionate to the stresses of daily living. The anxiety may occur periodically or it may be constant. Anxiety attacks may be brought on by even mild stress, or they may occur for no apparent reason.

The person with an anxiety disorder cannot relax. He becomes restless and irritable and continually overreacts to stressful situations. He may experience loss of appetite, heart palpitations, and increased respirations. If the anxiety is severe or prolonged, these symptoms intensify and the person may need to be hospitalized. Anti-anxiety medication may be given (Table 12-1).

Anxiety attacks may be caused by repressed feelings of anger and frustration. They may also be caused by trying to achieve unrealistically high goals and standards.

278  MENTAL HEALTH CONCEPTS

**Anti-Anxiety Medications**

| TRADE | GENERIC |
|-------|---------|
| Xanax | Alprazolam |
| Ativan | Lorazepam |
| Valium | Diazepam |
| Librium | Chlordiazepoxide HCL |
| Benefit Gained: | Short-term relief from intolerable anxiety |
| Side Effects: | incrased appetite<br>headache<br>muscular weakness<br>poor coordination<br>impaired judgment<br>menstrual irregularities |
| Caution: | NEVER drink on this medication<br>Watch for drowsiness—do not drive a car<br>or operate heavy equipment<br><br>can be ADDICTING<br>abrupt discontinuance may results in:<br>    insomnia<br>    agitation<br>    nervousness with trembling<br>    seizures |

Anxiety disorders include several subtypes. Two of these subtypes, phobic disorders and obsessive-compulsive disorders, are discussed in this chapter.

**Phobic Disorder.** A *phobia* is an abnormal, excessive fear of a specific situation or object. The person with a phobia realizes that the fear is unreasonable, but he is not able to control it. Phobias usually begin with repressed conflicts which produce anxiety. In an effort to control the anxiety, the person converts the anxiety into fear of a specific object. The person can then avoid the object and thus control the anxiety.

When a phobia is limited, the person can live a reasonably comfortable life simply by avoiding the object of fear. However, phobias often spread to include associated objects. When this happens, it may be difficult or impossible to keep the phobia from interfering with daily living. One treatment often used to help people overcome phobias is desensitization.

Phobias include exaggerated fears of death, snakes, dogs, open spaces, confinement, or heights. Table 12-2 lists some common phobias.

TABLE 12-2
Some Common Phobias

| PHOBIA | FEAR OF | PHOBIA | FEAR OF |
|---|---|---|---|
| acrophobia | heights | laliophobia | speaking |
| agoraphobia | open spaces | necrophobia | death |
| algophobia | pain | olfactophobia | odor |
| androphobia | man | ophidophobia | snakes |
| claustrophobia | being closed in | pharmacophobia | medicine |
| cynophobia | dogs | phasmophobia | ghosts |
| demophobia | crowds | ponophobia | work |
| gamophobia | marriage | pyrophobia | fire |
| hodophobia | travel | traumatophobia | injury |
| kainophobia | change | triskardekaphobia | number 13 |
| kakorrhaphiophobia | failure | vaccinophobia | vaccination |

**Obsessive-Compulsive Disorder.** Although different in meaning, obsession and compulsion often occur together. An *obsession* is a persistent, re-curring thought or feeling that is overpowering. A *compulsion* is an irresistible urge to engage in a behavior. Compulsion may be in the form of frequent handwashing or shoplifting. Whatever the compulsion may be, it has a symbolic meaning. The behavior is engaged in because it lowers anxiety. When the anxiety level builds up, the obsessive-compulsive act is performed again. This process is cyclic and may occupy the person's entire life.

It is not unusual for a person to experience recurrent thoughts periodically or to engage in ritualistic behaviors (handwashing, counting and re-counting, checking and re-checking). However, the person with an obsessive-compulsive disorder lets these thoughts and ritualistic actions interfere with his daily living. The person is unable to control his thoughts and actions even though he knows they are irrational, yet they release pent-up anxiety and tension.

Obsessive-compulsive behavior is often caused by repressed thoughts and feelings. It is an attempt to relieve anxiety and is another example of converting anxiety into other symptoms.

## Somatoform Disorder

Somatoform disorders are characterized by a loss or an alteration of physical functioning that has no physical basis. It is thought that the physical impairment is caused by a psychological conflict or need of the person. However, it must be remembered that the symptoms are very real—the person does not have conscious control over them. Somatoform disorders are divided into several subtypes. Two common subtypes are conversion disorder and hypochondriasis.

**Conversion Disorder**. Conversion disorder was formerly known as hysterical neurosis. In conversion disorder, the person converts his overwhelming anxiety into physical symptoms. This is an unconscious re-sponse. The person may experience paralysis of an extremity, blindness, deafness, or numbness. The disability has no physical basis. The individual usually complains about his pain and discomfort but is usually calm and indifferent about his symptoms. The physical symptom is symbolic of the unresolved anxiety producing the conflict. The symptoms enable the person to avoid an action that is unacceptable to him. They also enable the person to get attention and support from others that he might not get otherwise.

**Hypochondriasis**. Hypochondriasis is an abnormal anxiety about one's health. This disorder was formerly known as hypochondriacal neurosis. The person with hypochondriasis is preoccupied with his body and his imaginary illnesses. He has an unrealistic fear or belief that he is ill despite medical assurance that this is not so. This person has difficulty establishing meaningful relationships with others since much of his time and energy is spent worrying about himself. Hypochondriasis can affect both social and occupational functioning.

## Affective Disorder

As the name may suggest, affective disorders deal with the emotions. Included in this category are the subtypes of dysthymic, cyclothymic, and bipolar disorders. The dysthymic disorder (formerly called depressive neurosis) is characterized by depression. The cyclothymic disorder (formerly called cyclothymic personality) and the bipolar disorders deal with alternate moods of depression and elation.

The National Institute of Mental Health (NIMH) estimates that 36 million Americans are depressed at some time in their lives. Research is indicating a corollary between depression and biochemicals (i.e. norepinephrine deficiency). There is a problem with the transmissions of neurotransmitters across a synapse. Literature points to depression being biologically determined and influenced by multiple situational factors.

Researchers are gathering data on a seasonal affective disorder (SAD), whereby an individual is depressed in winter when there is less light available.

**Dysthymic Disorder.** The person experiencing a dysthymic or depressive disorder has a prolonged feeling of extreme sadness which is accompanied by guilt feelings, self-depreciation, and social withdrawal. The disorder is usually associated with a loss, such as loss of a loved one, loss of a possession, or loss of self-esteem. The person feels rejected, helpless, and worthless. He is indecisive and disinterested in his surroundings and unable to experience pleasure in life. He has a low energy level and is always tired. He may either be unable to sleep or may sleep excessively. The depressed person dwells on the negative aspects of life, which only add to his feelings of displeasure and guilt. He may cry often and easily. This person may have serious thoughts of suicide.

A dysthymic or depressive disorder often results from the person feeling: (1) that he has no control over his life, (2) that he is a failure because he has been unable to attain a desired goal, or (3) internal anger. Critical periods in the life cycle when a dysthymic disorder is more likely to occur are adolescence, menopause, and old age.

During adolescence, depression must be differentiated from temporary states of sadness. Adolescents are subject to emotional ups and downs. However, when a lack of feelings or a sense of emptiness becomes a dominant mood, this is considered a dysthymic or depressive disorder. The adolescent with a dysthymic disorder is unable to deal with or express his feelings. Boredom and restlessness can result. Drug use and unwarranted risk-taking can be symptoms of hidden depression.

During menopause, women must cope with physical changes as the aging process occurs. Menopause may have physical symptoms such as hot and cold flashes, pressure headaches, heart palpitations, insomnia, and persistent fatigue. Some of these symptoms are caused by the changed hormonal balance between estrogen and progesterone. Depression can be caused by a perceived loss of womanhood and childbearing abilities.

Women are not the only people who must contend with the effects of menopause. Men may also experience menopausal changes, which may accompany the normal diminution of sexual activity that occurs with advancing age. They may reduce their social interaction at this time, and may become preoccupied with feelings of guilt. They may communicate depression via facial expressions of sadness or negative verbal remarks. Daily stressors encountered on the job may have an increasingly negative impact on their outlook. The effects of the aging process on men may also become cause for heightened concern.

Social isolation and boredom may be symptoms of a dysthymic disorder. The individual has a facial expression of sadness and decreased verbal communication. With lessened energy levels and migratory aches and pains, they frequently withdraw from activity. With social interactions reduced, feelings of guilt and sadness prevail. Some people experience agitation and restlessness which result in pacing the floor and wringing the hands. The menopausal person who feels less attractive and useless turns feelings of rejection inward. These feelings of self-anger and destruction can make a person with a serious dysthymic disorder a real suicide risk. Any indications of suicidal thoughts should not be ignored.

The elderly often experience depression. The elderly person's self-perception may become distorted and he may feel worthless and ashamed. A decrease in self-confidence and loss of self-esteem may occur. A negative self-concept results in irritability, apathy, and a lack of humor. Activities of daily living become a problem and hair and clothing may appear disheveled. Movements are slow, posture is stooped, the brow is furrowed, and crying spells may be frequent. In the depressed elderly, there is an intense preoccupation with health. Complaints of vague aches and pains, constipation, and anorexia are common. The severely depressed can become extremely agitated and appear totally miserable. Some antidepressant medications are listed in Table 12-3.

**Cyclothymic Disorder**. The person with a cyclothymic disorder experiences alternating moods of depression and elation. During the elation stage, the person is warm and friendly. During the depression stage, the person isolates himself and withdraws from social activity. The person may experience normal moods between or intermixed with the elation and depression. The person is oriented to reality and has no delusions or hallucinations.

A cyclothymic disorder is a mild form of manic-depression. If the person is not treated, the disorder can become more serious.

**Bipolar Disorders**. Bipolar mood disorders are complex. Researchers are looking at biochemicals (i.e. melatonin, phenylethlymine) that influence brain function. A deficiency of dopamine and serotonin transmitters has been discovered in mania. Internal biological rhythms (circadian) are being carefully observed. Other studies are focused on the effect of light on mood patterns. It has been found that people with mood disorders may have abnormal thyroid studies: T3, T4, and TSH. Electroencephalograms may indicate a picture of a complete or partial seizure. In England (1988), DNA makers for bipolar disorder were located on the chromosome II, thus increasing our knowledge of the role of genetics. Bipolar disorders deal with moods of elation and depression. They are subtyped as bipolar disorder, manic; bipolar disorder, depressed; and bipolar disorder, mixed.

**TABLE 12-3**
**Antidepressant Medications**

| TRICYCLIC AND TETRACYCLIC | |
|---|---|
| **TRADE** | **GENERIC** |
| Tofranil | Imipramine |
| Norpramine | Desipramine |
| Elavil | Amitriptyline |
| Aventyl | Nortriptyline |
| Sinequan | Doxepin |
| Trazadone | Desyrel |
| Prozac | Fluoxetine |
| Benefit Gained: | improved outlook on life<br>better concentration<br>improved sleep, appetite<br>increased energy level |
| Side Effects: | blurred vision<br>dry mouth, drowsiness, nausea,<br>dizziness, light-headedness |
| Caution: | medication is HIGHLY LETHAL<br>non-addicting |
| | be alert to suicidal patients<br>stockpiling medication for a<br>lethal overdose. |
| | advise patient to get up from<br>a lying down or sitting position<br>slowly as he may experience dizziness.<br>With patient on in-patient monitor<br>B/P in sitting and standing positions<br>may have orthostatic hypotension |
| | keep all medication out of reach of<br>children |
| | watch for drowsiness — do not drive<br>a car or operate heavy machinery |

In the manic phase, the individual's appearance and behavior are hyperactive. He speeds up physically, mentally, and emotionally. He generally feels himself too busy to waste time on eating and sleeping. His thought processes may be so rapid that they are difficult to follow. This is called a *flight of ideas*. The person is happy and witty. His mood may shift from euphoria to exaltation to frenzy. He has an overoptimistic, perhaps delusionary, view of his own powers. This patient often meddles in the affairs of others and is aggressive in his social behavior. His angry outbursts, loudness, and manipulative ploys only increase their sensory overload.

The depressed phase is characterized by moderate to severe depression. The level of depression may fluctuate spontaneously throughout the day. These patients are high suicide risks even though depression appears to be only moderate. During the depression stage, the individual's appearance and behavior are hypoactive. Feelings, thoughts, and actions are abnormally decreased. He complains of being tired. Body functions slow, so anorexia and constipation are common. He is negative and hostile. His actions are characterized by agitation, restlessness, pacing, and wringing of the hands. He has the appearance of being sad, remorseful, and dejected. After each episode of misery, the depression slowly lifts. Lithium is a medication frequently given for bipolar disorder (Table 12-4).

## Dissociative Disorder

Dissociative disorders were formerly classified as hysterical neuroses. This disorder is characterized by changes in consciousness and identity. Psychogenic amnesia, psychogenic fugue, multiple personality, and depersonalization disorder are included in this category.

**Psychogenic Amnesia**. The person with psychogenic amnesia has a sudden loss of memory regarding important personal information that is too extensive to be considered ordinary forgetfulness. There is no damage to the nervous system. Psychogenic amnesia usually follows a stressful event and is thought to be a way of escaping conflicts and relieving overwhelming tension.

**Psychogenic Fugue**. Psychogenic fugue involves sudden and unexpected travel away from home or work with the inability to remember the past. The person experiencing psychogenic fugue assumes a new identity. Fugue often occurs following severe stress. Usually, it lasts for several hours to several days and involves only limited travel. In some rare cases, however, it may last for many months and involve extensive travel. The recovery is rapid and recurrences do not usually occur. This disorder is more common after a natural disaster or during wartime. There is no damage to the nervous system involved.

**Multiple Personality**. Multiple personality involves the existence of two or more distinct personalities within the same individual. Each of these personalities is dominant at a particular time. The personality that is dominant determines the behavior of the individual. Each personality is complex and has its own behavior patterns. The secondary personalities are usually quite opposite the original personality. The original personality is not aware of the other personalities, although the secondary personalities are often fully aware of the thoughts and actions of the original personality. Transition from one personality to another is sudden and usually follows stress. This disorder is extremely rare.

**TABLE 12-4**
**Lithium Medication**

| TRADE | GENERIC |
|---|---|
| Lithobid | Lithium Carbonate |
| Benefit Gained: | controls episodes of mania<br>long-term use prevents recurrences of<br>mania and depressive episodes<br>continue to experience emotions |
| Side Effects: | Diarrhea, Dizziness, Dry Mouth, Increased<br>thirst, increased urination<br>CNS symptoms and toxicity:<br>tremors, lethargy, confusion, nausea,<br>diarrhea, slurring of speech, muscle<br>weakness, blurred vision |
| Caution: | take this medication immediately after<br>meals or with food or milk to lessen<br>stomach probems |
| | contraindicated in pregnancy, breastfeeding |
| | Lab tests are necessary to determine that the<br>proper amount of medication is in the<br>patient's system. The blood drawn for a<br>Lithium level should be secured 8–12 hours<br>after the last Lithium dosage. |
| | Dietary: drink 8–12 full (8 oz) glasses<br>$H_2O$ or other fluids each day. Use<br>normal amounts of table salt on your<br>food. |
| | Lithium Toxicity: mild to moderate can<br>be reversed by discontinuing or decreasing<br>the dosage. Acute toxicity can lead to<br>coma and death. |

**Depersonalization Disorder**. Depersonalization disorder involves a change in the person's perception of himself. A sense of the person's own reality is lost. The person is cut off from his own awareness. He feels dissociated from his mind and body and may view himself from a distance. He functions in a dream state or in a mechanical fashion. His senses are dulled and he has a feeling of not being in complete control of his speech and actions.

This disorder often occurs after severe stress, depression, recovery from intoxication, fatigue, toxic illness, or physical pain. Onset is rapid but recovery is gradual. The person with a depersonalization disorder may experience dizziness, anxiety, hypochondriasis, and a disturbed sense of time. He may even feel that he is going insane.

## Nursing Care

Coping with the individual with a psychological disorder may be very difficult for the nurse. Nurses often feel that this person is a malingerer or fake. It must be recognized, however, that this individual needs help. The nurse should never deny the patient's illness. All complaints should be recognized as legitimate. A medical examination should be done to rule out the possibility of physical illness.

Nursing care of the psychological patient focuses on reducing anxiety. The person with a psychological disorder is often treated with minor tranquilizers and/or psychotherapy. The patient often feels that medication will help him. On the unit, the psychological patient needs to be involved in making his own decisions. This decreases his fears and anxieties. The nurse can increase the patient's ability to socialize by encouraging participation in unit activities. Keeping the psychological patient busy and giving verbal praise for achievements increases the patient's self-esteem. Verbalization is very important for this patient. The patient should be encouraged to talk freely concerning himself and his experiences.

The nurse should not ridicule the patient's ritualistic behaviors. It would be better to set limits that the patient can tolerate or attempt to distract the patient with diversional activities geared to his particular interests. If the nurse can gain insight into what motivates the patient's behavior, she can be observant of precipitating factors and plan appropriate nursing interventions.

The patient suffering from a bipolar disorder needs acceptance and approval to diminish his fears of inferiority and rejection. While in the manic state, he can be very dramatic and exhibit overwhelming enthusiasm and talkativeness. In contrast, he can also be very critical, sarcastic, and dominating. The nurse should reinforce positive behavior.

The nursing care plan for bipolar patients must be consistently carried out by all nursing personnel. The ability to recognize manipulative behavior and set firm limits is essential. Manipulation is any action/behavior that the individual purposefully directs toward others in order to meet a need of their own. Remember, manipulation can be viewed as a positive or negative action. The individual who engages in manipulation frequently evokes anger in others, yet their behavior is a form of guarding a very fragile self by attempting to control others. Therefore, our goal is to strengthen the individual's inner, personal control. All staff must approach the patient with a firm, consistent manner. Avoid acting in a judgmental way toward the patient; rather recognize your own underlying feelings of resentment. Our goal is directed toward maintaining the self-esteem of our patient. Begin by stating clearly our own expectations of the patient at an interdisciplinary meeting where everyone should agree on one planned approach. Clarify with the patient if there is a reason for this behavior and then state clearly why the behavior is unacceptable. Clearly state the team's expectation. Offer alternatives by stating choices or options (either/or statements). By giving choices, the patient will begin to feel more in control and will learn how to choose alternatives that work positively for him. The staff must practice attentive listening (what is this patient really trying to say?). Help the patient verbalize his feelings in a more appropriate way. Be alert for increased anxiety and refocus the patient when he becomes distracted. Remember that you are working together to achieve a change in behavior. Frequently a written contract works best. A contract clearly states the mutually agreed upon expectations and the way to arrive at this goal. Look at the patient's strengths, resources, and energy for change. Maybe the patient is currently in just a "survival" pattern and that will need to be addressed. We want to make reasonable requests so that the patient can be held accountable and we want small success experiences so that we can give the patient positive feedback. Areas to consider when writing a contract are: personal safety, amount of sleep and rest, food intake, structured time, activities of daily living, problem-solving techniques, and the patient's level of social interaction.

The bipolar patient's concentration is lessened and he is easily distracted and provoked. Social activities must be planned with this in mind.

Exercise can be advantageous, but competitive activities may increase anxiety and frustration levels. Many patients enjoy writing down their thoughts. These thoughts are usually fragmented.

During the depressed stage, the patient becomes weary and despondent. His feelings of hostility are directed inward. Safety of the patient is one of the major responsibilities of the nurse. Whenever there is a suspicion that a patient may be suicidal, he must be observed carefully. Showing a genuine caring attitude may help prevent a suicide attempt.

The bipolar patient needs sufficient rest to avoid fatigue and irritability. He may become so absorbed in his overenthusiasm or pessimism that basic hygiene is not remembered.

The psychological patient usually has poor eating and sleeping habits. The nurse should not allow the patient to manipulate her into accepting this behavior. Guidelines such as no eating between meals should be set. The nurse should make certain that the patient does not have a supply of his favorite snacks stored in his closet.

In dealing with the psychological patient, the nurse needs to frequently re-evaluate her nursing goals and their effectiveness. She also needs to be aware of her own feelings of frustration and helplessness.

## EATING DISORDERS

In our culture, much emphasis is placed on the ideal female figure. The modern female is believed to be influenced by multiple cultural and social pressures to be physically attractive or slim. To attain this ideal figure, females very often engage in reduced food intake. At times, dieting can go too far and a clinical syndrome characterized by a voluntary refusal to eat occurs. This is called *anorexia nervosa*. The incidence of anorexia nervosa has been estimated at between 0.24 and 1.6 annually per 100,000 population. Mortality rates range from 3 to 5 percent. This disease is most prevalent (95 percent) in females—adolescent girls and young women. Anorexia nervosa is described as "a relentless pursuit of thinness" (Bruch). Characteristics of anorexia nervosa include:

- Excessive weight loss with refusal to maintain weight
- Body image distortion with intense fear of becoming fat
- Obsessional thoughts
- Hyperactivity (excessive exercising)
- Shy and introverted
- Sense of inadequacy

- Conscientious and perfectionistic behavior
- Inability to trust the reliability of own emotions
- Amenorrhea

People with anorexia nervosa will rigidly and severely restrict their food intake and genuinely feel this is a positive achievement. The starvation syndrome simplifies their living. The anorexia nervosa's excessively thin body that looks like a prepuberty figure can help them avoid the conflicts of autonomous growth, competition, sexual identity, and social independence. Many anorexia nervosa patients have experienced a super togetherness in their family life with overprotectiveness, conflict avoidance, and rigidity. This family experience has been described as *enmeshment*. The family input fails to verify the developing female child as a competent person who can function in an independent way.

*Bulimia* is an eating disorder characterized by the consumption of a large amount of food in a short period of time (one to two hours, 50,000 calories) followed by self-induced vomiting. This cycle is called binging and purging. Other characteristics of bulimia include:

- Extreme dieting
- Laxative abuse
- Diuretic (water pill) abuse
- Preoccupation with food and eating
- Extreme sensitivity to body, shape, and weight
- Self-deprecating thoughts
- Impulsivity
- Depression
- Proneness to addiction
- A possible suicide risk

There are serious physical complications to eating disorders. Complications include the following:

- Electrolyte imbalance (potassium, chloride, sodium)
- Cardiac irregularities
- Kidney dysfunction and/or kidney failure
- Neurological disturbances
- Edema and dehydration
- Gastrointestinal disturbances

With bulimia, the person can experience painless swelling of their salivary glands. It is speculated that the swelling is caused by a combination of nutritional deficiencies, electrolyte imbalances, and trauma caused by excessive vomiting. Also, the gastric acid from self-induced vomiting in bulimia can cause gum and teeth deterioration.

Many of the deaths in anorexia nervosa and bulimia result from compromised cardiac functioning. With the profound depletion of the electrolytes—potassium, chloride, and sodium—these electrolyte abnormalities can result in serious heartbeat irregularities (arrhythmias) and sudden death.

Some researchers believe that anorexia and bulimia are compulsive-obsessive disorders. Patients with these disorders appear to have difficulty separating and individuating from their families. One sees much ambivalence and unexpressed anger. When taking a family history, the professional may note that the family has continuously used food to express their love and/or to gain control. Many eating disorder patients have been the well-behaved, perfectionistic youths who restricted their personal feelings and did not verbally communicate. A self-sacrificing attitude prevails. Initially, eating disorder patients must be closely evaluated. Do they need an in-patient admission to stabilize them metabolically? Will close observation with a behavioral approach be beneficial? Couple or family therapy can be indicated. Bulimics appear to progress with group therapy. Community educational programs are a necessity in a time when eating disorders are of epidemic proportion.

## SCHIZOPHRENIC DISORDER

The National Institute of Mental Health (NIMH) describes schizophrenia as the most prevalent, malignant, and baffling of all mental illness. It can be severe, persistent, and disabling. An estimated 2 million Americans will be stricken with schizophrenia. Current research into the contributing factors to the disease of schizophrenia include: molecular pathology, cerebral atrophy, ventricular enlargement, and evidence of neurological disease. A dysfunction of the dopamine system may be involved in schizophrenic symptoms. A link is being sought between genetic factors and biological vulnerability. In 1989, NIMH's National Plan for Schizophrenia Research Data derived that schizophrenia occurs at an equal rate among various ethnic and racial groups; however, limited information is available on Blacks, Hispanics, and Native Americans. Important data pointed to the fact that schizophrenia is found among the poor in disproportionate numbers (eight time higher). Poverty destroys the chance of earning a living and thereby, some sense of job satisfaction or the maintenance of a decent standard of living. Unemployed, uninsured, indigent people have increased environmental stressors, greater biological risk, and a diminished quality of life. Kraeplin's (1919) studies described dementia praecox (a premature brain deterioration). Bleuler (1950) stated that schizophrenia describes the splitting of the mind's functions and introduced the 4 A's of schizophrenia: *associative looseness,* autism, ambivalence, and change of affect. Associative looseness is defined as the personalized interpretation of reality that is usually disorganized and fragmented. *Autism* is characteristic of a person who is focusing exclusively on his own feelings.

When positive and negative feelings toward a person or object occur simultaneously it is called *ambivalence. Affect* describes a feeling state; usually flat with no expression and/or inappropriate giggling and laughing. Basically, schizophrenia is a thought disorder with disorganized thinking and faulty communication and social interaction.

One of the most important factors in a schizophrenic disorder is loss of self-esteem. This may be manifested in sudden and violent outbursts. It may result in dissociation or an exaggerated concern over body functions and appearance. Disturbances in thinking may range from a lack of clarity in the person's ideas to total incoherence. His thoughts are illogically connected, so they are difficult to understand. He may jumble words so they make no sense. This is called *word salad.* He may make up words to express his confused thoughts. These are called *neologisms. Echolalia* is the purposeless repetition of a word or phrase.

Characteristics of schizophrenia include: delusions, hallucinations, disturbed thought processes, and peculiar behavior. *Delusions* are false ideas that cannot be changed by logical argument. Delusions are often associated with hallucinations. They may occur in any type of psychotic reaction.

Delusional ideas may be in the form of guilt or persecution. The patient may feel that he has committed a grave sin or he may exaggerate a slight misdeed. The person with delusions of persecution believes that an organized group intends to harm him. He may perceive all happenings in relation to his delusion, using even unrelated events as proof of the delusion. The schizophrenic may also have delusions of grandeur. The patient believes that he has great power. He may see himself as Napoleon or Jesus Christ.

Hallucinations are perceptions that occur in the absence of stimuli and have no basis in reality. They include hearing nonexistent voices (auditory), having visions (visual), smelling (olfactory) or tasting things (gustatory), or having a sensation of being touched (tactile). Command hallucinations can be very frightening for the patient and may command the patient to do something dangerous to self and/or others.

An important part of behavior disturbance of the schizophrenic is his progressive withdrawal. He substitutes fantasy for real life. His actions may seem inappropriate to the situation as he becomes increasingly indifferent to his outside environment. This is described as an *inappropriate affect*. He feels alienated and isolated.

In an acute onset of schizophrenia, there is usually normal IQ, a normal brain functioning, the absence of negative symptoms (Table 12-5), and a good response to antipsychotic medications. With a slow onset, there are enlarged central ventricles, prominent negative symptoms, and a poor response to antipsychotics.

Antipsychotic medications possess many side effects that need to be carefully assessed by the nursing staff and reported to the psychiatrist (Table 12-6). A serious, irreversible side effect is Tardive Dyskinesia (TD). In order to detect TD at its earliest stages, an abnormal involuntary movement scale (AIMS) needs to be done at a minimum of every six (6) months (Table 12-7).

All patients on antipsychotic medication need to be observed for neuroleptic malignant syndrome (NMS). It is a serious, life-threatening syndrome of sudden onset with the following symptoms: increased temperature, increased B/P, diaphoresis, tachycardia, disorientation, and confusion. Immediate intervention must be made before death occurs.

### TABLE 12-5
### Negative Symptoms of Schizophrenia

| | |
|---|---|
| Affect | Flattened, Restricted |
| Emotions | Blunted—diminished range<br>Anhedonia—inability to express joy or pleasure |
| Thought | Content—poverty of content disorganized<br>Profess—Hallucinations, Delusions, Ideas of Reference |
| Personal | social withdrawal<br>psychomotor retardation<br>lack of sense of purpose, direction<br>impaired self-care<br>bizarre behaviors |
| Judgment | poor |
| Insight | poor |

### TABLE 12-6
### Anti-psychotic Medications

| TRADE | GENERIC |
|---|---|
| Haldol | Haloperidol |
| Prolixin | Fluphenazine HCL |
| Mellaril | Thioridazine |
| Thorazine | Chlorpromazine |
| Stelazine | Trifluoperazine |
| Navane | Thiothixene |
| Loxitant | Loxapine |
| Trilafon | Perphenazine |
| DEPOT NEUROLEPTICS | |
| Haldol deconate | Haloperidol Dec. |
| Prolixin deconate | Fluphenazine Dec. |
| Depot neuroleptics are designed for individuals who need antipsychotic medication yet have difficulty remembering to take them. Medication is injection-form and usually given every 2 weeks for Prolixin Dec. and every 4 weeks for Haldol Dec. | |
| Benefit Gained: | think more clearly elimination of/ significant reduction of: hallucinations, delusions, anxiety, and troublesome thoughts, feelings, behaviors |
| Side Effects: | blurred vision, dry mouth, constipation, urinary retention |
| Neurological: | *akinesia*–changes in posture, shuffling gait, muscular rigidity, drooling, slowed movements *akathesia*–squirming, restlessness, fidgeting, agitation *dystonia*–uncoordinated movements |
| Tardive Dyskinesia: | sucking movements, involuntary chewing, tongue protrusion, this is Irreversible |
| Caution: | do not use alcohol avoid prolonged exposure to sun. If outside, use a sunscreen with PABA—the higher the number, the greater the protection. |

There are several types of schizophrenia: disorganized, catatonic, paranoid, and undifferentiated. Again, the nurse must be cautioned that schizophrenics do not exhibit clear-cut patterns. Each patient responds with his own characteristics. As his anxiety increases, he turns from the real world and withdraws into a world of his own.

## TABLE 12-7
### Aims—Abnormal Involuntary Movements

| PATIENT ACTION | STAFF OBSERVATION |
|---|---|
| open mouth<br>protrude tongue | tongue at resting<br>tongue movements |
| tap thumb with each<br>finger as rapidly as<br>possible (approx.<br>10–15 seconds) | facial and leg movements |
| extend both arms in<br>front, palms down | trunk, leg, mouth<br>movements |
| walk a few paces<br>turn and walk back | hand and gait |
| sit in chair with<br>hands positioned<br>on knees, legs<br>slightly apart | entire body for<br>movements |
| record abnormalities on scale of:<br>minimal, mild, moderate, severe<br>check mouth for: candy, gum, dentures ||
| adapted from The Abnormal Involuntary Movements Scale ||

**Disorganized Type**. This category was formerly classified as hebephrenic schizophrenia. The disorganized schizophrenic exhibits inappropriate behavior. He smiles and giggles frequently at everything or nothing at all. There are gross thought disturbances, including the use of word salad and neologisms. Delusions and hallucinations are common, as is extreme social withdrawal.

**Catatonic Type**. The catatonic person's behavior varies, but there is usually an acute onset. Behavior may take the form of stupor or excitement. In catatonic stupor, the patient is immobile, mute, and negative. There is no interest in the environment; this apathy completely cuts off the patient from outside stimuli. He may remain in one position with very rigid muscles or he may possess *waxy flexibility* (a condition in which a limb remains in one position, even a very uncomfortable one, for a period of time).

The catatonic person exhibits unpredictable behavior because his behavior is controlled by his delusions and hallucinations. Stupor may change rapidly and unexpectedly to excitement. At these times, he is extremely restless and often violent. The catatonic schizophrenic exhibits two peculiar mannerisms—echolalia and echopraxia. *Echolalia* is an involuntary repetition of words spoken by others. This is often accompanied by muscle twitching. *Echopraxia* involves imitating the motions of others.

**Paranoid Type**. The paranoid schizophrenic is suspicious, aggressive, and hostile. He suffers from suspicion and jealousy, and delusions of grandeur and persecution. Hallucinations are common. The patient often hears voices commanding him. He often becomes combative. For example, he may break the television set because he believes it is sending him bad messages or perhaps reading his mind. At the beginning, other symptoms may be difficult to detect. As the condition progresses, behavior becomes more inappropriate and unpredictable. Since his delusions are often bizarre, he can be dangerous.

**Undifferentiated Type**. Undifferentiated schizophrenia is diagnosed when the symptoms do not fit in other categories for schizophrenia. Symptoms may include delusions, hallucinations, incoherence, and grossly disorganized behavior.

## PARANOID DISORDER

The patient with a paranoid disorder, like the patient with schizophrenia, suffers from persistent delusions. These delusions are generally delusions of jealousy, persecution, or sometimes grandeur. The paranoid patient does not have hallucinations but possesses a heightened suspiciousness that may progress to psychosis. The patient is fearful, guarded, and uses the mental mechanism—projection.

The paranoid patient usually does not show disorganization of his personality, other than the delusions. His actions seem to be appropriate to his delusionary experience. There is seldom further deterioration in his personality. He speaks and acts rationally and is well oriented to time and place. He may be able to carry on a productive occupation even when his condition is well developed. However, social and marital functioning are usually adversely affected.

Feelings of anger and resentment are common with a paranoid disorder. This patient can be dangerous as he may strike out in self-defense. Bizarre deterioration or incoherence is not seen in this patient.

## NURSING CARE

Nursing care for the patient suffering from a schizophrenic or paranoid disorder must be based on an assessment of behavior and problems as these patients have an individualized array of symptoms. The schizophrenic has a pattern of isolation. This is motivated by a fear of rejection. His behavior reflects his lack of self-confidence. The nurse needs to demonstrate a hopeful attitude consisting of acceptance, security, and confidence. Avoiding the patient only reinforces his feelings of low self-esteem. The nurse should observe the schizophrenic patient for any special interest. Involving him in a variety of activities such as checkers, card games, crafts, or hobbies can be a method of stimulating his senses. Genuine praise can reinforce confidence. It may be therapeutic to change the environment by walking outdoors or taking a ride in the country.

For a patient with a paranoid disorder, a flexible but consistent approach should be maintained at all times. This patient's trust in others must be strengthened. It is important for the nurse to be aware of her own behavior. Whispering or pointing when in the patient's environment must be avoided. Probing questions may provoke paranoid behavior. The paranoid patient requires calm, soothing voice tones at all times.

The nurse's goal is to provide support and structure for the patient in order to decrease his anxiety and decompensation. A firm, consistent environment will facilitate the patient's recovery from a state of inner disorganization.

In preparation for a return to the family and their community, the schizophrenic patient needs to be educated about the warning symptoms of a relapse of the disease. A signs of relapse checklist would be beneficial for the patient and his family and would be an excellent method of education as part of discharge planning. Warning signs of relapse include: a loss of interest in doing things, and eating and attending activities of daily living; trouble concentrating or thinking straight; fast thoughts; increased trouble with decision-making; preoccupation with religion; fear of others hurting them or that others are playing with their mind; increased irritability over little things; thoughts of hurting or killing self; and an increased use of alcohol or drugs. These warning signs indicate that a relapse may be coming and the patient needs to seek professional help. In extreme presentation of symptoms, the patient needs to go to the emergency room of their hospital. Each patient needs an emergency plan for severe relapse.

Hildegarde Peplau (1962) stated that to help the patient is to remember and understand fully what is happening to him in the present situation. You want to assist the patient to integrate this with other experiences in his life. Avoid isolating the experience as that will only increase thought fragmentation. Assist the patient to recognize maladaptive behavior: the causes, motives, and consequences. Assist the patient to look for alternative choices for his behavior and increase his constructive, productive lifestyle. The nurse is building trust and nurturing the patient. This is called a corrective emotional experience.

## PERSONALITY DISORDER

Personality can be defined as an individual's character traits, attitudes, thoughts, behaviors, and habits. It encompasses the individual's behavioral and emotional tendencies. It also involves the individual's adaptation to internal and external problems.

Personality disorders are maladaptive patterns of seeing, relating to, and thinking about the environment. Since the patterns are inflexible and deeply ingrained, there is impairment in adaptive functioning. Disturbances in emotional development and equilibrium are seen. There is a maladjustment to the social environment.

The American Psychiatric Association's Diagnostic and Statistical Manual (DSM-III) lists several subdivisions under the category of Personality Disorders. These subdivisions and characteristics are shown in Table 12-8. Personality disorders can begin in childhood, but usually are manifested at adolescence. They may or may not interfere with social or role functioning.

### Nursing Care

People with personality disorders are very difficult to deal with and treatment may be ineffective. In caring for these patients, the nurse should be able to handle the frustrations caused by their behavior. She also should be aware that some patients may be very manipulative. The manipulative patient wants his every need to be met immediately and may become aggressive or hostile when they are not met. Respond to manipulation with consistent reinforcement of limits.

The nurse might directly tell the patient with a personality disorder that his blaming, accusing, and intimidating manner alienates people. Peer pressure can frequently be used to modify behavior. Guidance in assertiveness is helpful for some patients. These patients need positive feedback for open, direct communication. The nurse should encourage relaxed rather than hostile exchanges. She should set appropriate limits and be

## TABLE 12-8
## Personality Disorders

| DISORDER | SPECIFIC CHARACTERISTICS | GENERAL CHARACTERISTICS |
|---|---|---|
| Paranoid | uwarranted suspicions and mistrust; hyper sensitivity; exaggeration of difficulties; inability to relax; cold and unemotional | odd |
| Schizoid | lack of warm, tender feelings for others; indifferent; few close friends; "loner" | difficulty in maintaining satisfactory relationships |
| Schizotypal | social isolation oddities of thinking and speech; illusions; suspicious; hypersensitivity | eccentric |
| Histrionic | overly dramatic expressions of emotion; overraction to events; self-indulgent; constant drawing of attention to self; irrational outbursts; inconsideration of others; vain and demanding; constant seeking of reassurance; lack of genuiness; craving of excitement | dramatic and emotional |
| Narcissistic | exaggerated sense of self-importance; need for constant attention and admiration; preoccupied with fantasies; vacillates between emotional extremes; lacks ability to recognize how others feel | self-centered |
| Antisocial | seeks immediate pleasure; selfish; poor occupational performance; unable to maintain lasting relationships; poor sexual adjustment; failure to accept social norms; irritability and aggressiveness; failure to plan ahead (impulsive); disregard for the truth; reckless; violation of the rights of others | defective judgement at risk of substance abuse |
| Borderline | impulsive and unpredictalbe; unstable interpersonal relationships; frequent displays of anger; identity problems, shifts in moods; intense discomfort when alone; physically self-damaging acts; recurring feelings of boredom and emptiness | erratic |
| Avoidant | hypersensitivity to rejection; social withdrawal; low self-esteem | anxious |
| Dependent | lacks self-confidence; avoids relying on self; allows others to assume responsibilty | fearful |
| Compulsive | preoccupation with trivial details; overly conventional and serious; insists on "own way"; indecisive | perfectionist |
| Passive-aggressive | indirectly resists demands for adequate performance; intentional inefficiency; forgetful; stubborness; procrastination; dawdling; resentful | incompetent overly dependent |

sure the patient knows the limitations. Diversional activities are important. The nurse might help by presenting growth opportunities, chances to assume responsibility, and small success experiences, Figure 12-1. There is now a move toward special residential homes for some patients with personality disorders.

Fig. 12-1 A small success experience for patients may be seeing their work displayed; this builds self-esteem.

## MILIEU THERAPY

Milieu includes all surroundings in the physical environment and those interpersonal interactions that contribute to the individual's personal growth and adaptation. The environment is structured to provide security and safety. On admission to the ward, the stimuli may be decreased while trust is built but gradually increased responsibility and involvement is encouraged. The environment is flexible yet limit setting is consistent. Personal respect and cooperation modelled by the staff increases the self-confidence and sense of autonomy of the patient. The eventual goal for the patient is increased motivation and socialization. The milieu aids in the recognition of maladaptive behaviors and allows for confrontation of the patient when these behaviors are observed.

The physical environment needs to be clean and safe. Harmonious colors and comfortable and safe furnishings contribute to the overall sense of well-being. Milieu includes many therapy modalities: group therapy, art and music therapy (a means to socialize and structure free time and increase self-confidence), pet therapy (comfort with the expression of caring through touching), horticulture (gardening and its responsibilities), nutrition counseling, occupational therapy (maximizing strengths and one's response to the environment), vocational work (counselor explores work/job options), and educational groups (communication skills, self-esteem, social interaction, financial planning). An interdisciplinary team coordinates these treatment activities and evaluates the patient's participation and progress at weekly team meetings. An individualized care plan facilitates the patient's participation through the patient's review of the plan and consent (either verbal or per written signature) that he accepts the plan.

Another aspect of the milieu is the community meeting. A community meeting is a scheduled meeting with a set time and predetermined decision that there will be no interruptions per staff or patients. The patient on admission to the ward is an observer at the meeting but develops as a participant. The community meeting gives everyone a voice in decision making. It provides a time to review problems and tensions on the ward and decreases conflict through discussion. Ward rules and roles are clarified and enforced in a consistent manner. At times, unit upkeep may be the meeting focus with assignments of chores or tasks. The main concept is to increase patient responsibility and accountability and thereby increase self-awareness and self-esteem.

Frequently requests for a therapeutic pass are generated at the community meeting. A therapeutic pass is a leave of absence from the hospital for two (2) or more hours. It is authorized by the physician. Some facilities call this a leave of absence (LOA). Prior to the pass, a nursing staff member meets with the patient and they decide on the purpose of the leave. Papers are given to fill out and hand in upon return that reflect the positive and negative aspects of the LOA. The patient may visit with family, run errands, or seek aftercare placement. This is an important part of the discharge plan as it promotes the patient's resocialization, assists him to identify and cope with stressors, and begin to utilize community support.

## TREATMENT FACILITIES

Treatment facilities for the mentally ill include: outpatient services, residential treatment centers, sustaining care centers, day treatment centers, and mental health units. Outpatient services are usually available through the local mental health department. Community centers provide therapy through psychiatrists, psychologists, and nurses. The services vary according to the financing available to the community. Payment for service is based on the individual's ability to pay. Appointments are made at the convenience of the patient.

Residential treatment centers provide for the individual's day-to-day living. The treatment center may be a private home or a foster home which has met state guidelines for the care of the chronically mentally ill. Patients are placed in the home after a period of hospitalization. The patient must be evaluated and his condition stabilized before being placed in a residential treatment center.

A sustaining care center is similar to a nursing home environment. The individual resides at the center. He has some functional skills and is further guided by professional personnel. There is usually a structured program of social activities.

Day treatment centers are concerned with patients who are emotionally dysfunctional. This includes patients who experience daily living problems and are in need of an intermediate step toward independent functioning. The goal is to increase the patient's self-responsibility and self-esteem. The patient comes to the center during the day to learn basic living skills. Educational and vocational training may be provided. Functional living skills are explored. Assertiveness training, problem solving, goal formulation, and decision-making skills are reaffirmed. Any of the psychotherapies may be used. Day treatment centers attempt to help the individual to manage himself in a way that is meaningful to him. Acceptance into the program is on a referral basis.

Mental health units are frequently located in the local community hospital. The care is usually geared toward short-term or emergency needs. Self-direction and personal initiative are among the goals. Care is given until the individual can return to the community.

Take time to assess your patient's financial status. Many patients may need assistance to file for social security benefits. The patient who has worked long enough may be eligible for SSDI (Social Security Disability Income) and if not, may meet Federal disability criteria for SSI (Supplemental Income). It is estimated that one-half of all the chronically mentally ill have not applied for these benefits due to feeling overwhelmed by the severity of their problem and their inability to work through all the laborious details required to file a claim.

## SUMMARY

Maladaptive behaviors can develop anytime from infancy through old age. Three critical times are adolescence, menopause, and old age. Coping activity is required throughout the life cycle.

The word *normal* can be viewed in a social, clinical, moral, or statistical way. There is no sharp distinction between normal and abnormal. Psychiatry categorizes patterns of behavior, but it must be remembered that patients do not fit neatly into these categories. Each patient has an individual reaction to stress and, therefore, an individual pattern of behavior.

Psychological disorders are disturbances that are characterized by maladaptive behavior aimed at dealing with high levels of anxiety. Anxiety disorders, somatoform disorders, affective disorders, and dissociative disorders are some common psychological disorders. Nursing care focuses on reducing anxiety.

Affective disorders deal with the emotions. This category includes dysthymic (or depressive), cyclothymic, and bipolar disorders. Bipolar disorders are subtyped as manic, depressed, or mixed. Dissociative disorders are characterized by changes in consciousness and identity. This category includes psychogenic amnesia, psychogenic fugue, multiple personality, and depersonalization disorder. Schizophrenia is characterized by delusions, hallucinations, disturbed thought processes, and peculiar behavior. Schizophrenics experience conflicting feelings and demonstrate inappropriate affect, word salad, neologism, delusions, and hallucinations. The types of schizophrenia are: disorganized, catatonic, paranoid, and undifferentiated. The patient with a paranoid disorder suffers from persistent delusions. These delusions usually are jealousy, persecution, or grandeur. Personality disorders involve an individual's adaptation to internal and external problems. The disorder may or may not interfere with social or role functioning.

Many psychiatric patients are a high risk for suicide. The depressed patient is the most likely to commit suicide. The nurse should be able to recognize indirect cues that the patient may be considering suicide. Talking about suicide is a plea for help and must be recognized as such.

Treatment facilities for the mentally ill include outpatient services, residential treatment centers, sustaining care centers, day treatment centers, mental health units, and mental hospitals.

### SUGGESTED ACTIVITIES

- Visit a mental health center. Observe the nurse as she relates to patients.

- In a class discussion, correlate the developmental stage of adolescence with the development of an eating disorder.
- Investigate the admission procedure to a day treatment center or mental health unit in your community. Report your findings to the class.

## REVIEW

A. Multiple choice. Select the best answer.

1.  An abnormal excessive fear of a specific situation or object is called a (an)
    a. obsession.
    b. compulsion.
    c. phobia.
    d. psychosis.

2.  A recurring overpowering thought or feeling is called a(an)
    a. obsession.
    b. compulsion.
    c. phobia.
    d. psychosis.

3.  An irresistible urge to engage in a behavior is called a (an)
    a. obsession.
    b. compulsion.
    c. phobia.
    d. psychosis.

4.  The type of schizophrenic disorder characterized by stupor and waxy flexibility is called
    a. disorganized.
    b. catatonic.
    c. undifferentiated.
    d. paranoid.

5.  The affective disorder that deals with alternate moods of depression and elation is the
    a. dysthymic disorder.
    b. depersonalization disorder.
    c. psychogenic fugue.
    d. bipolar disorder.

6.  The basic reason for compulsive behavior is to
    a. occupy the mind.
    b. manipulate the environment.

    c. lower anxiety.

    d. prevent mistakes.

7. Psychogenic amnesia is classified as a(an)
   a. affective disorder.
   b. personality disorder.
   c. dissociative disorder.
   d. conversion disorder.

8. The person with a conversion disorder
   a. converts anxiety to bodily symptoms.
   b. experiences severe mood swings.
   c. is cut off from his awareness.
   d. all of the above.

9. Behavior that the antisocial personality is likely to display is
   a. withdrawing from group activity.
   b. mechanical obedience.
   c. manipulation of others.
   d. ritualistic behavior.

10. The patient most likely to commit suicide is the
    a. schizophrenic.
    b. sociopath.
    c. depressed.
    d. hypochondriac.

B. Match each item in column II with the statement describing it in column I.

| Column I | Column II |
|---|---|
| 1. inability to act or react in an appropriate manner | a. delusion |
| 2. having positive and negative feelings simultaneously | b. dysthymic disorder |
| | c. maladaptive behavior |
| 3. characterized by maladaptive behavior aimed at avoiding anxiety | d. echolalia |
| | e. echopraxia |
| 4. prolonged feeling of extreme sadness accompanied by guilt feelings and social withdrawal | f. hallucinations |
| | g. psychological disorder |
| | h. ambivalence |
| 5. false ideas that cannot be changed by logical argument | i. anxiety disorder |
| | j. neologism |

6. perceptions which occur in the absence of stimuli
7. imitating motions of others
8. involuntary repetition of words spoken by others
9. made-up words to express confused thoughts
10. characterized by anxiety that is disproportionate to the stresses of daily living

C.   Briefly answer the following.

1.   What are the four aspects of the word *normal?*

2.   List the common psychological disorders.

3.   Differentiate between moderate and severe anxiety.

4.   List four types of schizophrenic disorders.

5.   List four significant behavioral cues which may indicate a potential suicidal person.

6.   Describe sustaining care centers and day treatment centers.

# CHAPTER 13
# VIOLENCE AND
# DISTURBED BEHAVIORS

## OBJECTIVES

After studying this chapter, the student should be able to:

- Identify predisposing signs, socio-cultural variables, and precipitating factors to violence.
- Recognize the importance of understanding anger and alienation.
- Identify verbal intervention techniques.
- Identify important criteria for placing patients in seclusion and/or restraints.
- Describe techniques needed to restrain an assaultive patient.
- Identify important areas of nursing documentation.
- Assess the suicidal/homicidal patient and identify intervention techniques.
- Describe nursing interventions in the planning of the care of the rape victim.
- Describe nursing interventions in the planning of the care of a victim of incest.

Violence is an urgent public health concern, with homicide being the second leading cause of death in our society for those people between the ages of 15 and 30. The management of violence, both physical and psychological, is a neglected problem in America. Violence is seldom addressed in textbooks; you may see suicide listed but not other topics i.e. homicide, violence, assault or agitation. Frequently, if textbooks deal with violent outbursts, they simply state, "call a psychiatrist."

There are also rampant acts of victimization (i.e. spouse, child and elderly abuse, and rape and incest) which are forms of perpetrated violence. Violent behavior among hospitalized medical and surgical patients has been on the increase, and the incidence of patients approaching facilities with concealed weapons is now a known fact.

We may expect the sick, suffering patient to become suicidal or depressed but are taken aback when the patient rejects our help or makes unreasonable demands and become caustic, obstreperous, and angry. Additionally, many psychiatric patients have a dual diagnosis (i.e. paranoid schizophrenia and substance abuse), which increases the risk of violent behaviors.

The management of disruptive, assaultive, or out-of-control behavior requires the development of a sound knowledge base, practical intervention skills, as well as training in and the practice of techniques for the patient with disturbed behavior. Prevention of violent episodes before they escalate is the best way to intervene.

## AGGRESSION

There are many points of view concerning aggression. Freud viewed aggression as an inborn drive or an impulse, with the aim of destruction, which requires discharge either directly or indirectly. Horney rejected this theory and stated that aggression and hostility are a response to basic anxiety. Horney believed that aggression is hostility turned inward and is self-destructive behavior, whereas, hostility turned outward is an aggressive act toward others.

Lorenz correlates genetics with the environment and believes that aggressive behavior is innate (inborn), demands expression, and stems form the internal excitation which increases aggression, impulsivity, and criminal violence. However, this evidence is fragmentary and Lorenz's XYY genotype has never been proven. Lorenz did state that aggression can be beneficial if slowly siphoned off or subliminated. However, if it is stored up it can be explosive and destructive.

The frustration-aggression view states that aggression is the result of frustration. When the achievement of a goal is blocked and frustration builds it is released as aggression because the tension is too much for the individual to endure. Environmental, behavioral, and learning theories are addressed in the frustration-aggression view.

Social learning theory states that aggression is acquired through direct experience or by imitating the behaviors of others. Social learning theorists believe that positive and negative reinforcers are more responsible for aggressive behavior than internal, inborn processes.

## ANGER AND ALIENATION

Anger is an emotion/feeling which usually follows a person's realization that "I don't like what is happening and it will just have to stop."

It is often our own anxiety and anger that makes rebellious people look so threatening to us, and compels us to take flight or fight. We need to reflect about the nature of our anger, anxiety, and fears. They tend to reinforce these same feelings in our patients and possibly will lead to violent behaviors. Remember that none of us are strangers to anger and its destructive power. Self-righteousness and self-deception arising from anger can give us an excuse to carry out a decision that has been made in anger.

Anger can be destructive; it can however, also be constructive (which we rarely recognize), Table 13-1. A key to use in reducing anger is to give the angry person/patient something he can settle for. Since anger is usually based on an unrealistic expectation of one-self, someone, or something else, courtesy, tolerance, and a willingness to help makes de-escalation work.

Conflict resolution is a method of resolving these feelings of alienation and anger. Conflict resolution contains the following: a direct message, active listening, negotiation, and a contract. Each of these areas can be defined as follows:

- *direct message*: clear message of what you want, don't want, or what you feel; "I want you to stop yelling obscenities."
- *active listening*: being attentive, verifying by stating; "I heard you say. "
- *negotiation*: consider alternatives and look at possible options
- *contract*: either a verbal or written contract. The objective is that both people clearly understand and agree upon alternatives and are committed to following through on them.

## TALK DOWN

The prevention and management of disturbed behavior is based on early, safe, effective interventions accompanied with assessment of the patient, self, and the environment. Talking down is verbal de-escalation.

It is very important to be aware of sudden changes in the normal behavior patterns of the patient. These can include: pacing, restlessness, wringing of the hands, kicking, throwing things, grimacing and withdrawal, fault-finding, shouting, unwarranted joking at another's expense, refusing medications, arguing, refusing to obey ward rules and schedules, cursing, sarcasm, and constant demands on the staff.

**TABLE 13-1**
**Anger: Constructive and Destructive Uses**

| ANGER | |
|---|---|
| **CONSTRUCTIVE USE** | **DESTRUCTIVE USE** |
| 1. View as normal, natural healthy | 1. Makes you distrustful |
| 2. Own responsibility for your own feelings | 2. Weakens self-esteem |
| 3. Remember you have control over your anger and how you handle it. | 3. Masks "real" feelings |
| 4. Recognize what triggers your anger | 4. Stops communication |
| 5. De-fuse self | 5. Destroys relationships |
| 6. Increase assertiveness skills | 6. Leads to physiologic problems |
| 7. Deal with issues as they arise | 7. Increases feelings of isolation |
| 8. Increase personal self-esteem | 8. Accumulates and leads to hostility and rage |
| 9. Develop mutual understanding and forgiveness | |

Physical changes caused by a chronic illness and the prolonged use of therapeutic drugs increase the incidence of assaultive behaviors. Organic brain syndrome, brain lesions, and metabolic or endocrine disorders can also cause disruptive behaviors. One needs to carefully assess the patient's condition and drug regime, as an agitated patient may be manifesting symptoms of toxic drug levels or interactions and a delirium syndrome, Table 13-2.

**TABLE 13-2**
**DELIRIUM: Therapeutic Drugs Associated with Delirium**

| | |
|---|---|
| Acth | Lithium |
| Alprazolam | Meperidine |
| Amantadine | Naproxen |
| Aminophylline | Prednisone |
| Amphetamines | Propanalol |
| Amphotericin B | Theophylline |
| Cimetidine | Clonidine |
| Digitalis | Ephedrine |
| Isoniazid | Lidocaine |

ANTICHOLINERGICS: produce delirium
CNS STIMULANTS: produce paranoid psychosis
CORTICOSTEROIDS: affective (mood) changes
BETA BLOCKERS: produce depression

Research reveals that causes of disruptive behaviors include fear, frustration, reality testing, rejection, feelings of inferiority, intrusion of personal space/lack of privacy, and grief. Common behavioral disorders can occur as either defensive or offensive actions. A patient's feelings of fear and helplessness are motivated by a sense of self preservation. Offensive actions are actually meant to destroy or punish one's self. It is possible that this can result in suicide. Sarcasm, arguing, and physical aggression to self or others is seen. On the other hand, a patient with passive behaviors are unable to accept and acknowledge their feelings of anger. This patient will usually withdraw.

Disturbed behavior moves along a continuum from verbal to physical violence to destruction of self or others. There is usually a hierarchy of violent behaviors, Table 13-3. An important aspect of the control of the anger and alienation is personal self-awareness. This self-awareness can prevent escalating anger and alienation. Learn to trust your own feelings and judgments.

From our own viewpoints, when you have a gut feeling of uneasiness, look at the following feelings: fear, anger, anxiety, need to act-out, frustration, helplessness, guilt, denial, withdrawal. Environmentally, assess the milieu and assess factors that influence that milieu.

**TABLE 13-3**
**Hierarchy of Dangerous Behaviors**

- Assault with gun or knives
- Punching, kicking
- Slapping, biting
- Throwing objects
- Spitting, pushing
- Cursing, overt threats
- Veiled threats

With regard to patients watch for periods of increased activity followed by periods of inactivity on your units (i.e. during shift report or the idle time before bedtime where limits can be tested). Observe the ward organization of males and females and the age variable. On the psychiatric unit, there will develop a patient hierarchy of social status and power influence. This can be assessed at ward community meetings.

We, as health professionals, can inadvertently re-enact destructive patterns in the patient's history and increase the insecurity that duplicates relationships outside the hospital. So one concept important to understand is *therapeutic neutrality*. Therapeutic neutrality is not a blank screen, not a deprivation, not unresponsiveness; it is a response that is neutral and devoid of needs, values, and morality. It is predicated on what is helpful to that particular patient, not us.

As staff on a psychiatric unit, we need to review our behavior regularly and process our feelings. We need to assess whose need this is, ours or theirs. We need to ask: Is the patient making me feel powerless? Do I fear loss of control? Finally, we need to remember that powerlessness is difficult to deal with in our culture as we do not value weakness and vulnerability.

An important characteristic of the ward milieu is the allowance of open dialogue. Communication needs to be undistorted and unconstrained. In open dialogue, no topics are off limits. There are always four directions of communication: patient-staff, staff-patient, staff-staff, patient-patient.

Sometimes, we model our patient's communication patterns rather than offering a new communicative style. In our self-assessment we need to find out what pushed our button. Is one pushed by hostility, profanity, out-of-control people, or seductiveness? Does the neurotic patient make you feel competitive and the psychotic patient make you feel empty?

Staff also need mutual support so that they can individually and together work on issues and begin to deal with them. Increasing your knowledge base of psychopathology is very helpful, as is the development of treatment interventions. Remember that inappropriate or negative staff behaviors can lead to violence, Table 13-4.

Working with a violent patient is less anxiety-provoking when a systematized approach to assessment is followed. Even a thumbnail assessment of violence can be most helpful. Collect data on:

- *previous history of violence*: ask non-judgmentally—do you tend to be a fighting person? What is the most violent act that you have engaged in?
- *methods of violence available*: knives, guns, black belt in Karate?
- *problems with impulse control*: a history of substance abuse, difficulty keeping a job, multiple AMA (against medical advice the patient leaves the hospital)
- *a recent or threatened loss*: illness, death, abandonment, divorce, unemployment
- *a macho image*: tough, brave, fearless, volatile, abandonment, unpredictable—can be male or female
- *suicidal ideation*: suicide often is the acting out of rage felt toward someone else and directed toward the self. Remember that suicide and homicide are the opposite sides of a coin.

### TABLE 13-4
### Staff Behavior Increasing Possibility of Violence

| |
| --- |
| • Not setting enough limits or limits with unclear expectations |
| • Staff approaches that are inconsistent |
| • Offensive attitudes |
| • Arguing, joking, ridiculing |
| • Veiled hostility . . . Mask of kindness |
| • Seductive behavior |
| • Labeling a patient |
| • Inappropriate touching |
| • Pushing for disclosure |
| • Attention given only when inappropriate or out-of-control |

- *tension in a relationship*: teasing in a hostile way, caustic humor, provocative and unpredictable behaviors
- *psychosis*: assess history of hallucinations, delusions and thought processes—is the patient logical, sequential, and relevant?
- *cognitive impairment*: assess confusion, disorientation, impaired judgment, and concentration
- *history of victimization*: assess for child/adult abuse, neglect, incest, or witnessing victimization.

## SECLUSION

Seclusion is the placement of a patient, alone, in a specifically designated, lockable room with direct observation available through a window. Seclusion should be considered a treatment intervention before progressing to the ultimate act of restraining the patient. Remember that we are always looking for the *least restrictive mode* that provides verbal/chemical intervention prior to initiating seclusion.

Seclusion is influenced by: unit philosophy, staff attitude, staff availability, staff/patient ratios (increased census, decreased staff), general milieu (anxiety, hostility), and the staff's regular, routine training in the prevention and management of disturbed behavior. The goal of seclusion is to get the patient to settle down, be cooperative, and usually sleep. Serious consideration must be given to the outcomes—the calming effect of the room versus the sensory deprivation which may lead to increased mental deterioration.

Two factors are to be considered when considering seclusion: the patient's potential for harm to self or others, and the ward environment that accelerated the patient's agitation. Each unit also needs a clinical indicator check list to initiate seclusion and a readiness to release from restraints guideline, Table 13-5.

Each facility has a policy and procedure that directly addresses seclusion and restraint policies. The procedure might involve calling a nursing alert for a violent patient and a number to dial (i.e. 511), or announcing a *Code Red*. This information needs to be posted where all staff have ready access to it.

At times, the facility security officers need to be called; however, the officers will only take part in the action when specifically requested to do so by the clinical staff member directing the action or take-down. Remember the take-down and the placing of the patient in restraints is equivalent to the Code 99 procedure on your medical-surgical units. A take-down is based on speed, surprise, and the break and escape methods. Be certain to have sufficient help for physical restraining. Team work is important; however, one leader will direct the situation as the charge person. Be ready!

**TABLE 13-5**
**Readiness to Release Patient from Leather Restraints Guidelines**

- Orientation—Responds to name, direct eye contact
- Hallucinations/delusions—No longer active
- Medication—Effective response
- Threats—No longer making physical/verbal threats
- Self control—
  1. Able to state what self control means for him/her
  2. Cooperate with simple instructions
  3. Noted decreased impulsivity
- Readiness—
  1. Patient able to state he/she is ready to be released from restraints
  2. Confer with staff for assessment of readiness

Have the team ready and the restraints keys and a complete set of leather restraints ready. The staff must have confidence with their personal safety techniques: i.e. providing personal space and lunge room, punch blocking, handling grabs, and hair pulls.

A new technique utilized by some facilities is the hang technique. Three persons are needed for this technique: Two grab one arm each and hang with their dead weight; the third person steers the patient by holding the disruptive patient's belt. The hang technique is used until the patient drops to one knee, is then in a control position, and can be carried to the seclusion room where the leather restraints are applied. A clinical record of visual patient checks made every fifteen minutes (q15m) are initiated. Remember that these checks are mandatory, Table 13-6.

A registered nurse (RN) initiates the restraint procedure and is legally responsible. An order for restraint then must be obtained from the physician and must be rewritten every twenty-four hours. The time of initiating restraints and the time of the notification of the physician must be carefully noted. Clear, concise charting is especially important. There are many critical documentation areas in the seclusion/restraint procedure, Table 13-7. For documentation purposes, many facilities require an *RN progress note* in the chart every two hours.

**TABLE 13-6**
**Clinical Record: Seclusion and Leather Restraints,**
**Visual Checks Made on Patient Every 15 Minutes**

DATE _____
CODE # AND ACTIVITY

| | NIGHTS | DAYS | EVENINGS |
|---|---|---|---|
| 1. Yelling or screaming | 12:00 ____ | 8:00 ____ | 4:00 ____ |
| 2. Cursing | 12:15 ____ | 8:15 ____ | 4:15 ____ |
| 3. Standing still | 12:30 ____ | 8:30 ____ | 4:30 ____ |
| 4. Lying down on cot | 12:45 ____ | 8:45 ____ | 4:45 ____ |
| 5. Sleeping | 1:00 ____ | 9:00 ____ | 5:00 ____ |
| 6. Fluids given | 1:15 ____ | 9:15 ____ | 5:15 ____ |
| 7. Restraints released | 1:30 ____ | 9:30 ____ | 5:30 ____ |
| a. right wrist | 1:45 ____ | 9:45 ____ | 5:45 ____ |
| b. left wrist | 2:00 ____ | 10:00 ____ | 6:00 ____ |
| c. right leg | 2:15 ____ | 10:15 ____ | 6:15 ____ |
| d. left leg | 2:30 ____ | 10:30 ____ | 6:30 ____ |
| 8. Range of motion | 2:45 ____ | 10:45 ____ | 6:45 ____ |
| a. right arm | 3:00 ____ | 11:00 ____ | 7:00 ____ |
| b. left arm | 3:15 ____ | 11:15 ____ | 7:15 ____ |
| c. right leg | 3:30 ____ | 11:30 ____ | 7:30 ____ |
| d. left leg | 3:45 ____ | 11:45 ____ | 7:45 ____ |
| 9. Medication | 4:00 ____ | 12:00 ____ | 8:00 ____ |
| | 4:15 ____ | 12:15 ____ | 8:15 ____ |
| | 4:30 ____ | 12:30 ____ | 8:30 ____ |
| | 4:45 ____ | 12:45 ____ | 8:45 ____ |
| | 5:00 ____ | 1:00 ____ | 9:00 ____ |
| | 5:15 ____ | 1:15 ____ | 9:15 ____ |
| | 5:30 ____ | 1:30 ____ | 9:30 ____ |
| | 5:45 ____ | 1:45 ____ | 9:45 ____ |
| | 6:00 ____ | 2:00 ____ | 10:00 ____ |
| | 6:15 ____ | 2:15 ____ | 10:15 ____ |
| | 6:30 ____ | 2:30 ____ | 10:30 ____ |
| | 6:45 ____ | 2:45 ____ | 10:45 ____ |
| | 7:00 ____ | 3:00 ____ | 11:00 ____ |
| | 7:15 ____ | 3:15 ____ | 11:15 ____ |
| | 7:30 ____ | 3:30 ____ | 11:30 ____ |
| | 7:45 ____ | 3:45 ____ | 11:45 ____ |

STAFF SIGNATURES & INITIALS

_____   _____   _____

_____   _____   _____

_____   _____   _____

### TABLE 13-7
### Seclusion/Restraint Documentation

- Seclusion used only as last resort, and only after *FAILURE OF LESS RESTRICTIVE MEASURES*
- Use facility's policy/procedure standards as guidelines
- Alternatives and/or interventions and results
- Patient's behavior necessitating seclusion/restraints
- Time placed in restraints
- Medications effectiveness, any changes in meds, any side effects
- Time physician notified
- 15 minute checks and interventions
- Progress note every two hours
- Assessment note at the beginning and end of *each* shift
- Nursing conference
- Nursing conference recommendations and posting on ward

Remember that the patient in restraints is now an intensive care patient. Tell the patient in a calm manner that he is now safe and protected and that close supervision will be provided.

Immediately following a seclusion or restraint action, the nurse in charge needs to conduct a conference with all staff members involved to evaluate the manner in which the action was carried out. The conference notes will be used as guide to assess the restraint action and any need for improvement. Continual monitoring and assessing of the use of seclusion and restraining will ensure that this treatment alternative is utilized judiciously, safely, and therapeutically.

If a patient remains in seclusion/restraints for a period of twenty-four hours, a nursing care conference should be held. The conference includes the nursing staff, the clinical nurse administrator, and the clinical nurse specialist assigned to that unit. An evaluation would consist of indicators similar to the following:

- What is the need for continued seclusion/restraint?
- Does an objective assessment verify this decision?
- Is the documentation clear; can it meet review criteria?
- Is the medication regime effective?
- Does the documentation state that the seclusion/restraint action occurred *after* least restrictive measures were utilized?

- Are the facility's policy/procedure standards met?
- Have attempts been made to remove the patient from restraints or reduce the level of restraints?

Results of this nursing care conference will be posted for all staff to read and initial. This conference provides objectivity and peer support as well as an opportunity to ventilate feelings. Many facilities have a monthly report of restraint and seclusion which must also be completed and submitted to a Prevention and Management of Disturbed Behavior Committee. Lately facilities have been marking charts or designating on computer entries when a patient has a history of assaultive behavior. This is called *behavioral flagging* and remains a controversial issue.

## SUICIDAL PATIENTS

Many patients under psychiatric care pose some risk for suicide. Suicidal patients have feelings of depression and guilt, and frequently relate feelings of hopelessness and helplessness. Their self-esteem is also very low. The suicidal patient turns his hostility inward until it becomes self-destructive.

Genuine caring and making the patient feel worthwhile may help prevent an attempt at suicide. Letting the patient know that there are alternatives and that others are willing to help find solutions may be beneficial.

However, patients seem determined to destroy themselves. They secretly collect razors (or any other sharp items), ropes, pills or belts, and attempt suicide the first change they get. These items are contraindicated on the psychiatric unit and are called *contraband*. Contraband checks are very important when patients are initially admitted to a unit or if a patient is returning from a pass. Contraband may be sent in the mail or included in a present to the patient.

The majority of suicidal patients are not so intent on ending their lives, they are giving a cry for help. The nurse must watch for the direct or indirect pleas for help. The suicidal patient may give some indications of his intention, perhaps by saying, "Life isn't worth living," or "Here, take my camera, I won't be needing it anymore." Others may openly or jokingly mention suicide. The old notion that a person who talks about suicide will never do it is simply not true. Other significant behavioral clues include the following:

- a despairing mood
- prolonged depression
- change in eating or sleeping patterns
- problems with school grades for the adolescent
- lack of previous interest in social situations
- uncharacteristic behavior such as reckless driving, or serious drug abuse
- a vacant stare

As previously stated, adolescence, menopause, and aging are critical events in the life cycle. During these stages there are many stressors that culminate in suicidal tendencies. Immediate precipitating factors may include: loss of a loved one, rejection, divorce, or fear of a physical or mental breakdown. These factors plus a sense of social isolation and nothingness can provoke a suicide response.

There has been an increase in youth suicide in the United States. School personnel, parents, and students need to be more aware of the maturational stresses that the adolescent is experiencing. Adolescents are challenged but confused by the ambiguity in our society. They feel increasingly alienated, depressed, and despondent. Youth who are depressed, have a history of alcohol/drug abuse, or have been sexually or physically abused as children are at a very high risk for suicide.

The nurse must connect with the suicidal patient and attempt to build a relationship. To prevent self-destructive actions, the nurse first observes the patient closely. Assessment is frequently made for the lethality of the patients thoughts and/or plans. Time is then planned to sit with the patient and encourage verbalization. This will acknowledge the person's feelings of helplessness and provide an opportunity to discuss alternatives to suicide. Listening and reflecting back feelings expressed demonstrates to the suicidal person that you are aware of his pain and willing to stay with him to provide a safe environment.

Suicide assessment includes: the level of lethality (low, moderate, high), a distinct plan (client states, "I will take this ballpoint pen and stab myself in the chest"), and gathering family history of suicide attempts and patient's history of previous attempts.

Look at the history of impulsive acting-out by this patient and his current life stressors. Are thought problems present: hallucinations, delusions, thought broadcasting? Has the patient been finalizing his life by giving things away? What are this particular patients personal strengths, resources and support systems.

If the patient appears to have no energy to act, do not decrease vigilance as the patient remains at serious risk. Place the patient on Suicide Precautions to insure protection and safety. A patient placed on high risk precautions needs a staff member on a one-to-one basis. This places the patient under constant observation and the staff member stays directly with the patient. A previous attempt(s) i.e. suicidal gesturing, manipulative or serious suicidal attempts is the best predictor of a patient at risk. Research indicates that suicide occurs at a far greater rate among alcoholics and other substance abusers than it does among the general population.

When the patient is being discharged from the hospital to the community, check the patient's resources: family, relatives, close friends, physicians, clergyman, professional therapists, and agencies. Does this patient have other people to communicate with? Is there a support system? Are there positive thoughts about the future or an attitude that there is no point in living?

In the future, suicide research is needed in certain specific areas. These include genetic factors and the part that they play in suicide, and differences in suicide in a variety of subcultures—men, women, young, old, white, Hispanic, oriental and black.

## HOMICIDE

Homicide is an act of violence directed toward another with an intent to kill. It is our responsibility to focus attention on the patient's mental status and look for increased agitation, specific threats, and their view of this violent act as their only recourse. Assessment must be made of the availability of a weapon and the availability of a victim. An open-ended approach where the patient is asked directly about his desperate thoughts is an effective and safe way to handle patient care.

A landmark case, Tarasoff vs. Regents of University of California, California Appellate Court, 141 Cal. 92(1977) brought to focus the rights of the patient versus the rights of the public. A patient communicated to the provider (a psychiatrist), an actual threat of violence or the means of harm to a reasonably identifiable victim/victims. Statements were made to the psychiatrist indicating imminent danger to that person and that physical violence would be used to cause serious personal injury. In this particular the victim was murdered, and the family brought suit against the psychiatrist. This court decision brought about (in most states) the health provider's *Duty to Warn*.

In September 1987, the State of Indiana stated that providers of mental health services have a duty to warn of a patient's violent behavior. Providers include: hospitals, private institutions, physicians, psychologists, social workers, nurses, and college counseling centers. Reasonable efforts must be made to notify a police department or other law enforcement agency having jurisdiction in the patient's or victim's place or residence. A civil commitment to take custody of the patient may need to be sought. The mental health provider who provides information that must be disclosed to comply with this act is immune from civil and criminal liability under state statutes that protect that patient's privacy and confidentiality. If the victim is a minor, the parents must be notified. Current hospital policies and procedures need to reflect the provisions of this new act, and mental health providers must research the laws of their particular state.

## ABUSE

With increased media coverage, there is awareness and emphasis on family and social violence. It a complex social problem. A violent act has a victim, a perpetrator, and frequently witnesses. There are female and male perpetrators. Multiple stressors contribute to violence, Table 13-8.

### Patient Abuse

Patient abuse includes mental, physical, sexual, and verbal abuse. This act is forbidden: No patient is to be mistreated or abused in any way. Patient abuse is still not allowed even if the employee feels provoked by the actions of the patient. Abuse considered to be of a minor nature (teasing a patient, speaking harshly, rudely) can result in reprimand, suspension, or demotion. The penalty of serious abuse is removal from the facility. Further, any employee who witnesses any unkindness, rudeness, or violence of any kind toward the patient and does not promptly report it is also subject to disciplinary action. Employees need to be closely advised of the patients' rights. Remember that intentional omission of care is also abuse and disciplinary action is warranted.

### Sexual Abuse

Rape is a sexual assault: a forceable, degrading and humiliating act. It is sexual intercourse by force, without consent of the partner. It is an act of aggression and a violent sexual crime.

**TABLE 13-8**
**Stressors**

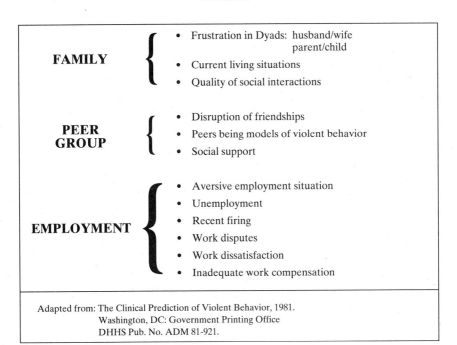

| FAMILY | • Frustration in Dyads:  husband/wife<br>                              parent/child<br>• Current living situations<br>• Quality of social interactions |
| --- | --- |
| PEER GROUP | • Disruption of friendships<br>• Peers being models of violent behavior<br>• Social support |
| EMPLOYMENT | • Aversive employment situation<br>• Unemployment<br>• Recent firing<br>• Work disputes<br>• Work dissatisfaction<br>• Inadequate work compensation |

Adapted from: The Clinical Prediction of Violent Behavior, 1981.
Washington, DC: Government Printing Office
DHHS Pub. No. ADM 81-921.

The nurse in the emergency room may be confronted with a patient who has experienced a sexual assault of rape. The emergency care for the rape victim needs a multi-faceted approach, Table 13-9. The need for sedative medication must be carefully evaluated. The patient's psychological needs are also great. She feels frightened and vulnerable. Her self-esteem is damaged and she often feels deeply embarrassed. Often, she feels guilty ("What has happened to me is my own fault").

Frequently, her thought processes are disorganized. When talking to the victim, the nurse should speak slowly and allow time for comprehension.

The police must be notified at once. They will also question her in the emergency room. She needs emotional support during this questioning as it is often a traumatic experience for her.

As part of the medical process, any wounds must be dressed and medication must be given to prevent pregnancy and venereal disease, even though pregnancy seldom results from rape. (Scientists suspect that the hormonal balance of the victim is upset by the rape, thus preventing conception.)

**TABLE 13-9**
**Emergency Care for the Rape Victim**

- Attention to psychological needs
- Care of wounds
- Notification of police
- Emotional support during police questioning
- Medication as ordered
- Obtaining sperm, nail, and hair samples
- Clear explanation of procedures
- Contacting the victim-advocate program
- Referals
- Follow-up

Rape kits are now available in emergency rooms. These kits contain materials for collecting proof of the occurrence of a rape (such as sperm). The emergency room staff must be careful about collecting and handling evidence. This proof, such as clippings of fingernails and combings of pubic hair might be compared by the police to the skin and hair samples of a possible suspect.

It is extremely important that the victim understand each procedure and the reason for it. No one other than the doctor, nurse, and police are allowed access to the evidence. All slides and smears must be protected. If there is a victim advocate program in the area, the staff should be contacted. Someone from the program will usually come to the emergency room to provide support for the victim. Later, someone from the program visits her for counseling and referral.

The nurse should be aware of the sociological aspects of rape. From the point of the rapist: The attacker is usually a person with a strong hostility toward women. He has the need to control by sexually dominating a women. Rape may give the man a sense of power, and he feels that power will ensure potency, since many rapists have difficulty with erection or ejaculation.

From the woman's point: rape inflicts a feeling of loss upon the victim. She may develop a wide range of feelings—anger, mistrust, and anxiety. This internalized rage can lead to depression. The nurse should anticipate the victim's grief due to the degradation of the self. It is important to also note that she may not receive loving and supportive responses from significant persons in her life. Some husbands or fiancees may withdraw from her. Others reject the woman, using a blaming statement such as, "Things like this just don't happen to good girls." Even family members may ask questions such as, "Why did you walk alone in the dark?", "Couldn't you have screamed louder?" or "Didn't you fight back?"

The nurse needs to recognize that significant others may need to ventilate their feelings as they search for a rational explanation for such violent behavior against someone they love. Rape victims and their significant others can suffer a traumatic disruption of their life-style. Counseling may be necessary for the woman, spouse, and family. The long-term goal is for the woman to return to independent functioning in all phases of her life.

## INCEST

Information is scant in medical literature concerning the practice of incest. Incest is defined as a sexual relationship between blood relatives. It can be either a forced relationship or a consensual one. These relationships may involve father and daughter, mother and son, or brother and sister. This section will deal only with forced incest. The sexual relationship may include foreplay, caressing, kissing or mutual masturbation.

This experience can be a very traumatic one for young children and adolescents. It may predispose them to sexual maladjustments or psychological problems such as phobias and depressive reactions. According to Briere (1989), post incestuous relationships have three phases: reaction, adaptation, and survival. During these phases the victim is going to deal with intrusive (flashbacks, nightmares, reliving of the incest) and avoidant symptoms (withdrawal and dissociation). Anxiety, depression, and anger are the emotional effects. Impulsive behaviors, i.e. self-mutilation, drug/alcohol abuse, hypersexual activity or suicide, may occur.

In therapy, the victim needs to be reminded how far they have come and how much they have accomplished. It must be realized that there is much numbing emotionally and sexually. Briere (1989) discusses an impaired self reference (Where do I start? Where does he/she stop?) The victim, who is now the survivor, will have difficulty with the consolation of self; therefore, the therapist must align with the survivor's strong, healthy parts.

Understand two things when approaching the patient: stay with reality and provide concrete information. Many of the survivor's symptoms have served a purpose and provided them with a more adaptive way of dealing with their abuse. The basis philosophy of their treatment is respect, positive regard, and the assumption of their own personal growth.

## SUMMARY

Violence in our society is rampant. We must learn to understand our roles in the prevention and management of our patient's violent behaviors and also our roles in the nursing care of the victims. The care provider's own fear and anger must be appropriately dealt with and personal safety issues explored.

Violent, assaultive behavior is a true emergency. A safe, systematized approach and learned and practiced management techniques will provide therapeutic interventions of the violent patients. If necessary, this will involve restraint. Post-conferences after a violent episode allows time for the staff to discuss their personal safety needs and feelings. During the seclusion/restraint time period, careful and thorough documentation must be followed.

Family and social violence are complex issues in our culture. As health professionals we need to deal with our own beliefs and biases. Rape and incest are difficult areas for care providers and knowledgeable, supportive care must be given.

### SUGGESTED ACTIVITIES

- Collect newspaper articles in your community over the period of a week and look at the most reported areas of violence.
- Look at your anger in the present and your anger in the past and allow yourself to view the differences. List constructive-destructive elements of your own personal anger.
- Write a script and role play a specific aggressive, acting-out behavior and way of de-escalating the behavior.
- Role play a post-conference on a psychiatric unit after a vigorous take-down and placement of the patient in leather restraints. A team member has been injured and is currently in the emergency room.
- Discuss current issues of consensual sex and rape. Look at the myths versus reality.
- Invite a guest speaker to discuss child abuse and the problems in you own community. Recognize available community resources.

### REVIEW

A.   Multiple Choice. Select the best answer.

1. The second leading cause of death in our society for those people between the age of 15 and 30 is
   a. suicide
   b. homicide
   c. cardiac arrests
   d. cancer

2. Theories of aggression include
   a. inborn drive/impulses
   b. blocked goals
   c. positive and negative reinforcers
   d. all of the above

3. A staff behavior that can increase the possibility of violence is
   a. negotiating with a patient
   b. contracting with a patient
   c. labeling a patient
   d. actively listening to a patient

4. Constructive uses of anger include all of the following except
   a. increasing assertive skills
   b. increasing feelings of isolation
   c. developing mutual understanding
   d. increasing personal self-esteem

5. Nonverbal techniques for controlling disruptive behavior include all of the following except
   a. respecting personal space
   b. interpreting body language
   c. controlling your tone of voice
   d. providing the most restrictive environment

6. When caring for a rape victim, the nurse can help by
   a. telling her what is being done and why
   b. showing empathy
   c. notifying the victim advocate program
   d. all of the above

B. Briefly answer the following.

1. List the three chief life stressors that contribute to violent behavior.

2. List the hierarchy of dangerous behaviors.

3. List the three components of a suicide assessment.

4. List and briefly describe the three phases of post-sexual abuse.

5. Describe the Tarasoff Duty to Warn of a Patient's Violent Behavior for the mental health provider.

## BOOKS

Bass, E. Davis, L. *The Courage to Heal: A Guide for Woman Survivors of Child Sexual Abuse.* Perennial Library: N.Y., 1986.

Bowlby, J. *Attachment and Loss: Vol. 2 Separation: Anxiety and Anger.* Hogarth: London, 1973.

Briere, J. *Therapy for Adults Molested as Children Beyond Survival.* Springer Publishing Co.: N.Y., 1989.

Brown-Miller, S. *Against Our Will: Men, Women and Rape.* Simon & Schuster: N.Y., 1975.

Lerner, H.G. *The Dance of Anger: A Woman's Guide to Changing the Patterns of Intimate Relationships.* Harper Collins Publishers, Inc.: N.Y., 1989.

Madden, D.J. & Leon, J.R. *Rage, Hate, Assault and Other Forms of Violence.* Spectrum Publishers: N.Y., 1976.

## ARTICLES

Abrams, G.H. Setting limits. *Archives of General Psychiatry* 19: 113-119, 1968.

Becker, J. et al. Incidence and types of sexual dysfunction in rape an incest victims. *Journal of Sex & Marital Therapy* 8:65-74, 1982.

Boettcher, E. Preventing violent behavior: an integrated theoretical model for nursing. *Perspectives in Psychiatric Care* 21:2, 54-58, 1983.

Briere, J. Symptomatology in men who were molested as children: a comparison study. *American Journal of Orthopsychiatry* 58: 457-61, 1988.

Burgess, A. and Holstrom, L. Rape trauma syndrome. *American Journal of Psychiatry*, 131: 981-86, 1984.

Cantwell, D.P. Hyperactivity and antisocial behavior. *Journal of American Academy Child Psychiatry* 17:252-262, 1978.

Carmel, H. et al. Compliance with training in managing assaultive behavior and injuries from inpatient violence. *Hospital & Community Psychiatry* 41(5): 558-60, May 1990.

Carpenter, M.D., Hannon, V.R. et al. Variations in seclusion and restraint practices by hospital location. *Hospital and Community Psychiatry* 39(4), 418-43, April 1988.

Chitty, K. and Maynard, C. Managing manipulation. *Journal of Psychosocial Nursing* 24(6): 9-13, June 1986.

Collins, J.J. and Schlenger, W.I. Acute and chronic effects of alcohol use in violence. *Journal of Studies on Alcohol* 49(6): 516-520, 1988.

Convit, A., Jaeger, J. et al. Predicting assaultiveness in psychiatric inpatients: a pilot study. *Hospital & Community Psychiatry* 39(4): 429–34, April 1988.

Convit, A., Jeager, J. et al. Characteristics of repeatedly assaultive psychiatric in-patients. *Hospital & Community Psychiatry* 41(10): 112-5, October 1990.

Crockett, M. A case of anger and alienation. *American Journal of Nursing* 86(3): 294-298, March 1986.

Dang, S. When the patient is out of control. *RN* 53(10): 57-58, October 1990.

Davis, S. Violence by psychiatric inpatients: a review. *Hospital & Community Psychiatry* 42(6): 585-589, June 1991.

Dooley, Z. Aggressive incidents in a secure hospital. *Medical Science Now* 26(2): 125-130, April 1986.

Drummond, D., Sparr, L. et al. Hospital reduction among high-risk patients. *Journal of the American Medical Association* 216(17): 2531-2534, 1989.

Engel, F. Helping the employee victim of violence in hospitals. *Hospital & Community Psychiatry* 37:2, February 1986.

Ferran, C. and Keane-Hagerty, E. Communicating effectively with dementia patients. *Journal of Psychosocial Nursing* 27(5): 13-16, June 1990.

Flannery, R.B., Fulton, P. et al. A program to help staff cope with psychological sequelae of assaults by patients. *Hospital & Community Psychiatry* 42(9): 935-936, September 1991.

Goodwin, J. Family violence: principles of intervention and prevention. *Hospital & Community Psychiatry* 36(10): 1074-1070, October 1985.

Kirkpatrick, H. A descriptive study of seclusion: the unit environment, patient behavior and nursing interventions. *Archives of Psychiatric Nursing* III:1, 3-9, February 1989.

Lee, H.K. et al. Characteristics and behavior of patients involved in psychiatric ward incidents. *Hospital & Community Psychiatry* 40(12): 1295-1297, December 1989.

Lion, J. Training for battle: thoughts on managing aggressive patients. *Hospital & Community Psychiatry* 38(8): 882-884, August 1987.

Loomis, M.E. Levels of contracting. *Journal of Psychosocial Nursing and Mental Health Services* 23(3): 8-14, 1985.

Morrison, P. A multidimensional scalogram analysis of the use of seclusion in acute psychiatric settings. *Journal of Advances in Nursing* 15(1): 59-66, January 1990.

O'Brien, A. *Seclusion Imprint* 36(4): 79-80, November 1989.

Sparr, L. F., Drummond, D. L. et al. Managing violent patient incidents, the role of a behavioral emergency committee. *Quality Review Bulletin* 14(5): 147-153, 1988.

Turnbull, J. et al. Turn it around: short-term management for aggression and anger-training for nurses. *Journal of Psychiatric Nursing and Mental Health* 28(6): 6-10, June 1990.

Van Dongen, C. J. Agonizing questioning: experiences of suicide victims. *Nursing Research* 39(4): 224-229, July-August, 1990.

Way, B. B., Braff, J. et al. The relationship between patient-staff ratio and reported patient incidents. *Hospital & Community Psychiatry* 43(4): 361-364, April 1992.

# CHAPTER 14
# HUMAN SEXUALITY

## OBJECTIVES

After studying this chapter, the student should be able to:

- State three aspects of sexuality
- Name three surgical procedures that may threaten sexuality.
- List three medical problems that may affect sexuality.
- Describe emergency care for the rape victim.
- State the possible meaning of rape to the attacker, the victim, and the victim's family.
- Name four psychosexual disorders.

The nurse who accepts the concept of total care must consider human sexuality as a significant part of the patient's identity. Sex is not an isolated activity; it involves many aspects of the patient's life, such as identity, social role, and physical functioning. Sexuality is a facet of personality and is self-affirming. It encompasses the individual's personal value system and philosophy of life. Sexuality is an integral part of self-concept. An individual is a sexual being at birth. However, sexuality is not just the difference between male and female.

Sexual behavior includes how a person acts regarding sexual intercourse, reproduction, and childbirth. This is based on boundaries set by a particular culture. The basic sexual identity, however, is taught by society as children learn what role is expected of boys and girls. Sexual roles are taught and reinforced throughout life. Boys and girls are frequently given toys that are gender-specific; i.e., trucks for boys and dolls for girls, Figure 14-1. Sexual identity and the behavior that goes with it are part of the total being. Thus, sex is part of what a person is, as well as what the person does. Sexual well-being can contribute to a positive mental attitude. The person who is able to accept himself or herself in totality is better able to maintain a level of wellness.

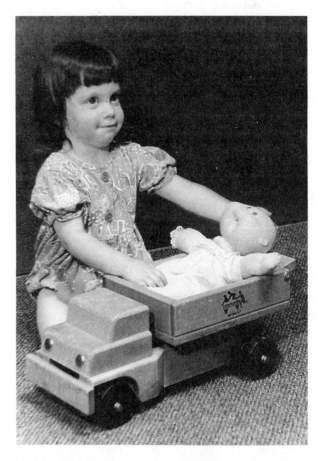

Fig. 14-1 Toys that were once considered gender-specific are a playful combination for this little girl.

Until recently, sexuality and the physical acts of sex were seldom discussed openly in our cultures. These subjects were shrouded in secrecy and embarrassment. Some types of sexual activity brought punishment. Today, in spite of the more permissive attitudes toward sexuality, society still condemns many aspects of sexual behavior. Fear and embarrassment still add to the general lack of knowledge. People with questions about sex are often reluctant to seek help or advice. Hospital patients with such questions may be hesitant to seek answers. Nurses may have problems responding to such questions.

The nurse must re-evaluate her attitudes about sexual matters. She should recognize any biases and any areas which make her uncomfortable or embarrassed. Angry or sarcastic remarks only interfere with the nurse-patient interaction. The nurse must learn to cope with her own fears and anxieties. Her attitudes, beliefs, and behavior either curtail discussions with patients or create an atmosphere that contributes to open and spontaneous discussion.

There is a great deal of controversy surrounding sexual behavior and personal rights. A person's social and religious background helps to determine his attitudes. Nurses need to investigate their own value systems in relation to these and other controversial issues involving human sexuality. They must be able to care for people with differing values. This requires a nonjudgmental attitude.

## SEXUALITY AND PHYSICAL ILLNESS

Illness brings about a disturbance of physical and emotional equilibrium. This affects all aspects of the person, including his sexuality. Patients may not need in-depth counseling. They may only need someone with whom they can talk. A sympathetic ear might be enough. Having a knowledgeable person give reassurance or assistance in problem solving may be a great help.

Patients often avoid mentioning sexual problems or concerns because they feel embarrassed. However, they may give nonverbal and verbal cues that they are worried. The nurse who wishes to be of assistance should look and listen for these cues. The patient can then be approached, and the nurse can try to discover what is worrying him. When encouraging a patient to express his feelings, an open, nonjudgmental approach is important. Really  listening to what the patient is saying can show the nurse if the patient seems uninformed or misinformed. The nurse can then offer correct information and respond with facts and not opinions. Good communication skills are essential. The nurse needs to know when she has met her own limitations and should seek qualified assistance. The nurse cannot be expected to do highly specialized counseling. An appropriate referral to counselors, gynecologists, or urologists in the community may be necessary.

The nurse may encounter other communication problems. Older patients may resent younger nurses giving them sexual instruction. Male patients may be hesitant to discuss sexual concerns with a female nurse.

Although it is good practice to use anatomical terms in teaching, the nurse should make sure the patient understands her message. It may be necessary to avoid using technical words. The nurse also needs to be aware of street language the patient may use, and not overreact to it. The nurse should assume nothing and seek clarification as necessary.

Patients may have questions or problems concerning sexual intercourse or reproduction. At times, their problems are broader and may encompass the patient's total relationship with his or her sexual partner. For example, illness can be a threat to a sexual relationship. Illness, as well as medications, can decrease the sex drive. The hospital environment lacks privacy, and marital or romantic partners sense a loss of intimacy. Hospital gowns tend to alter the body's image, making the patient feel unattractive.

Because of dependency and loss of physical strength following illness or surgery, many patients fear sexual inadequacy. Mass media advertising and entertainment impress upon the public the importance of being young and attractive. The message received is: "Happiness is being sexy." Sick people do not usually see themselves as sexy. They feel "bad all over," not sexy.

The nurse may also encounter a situation in which the patient makes a sexual advance. The best approach to this situation is to confront the patient with his behavior. If the nurse goes about her nursing care and pretends the sexual advance did not occur, the patient may interpret this as encouragement. The nurse should verbalize that the sexual advance is inappropriate and may interfere with the patient's needed nursing care. This statement should be made in a calm, objective manner and not in judgmental tones. It is important for the nurse to assess her own dress and behavior.

When dealing with patient's sexual problems, the nurse should be objective, sensitive, and emphatic. She must reach out to patients who need help.

## MEDICAL PROBLEMS AND SEXUALITY

Some medical conditions can have a direct effect on the patient's sexuality, including cardiac conditions, diabetes, hypertension, arthritis, and spinal cord injuries. These conditions can alter the patient's strength, range of motion, sexual desire, and body image. The nurse should watch for hidden fears and unasked questions. An open and accepting approach is necessary to encourage discussion and reassure the patient.

Sexual intercourse in an important part of a marriage relationship; it contributes to total well-being. A patient with a medical condition that affects sexual functioning requires extra sensitivity. The meaning and importance of sex to the patient should be explored. An honest discussion of the severity and permanence of any sexual impairment is needed. Personal fears and anxieties must be verbalized. It is vital that the feelings of the patient's sexual partner be considered. With the understanding and cooperation of patient and partner, solutions may be found.

## Cardiac Conditions

With a cardiac condition, such as a myocardial infarction, the patient may have to assume a dependent and passive role. Many of these patients have a fear of sexual intercourse. Sexual activity may be perceived by the patient or his sexual partner, or both, as too much strain on the patient's heart. Either partner may be afraid of a recurrence of the chest pain or may fear an inability to function; therefore, all sexual advances of the other partner may be discouraged. Some cardiac patients are in need of sexual counseling.

Cardiac patients may be advised by their physician to refrain from intercourse for two to four months. It has been shown, however, that sexual activity does not put an excessive strain on the heart. The cardiac patient should be instructed to check with his physician before engaging in sexual intercourse. He should watch for fatigue and take special note of chest or arm pain during or after intercourse. Extreme fatigue the following day is a symptom that should be reported. Alternative positions for intercourse may prevent overburdening the cardiovascular system. A stressless environment is encouraged.

Before resuming sexual activity, the patient and his partner must first accept the patient's condition and its limitation. They can then set realistic goals for a satisfactory sexual adjustment. Adaptation need not be difficult. Intercourse can be a part of the cardiac patient's life.

## Diabetes

Diabetes is a chronic disease that can cause sexual problems. Many diabetic men suffer from *impotence* (the inability to have an erection).

Some problems may be caused by *neuropathy* (disease of the nerves) which may occur in the later stages of diabetes. One physiological problem of diabetic men is *retrograde ejaculation* (a sexual dysfunction in which semen ejaculates into the bladder). Men with these sexual difficulties may need professional counseling.

Women with diabetes have an increased incidence of vaginal infections. *Dyspareunia* (painful intercourse) may occur. The vaginal infection requires treatment. Many diabetic women express a fear of pregnancy. This is because there is an increased incidence of stillbirths among diabetics. However, modern medical technology has improved the chances for a successful pregnancy. The diabetic woman should be encouraged to express any fear and anxiety she feels about sexual matters.

## Hypertension

Sexual problems associated with hypertension are sometimes brought on by treatment measures. Impotence can be a side effect of certain drugs prescribed for hypertension. Reserpine, a common antihypertensive medication, decreases sexual desire. Ismelin, another often-used drug, can cause ejaculatory dysfunction. Since uncontrolled hypertension can lead to more severe medical conditions, use of the proper medication is vital. The physician should inform the patient of any possible sexual dysfunction resulting from medication. If a problem occurs, the patient should be encouraged to consult the physician. A combination of medications can be tried, which may relieve the problem. Sexual counseling may also be advantageous.

## Arthritis

Arthritis is a chronic disabling and deforming disease that affects more women than men. The disease causes inflammation of the joints of the hands, wrists, and knees. In a more advanced stage, all joints may be very painful. The joints become stiff and immobile, particularly the hip joint. The appearance of the joint changes. If surgery is done, there are scars. With these deformities, the patient's self-image may change, or at least, he may feel more vulnerable.

Rehabilitation of the arthritic patient should include restoring sexual functioning. It is best if both members of a sexual partnership are involved. They should be helped to realize the importance of sex in their relationship. Sexual counseling should include a frank discussion of potential problems.

Relaxation exercises may be helpful. Motion exercises done daily are an important part of routine care. Partners may need to develop their communication skills so they can better understand each other's needs.

Much practical advice can be offered. For example, variations of sexual positioning might be considered. A discussion of family planning may be of value. Family planning encompasses social, psychologic, economic, physical, and religious concerns of the couple and their decision regarding children. Information can be given in an objective and nonjudgmental way.

The patient needs to know that corticosteroids may decrease sexual desire. The timing of intercourse is also important. Early morning may be a poor time for intercourse because of stiffness and pain of the joints. By evening, the arthritic person may feel too tired for sexual activity.

Adequate sexual counseling can dispel some of the patient's psychological stress. It could prevent a divorce or the partner's seeking pleasure elsewhere. A loving, understanding response from a partner and a feeling of sexual fulfillment can decrease the incidence of depression in the arthritic patient.

## Spinal Cord Injuries

The functioning of the genital area may be altered by a spinal cord injury. If the male patient can voluntarily empty his bladder, he is probably capable of an erection. The patient with an injury to the sacral segment of the spinal cord is least likely to have an erection. Penile erection may be unpredictable and of short duration. Few patients are capable of an ejaculation. When patients realize they have these problems, they usually feel angry and depressed.

Some patients, both males and females, suffer from bladder spasms. The patient can take antispasmodic medication to control the spasms. Some patients must wear urinary catheters. This need not limit sexual intercourse. Most catheters can be removed before and reinserted following intercourse. The patient or partner can be taught to do this.

Because of possible bowel and bladder dysfunction, both the patient and his sexual partner need to be included in frank discussions. Alternatives to coitus may need to be explored. There are a variety of body sensations and possible responses that can give sexual pleasure. The partners need to discuss what is satisfactory to each of them. It is important that each knows the types of lovemaking with which the other feels comfortable. Emotional closeness is a satisfying element in loving.

The patient who has suffered spinal cord injury also needs sexual counseling. Group discussion with other victims of spinal cord injuries can provide a much needed opportunity for sharing problems, especially sexual ones.

## SURGERY AND SEXUAL PROBLEMS

Sexual procedures can represent a threat to the patient's sexuality, Table 14-1. Some procedures, such as mastectomy and amputations, subject the patient to body distortion. Patients may feel undesirable. These patients need to be able to explore their feelings. They also need to be reassured of their sexual attractiveness and capability.

Although the nurse should be concerned with the sexual adjustment of all patients, some need special consideration. These include persons who have undergone ostomy surgery, a hysterectomy, a mastectomy, or a prostatectomy.

### TABLE 14-1
### Medical and Surgical Problems That Can Affect Sexuality

| Medical Problems | Surgical Problems |
|---|---|
| cardiac conditions | ostomy |
| diabetes | hysterectomy |
| hypertension | mastectomy |
| spinal cord injuries | prostatectomy |
| arthritis | |

## Ostomy

Colostomy and ileostomy surgery have a physical and emotional impact of the patient's self-esteem. It is difficult to accept bowel elimination through a stoma on the abdomen. Counseling of the sexual partner is important because the partner's attitude and understanding influence the patient's adjustment.

Sexual intercourse does not injure or damage the stoma. Psychic problems, however, especially those concerning continuous fecal draining, can contribute to impotence or a nonorgasmic response. The nurse should reassure the patient that a colostomy does not drain continuously and sexual encounters can be timed accordingly. The ileostomy patient can be reassured that the appliance he wears does not come loose during intercourse. A patient who has had an abdominal perineal resection may in some cases be impotent if nerves have been severed.

Many patients worry about how their partners will react to seeing the stoma. The nurse should try to prevent a possible avoidance and denial syndrome. If the patient remains uniformed and fearful, becoming a desirable sexual partner will be difficult. Some patients worry about possibly becoming pregnant. Frequently, a member of the local ostomy association can be of great assistance in helping the patient achieve a healthy approach to living and loving.

## Hysterectomy

A hysterectomy is one of the most common surgical procedures for women. Many women suffer postoperatively from an identity crisis and exhibit depression. They feel they have lost their femininity or their sexuality. Misconceptions about hysterectomy abound. The patient may have heard, "You turn old because the vagina dries up" or "You get fat when the uterus is gone."

The patient should be encouraged to discuss her anxieties. Misconceptions should be accepted as the patient's point of view. Refusing them usually does not persuade the patient that the notions really are wrong. Instead, the observant nurse should listen for remarks that may lead to discussion. The nurse should remember that the patient is going through a time of heightened emotional sensitivity. The nurse's interest, concern, and willingness to listen will help the woman see her body in proper perspective.

The nurse should help the patient to think positively. Some women like the idea of not having a menstrual cycle following a hysterectomy. Other women are pleased to be free of the risk of pregnancy. Focusing attention on positive aspects decrease the woman's preoccupation with her disability.

## Prostatectomy

Many men must undergo surgery for removal of the prostate gland. These men may fear that the surgery will affect their sexual functioning. A prostatectomy usually does not cause impotence. However, sexual activity should be delayed for six to eight weeks until healing has occurred.

Potency is retained when the prostate is removed by one of the usual procedures. If a perineal incision is made, the patient may have difficulty with retrograde ejaculation and sterility. He is likely to become impotent if there is a radical excision due to cancer. Preoperative preparation and counseling aid the patient in postoperative adjustment.

## Mastectomy

The patient who undergoes a mastectomy needs a competent nurse who can promote a favorable body image. Television, movies, and stories are constantly emphasizing the female breasts. The mastectomy patient needs reassurance that she is still sexually attractive despite removal of a breast. This patient needs preoperative counseling and postoperative support. Her sexual partner also should be involved in the counseling. Even with counseling, the patient should be allowed to adjust to the surgery at her own pace. She usually starts the adjustment by looking at the scar. If the patient is reluctant to look at the incision site, however, her resistance must be respected. She will eventually work up to touching the scar.

The nurse should demonstrate that she cares about the patient through talking, listening, and encouraging the patient to verbalize her feelings. The mastectomy patient usually has many questions. The best person to suggest answers is another woman who has adjusted to a mastectomy. Women from the group, Reach for Recovery, sponsored by the American Cancer Society, are available to visit the patient. They offer reassurance and suggestions concerning clothing. These women share their own emotional adjustment phases to their mastectomy and altered body image with the new mastectomy patient.

Many types of breast prostheses are available. These include the fluid-filled type, the air-filled type, and those made of sponge rubber. The fluid-filled type is the most satisfactory. This type of prosthesis is filled with a thick, slow-flowing fluid. In order to have any prosthesis fit well, a properly fitted brassiere is necessary. Prostheses may be made specifically for the individual, or they may be purchased ready-made. Many department stores now have mastectomy boutiques.

Breast reconstruction is possible following a mastectomy. During the initial surgery, if biopsies of the nipple are negative, the nipple areolar complex can be temporarily attached to the patient's anterior abdominal wall. Six months to one year later, surgery can be scheduled for reconstruction of the breast utilizing the pectoralis major muscle and an inflatable prosthesis. The patient's own nipple is then attached to the reconstructed breast. Other innovative surgeries are available to help the mastectomy patient regain a positive body image.

## PREMENSTRUAL TENSION SYNDROME (PMTS)

PMTS comprises a group of emotional and behavioral changes reported by some women during the premenstrual phase of their menstrual cycle. Characteristics of this syndrome include: depression, increased irritability and liability of moods, tension, impulsivity, and distractibility, and impaired concentration. It is important to note that these symptoms are time limited. Diagnosis may be difficult. It is important to assess the timing of symptoms in regard to the menstrual cycle (i.e., "I shout at my children and hit them five to seven days before my period occurs.") Physical symptoms such as abdominal bloating, headaches, breast swelling and tenderness are also reported. Many outpatient clinics are providing support groups for women with PMTS.

## SEXUALITY AND THE AGED

Aging is a phase of human development. As in all other phases of life, loving and giving are important for the elderly, Figure 14-2. Sexual desire or ability do not end with old age. Anxiety, depression, and irritability may occur during menopause. These symptoms are usually related to hormonal imbalance and the woman's acceptance of the new phase. Men often experience similar feelings. They may feel less sexually responsive. Emotional and adjustment problems may also occur.

It is most important for nurses to re-evaluate their ideas concerning sex and the aged. The chief source of sexual desire is the mind. Therefore, deterioration of the body due to age need not mean an end to sexual activity. Because people associate youthfulness or the ability to reproduce with sex, it is difficult for some people to see the elderly as sexual beings. Nonetheless, the elderly need love. The aged need to touch, to be close to someone, to express affection. They should be encouraged to assess their needs realistically. The elderly should never be considered abnormal for choosing intercourse.

Some elderly men have difficulty with erection. The vagina is drier in the aged woman. The application of a lubricant by either sexual partner makes penetration easier. Chronic illness and vascular insufficiency also can cause sexual difficulties. Suppression of sexual needs may lead to frustration and depression. As in any other age, the sexual drive can be satisfied in nongenital ways.

If the aged person is living an independent life, he may feel free enough to develop a relationship. In the nursing home environment, the elderly need privacy. A judgmental, negative approach by the nurse can only contribute to lower self-esteem for the patient. Full and satisfying lives for the elderly should be among the nurse's goals.

Fig. 14-2 The elderly need love and affection.

## PSYCHOSEXUAL DISORDERS

The nurse should be aware of the following psychosexual disorders.

- **fetishism** - sexual excitement and gratification from touching or fondling certain objects or clothing. It occurs primarily in men and is a substitution for a normal love object.

- **voyeurism** - sexual pleasure derived from secretly watching people involved in sexual acts, or by looking at their bodies and sex organs without their knowledge. This person is know as a "Peeping Tom." This occurs mainly in men.
- **exhibitionism** - a sexual desire to display the genital area to the opposite sex in socially inappropriate situations. The exhibitionist usually does not talk or touch his victim; he gets his gratification from the shock shown by the female. Exhibitionism occurs primarily in men.
- **pedophilia** - unnatural desire for sexual relations with children.
- **transvestism** - adopting the dress and often the behavior for the opposite sex. There is no desire to change sex, or to be homosexual. Men dress in women's clothing and women dress in men's clothing. An example of transvestism is a man wearing a bra and garter belt under his business suit. This is usually done in a private and secretive manner.
- **transsexual** - a person that is biologically one sex, but has a psychological urge to be the opposite sex. A transsexual may seek help through requesting a sex change operation.

The nurse assigned to care for a patient with a psychosexual disorder may feel afraid or uneasy. She should not let her personal feelings about different sexual behavior affect the care she gives the patient. This patient has health needs apart from his sexual preference. Fellow employees also should be evaluated on work performance and not sexual preferences.

The nurse should be aware of her own feelings, values, and beliefs regarding unconventional sexual behavior. Does the nurse feel that patients with psychosexual disorders are queer or perverted? The nurse must be able to develop a tolerant attitude toward patients with unconventional sexual behaviors.

## SEXUAL ASSAULT

The nurse in the emergency room may be confronted with a patient who has experienced a sexual assault or rape. Rape is sexual intercourse by force. It is a violent sexual crime. Although male (homosexual) rape also occurs, our discussion will be limited to rape of a female.

The emergency care for the rape victim needs a multi-faceted approach (Table 14-2). The patient's psychological needs are great. The woman feels frightened and vulnerable. Her self-esteem is damaged and she feels deeply embarrassed. Often she is made to feel guilty. Frequently, her thought processes are disorganized. When talking to the victim, the nurse should talk slowly and allow time for comprehension.

**TABLE 14-2**
**Emergency Care for the Rape Victim**

Attention to psychological needs

Care of wounds

Notification of police

Emotional support during police questioning

Medication as ordered

Obtaining nail and hair samples

Clear explanation of prodedures

Contacting victim advocate program

Referrals

Follow-up

The police must be notified at once. They will question the victim in the emergency room. The victim needs emotional support during this questioning as it is often a traumatic experience for her. The need for sedation must be carefully evaluated. Wounds must be dressed. Medication may be given to prevent pregnancy and venereal disease. Pregnancy seldom results from rape. (Scientists suspect that the hormonal balance of the victim is upset by the rape, thus preventing conception.)

Rape kits are now available in many emergency rooms. These kits contain materials to collect date necessary to detect the presence of sperm. The emergency staff must be careful about collecting and handling evidence. Clippings of fingernails and combings of pubic hair might be compared by the police to the skin and hair samples of a possible suspect. It is extremely important that the victim understand each procedure and the reason for it. No one other than the doctor, nurse, and police are allowed access to the evidence. All slides and smears must be protected.

If there is a victim advocate program in the area, the staff there should be contacted. Someone from the program will usually come to the emergency room to provide support for the victim. Later, someone from the program visits the woman for counseling and referral.

The nurse should be aware of the sociological aspects of rape. The attacker is usually a person with a strong hostility toward women. He has the need to control by sexually dominating a woman. Many rapists have difficulty with erection or ejaculation. Rape may give the man a senses of power, and he feels that power will ensure potency. Rape inflicts a feeling of loss upon the victim. The woman develops a wide range of feelings— anger, mistrust, and anxiety. Internalized rage can lead to depression. The nurse should anticipate the victim's grief due to degradation of self.

It is important to note that the victim may not receive loving and supportive responses from significant persons in her life. Some husbands or fiancees may withdraw from the woman. Others reject the woman, using a blaming statement such as, "Things like this just don't happen to good girls." Even family members may ask questions such as, "Why did you walk alone in the dark?" "Couldn't you have screamed louder?" or "Didn't you fight back?" The nurse needs to recognize that significant others may need to ventilate their feelings as they search for a rational explanation for such violent behavior. Rape victims and their significant others suffer a traumatic disruption of their life-style. Counseling may be necessary for the woman, spouse, and family. The long-term goal is for the woman to return to independent functioning in all phases of her life.

## INCEST

There is very little information in medical literature concerning the practice of incest. Incest is defined as sexual relationships between blood relatives. These relationships may involve father and daughter, mother and son, or brother and sister. The sexual relationship may include foreplay, caressing, kissing, or mutual masturbation. Incest usually refers to sexual intercourse in which there is penetration of the vagina by the penis. This experience can be a very traumatic one for young children and adolescents. It may predispose them to sexual maladjustments or psychological problems such as phobias, depressive reactions, and chemical dependency. The literature estimates that 250,000 children are molested yet we know that this problem crosses all cultures and all socio-economic strata. Incest cannot be stereotyped. Increased media coverage of this issue has increased public awareness and concern.

## MASTURBATION

Masturbation is manipulation, by fondling or touching, of one's own genital area for sexual gratification. Although masturbation is considered normal, there are many cultural taboos forbidding the practice. Some people at a young age are warned by a parent that masturbation leads to serious illness, even insanity. People masturbate to meet their own needs.

The nurse may come upon a patient who is openly masturbating. The best approach is to leave the patient and then provide privacy. The nurse should be prepared for the possibility of such a situation occurring in all age groups. In the hospital environment, this behavior may be a response to sensory deprivation. *Sensory deprivation* is a lower level of sensory input than what that individual requires in order to function at an optimal level. The nurse can intervene by offering a variety of stimulation, such as a radio or television. Music enhances sensory awareness. Personal contact with other people is very therapeutic. The nurse should discover the patient's interests and provide pictures, posters, or books about those subjects.

## HOMOSEXUALITY

Homosexuality is engaging in sexual relations with a person of the same sex. The term gay usually refers to a man whose sexual desire is directed toward men only. The term lesbian refers to a woman whose sexual desire is directed toward women only. The American Psychiatric Association has stated that it no longer considers homosexuality a mental disorder. Some people experience a strong, yet irrational fear of their own homosexual feelings and do not seek out a professional counselor to work out these issues. Instead they speak in a disparaging manner about those who seek a variation in sexual expression.

It is a myth that all homosexuals are promiscuous. They are not all unhappy, guilt-ridden individuals. Some have committed themselves to lasting effective relationships. Homosexuals are now working toward understanding and acceptance through a movement called Gay Liberation.

## ACQUIRED IMMUNODEFICIENCY SYNDROME (AIDS)

In the past 12 years, a new and serious challenge for the health profession has become the AIDS and HIV-infected patient. The Center for Disease Control in Atlanta estimates that 1.5 million people are infected with the HIV virus. Many of these people will develop AIDS and ARC (AIDS-related complex). Although there have been medications developed to slow the disease process, AIDS is fatal; there is no cure. All are at risk. Higher risk populations are the male homosexuals and the intravenous drug users (IVDU). IVDU are shooting drugs, sharing and reusing needles, and frequently using other drugs; i.e., alcohol, amphetamines, marijuana in combination with cocaine, crack, or heroin. Judgment is impaired and risky sexual behaviors are practiced. Public hysteria has caused much media coverage and this has generated increased public education for safe sex practices. Safe sex is sex with the use of a latex condom with a germicidal gel (oxy-9). In reality, safe sex minimizes your chances of contacting the HIV virus by contact with semen, blood, or vaginal cervical secretions. However, one is always at risk. Sweat, tears, and urine do not transmit the HIV virus. As life is prolonged with new drugs, and more long-term facilities will be treating PWA's (Persons with AIDS). Inpatient pschiatric units will admit patients with the psychiatric complications of AIDS: stress responses, depression with suicidal ideation, and organic and/or delusional syndromes. Problems will exist in providing care for these patients. Universal precautions need to be strictly followed and enforced by facilities and by the Occupational, Safety and Health Administration (OSHA). Areas of concern include: needle disposal, disposal of certain contaminated equipment and linens, blood spills, and securing protective barrier equipment. For the staff, education programs must include discussion of stigmatization and information concerning transmission. Health care providers express fear of infection and many will relate pressure from their families and friends to actually change jobs. Support groups that allow verbalization of these fears are important and will decrease the incidence of burnout with its emotional exhaustion and job dissatisfaction.

The professional will have to develop ease at sexual counseling as explicit questions may be asked and changes in sexual behavior may need to be recommended.

Currently, respite care programs are providing relief to families caring for loved ones with these special needs. Respite care gives a family member a break from the 24-hour-a-day job and much needed time-out. There are AIDS counseling, testing sites, and AIDS hotlines. Free anonymous testing is available. Literature is geared specifically toward cultural communities—black and Hispanic. Remember the AIDS patient lives in a world of uncertainty because he/she does not know when the time bomb might explode and an opportunistic infection set in. They are dealing with a terminal disease process and multiple losses; employment, the right to privacy, intimate relationships, questionable insurance benefits, and eventually the loss of life, itself. We need to deal with our own strong reactions in order to approach the patient with care and compassion and not with fear or prejudice.

## ABORTION

Abortion is a very controversial issue. The nurse may be assigned to the patient undergoing an abortion either before or after the procedure. A nurse who is assigned to care for the patient who has undergone an abortion may need to explore her own feelings and values about abortion. Some nurses who oppose the procedure have a great deal of difficulty relating to such patients. The abortion patient should be viewed by the nurse as a person who needs health care. Refusal to give care has been tested in some courts. Nurses who refuse to give care may, in some states, jeopardize their own jobs.

There are many reasons for choosing abortion. Each patient is unique, but the decision is seldom easy. Some women who undergo abortion have little choice, since it may be a therapeutic necessity. The abortion may be necessary in order to preserve the life of the mother. Before an abortion is performed, the pregnant woman should receive counseling. Counseling should help the woman voice her concerns. A counselor will help her to understand the pros, cons, and alternatives to abortion, and the types of abortion need to be explained.

The patient who has an abortion frequently experiences loneliness, depression, and alienation. She needs the understanding, acceptance, and caring of the staff. Postabortion care is important. The nurse may need to explain contraceptive methods. A follow-up visit to a doctor or psychologist if emotional problems develop is essential.

## SUMMARY

The concept of human sexuality must be considered when caring for the whole person. Sex is not just an isolated activity; it includes identity, social role, and physical functioning. The nurse should become knowledgeable in discussing human sexuality.

Illness may affect sexual functioning. Patients may be worried about intercourse or reproductive ability. Usually the patient's concerns are broad and encompass the total relationship with the sexual partner. The nurse who deals with sexual problems must be objective, sensitive, and empathetic.

Some medical conditions may have a direct effect on the patient's sexual functioning. These conditions include cardiac conditions, diabetes, arthritis, spinal cord injuries, and hypertension. These conditions can alter the patient's strength, range of motion, sexual desire, and body image. Counseling and help with problem solving are important aspects of nursing care.

Surgical procedures can represent a threat to the patient's self-image. Patients having ostomy or a hysterectomy, mastectomy, or prostatectomy are in need of special help. These procedures alter the body image and may make the person feel undesirable.

It is important for nurses to re-evaluate their ideas concerning sex and the aged. Sexual closeness is a realistic need of the elderly. A sympathetic nurse who recognizes this need can help the elderly to a fuller and more satisfying life.

Some patients evoke negative reactions from the nurse. A nurse who feels fearful or uncomfortable in caring for a patient must clarify her own feelings and values. The nurse should accept the patient as a person who needs her help and a great deal of psychological support.

## SUGGESTED ACTIVITIES

- Find out what information sex education programs in your community have to offer patients with particular problems.
- Write for literature from:

    Reach for Recovery
    American Cancer Society
    777 Third Avenue
    New York, New York

- Role play the following:

    a. Counseling a man, age thirty-five, who has suffered a myocardial infarction, to consider his sexual functioning. The nurse is twenty years old and unmarried.

    b. Counseling an arthritic woman age thirty-five, concerning her sexual functioning.

    c. Counseling a young black woman who has recently discovered her husband is an intravenous drug user.

## REVIEW

A. Multiple choice. Select the best answer.

1. When the cardiac patient expresses concern about sexual intercourse, the nurse should advise the patient to
   1. refrain from sexual activity for six to eight months.
   2. consider alternate means of sexual pleasure.
   3. check with the doctor, but sexual activity does not usually put
      added strain on the heart.
   4. avoid discussing the subject.
      a. 1, 2
      b. 2
      c. 3
      d. 3, 4

2. If a diabetic patient mentions he does not feel like a man, the nurse
   should:
   1. assume he is talking about intercourse and refer him for counseling.
   2. discuss alternate means of obtaining sexual pleasure.
   3. tell him it is only temporary.
   4. encourage more discussion about his feelings.
      a. 1
      b. 2, 3
      c. 4
      d. 2, 4

3. The sexual problems of the arthritic patient usually concern
   a. immobility of the joints.
   b. dyspareunia.
   c. impotence.
   d. retrograde ejaculation.

4. The victim of spinal cord damage can function sexually
   a. as a passive partner.
   b. by avoiding the issue.
   c. using alternative techniques to intercourse.
   d. none of the above.

5. A patient who has had a mastectomy states that her husband will
   probably divorce her now. The nurse should
   a. advise her to wear a bra under her nightgown.
   b. suggest that she discuss this with her husband.

c. encourage her to express her fears.

d. refer her for psychiatric counseling.

6. Which of the following statements is true?

a. Impotence is only psychological in nature.

b. Masturbation is an abnormal activity.

c. Incest is not a problem in our culture.

d. Sexuality includes a person's value system and philosophy of life.

7. When caring for an AIDS patient, the nurse:

a. uses good handwashing techniques.

b. shows empathy.

c. assists with the grieving process.

d. all of the above.

B. Briefly answer the following:

1. Name three medical problems that may affect the patient's sexual functioning.

2. List three surgical procedures that the patient may view as a threat to sexuality.

3. Name three aspects of sexuality.

4. State the possible meaning of rape to the:

a. attacker

b. victim

c. victim's spouse/partner

d. victim's family

5. Name four psychosexual disorders

6. Discuss safe sex and the use of alcohol and drugs

## BOOKS

Briere, J *Therapy for Adults Molested Children: Beyond Survival.* Springer Pub.: N.Y., 1989.

Fromer. M.J. *Aids: Acquired Immune Deficiency Syndrome.* Pinnacle Books: N.Y., 1983.

Kaplan, H.S. *The New Sex Therapy.* Bruner-Mazel: N.Y., 1974.

## ARTICLES

Aruffo, J.K. et al. Knowledge about AIDS among women psychiatric patients. *Hospital & Community Psychiatry* 41(3): 326-328, Mar. 1990.

Baer, J.W., et al. Challenges in developing an inpatient psychiatric program for patients with AIDS and ARC. *Hospital & Community Psychiatry* 38: 1299-1303, 1987.

Cohen, J.A. Sexual counseling of the patient following a myocardial infarction. *Critical Care Nurse* 6: 18-26, 1986.

Davidhizar, R. et al. Teaching safer sex in a long-term psychiatric setting. *Perspectives in Psychiatric Care* 27(1): 25-30, Nov. 1, 1991.

Greenfield, M. Disclosing incest: the relationship that makes it possible. *Journal of Psychiatric Nursing and Mental Health Services* 18(7): 20-23, 32-33, July 1990.

Gwartley, D.L. et al. PWAs in the long-term facility attitudes, policies, and preparations. *AIDS Patient Care* 6(1): 18, Feb. 1992.

Hatchett, D. The Impact of AIDS on the black community. *Crisis*, 97(9): 28-30, Nov 1990.

Jacobs, P. & Bobeck, S. Sexual needs of the schizophrenic client. *Perspectives in Psychiatric Care* 27(1): 15-21, Nov. 1, 1991.

Kernberg, O.F. Mature love: prerequisite and characteristics. *Journal of American Psychoanalysis* 22: 743-768, 174.

Manley, G. Diabetes and sexual health. *The Diabetes Educator* 12: 366-369, 1986.

Martin, H. The coming-out process for homosexuals. *Hospital & Community Psychiatry* 42(2): 158-162, Feb. 1991.

Martin, C.E. Factors affecting sexual functioning in 60-79 year olds. *Archives Sexual Behavior* 10: 399-403, 1981.

Perry, J.W. & Markowitz, J. Psychiatric intervention for AIDS spectrum disorders. *Hospital & Community Psychiatry* 17: 1001-1106, 1986.

Polk-Warner, G.C. Treatment of AIDS in a psychiatric setting. *Perspectives in Psychiatric Nursing* 25(2): 9-13, Mar. 1990.

Renshaw, D.C. Sexuality: making adjustments for illness, disability and age. *Consultant*: 81-107, 1986.

Sacks, M.H., et al. HIV-related risk factors in acute psychiatric inpatients. *Hospital & Community Psychiatry* 41(4): 449-451, Apr. 1990.

Silbert, D.T. Human sexuality growth groups. *Journal Psychiatric and Mental Health Services*, 19(2): 31-34, 1981.

Swanson, B., et al. Dementia and depression in persons with AIDS: causes and care. *Journal of Psychiatric Nursing and Mental Services* 28(10): 33-41, Oct. 1990.

Wasow, M. Sexuality and the institutionalized mentally ill. *Sexuality and Disability* 3(1): 3-16, 1980.

————— Psychiatric support for AIDS sufferers. *Nursing Times* 86(27): 65-67, Jul. 4-10, 1990.

————— The hospitalized AIDS patient and the psychiatric liaison nurse. *Archives of Psychiatric Nursing* 2(1): 35-39, Feb. 1988.

————— The uneven odds—minorities are afflicted with AIDS in significantly dispropriate numbers. *US News & World Report*: 31-34, Aug. 17, 1987.

# CHAPTER 15
# GRIEVING AND PAIN

## OBJECTIVES

After studying this chapter, the student should be able to:

- Identify stages of the grief process.
- State ways the nurse can help the dying patient and his family through the grief process.
- State the importance of completing the grief process.
- State three reasons why children need added help to cope with death.
- Name three concerns of the dying patient.
- State ways the nurse can help the patient cope with pain.
- List the objectives of the hospice program.

Grieving is a major stressor that most people experience at some time in their lives. Many people experience difficulty working through loss and grieving. Grief occurs after many different types of losses: divorce, loss of a job, amputation of a limb, or loss of a loved one. Special circumstances can affect the grieving; i.e., death of a child, mourning and dying teen-ager, widowhood in early life, death after a lingering illness, and long vigils at the bedside of a friend with an advanced state of AIDS. Throughout the life span, there are loss experiences. The grief process must be successfully coped with and completed for good mental health. If the individual is unable to do so, anxiety and depression may result. People usually need help in completing the grief process. Since many loved ones die in hospitals, the function of helping the family becomes a responsibility of the nurse. To help the patient and family cope with impending death, the nurse must first be aware of her own feelings about death. Some questions the nurse may ask herself to determine her attitudes about death are found in Figure 15-1.

1. Does a dying patient make me very uncomfortable?
2. Do I have difficulty controlling my feelings when I know a patient is dying?
3. Am I afraid of dying because I fear the unknown?
4. Should children be shielded from death?
5. Does being with someone who is dying frighten me?
6. Is pain the most difficult part of dying?
7. Do I believe that death is the end, and there is nothing more?
8. If a person has lived a good life, should he fear death?
9. Should time be spent on the dying patient when there is nothing more that can be done?
10. Is taking care of a dying patient satisfying?

Fig. 15-1 Questions the nurse may ask herself to determine her attitudes about death.

Years ago, death was considered a natural phenomena. An elderly family member became very ill and was cared for in the home. When death came, the viewing (wake) was also held at the home. Dying was a familiar and accepted sight. Fear was not associated with death. Today, was have moved dying to hospitals and wakes to funeral homes. We have become uncomfortable with the thought of death. Our present life styles effectively shield us from the finality of death. Phrases such as "now that she's gone" or, as nurses frequently state, "He's terminated," avoid actually verbalizing death.

Death has become a controversial issue of the 1990s. Natural death occurs as a natural response (inevitable) to aging or a disease process. However, much discussion now evolves around euthanasia and mercy killing. Euthanasia is the withdrawal of therapeutic means and death occurs. Mercy killing is an act of taking another's life. Debates have occurred in hospital settings over criteria and ethical issues surrounding DNR (do not resuscitate) orders for terminal patients. A document called a Living Will has evolved. In a Living Will a person gives direction about the use of life-prolonging medical procedures. The statement usually reads that no heroic or artificial means are to be taken in the event of terminal illness.

Reactions to death are influenced by cultural and religious beliefs. The nurse is conditioned by her own background and her own experiences with the deaths of others. Nurses who have come to terms with the thought of their own deaths are better able to help the dying patient. Some nurse tend to ignore the dying person because they do not know what to say. This is made more difficult when the patient has not been told about the prognosis.

Nurses are taught that one of their goals is to save lives. In spite of what is done for the patient this goal cannot always be met. Because of this, some nurses feel anger; others become discouraged or depressed. In working with the dying patient, the nurse must set different goals. Satisfaction must come from knowing that the patient has been helped to a more peaceful death and that needed support, care, and attention to the patient and family have been given.

## THE GRIEF PROCESS

*Grief* is the process of coping with a loss. The loss may be one's own imminent death, the death of a loved one, or the loss of a limb, prized object, or image. The grief process must be completed, Figure 15-2. A person who is unable to complete the grief process often has difficulty coping with the simple stressors of living.

Fig. 15-2 The grief process must be completed.

Families of servicemen killed overseas sometimes experienced anxiety until the bodies were returned. Even though it may have taken years, the grief process continued until the family could see to the burial themselves. Mothers who have stillborns or who place their infants for adoption without contact with them often have anxiety and guilt feelings for the rest of their lives. They are unable to complete the mourning process because they were never allowed to see and touch their infants.

It is always difficult to decide if a patient should be told he is dying. Some doctors and families request that the patient not be told. They feel the individual will not be able to cope with the truth. Some patients do respond by giving up. They become so overwhelmed by fears that they cut off all stimuli and become unfeeling. They cooperate but no longer care. Other patients who are told that they are dying choose to discuss their deaths openly. They struggle with their feelings and fears, but continue to participate actively and to maintain control over their lives.

Nurses may find that patients suspect their prognosis even if they have not been told. Patients recognize nonverbal cues. They can also feel the changes occurring in their bodies. It may be very difficult to care for a patient who has not been told of his diagnosis or prognosis. Because death is unspoken, there is no sharing of grief. The patient, the family, and the nurse all grieve alone.

According to Kyes and Holfing, the grieving survivors of the deceased adjust to the loss in gradual steps.

- Total preoccupation with the deceased. This preoccupation may last three months. It includes normal grieving behavior.
- A period of redistribution of emotions. There is a marked detachment from the deceased, with a gradual letting go of emotional ties. Much of the bereaved person's time may be spent with projects or organization.
- A period of gradual reattachment of emotional ties to an activity or to significant others. The grief process is completed and the loss have been accepted.

Most people need assistance to complete the grief process. The nurse needs to understand and respect the importance of grieving for herself and others. To avoid feeling of isolation and abandonment, people experiencing grief need outlets and emotional support. Some people need to cry; others feel better by shouting. Emotional stability may be supported by religious faith. A social network of family and friends with whom problems can be discussed and possible solutions verbalized is an important facet of the grief process. As the reality of death penetrates, this sharing network helps the grieving person attain security, self-confidence, and a sense of well-being. Without a sharing network, a person can become detached and unfeeling because of emotional depletion. Many people express a feeling of numbness. Nurses who work with the terminally ill need to establish support groups so communication networks are open to them on a daily basis.

## Stages of the Grief Process

Dr. Elisabeth Kubler-Ross describes five stages in the grief process, when a person knows he is dying. Although not absolute, the stages serve as a basis for understanding the process. The stages are denial, anger, bargaining, depression, and acceptance, Table 15-1. A person may experience all five stages in rapid succession. He may move back and forth between stages or remain for some time within a single stage. Stages should be recognized, but never rushed.

### TABLE 15-1
### Nursing Interventions for the Stages of Grief

| STAGE | INTERVENTION |
| --- | --- |
| Denial | Use reflective responses. |
| Anger | Give understanding and support; listen. Meet needs and requests immediately. |
| Bargaining | Act upoon requests, if possible; listen. |
| Depression | Avoid reassuring clichés. Demonstrate caring |
| Acceptance | Remain close to the patient. |

**Denial**. Denial begins when the person is made aware that he is going to die. Initially, there is shock. The person feels numb. He is unable to allow the information to be processed further. Lather, he begins to deny the information. He may state, "This isn't happening to me" or "Doctors have been wrong before." The patient may turn to quackery that promises a cure, or look for another doctor.

When a patient is in the denial stage, he knows he is dying. He does not want confirmation. It would not help for the nurse to say, "Yes, I am afraid you are dying" or "I'm awfully sorry." It also does not help to say,

"No, you are not going to die." Instead, the nurse might reflect the statement, e.g., "Do you think you are?" or "You must be pretty frightened." Patients' statements such as, "I can't have cancer; I'm too healthy" or "I'm too young to die" may be indications of denial. As health deteriorates, denial becomes more difficult.

**Anger.** Eventually, the patient is no longer able to deny the fact that he is dying. He then becomes angry. The patient is desperate because he realized he is losing his hold on life and is fearful of what is to happen to him. He is frustrated because he cannot change events. His anxiety and frustration are turned into anger toward anyone around him. Even small added stressors are difficult to handle.

When the patient becomes angry, he may lash out at the nurse by saying, "It's all your fault. You made me sign for that biopsy and now the found I have a malignancy." The nurse must understand the source of the anger. The patient requires understanding and support. His needs and requests must be met immediately because he cannot handle added stressors. The nurse must take time to listen to his frustrations. The patient should be allowed and encouraged to vent his anger. Attempts should be made to convince him that his anger is acceptable.

**Bargaining.** During the third stage, the person accepts the fact that he is dying but bargains for more time. He may bargain with God or with the staff. "God, if you will let me live just a little longer, I will donate all my money to the church" or "You have to let me go home to finish this task before I die." The requests are for more time: "I am ready to die, but not yet."

If it is possible to do as the patient requests, it should be done. If the patient is bargaining with God, the nurse can only listen quietly as the patient attempts to work through this stage.

**Depression.** Depression marks the fourth stage. There is a full realization that death is near. The person is sad because he realizes that he will no longer be able to see his family or friends and that he will not be able to do things that were planned. This is a lonely time for the patient.

The nurse should avoid using reassuring clichés with the depressed patient. There is a real cause for depression and the patient "needs" to be depressed. Things are bad and depression is appropriate. The depressed patient needs to know that someone else cares that he is dying. Touching the patient and even crying in his presence are ways of letting him know the nurse cares.

**Acceptance**. When the person begins to prepare for death, he is in the stage of acceptance. He may complete unfinished business and comfort those he will leave behind. He has accepted the fact that he is to die. Even when the patient has accepted his fate, he is still afraid. He needs someone with him until the end.

Although our lives may not be as rhythmic as the following biblical passage, throughout life we must accept the press of change.

> For everything there is a season, and a time to every purpose under heaven:
> a time to be born and a time to die;
> a time to plant, and a time to pluck up what is planted;
> a time to kill, and a time to heal;
> a time to break down, and a time to build up;
> a time to weep, and a time to laugh;
> a time to mourn, and a time to dance;
> a time to cast away stones, and a time to gather stones together;
> a time to embrace, and a time to refrain from embracing;
> a time to seek, and a time to lose;
> a time to keep, and a time to cast away;
> a time to rend, and a time to sew;
> a time to keep silence, and a time to speak;
> a time to love, and a time to hate;
> a time for war, and a time for peace.
>
> Ecclesiastes 3:-18

## Helping the Family

The family that has lost a loved one goes through the same stages as the grieving patient. If the death is sudden, the grief process begins after the death. If the illness has been long and death has been anticipated, the family may be helped in the grief process before the death actually occurs. Anticipatory grief occurs when one is prepared for the death.

The family should be allowed to help in the care of the patient as much as possible. Becoming involved in the patient's care helps the family members express love. It increases their self-esteem and lessens guilt. Being able to stay with the patient, even during the night, helps the patient and the family. The nurse must be watchful that the family is not overtaxed as fatigue lessens the ability to handle stress. The nurse should make the family aware that the patient's hearing is commonly the last sense lost and that even whispering frequently can be heard.

Like the patient, the family members need an opportunity to express their concerns and vent their feelings. Observe for the absence of grief. Some people see tears as weak. Those who repress their emotions may experience physical symptoms, i.e., chest pain, nausea, headaches, and depression. Relatives do not see themselves as the nurse's responsibility, so the nurse must recognize their needs. She must seek them out and encourage communication. The nurse should not say, "Oh, you are so strong." The family member should not feel the need to maintain constant composure. Crying can be a desirable emotional release. Some people have difficulty expressing their grief publicly. The nurse may convey more caring through a gentle touch than through words. The fact that the nurse cares is important to the family.

After the death of a loved one, the family members need comfort and guidance. There are immediate decisions that can be difficult such as a possible autopsy or locating the name of a mortician. Telephone calls need to be made and the family's privacy maintained. If family members are extremely distraught, it may be necessary to arrange for transportation home. Optimally, a follow-up call is made to the family within the next few weeks. Encourage the family member to reminisce, and verbalize feelings, and remind them that anniversary times and holidays can reactivate grief feelings. Planning time with family and other supportive people can be helpful.

Children need added help to cope with the death of a loved one. Parents tend to shield their children from death. The more parents avoid talking about it, the more children fear it. When children are told about death, they are usually not told the truth. Statements such as "Daddy has gone to sleep," "God has taken Mommy away," or "Aunt Liz has gone on a long trip" confuse the child.

Children need special attention because they need a concept of death in order to grieve. Most children do not understand the finality of death. The young child has difficulty differentiating death from sleep. Children are often forgotten as the adult members work through their own grief. A child needs open, relaxed communication concerning death. Many excellent books explaining the meaning of death are available for children. These books help to open further discussion about death.

## The Dying Child

Society tends to protect children even from their own deaths. When children are seriously ill, they may not be told the seriousness of their illness. However, nurses who work with these children say that children, like adults, sense the truth. Many seem to want open communication. Secrecy is an added burden; it means the child must die alone without the support of his family.

The death of a child is not easily accepted in American society. For this reason, it is much more difficult for family members to watch a young person die. Children withdraw from their parents in the latter stages of the death process. This is difficult for parents to understand and they often see it as rejection. It is really the child's attempt to let go. Parents fear the suffering of their child even more than death. They feel guilty in not being able to relieve pain.

The nurse must consider the child's concept of death. The toddler usually has none. He may hurt and feel anxiety about his pain, but has no idea of what is happening to him. The preschooler begins to consider death. It may be a long journey, going to sleep, or going to heaven. His concept depends on what he has heard about death. He does not understand it. This child has a great deal of faith in his parents. He looks to them to solve all problems. He tells himself that his parents will see that he gets better.

To the school-aged child, death becomes more permanent. He seems to be more concerned with death and violence. Death is more frightening to this age group. There may be a concept of the soul leaving the body. There is often a fear of what will happen to the body. There is fear of being abandoned and alone.

The preteen is frightened at the thought of death. Unable to cope with the fears, he may joke, tell ghost stories, or act brave. The preteen's fear also seems mostly concerned about what happens to the body when it is buried. The adolescent seems to have a need to prove his immortality. He seems to take risks just to prove that death cannot take him. The adolescent needs open, relaxed communication networks.

The dying child must go through the same grief process as the adult. The ease with which he goes through this process depends on many factors. Some of these factors are his concept of death, his religious beliefs, and his family's support. The child's desire to voice his fears should be encouraged. He should be given as much information as possible. He should be allowed the amount of activity he wants, even though he may not seem capable of handling it.

Children are sometimes taken home to die. This seems like an added burden on the family, but it actually helps the family in the grief process.

The family seems better able to cope with the death if the child has died within the family unit. They know they have done all that is possible for him.

## NURSING INTERVENTIONS

The most frequently voiced concerns of the dying are pain, isolation, and the fear of the unknown. The dying person should be made as physically comfortable as possible. Physical comfort can be offered through oral hygiene, repositioning every two hours, and good skin care. Hair and nail care, shaving, shampooing, and applying makeup contribute to a sense of well-being. The nurse's touch conveys caring. A steady, smooth touch is therapeutic; jerky movements should be avoided. The nurse's goal is to maintain the patient's optimum level of functioning, comfort, and dignity until the time of death. This called *palliative care*.

Fear of the unknown is common in most people. One cannot adequately prepare for the unknown. Ideally, the dying person should never be left alone. Family and close friends should be encouraged to stay with him. The nurse should plan time for extended visits to the patient. A satisfying and productive interaction is very comforting. Frequently, the patient enjoys reminiscing. The nurse can facilitate this review of his life.

Spiritual needs should be considered. The nurse can offer to call the chaplain, priest, minister, or rabbi. Some patients find comfort in prayer or bible reading. The nurse should ask the patient if he would like her to pray or read to him. Expressions of human need can be found in scripture. The psalms of the Old Testament of the Bible can be an excellent source of comfort.

A new method of offering skilled, compassionate care for the dying patient is the hospice movement. Hospice means refuge. The hospice may be a facility in the hospital or may be a home care program. The goals of the hospice movement are to increase the dying patient's quality of life, to develop pain-control methods, and to help the family actively participate in the patient's care. Hospice services are available twenty-four hours a day. An awareness of the grief process is shared by the surviving family.

## THE CONCEPT OF PAIN

Pain is a subjective sensation ranging in intensity from mild discomfort to intolerable agony. Pain is a private experience. It is experienced by the individual; only its effects can be seen by the observer. Effects of pain are both physical and psychological in nature. The primary purpose of pain is protection. It serves as a warning that tissue damage is taking place in the body.

Pain is caused by stimulation of special nerve endings. A stimulus is picked up by the nerve endings and transmitted to the brain, where it is interpreted. The brain's interpretation of the stimulus depends on many factors, including prior conditioning concerning acceptable responses to pain. Previous experiences with pain, fatigue, and the state of health of the patient are contributing factors.

People learn about pain from families and experiences. They learn which stimuli to call pain, which to call discomfort, and which to call annoyance. They learn what are acceptable responses to pain in their culture. Prior experiences also teach people how to cope with pain. Perception and interpretation of pain vary with different individuals and even within the same individual. What is painful at one time may not be painful at another.

Perception and interpretation are affected by anxiety. The more frightened a person is, the more he is apt to interpret stimuli as pain. Anxiety leads to tension. Muscle tension results in fatigue. When a person is tired, he more apt to interpret a stimulus as pain. The ability to cope is also an important influence. The more stressors the person has, the more pain he feels. To ignore pain is inexcusable. Whether or not pain has a physiological basis, the pain is real to the patient who has it and should be accepted by the nurse.

## The Child and Pain

The small child's perception of pain is often confused; he does not understand it. His reactions are as varied as those of the adult. Some children rock rhythmically. Others become hostile and aggressive; many do not cry. Some children are restless and some quietly deny their pain. Anxiety and pain seem to be confused in the child's mind. Fear is often felt as pain. Pain is increased by anxiety. Many children confuse pain with dying.

The adolescent is struggling for independence. He sees pain as a hindrance to that independence. Pain is something he cannot control.

A loss also may be experienced as pain. The loss may be a loss of privacy, self-control, or a personal relationship. the child in pain must cope with these losses. At the same time, he must cope with the uncertainty that accompanies pain.

To help the child in pain, the nurse must know the meaning of pain to that child. Separation from parents increases anxiety. Feeling abandoned or unloved increases pain. Measures to relieve anxiety should be employed. Massages, warm baths, and relaxation exercises help relieve tension. Storytelling helps distract the small child. The nurse must be warm, understanding, and caring if she is to help the child who is in pain.

## Pain Medication

Appropriate medication should be given promptly for pain. Pain medications should be ordered every four hours and not given upon patient request (prn). Many patients refrain from asking for the medication until the pain has become severe. In caring for the terminally ill, the possibility of addiction should not be a priority. Frequently, morphine is ordered every four hours. A phenothiazine tranquilizer may be given for anxiety or a tricyclic antidepressant for depression. If morphine is to be used for an extended period of time, a bowel softener such as Peri-Colase is ordered. A preparation now being used successful for pain control is Brompton's Mixture of Brompton's Cocktail. It is an oral narcotic with the following constituents: diamorphine, cocaine elixir, and an aromatic elixir. Brompton's is given every four hours or as ordered around the clock. Initially, the patient is very drowsy, but in approximately three days this effect is diminished.

## Nursing Intervention

Realizing that the person is in pain is the first step in helping. Observation and listening are essential. Because of prior conditioning the patient may not be able to complain of pain; he may feel that it is a sign of weakness. This patient feels he must cope in silence. This type of person expresses pain in nonverbal ways. Restlessness, increased pulse rate, withdrawal, sadness, grimacing, and clenched fists are some of the signs of pain. The patient's statement, "Nurse, I have terrible pain," should be believed.

Many things can be done to relieve pain. The nurse should check for tight dressings, wrinkled sheets, and uncomfortable positioning. If the pain is mild or moderate, distraction methods can be used. Distraction focuses the patient's attention and concentration on other stimuli and prevents concentration on pain. Backrubs and repositioning can be effective.

Music, reading, or a hobby are other diversional activities. If medication is given, it is helpful for the nurse to say to the patient, "Mr. Jones, I have something to give you for your pain."

Methods used to relieve anxiety also can be used to relieve pain. When the reason for the pain is unknown, anxiety is increased. The more severe the anxiety, the more difficult it is for the patient to cope with pain. Relaxation techniques and emotional support lessen anxiety and increase the patient's ability to cope. Acknowledging that the patient has pain and allowing him to voice his frustrations may be helpful. The nurse should reinforce the fact that she will protect him from unnecessary pain, Table 15-2.

Sensory overload can accentuate pain. Lessening the number of stimuli the patient must handle may also help to relieve pain. A quiet room, soothing bath, and dimmed lights all help contribute to a restful atmosphere. It is important for the nurse to communicate her caring to the patient. The nurse's touch, attentive look, and genuine concern give support to the patient. The nurse should take time to sit with the patient experiencing pain; he may need to verbalize feelings of sadness, anger, frustration, or loneliness.

### TABLE 15-2
### Coping with Pain

| RELAXATION TECHNIQUES | EMOTIONAL SUPPORT |
|---|---|
| lessening of stimuli | gentle touch |
| quiet room | attentive look |
| soothing bath | genuine concern |
| dim lights | encourage verbalization |
| distraction activities | conversation |
| position change | communicate caring |

## Care Providers

On units where death, dying, and pain are everyday experiences, special attention must be given to the care providers. As the care provider offers comfort and strength to patients and families, they may begin to recognize feelings of hopelessness and helplessness within themselves. Watch that the care providers are not reverting to "couch potatoes" on their days off, with decreased contact with friends and family. Care providers are survivors, and hospitals, hospice centers, etc. would do well to provide them with support groups so they can express their grief and address their anger, depression, and sense of failure.

## SUMMARY

Grieving is a major stressor that most people experience at some time in their lives. If it is not successfully completed, anxiety and depression may result. Reactions to death are influenced by cultural and religious beliefs, background, and experience with death. Dr. Kubler-Ross describes five stages of grief: denial, anger, bargaining, depression, and acceptance.

Pain and isolation are two concerns of the dying. The dying person should be made as comfortable as possible and never left alone. The family of the dying patient also needs the support of the nurse. As the family members do not feel they are the nurse's responsibility, the nurse usually must seek them out and encourage communication. Children need added help to cope with death as their concept of death is often confused.

Pain is a subjective sensation that ranges in intensity from mild discomfort to intolerable agony. Effects of pain are both physical and emotional. Perception and interpretation of pain vary with different individuals and even within the same individual. Anxiety and fatigue increase pain. The nurse needs to observe for nonverbal signs of pain. Both emotional measures and medication can be used to relieve pain. When pain cannot be relieved, the patient must be helped to accept the discomfort.

## SUGGESTED ACTIVITIES

- Think about your first experience with death (it may have been an animal, relative, or friend). How did you feel? How did you resolve your feelings?
- Discuss the following questions with your classmates:
  a. Which type of dying patient would you consider that most difficult to care for?
     - a five-year-old with leukemia
     - a mother, age twenty-seven, with two preschool children
     - a retired gentleman, age sixty-eight
  b. Should the dying person be told he is dying?

c. How do you expect to react to your own death? Would you want
to know you are dying?

- Investigate religious beliefs on death by talking to various clergy.

## REVIEW

A.  Multiple choice. Select the best answer.
1.  In order to help a patient cope with death, the nurse must first know
a. the meaning of death.
b. how the patient feels about dying.
c. how the family feels about death.
d. how she herself feels about death.

2.  The dying patient is sometimes ignored because the nurse feels
a. he does not need as much care as other patients.
b. she does not know what to say.
c. time is needed for patients that can be helped.
d. nursing efforts would be wasted.

3.  Grief is the process of
a. coping with loss.
b. feeling sorry for oneself.
c. mourning the dead.
d. depression.

4.  When a patient begins to prepare for death he is probably in the
a. denial stage.
b. bargaining stage.
c. depression stage.
d. acceptance stage.

5.  When a patient asks, "Please doctor, help me to live just one more
year," he is in the
a. shock stage.
b. bargaining stage.
c. depression stage.
d. acceptance stage.

6.  If the patient looks for another doctor, he is probably in the
a. denial stage.
b. bargaining stage.
c. depression stage.
d. acceptance stage.

7. When the dying child withdraws from his parents, it is an indication of
   a. pain.
   b. withdrawal from reality.
   c. rejection of the parents.
   d. an attempt to let go.

8. The patient who says he is in pain although the pain is not physically justified should be
   a. ignored.
   b. believed.
   c. challenged.
   d. treated with placebos.

9. When pain cannot be relieved, the patient should be
   a. given a stronger medication.
   b. given medication more often.
   c. left alone.
   d. helped to accept the discomfort.

B. Briefly answer the following.

1. Name the three reasons children need added help to cope with death.

2. Why is it important for the grief process to be completed?

3. Name three concerns of the dying.

4. What is Brompton's Mixture?

5. List three objectives of the hospice program.

## BOOKS

Burns, N. *Nursing and Cancer.* W.B. Saunders: Phila., 1982.
Hansel, T. *You Gotta Keep Dancin' : in the Midst of Life's Hurts, You Can Choose Joy!* Cook Pub.: Illinois, 1985.
McCaffrewy, M. *Nursing Management of the Patient in Pain.* J.P. Lippincott: Phila., 1979, 2nd ed.

## ARTICLES

Beglinger, J.E. Coping tasks in critical care. *Dimensions of Critical Care*, 2: 80-89, 1983.
Bowlby, J. Attachment and loss: retrospect and prospect. *American Journal of Orthopsychiatry* 52: 644-678, 1982.

Collison, C. & Miller, S. Using images of the future in grief work. *Image* 19(1): 9-12, 1987.

Heiney, S.P. Sibling grief: a case report. *Archives Psychiatric Nursing* V(3): 121-127, June 1991.

Lindemann, E. Symptomatology and the management of acute grief. *American Journal of Psychiatry* 101: 141-148, 1944.

Ross, H.M. Societal/cultural view regarding death and dying. *Topics in Clinical Nursing* -: 1-16, Oct. 1981.

Rubin, S. A two-track model of bereavement. *American Journal of Orthopsychiatry* 51: 101-109, 1981.

Schubert, J. Comparing the grief reactions of a rehabilitation and a psychiatric patient. *Imprint* 37:59, 61-62, Feb.-Mar. 1990.

Steeves, R.H. & Kahn, D.L. Experience of meaning in suffering. *Image* 19: 114-116, 1987.

Stockdale, L. & Hutzenbiler, T. How you can comfort a grieving family. *Nursing Life* 6(3): 22-26, 1982.

Watt-Watson, J. What we need to know about pain. *American Journal of Nursing* 87: 1217-1218, 1987.

Zisook, S. & DeVaul, R.A. Grief, unresolved grief and depression. *Psychosomatics* 24(3): 247-256, March 1983.

# CHAPTER 16
# FACILITATING
# MENTAL HEALTH AND
# RE-ENTRY INTO
# THE COMMUNITY

## OBJECTIVES

After studying this chapter, the student should be able to:

- Name five ways that modern society contributes to mental illness.
- State four stressors that make the poor a high risk for mental illness.
- State how culture affects mental health.
- Name four ways that the family can help to improve the mental health of children.
- List four needs of the patient who is re-entering the community.
- Explain why it is more difficult to establish identity today than it was in the past.

Health is defined by the World Health Organization (WHO) as a state of complete physical, mental, and social well-being. Health is not merely the absence of disease or infirmity. Mental well-being involves functioning with emotional equilibrium in everyday life. People must function adequately within their roles in society. They must adapt to their environment and the environment must continually adapt to their needs—it is an ongoing, continuing process. The stresses of life create problems for individuals and society as a whole. Social, economic, and cultural factors that influence behavior can be complex. The nurse needs to develop a deep understanding and awareness of the complicated network that surrounds each individual's life.

Prevention is the ultimate goal in dealing with the problem of mental illness. In an effort to prevent mental illness, personal happiness and the ability to deal with stress must be enhanced. This is not an easy task in the vastly complex society in which we live today. Modern society has greatly increased the stress which precipitates mental illness. Our world has become impersonal and highly technical. The rapid changes that society is undergoing have contributed to social disorganization, disrupted family units, and disturbed parent–child relationships.

This rapid change in enhanced by the mobility in today's society. Fast travel, new opportunities, and changing jobs move people from place to place on a national and international scale. Each move is a new stress. Adaptation to the new environment includes family, friends, schools, and community resources. Feelings of alienation and loneliness become prevalent as people are separated from loved ones.

Everyone needs significant others in their environment. Hostile feelings can develop when the basic need of belonging is not satisfied by a support system. A significant other may be a parent, husband, wife, teacher, or friend. These significant others accept the individual with his own limitations and strengths and offer encouragement to take responsibility for his own actions. Significant others are the individual's support system; they frequently influence the person's behavior. These people are a necessary part in the creation of autonomous, satisfying lives.

Unemployment is another stress in society. It places a strain on the entire family unit. Long-term unemployment can erode the self-concept. Many who do have jobs are bored with them and feel no sense of pride or accomplishment. They often feel unfulfilled. A feeling of being powerless to control the environment or change events is common. Meaningful work contributes to a sense of well-being. Financial stability enhances personal status.

In an effort to obtain fulfillment, people often turn to materialistic objects. Finding no lasting satisfaction in objects, they constantly strive for bigger and better things—a new car, new home, or expensive jewelry. The constant striving and lack of lasting satisfaction only tends to increase stress and frustration.

Lack of identity is a large problem in today's society. Years ago, America was an agricultural nation. Extended families that included grandparents and relatives usually lived in the same community. There was a closeness and support that is seldom seen today. Children felt confident in their place in society and often worked along with their parents. Today, children usually do not see their fathers or mothers at work and may not know the nature of their occupation.

In the past, children accepted their parent's values and grew into their adult role with little questioning. Today, children are constantly confronted with choices. There is no single way of looking at situations. However, learning to choose from alternatives can give direction to a person's life.

Modern society has brought with it more freedom. Although there are several advantages to this, freedom also increases stress. Life is no longer simple. Families are constantly on the move and, therefore, may become fragmented. Roots are uncertain and support systems may not be readily available. The family and religious and political structures that once provided security have been weakened. One out of every five families is disrupted because of divorce, separation, death, imprisonment, or institutionalization. Even in two-parent families, approximately 75 percent of the mothers work outside the home. Parental employment and youth activities leave little time for family experiences. The child has more freedom, but less help in learning to use it wisely.

Although radio and television broaden the individual's world by exposing him to greater learning and enjoyment, they also expose him to greater stress. Television can be both entertaining and disruptive. Some people watch television to the exclusion of all other experiences. Although television provides an awareness of world difficulties, it may limit family interactions and detract from personal development. Spending absorbing hours before the television set divests people of valuable reading, writing, and talking time.

## CULTURE AND MENTAL HEALTH

Culture is defined as the customary beliefs, values, and ideas held by a racial, religious, or social group of people. There seems to be a correlation between culture and mental health problems. More research is needed to understand why this is so. There is more violence in the ghetto, fewer role conflicts among Mexican-Americans, and a problem of increased alcoholism and suicide among American Indians. If mental illness is to be prevented, consideration must be given to cultural influences. Culture affects an individual's total way of life as customs are passed down from one generation to the next. Culture is a complex phenomenon that is learned through interactions with others.

Cultural differences can cause problems in health care since a person's attitudes toward health and illness are influenced by cultural background. The language of a culture may contain words and phrases that have meaning only to the culture because of background, problems, or interests. This may make communication difficult between groups of different cultures. There are important steps in developing a culturally sensitive practice. Two areas deal with ourselves. Do we have an awareness and acceptance of our own racial/ethnic group? What are our cultural experiences that have impacted on us (as child/adolescent/adult?) A culturally competent person understands the dynamics in the helping process and assist the patient by recognizing the reality of the patient. We adapt our practice skills to fit our patients and not the reverse—our patient is expected to adapt or fit into our mold. Affirming our culturally different patient's problem-solving skills and their survival instincts reflects our caring and gives them power.

The nurse should also be aware of subculture differences. A subculture is an ethnic, regional, economic, or social group having similar behavior patterns that distinguish the group from others within the culture. For example, separating the aged from the rest of society creates a subculture. Singling out and discriminating against an ethnic group is also contributing to the growth of a subculture. People within a subculture interact chiefly among themselves.

Dealing with mental health problems must include a concern for the cultural and subcultural backgrounds of the patient. What may seem to be maladaptive behavior to the nurse may be normal behavior within the patient's subculture (see Table 16-1). The nurse only creates more stress for the patient if she tries to impose her own values on him. She must, instead, be attuned to the patient's expectations, needs, and life style. Empowerment is the keyword. Areas of empowerment include: families and effective support systems, problem solving techniques, communication skills, family rules, and roles. Identifying blocks in their power diminishes feelings of oppression and enhances therapy. The patient feels understood. When appropriate, bicultural and bilingual professionals need to be sought.

## POVERTY AND MENTAL HEALTH

The environment plays an active role in determining stress factors and the individual's ability to cope. There is also a definite correlation between socioeconomic levels and health. A low socioeconomic level often leads to poor nutrition, crowded living conditions, maternal deprivation, and a lack of self-esteem. Mental illness can develop as the person becomes more oppressed and more vulnerable.

**TABLE 16-1**
**Culture Variations**

| | |
|---|---|
| Acculturation | Uncomfortable with own cultural identity |
| | Join dominant culture** |
| Bicultural | Pride in racial identity |
| | Seeks racial diversity |
| | Experiences reflect both cultures |
| | Integrated setting for work and home |
| | Sense of "between cultures" |
| | Result can be pain and discord |
| Culturally immersed | Rejects dominant cultural norms and values |
| | Pro their culture |
| | Attempts to meet all needs in culture** |
| | May blame society for all problems |
| Traditional | Dominant culture is not accepted or rejected |
| | Community is church |

Adapted from the writings of Peter Bell, 1981

** language, music, art, entertainment

The poor are a high risk for mental health problems as they are exposed to many more stressors that the average person, Table 16-2. Their biggest problems concern finances, employment, and social isolation—all of which limit their access to health care. Lack of adequate housing, schools, and available living space, and a high crime rate also contribute to metal health problems. If health care is provided, the clinics may be far from home. Even though health care is often free or inexpensive, there may be no money for transportation and/or baby-sitters. Transportation and baby-sitters may even be unavailable. Seeing a different health care person at each clinic visit only adds to the patient's stress. The questions and paperwork at the clinic may be frustrating and overwhelming.

Lack of stable employment is a particular stress for the poor as it blocks efforts to provide basic needs of food, shelter, and clothing. Many who have tedious, task-oriented jobs become frustrated and bored. There is no sense of pride or accomplishment. Having no power to control the environment or to bring about change can be devastating. Continued frustrations often cause people to withdraw and become apathetic. This is a way of warding off stress, but it is also a cause of added stress. Health care workers often turn away from the apathetic poor because they feel the poor don't really care or want to help themselves. This type of attitude places more stress on the already overburdened person.

**TABLE 16-2**
**Stressors of Poverty**

- Social isolation
- Maternal deprivation
- High crime rate
- Lack of adequate:
  Employment
  Finances
  Housing
  Nutrition
  Schools
  Living space
  Child care
  Health care
  Transportation

The chronic mentally ill (CMI) have severe and persistent symptoms of mental or emotional disability. Recent studies have pointed to a serious problem with the lack of treatment of medical illness in the chronically mentally ill. There is a diminished level of functioning in regard to their daily living skills. Some primary aspects include: personal relations, living arrangements, and work skills. An isolative approach and the avoidance of minimal stresses can enable them to remain in their homes, in the community. The chronic mentally ill are sometimes referred to as the wanderers of our cities who can be characterized as highly impulsive, reactive, and frustrated.

The chronic mentally ill are found housed in many areas: the YW-YMCAs, boarding houses, soup kitchens, bus stations, skid row, and jails. Approximately one-third of nursing home (intermediate and personal care) residents have a psychiatric diagnosis. If the mentally ill person is in a residential housing, what is the quality of the neighborhood? Do the neighbors accept this population of people and are they viewed as contributing to a neighborhood blending? Aren't some of these live-in board and care homes also segregated, removed from the community and there-fore similar to the state hospitals? Before admission to the residential housing, the following data should be collected: is the patient able to maintain personal hygiene and physical activity; shop, cook, and clean; seek out and use public transportation. If we can identify the person's strengths, we can help him cope with his limitations.

In New York state, a project called CLUE (Community Link-Up Experiences) is underway that consistently works with the mentally ill person on the following: job abilities, money management, job seeking, interviewing, and filling out a job application. This approach creates suc-cess experiences for the chronic patient. Social and economic changes have soared the number of homeless in our country . . . approximately 350,000 or a very high 2,000,000 when families and children are included. Innovative programs have begun for the homeless. In Portland, Oregon, an inner city residential facility provides a continuum of medical, psychi-atric, and rehabilitative services in a homelike atmosphere. The Depart-ment of Veterans Affairs has initiated Homeless, Chronically Mentally Ill Veterans Programs to provide aggressive outreach services and on-site assessments and referrals to homeless veterans. The Department of Housing and Urban Development (HUD) supports Shelter-Plus Care. It provides permanent supportive housing for the homeless people who are severely mentally ill, chronic alcohol/drug abusers, or have AIDS. Supportive services are linked to rental assistance through the Affordable Housing ACT, 1990. Supportive care is also matched to culture with con-sideration for traditions, life style, identity, standards, and values.

Some mentally ill people who are living in the community attend day care four days per week. It provides a structured environment, daily group therapy, and educational activities. This program fosters and en-courages noninstitutional living patterns.

In order to pay for and facilitate placement in these areas, the men-tally ill person needs Supplemental Security Income (SSI). SSI is a result of being certified as a person with a psychiatric disability. The applicant must have a specific mental disorder that is expected to last a minimum of twelve months and will result in an inability to work.

## PREVENTION OF MENTAL HEALTH PROBLEMS

Primary prevention of mental health problems is aimed at lessening stress and  developing improved coping mechanisms. Prevention must begin in the family. Studies show that parent–child relationships influence all future relationships. It is through the parent–child relationship that the child develops his self-concept. A higher self-concept is associated with a close family bond that has been established at birth. This bond must be fostered throughout life. Ways must be found to strengthen the family unit and to support family members. Families must see the importance of being together; family discussion and positive interactions increase the self-concept of each member, Figure 16-1.

Fig. 16-1  This family enjoys being together.

Parents are the child's most important teachers. Parents cannot effectively delegate their responsibility to teach the child about himself to anyone else. The family is still the most effective place for strengthening its members. It is within the family that sensitivity to others is learned. Coping mechanisms and values are also acquired within the family. Children need to learn responsibility and to make decisions within the family in order to properly prepare them for adulthood. Children who are given reasons for restrictions are more apt to accept themselves as worthwhile.

Children, like adults, feel frustration, anger, insecurity, and a need to express their feelings, Figure 16-2. They need to know that these feelings are normal and acceptable. Seeing children as people, listening to them, and considering their ideas are new concepts. Talking with children instead of at them is difficult for many parents. Some communities have recognized this difficulty and have instituted programs to help parents communicate with their children.

Many of these programs are based on Thomas Gordon's *Parent Effectiveness Training*. Gordon believes that the child must feel accepted. He teaches parents to listen and hear what the child is saying and to accept the child's feelings. Solutions to problems should not be imposed. Greater growth is accomplished if solutions are mutually sought and agreed upon. A child's problems are important to the child, no matter how insignificant they may seem to others. The child should never be belittled.

Fig. 16-2 Communication between adult and child is important.

Open communication between parent and child at any age is essential. Blocks to communication should be avoided. Openness and honesty are important. Reasons should be given for demands or restrictions. Sometimes a parent cannot compromise and cannot give a reason. In these instances the parent might say, "I may be wrong, but this decision is my responsibility. You will just have to accept it this time." Parents sometimes are under too much stress to cope with a child's problem immediately. The child should be told honestly, "I can't cope with it right now." Sincere honesty does not hurt the child's self-concept. Being honest helps the child to understand. Honesty contributes to a realistic perspective.

Support services for families are available and should be used if needed. These services include crisis counseling, hot lines, drug counseling, suicide prevention centers, abortion and Pro Life counseling, child and family services, family service agencies, and runaway services. Many people do not contact mental health agencies. They feel more comfortable seeking help from family members, the clergy, or friends.

Single parents may require more help, as they must cope with day-to-day problems alone. As problems accumulate and multiply, the person may become more vulnerable. Day-care centers, the Big Brother and Big Sister organizations, and Parents Without Partners are groups that provide support for single parents. These supportive services can cushion the effects of a crisis and help the family feel a part of the community.

A new idea in prevention of mental illness is home care. Mental health workers work with high-risk families by initiating discussions and problem solving in the home. This is thought to be effective because the problems are viewed within the actual home setting. This facilitates working out available alternatives. Positive areas and strengths are reinforced and feedback can be received. By talking through a situation, obstacles that may cause a potential crisis can be more easily seen and thus averted.

Small drop-in facilities have been established throughout the country in such areas as shopping centers, airports, and bus terminals. Individuals can stop by at any time and find an empathetic and receptive listener. Mental health problems require creative solutions

Because the majority of the mentally ill return to their families, family approaches that will attempt to decrease the tremendous physical, mental, and emotional family burden need to be carefully considered. The following approaches can prove to be beneficial: family therapy, interpersonal skill improvement, patient/family education (especially concerning medication regimen and medication monitoring), and home visits by professionals. Major questions are: How do we prevent a family from feeling very depleted? Do we assess all available social supports? Is there an extended family, financial support, religious affiliations, or community contact people? What is the quality of this family's life?

## REHABILITATION

Before re-entry into the community, the patient may need rehabilitation. Rehabilitation is a process that enables an individual to return to the highest level of functioning. Brief stays at intermediate facilities can be helpful. Intermediate facilities include foster homes and halfway houses. The patient needs time to discuss and re-evaluate basic living skills. He must be able to adapt and survive in a new environment and function adequately. If he seeks employment, his ability to file an acceptable application needs to be evaluated. Interviewing techniques should be reviewed. In order to be independent in the activities of daily living, the patient may need assistance with budgeting, shopping, menu planning, and cooking.

Good health habits contribute to vitality. The patient needs to have an adequate diet and exercise. Exercise and relaxation help the person avoid fatigue and are essential components for good mental health. Exercise leads to better physical health and is a way of working out frustration. Relaxation techniques could be demonstrated and practiced. The physically healthy person is better able to handle stress. Adequate sleep is essential. Some people who have suffered a mental health problem escape from stress by sleeping. This is not recommended. Adequate sleep at night with an afternoon nap during the immediate re-entry period is sufficient. Effective use of leisure time is important. Enjoyable activities should be encouraged. Hobbies and interests need to be cultivated, Figure 16-3. Making leisure time productive adds to positive life experiences.

If the patient is capable of being responsible for his own drug therapy, medication instruction should be given. Drug dosage and possible side effects must be explained. Careful compliance to medication times needs to be evaluated. If a family member must administer the medication, teaching sessions need to be scheduled.

The patient and his family should be instructed to watch for overwhelming stressors. Too much stimulation can cause irritability. The individual will probably be better off with limited stimulation for a time after returning home. Each person also requires a certain amount of space for privacy in his environment. However, private moments need to be bal-

Fig. 16-3 A pet can be a special interest for an aging person.

anced with satisfying interactions. Satisfying interactions relieve feelings of loneliness and isolation. Community resources, such as museums, YWCA or YMCA, library, parks, and modes of transportation should be discussed. A brochure that covers these areas of interest in the community, times of availability, modes of transportation, and possible fees is an excellent method of making the patient aware of community resources.

During the rehabilitation phase, employment becomes an issue. We need to recognize that work can add great stress to the lives of the psychiatric patient and they will need adequate support and help with motivation. A wider array of vocational options which consider the variety of skills, personal wishes, and talents of these individuals is needed. Expecting all the mentally ill to engage in the same kind of employment is a denial of their individuality. One must reflect: does the failure of the chronically mentally ill at job sites reflect the restrictiveness of the offerings and the lack of additional provisions for support and motivation? Creative rehabilitation efforts are looking at greater flexibility and new ideas, i.e. shared jobs, shortened work schedules. With increased realistic expectations about what a particular mentally ill person is able to do, a more satisfying experience can result. Rehabilitation should prepare the individual to enter the community as a worthwhile, confident participator.

## RE-ENTRY

A person who had been confined or isolated for a period of time must go through a process called re-entry. This is a difficult process because of stereotyping. Many former patients are regarded as mentally ill or "crazy" the rest of their lives. They are often feared or ignored, which adds to their stress. Returning home can be very stressful. Neighbors and friends often avoid the former patient. They do not know what to say or how to act. This only makes the person's self-concept more negative. Families need assurance that the individual's behavior has changed and that the maladaptive behavior need not return. They should be informed of factors that may have contributed to the problem and how they can help the person cope in the future. Early symptoms of maladaption need to be explained so that early intervention and treatment can be provided. Community reception can be a factor in a return to maladaptive behavior. People who are re-entering need an adequate support system to offset these negative aspects. Hospitalization greatly disrupts the person's life style, and a difficult period of readjustment begins after discharge from the hospital. Lines of communication must be kept open. Communication occurs when talking to a person, not at him. Listening encourages frankness; people feel free to express their fears, insecurities, and disappointments. Social agencies, schools, churches, health care workers, and families need to work together to provide a support system. Professionals in both the private and public sector must be more aware of the full range of available community services and resources.

The person re-entering a community needs an adequate problem-solving approach. The person's problem-solving approach should be evaluated and alternatives discussed. General guidelines for approaching a problem include the following:

1. Place attention on the immediate problem
2. Write down possible solutions.
3. Look at personal strong points.
4. Determine the support system.
5. Choose an appropriate action.
6. Act.

Effective problem solving strengthens coping and adds to the individual's self-confidence and self-acceptance. This helps to make his life more consistent and stable.

If the person is going directly into the home situation, some type of home visit might be needed. The extent of burden on the family extends to many areas. Research points to five (5) specific areas of burden: financial, family routine, leisure, interaction, and the health of other family members. There is a disruption of routine in the family and home and increased arguing over the patient and the patient's irrational demands. A financial burden becomes evident as there is loss of the patient's income, increased expenses of the illness, and dipping into family funds to expand financial needs. Often family members miss important activities (school, work, outings) as they are designated to stay home and "watch" their family member. Fun and play are abandoned or postponed and the family's life becomes more absorbed in the patient. Frequently, families become isolated as friends refuse to drop by or families now are not comfortable entertaining at home. These stressors can have an adverse effect n the physical and mental health of all family members.

Weekly group meetings are sometimes arranged to reinforce new behaviors. Discussion groups can be excellent reinforcers of self-growth. Giving the individual an opportunity to voice his own opinion can increase his sense of confidence and competence. Group therapy can assist in resocialization and allow the patient to test out new behaviors safely. Sharing with others through group therapy helps the person to learn how to cope. It is also a way to develop new friendships and practice new social skills. Adequate support and encouragement help to motivate the patient toward recovery.

Returning to a previous work environment can be stressful. Sometimes fellow workers who pitched in to get the job done during the person's absence resent his return. The former patient is often discriminated against when it comes time for salary increases and promotions. The nurse who works in industry can act as a liaison between the hospital, home, and work environment. She can do much to promote healthful attitudes among the workers. The industrial nurse can arrange seminars that contribute to positive well-being, such as stress reduction seminars or retirement seminars. Recently, companies and businesses have developed Employee Assistance Programs (EAP) to offer help to the troubled employee. The employee can be self- or supervisor-referred. An assessment is done of personal problems and the degree of these personal problems (i.e., absenteeism, substance abuse, family/marital conflicts, financial difficulties, or legal problems). The assessment can also include recommendations and referrals for help.

The elderly re-entering the community especially need frequent home visits. Re-entry can mean return to the same stressors the person left. The elderly should be introduced to drop-in centers, Golden Age Clubs, or Foster Grandparents.

Retirement and preretirement counseling are a new dimension to mental health for the aging. At these counseling sessions, the continued usefulness of the individual is reinforced. Various activities and future prospectives can be explored through utilizing therapeutic communication techniques and community resource people. Areas to be explored include: increased leisure time, decreased income, personal attitudes toward retirement, adaptability, community resources and activities, and support systems. A meaningful reorganization of the individual's life can help the retired person to adapt and adjust to this new stage in the life cycle.

The nurse in the community health setting needs to approach the patient through the nursing process. The nurse should observe the patient's behavioral patterns, interpersonal relationships, family role, communication skills, coping mechanisms, and social skills. Anticipatory counseling prepares the individual for problematic situations in his particular setting. The goal is to prepare the person for future coping. The nurse helps the person look at new ways of resolving problems. Social skills may require further developing. Adequate feedback is a necessity.

Appropriate interventions must be developed, as a crisis could be overwhelming. If the person is thoroughly prepared, crises can be avoided. Times of potential crisis should be anticipated. For example, adolescence, menopause and aging are times with added stressors. Other situations that need to be carefully observed include:

- Completion of school
- Changing residence
- Starting a new job
- Sudden loss (death of a loved one; loss of income)
- Childbirth
- Retirement

The rapport that the nurse establishes with the patient provides the patient with a significant other that he can turn to when problems arise. During the nursing process, the nurse needs to constantly re-evaluate both the long-term and the short-term goals. Individual needs of the patient must always be taken into consideration. All aspects of the person and his individual situation must be considered in order to make his environment as problem-free as possible.

Special community programs geared to contemporary services are a necessity. More research needs to be done to explore innovative programs and methods of service. The evaluation of community needs should include the following:

- Residential care
- Centers for the aged
- Custodial care
- Home visitation programs
- Acute treatment centers
- Effective leadership
- Youth seminars and services

A problem in some communities is the lack of centralization of available services. People must be properly referred to the service that will coordinate and facilitate resolution of their unmet needs, Figure 16-4. The goal of prevention is a fully alive, healthy person who can become a satisfied, functioning member of his family and community.

The levels of prevention can be described as: primary, secondary, or tertiary. In primary prevention, an intervention occurs before the health problem disrupts the person's life. In a secondary prevention, an intervention occurs promptly when a health problem is present and this intervention decreases the severity and duration of the problem. Tertiary prevention limits the disability related to the illness.

The National Advisory Mental Health Council of the National Institute of Mental Health has formulated a national plan and research strategy to improve services for people with severe mental disorders. Money allocations are estimated at $47 million in 1990 with an increase to $369 million by 1997. Systems of care that will benefit the patient are being explored. Two areas of study are clinical services and service systems. Assessment for severe mental illness will include: the characteristics of severe mental illness, outcomes (good and bad), diagnosis, and physical, social, and vocational functioning across cultural groups. Specific interventions in areas of treatment and rehabilitation will be observed and outcome studies done to assess effectiveness. Special interest areas are: risk factors, complication caused by physical health problems, preventive techniques, and the risk of HIV infection. Services needed by communities and their various populations will be identified and swift referrals implemented.

What type of care is given in the local hospital?
Does the staff identify with the patient?
Is work output hindered by stereotyping?
Is there a problem working with ethnic or racial groups?
How often is the patient seen by the doctor?
How is cost controlled?
Are there consultant services to schools and courts?
Is the public educated concerning mental illness?
What is the usual mode of care?
What is the method of treatment?
How effective is the method of treatment?
What is the method of rehabilitation?
What is socially accepted in the community?

Fig. 16-4  Questions that can be used to assess how well a community is meeting the needs of its residents.

Models of care management, continuous treatment teams, and the strengths and weakness of the community mental health centers will be observed and documented. Research priorities include:

- Quality of Care
    assessment
    treatment and rehabilitation

- Financing of Care
    coordination
    continuity
    mental health laws
    stigmatization

- Research
    capacity (skilled researchers—multidisciplinary) method of knowledge exchange

We are finally facing the extraordinary, complex problem of the chronically mentally ill and focusing attention on this problem. We are setting priorities and developing strategies based on scientific research in order to improve the quality of care, services, and hopefully the quality of life for these people.

## SUMMARY

Prevention is the ultimate goal in dealing with the problem of mental illness. Personal happiness and the ability to deal with stress are important factors in preventing mental illness. Modern society has greatly increased the stress which precipitates mental illness. Mobility, unemployment, culture, poverty, and broken homes are all stressors that add to the probability of mental illness. Primary prevention is aimed at lessening stress and improving coping mechanisms.

Prevention begins in the family. Positive family interactions are necessary for a positive self-concept. Parents cannot effectively delegate their responsibility for their children to others. Open communication between parent and child is essential. Many support services for families are available in the community. These support services include crisis counseling, hot lines, drug counseling, suicide prevention centers, abortion and Pro Life counseling, child and family services, family service agencies, and runaway services.

Re-entry into the community after mental illness is difficult because of stereotyping. Many former patient are often feared or ignored. The person re-entering the community needs an adequate support system to offset these negative aspects. Families of the former patient should be informed of factors that may have contributed to the problem and be advised how they can help the person cope in the future. Before re-entry, the patient may need some rehabilitation at an intermediate facility such as a foster home or halfway house. Referrals to special community programs should be coordinated.

## SUGGESTED ACTIVITIES

- Discuss how modern society contributes to mental health problems.
- Make a list of stressors and acceptable ways to relieve stress within your culture.

- View a popular television program and determine its negative and positive aspects.
- List several ways your family has influenced your coping mechanisms.
- Obtain a brochure of community-sponsored activities.
- Visit a local community resource center to gather information concerning "helping agencies" within the community.

## REVIEW

A. Multiple choice. Select the best answer.

1. Primary prevention of mental illness is aimed at
   a. lessening stress and developing improved coping mechanisms.
   b. working with rehabilitation centers.
   c. early detection and treatment of symptoms.
   d. prevention through genetic counseling.

2. A new idea in treatment of mental illness is
   a. homemaker services.
   b. runaway services.
   c. the training of bartenders in helping skills.
   d. home care.

3. Re-entry refers to the patient's
   a. return to the community.
   b. return to the hospital.
   c. return to reality.
   d. acceptance of his illness.

4. Discussion groups for former patients provide
   a. help in learning how to cope.
   b. reinforcement of self-worth.
   c. support and encouragement.
   d. all of the above.

5. When caring for a patient from a culture different from her own, the nurse should
   a. use clear, simple explanations.
   b. not impose her values on the patient.

    c. be attuned to the patient's needs and life style.
    d. all of the above.

B.    Briefly answer the following.

1.    Name five ways that modern society contributes to mental illness.

2.    Why is the parent–child relationship so important?

3.    Why is it more difficult to establish identity today that it was years ago?

4.    List four stressors of the poor that make them a high risk for mental illness.

5.    Name four ways the family can help improve the mental health of children.

6.    List four needs of the patient who is returning to the community.

## BOOKS

Leiniger, M. *Transcultural Nursing: Concept, Theories and Practices.* Wiley Co.: N.Y., 1978.

Nat'l. Institute of Mental Health National Advisory Mental Health Council. *Caring for People with Severe Mental Disorders: a National Plan of Research to Improve Services.* U.S. Dept. of Health and Human Services, Public Health Service, Alcohol, Drug Abuse, and Mental Health Administration, #91-1762, 1991.

## ARTICLES

Austad, C.S. & Shapiro, R.S. Treatment implications of post-discharge contact. *Hospital & Community Psychiatry* 34: 215–226, 1983.

Backrach, L. Perspectives in work and rehabilitation. *Hospital & Community Psychiatry* 42(9): 890–91, Sept. 1991.

Bawden, E. Reaching out to the chronically mentally ill homeless. *Journal of Psychiatric Nursing and Mental Health Nursing* 28(3): 6–8, 10–13, 41–42, March 1990.

Beeke, L.H. Reframe your outlook on recividism-crisis stabilization unit in a community program - alternative to psychiatric hospitalization. *Journal of Psychiatric Nursing & Mental Health Services* 28(9): 31–33, 36–37, Sept. 1990.

Casphina-Bacote, L. Community mental services for the under-served: a culturally specific model. *Archives of Psychiatric Nursing* 4: 229–235, Aug. 1991.

Holstrom, C. Community living for the chronically mentally ill. *Canadian Journal of Psychiatric Nursing* 30(4): 6–8, Oct.—Dec. 1989.

Koyanagai, C. & Gildman, H.H. The quiet success of the National Plan for the chronically mentally ill. *Hospital & Community Psychiatry* 42(9): 899–905, Sept. 1991.

Kramer, H.B. et al. Development and validation of a level-of-care instrument for predicting residential placement. *Hospital & Community Psychiatry* 44(4): 407–412, April 1990.

Krauss, J.B. New conceptions of care, community and chronic mental illness. *Archives of Psychiatric Nursing* 5: 281–287, Oct. 1989.

Kruse, E.A. et al. Development of a comprehensive suicide protocol in a home health care and social service agency. *Journal of Home Health Care Practitioner* 2:(3): 47–56, May 1990.

Lawson, W.B. Racial and ethical factors in psychiatric research. *Hospital & Community Psychiatry* 37: 50, 54, 1986.

Lehman, A.F. , et al. The quality of life of chronic patients in a state hospital and in community residents. *Hospital & Community Psychiatry* 37(9): 901–907, 1986.

Lesseig, D.Z. Home care for psychiatric problems. *American Journal of Nursing* 87(10): 1317–1320, 1987.

Minkoff, K. Beyond deinstitutionalization: a new ideology for the post-institution era. *Hospital & Community Psychiatry* 38(9): 945–950, 1987.

Pai, S. & Kapuir, R.L. The burden on the family of a psychiatric patient: development of an interview schedule. *British Journal of Psychiatry* 138: 332–335, 1981.

Palmer, M.E. & DFck, E.S. Teaching your patient to assert their rights. *American Journal of Nursing* 87: 650–654, 1987.

Pittman, D.C. Nursing care management: holistic care for the de-institutionalized chronically mentally ill. *Journal of Psychiatric Nursing and Mental Health Services* 27(11): 23–27, 33–34, Nov. 1989.

Stravinsky, A.T. Psychiatric nursing in the year 2000: from a nonsystem of care to a caring system. *Image* 16(1):17–20, 1984.

Worlkey, N.K., et al. Improving the physical health-mental health interface for the chronically mentally ill: could nurse case managers make a difference. *Archives of Psychiatric Nursing* 4(2): 108–113, Apr. 1990.

# Glossary

**abstract thinking** – the ability to generalize and categorize things
**acute** – severe symptoms of a short duration
**adaptation** – the act of coping with or handling stressors
**addiction** – physical dependence on a drug to the extent that physical symptoms occur when the drug is withdrawn
**adulteration** – changing and weakening of a drug by mixing it with other substances
**affective** – pertaining to feelings or emotions
**aggression** – destructive behavior that results from feelings of anger
**alarm stage** – the first stage in the body's adaptation to stress in which the body's forces are mobilized; also called the crisis stage
**alcoholism** – physical dependence on the drug, alcohol
**alienation** – separation from a former attachment
**Alzheimer's disease** – a form of progressive dementia that is characterized by the presence of tangles and plaques
**amnesia** – sudden and total memory loss; the loss may be for a short or an extended time period
**anal stage** – second stage in the child's development in which bowel training is most important
**anorexia nervosa** – extreme form of fasting which usually affects female adolescents
**anxiety** – reaction to stress ranging from a feeling of uneasiness to panic, usually brought about by a nonspecific cause
**apathy** – lack of feeling or emotion
**assertive** – able to meet one's needs while also considering the other person's needs
**awareness** – noticing how the self behaves, thinks, and senses at any given time
**baseline** – measurement of behavior under normal conditions; used to determine effectiveness of behavior modification techniques
**behavior modification** – changing behavior by eliminating a reinforcer for undesirable behavior or increasing the reinforcer for desirable behavior
**behaviorism** – psychotherapy based on the concept that behavior is controlled by rewards and consequences in the environment
**belief system** – what an individual believes about events or circumstances
**bias** – personal distortion of judgment; prejudice

**blocks to communication** − statements that stop communication

**bonding** − process of establishing an intimate attachment, primarily between mother and infant or father and infant

**bulimia** − an eating disorder characterized by the consumption of a large amount of food in a short period of time (binging) followed by self-induced vomiting (purging)

**burnout** − a reaction to accumulated stress which overwhelms the individual

**catastrophizing** − personally viewing events as terrible

**catharsis** − a process of psychotherapy in which the individual is encouraged to talk and verbalize feelings

**child abuse** − maltreatment of a child by the child's caretaker

**client-centered therapy** − therapy based on the concept that every person wants to achieve self-actualization

**cognitive** − thinking processes such as judgment, reasoning, and understanding; factual knowledge

**coitus** − sexual intercourse

**communication** − sending and receiving messages between two or more people

**compensation** − mental mechanism in which a person develops an alternate ability in order to overcome a real or imagined defect

**compulsion** − irresistible urge to engage in a behavior

**conditioning** − previous learning that determines behavior

**conflict** − Freudian: a clash between opposing unconscious feelings Behaviorism: a clash between two opposing conditioned behaviors

**confusion** − responding inappropriately; being mixed up

**conversion** − changing an emotional problem into physical symptoms

**cope** − ability to deal with problems and stress

**Creutzfeld-Jakob's disease** − a form of rapidly progressing dementia

**crisis** − the first stage in the body's adaptation to stress in which the body's forces are mobilized; overwhelming stress

**cues** − nonverbal behavior used to communicate feelings

**custodial care** − caring for the patient's routine daily needs without rehabilitation or therapy

**defense mechanism** − method frequently used to lessen anxiety; mental mechanism

**dehydration** − loss of fluid from the intra- or intercellular spaces

**delusion** − false ideas that cannot be changed by logical argument

**denial** − mental mechanism in which the person unconsciously rejects the truth

**depression** − condition of sadness or dejection usually not proportionate to circumstances

**desensitization** − the process of describing stressful events over and over until the individual is able to tolerate them

**developmental disability** − the lack of mental development

**displacement** − Freudian: taking out hostility on someone other than the person for whom it is intended
Behaviorism: engaging in substitute behavior

**dissociation** − an unconscious escape from situations that would cause anxiety; the individual is cut off from his own awareness

**diversional activity** − activity planned to take an individual's mind off stressful situations

**drug dependence** – psychological or physical dependence on a drug

**echolalia** – involuntary repetition of words spoken by others

**echopraxia** – involuntary imitation of the motions of others

**ego** – the part of the personality that deals with reality; the conscious self

**Electra complex** – development stage in which daughter grows closer to her father and is jealous of her mother; same as Oedipus complex in males

**electroconvulsive therapy** – method of treatment in which electrical impulses are used to produce seizures in the mentally ill patient when the patient does not respond to drugs or other therapy

**electrolytes** – chemicals necessary for the effective functioning of all cells, including the nerve cell

**emote** – to express feelings

**empathy** – understanding the feelings of others

**endogenous depression** – a depression caused by factors inside the affected person

**environment** – circumstances, conditions, and objects that surround and influence an individual

**euphoria** – a sense of elation or well-being

**exaggeration** – purposefully making something larger, louder, or more important to increase self-awareness

**extinction** – the stopping of a conditioned response

**fantasy** – creation of the imagination; daydream

**fear** – anxiety reaction toward a known stimulus

**fetus** – developing infant in utero from about the eighth week after conception to birth

**flashback** – re-experiencing the effects of a hallucinogenic drug days, weeks, or months after using it

**flight of ideas** – the rapid succession of ideas that do not necessarily have a connection

**free association** – method of counseling that allows the person to say whatever comes to mind

**game** – relationships in which an individual engages to make his script turn out as planned

**general adaptation syndrome (G.A.S.)** – the measurable changes produced in the body in response to stress

**genuineness** – free from pretense; showing of sincere and honest feelings

**grief** – deep distress caused by a loss

**habituation** – emotional need or strong desire

**hallucination** – imaginary sense perception which may involve the five senses of hearing, seeing, feeling, smelling, or tasting

**heredity** – acquirement of qualities from parents through the genes

**hierarchy** – arrangement of needs, from lowest to highest

**holistic** – view of people as total beings, considering physical, social, and emotional aspects

**homeostasis** – condition of internal balance

**homosexuality** – sexual preference for an individual of the same sex

**hostility** – feeling of anger and pent-up energy which erupts in aggression

**humanism** – pertaining to and concern for human beings

**hypothermia** – loss of body heat and a lowering of body temperature

**hypoxia** – loss of oxygen to the brain cells

**hysteria** – maladaptive behavior due to overwhelming anxiety characterized by dissociation and conversion reactions

**id** – part of the personality that controls physical needs and instincts

**illusion** – mistaken perception of reality

**incongruent** – situation in which an individual sees himself as different from what he is experiencing; lacking internal harmony

**instincts** – inborn drive toward a behavior

**intellectualization** – mental mechanism in which one dissociates himself from a stressful problem by overuse of intellectual processes

**intervention** – action taken by a helping person

**introspection** – evaluation of why the self reacts as it does

**kleptomania** – compulsion to steal

**Kuru** – a form of dementia found in cannibal tribes that is caused by a slow-acting virus

**libido** – sexual energy available to an individual

**lysosome** – small body within the cell that contains destructive enzymes

**mainlining** – injecting a drug directly into a vein

**maladaptive response** – energy-wasting response to stress

**malformation** – disability or serious illness

**manipulate** – to play upon the emotions of others in order to get one's own way

**mental mechanism** – way of coping with stress

**milieu therapy** – technique used to help the patient through the use of the environment

**negativism** – strong opposition to advice, direction, or suggestion

**neologism** – made-up word that has no meaning except to the person who has made it up

**nursing process** – process of achieving patient care through deliberate systematic and individualized procedures; it consists of four major subprocesses: assessment, planning, intervention, and evaluation

**obsession** – recurring thought or feeling that is overpowering

**Oedipus complex** – a stage in development during which the boy falls in love with his mother and becomes extremely jealous of his father; same as Electra complex in females

**oral stage** – first stage in development in which the infant receives all of its pleasure through the mouth

**organic brain syndrome** – condition in which there is behavior change due to demonstrable brain damage

**orientation** – an awareness of time, place, and person

**panic** – disorganized behavior as a response to severe anxiety

**paranoia** – psychotic state characterized by delusions of persecution

**passive aggression** – use of passive behavior, such as pouting, producing guilt feelings, or intentional ineffectiveness, to express hostility

**pathogenic** – disease producing

**payoff** – reward for behavior

**peer** – belonging to the same group in society

**perfectionism** – need to behave correctly at all times; inability to accept mistakes made by the self

**personality disorder** – maladaptive behavior created by defects in the development of the personality

**phallic stage** – stage in which the child begins to develop sexual identity

**phenomenon** – fact or event

**phobia** – abnormal excessive fear of a specific situation or object

**physiological** – pertaining to the body's physical reactions

**plaques** – starchlike deposits in the brain tissue of Alzheimer's victims

**play therapy** – therapy in which children are helped to express themselves through play

**poetry therapy** – therapy using poetry to help patients express themselves

**positive regard** – acceptance of the patient as he is

**presentizing** – bringing past experiences into the present to increase self-awareness

**projection** – mental mechanism whereby the individual places blame for shortcomings on someone else

**psychedelic** – capable of producing hallucinations

**psychiatrist** – doctor of medicine who specializes in the diagnosis and treatment of mental illness

**psychoanalysis** – psychotherapy developed by Freud that attributes maladaptive behavior to repressions in the subconscious mind; technique involves bringing these repressed feelings and experiences to the conscious level where they can be dealt with

**psychodrama** – method of treatment allowing patients to act out their problems

**psychologist** – person who specializes in testing, diagnosis, and treatment of individuals with mental health problems. The person is not a medical doctor

**psychophysiological** – physical manifestations of emotional problems

**psychosurgery** – surgery on the brain for the purpose of relieving overwhelming stress when an incapacitating mental disorder does not respond to other therapies

**psychotherapy** – treatment of mental and emotional disorders

**rational** – able to reason and understand

**rational emotive therapy** – psychotherapy based on the theory that problems are not caused by events that happen, but are a direct result of what the person believes about the events

**rationalization** – mental mechanism whereby the individual denies his real thoughts by excusing behavior with more socially acceptable reasons

**reactive depression** – depression that results from some outside event

**reality orientation** – type of therapy that brings people back to awareness of reality

**reality therapy** – therapy developed by William Glasser in which clients are expected to take responsibility for changing their behavior

**reflecting** – repeating the patient's thoughts and feelings as understood by the helping person

**rehabilitation** – restoring to health or to useful, acceptable behavior

**reinforcement** – reward that continues a behavior

**rejection** – turning away from

**REM (rapid eye movement)** – movement of the eye during periods of sleep

**reminiscing** – encouraging the aged to think about and express events of the past as a starting point to bringing him or her back to reality

**repression** – unconscious mental mechanism that keeps unpleasant experiences from awareness

**resistance** – attempts to block the movement of unconscious thoughts to the conscious level

**response** – action as a result of a stimulus

**retrograde ejaculation** – dry ejaculation; sperm backs up into the bladder

**reward** – reinforcement for a specific behavior

**role** – the part one plays in society

**script** – the pattern of behavior which an individual follows

**self-concept** – the way in which a person feels, views, and thinks of himself; self-esteem

**sexism** – belief that one sex is inferior to and exists for the benefit of the other

**socialization** – ability to interact with other people

**soma** – the body

**status** – position or rank within a social group

**stillborn** – to be born dead

**stimulus** – something that causes action; may be internal or external

**stress** – nonspecific response to any demand made on the body

**stressor** – demand which causes the stress reaction

**sublimation** – mental mechanism in which unacceptable instincts are substituted for socially acceptable behavior

**superego** – internalized parental value system that is partly conscious

**suppression** – mental mechanism in which stressful events and feelings are deliberately blocked from awareness

**tangles** – a characteristic of Alzheimer's disease; the axons and dendrites of the nerve cell wrap themselves around the atrophied nerve cell

**time out** – physical withdrawal from an overwhelming stressful situation

**tolerance** – body's ability to endure the effects of a drug without showing effect; after tolerance has developed, an increased amount of the drug is needed to produce the desired effect

**tranquilizer** – drug used to reduce anxiety and tension

**transactional analysis** – psychotherapy based on the study of interpersonal communication

**transference** – attributing characteristics of significant others in the patient's life to another person

**values** – personal beliefs which are used in making decisions

**vulnerable** – open to attack or damage

**waxy flexibility** – waxlike rigid condition of the extremities that is characteristic of catatonic schizophrenia. Extremities remain in any position they are placed, no matter how uncomfortable the position may be.

**withdrawal** – group of symptoms that occurs as a result of stopping the intake of an addictive drug

**withdrawn** – form of behavior that characterizes a retreat from reality

**word salad** – words or phrases that have no logical connection or meaning

# Bibliography ═══════

## CHAPTER 1

### Books

Alexander, F.G., and Selesnick, S.T. *The History of Psychiatry.* New York: New American Library, 1974.

Beers, C. *A Mind That Found Itself.* New York: Doubleday & Co. (reprinted with additions), 1953.

Bullough, V.L., and Bullough, B. *The Emergence of Modern Nursing.* 2nd ed. New York: Macmillan Publishing Co., 1969.

Leininger, M., ed. *Contemporary Issues in Mental Health Nursing.* Boston: Little, Brown, & Co., 1973.

Manfreda, M., and Krampitz, S. *Psychiatric Nursing.* 10th ed. Philadelphia: F.A. Davis Co., 1977.

Sarason, I.G. *Abnormal Psychology.* 2nd ed. Englewood Cliffs, NJ: Prentice-Hall, 1972.

Schultz, R., and Johnson, A.C. *Management of Hospitals.* New York: McGraw-Hill Book Co., 1976.

Toffler, A. *Future Shock.* New York: Bantam Books, 1971.

### Periodicals

Callahan, C.L. "The White House Conference on Food, Nutrition and Health." *Nursing Outlook* 18:58, January 1970.

Crawford, B., et al. "Mental Hospitals — An Obituary?" *Psychiatric Nursing* 9:18 July–August 1971.

Horbin, V.K. "The Stress Phenomenon." *Journal of School Health* 48:507, October 1978.

Johnson, R.L. "Holistic Experiences of Stress Opportunity for Growth or Illness." *Occupational Health Nursing* 28:15–18, December 1980.

Keeler, J. "Nine Tips for Beating Stress." *American Operating Room Nurse* 30:138, July 1979.

Knowles, R.D. "Control Your Thoughts — Can Lead to Control of Emotions and the Behavior of Self." *American Journal of Nursing* 81:353, February 1981.

Ledney, D. "Psychiatric Nursing: Breakthrough to Independence." *RN* 34:29, August 1971.

Lewis, E., and Browning, M. "The Nurse in Community Mental Health." *American Journal of Nursing* (35 selected articles), 1972.

McRae, J. "Seen But Not Admitted at the State Hospital." *Psychosocial Rehabilitation Journal* 2:21–32, October 7, 1983.

News and Notes. "APA Endorses Right to Care and Treatment for All Patients." *Hospital and Community Psychiatry* 26:772, 1975.

News and Notes. "Department of Labor Issues Rules Governing Payment of Patient Workers." *Hospital and Community Psychiatry* 26:48, 1975.

Sharfstein, S.S. and Patterson, D.Y. "The Growing Crisis in Access to Mental Health Services for Middle-Class Families." *Hospital and Community Psychiatry* 34(11):1009-1010, 1014, November 1983.

Shubin, S. "Rx for Stress — Your Stress." *Nursing '79* 9:52-55, June 1979.

Silver, G.A. "A National Health Insurance, National Health Policy and the National Health." *American Journal of Nursing* 71:1730-1734, September 1971.

# CHAPTER 2

## Books

Larazus, R. *Psychological Stress and the Coping Process.* New York: McGraw-Hill, Inc., 1966.

Levinson, D. *The Seasons of a Man's Life.* New York: Ballantine Books, 1978.

Murphy, L., and Moriarity, A. *Vulnerability, Coping and Growth.* New Haven: Yale University Press, 1976.

Sheehy, G. *Passages.* New York: E.P. Dutton, 1976.

## Periodicals

Banard, P. "Crisis in Care: How to Reduce Stress." *Nursing Mirror* 19:47-48, November 6, 1985.

Bayer, M. "The Multipurpose Room: A Way Out Outlet for Staff and Clients: Our Security Room." *Journal of Psychiatric Nursing* 18(10):35-37, October 18, 1980.

Castedine, G. "Taking a Rest from Stress — Common Stressors Which All Nurses Experience." *Nursing Times* 81:22, March 20-26, 1985.

Chiarelli, M., et al. "Women and Mental Health: A Feminists View." *Canadian Nurse* 81:23, January 1985.

Clarke, M. "Stress and Coping: Constructs for Nursing." *Journal of Advanced Nursing* 9(1):3-13, January 1984.

————. "The Constructs of Stress and Coping as a Rationale for Nursing Activities." *Journal of Advanced Nursing* 9(3):267-275, May 1984.

Croley, J. "What Causes Stress?" *Your Life Health* 98(8):4-6, August 1983.

Daniels, L.A. "How to Understand and Control Stress." *Hospital Topics* 63(4):12-15, July-August 1985.

Hughes, G.H. "Stress: Sources, Effects, and Management." *Family and Community Health* 7(1):47-58, May 1984.

Kinsey, E. "Your Body and Stress." *Your Life Health* 98(8):6-8, August 1983.

Maier, S.F., et al. "Stress and Health — Exploring the Links." *Psychology Today* 9(8):44-49 August 1985.

Morton, Cooper A. "The End of the Rope — Stress in Nursing." *Nursing Mirror* 159(21):18-19, December 5, 1984.

# CHAPTER 3

## Books

Erikson, E.H. *Childhood and Society.* New York: W.W. Norton and Company, Inc., 1963.

Havinghurst, R.J. *Human Development and Education.* New York: Longman, Inc., 1953.

Maslerson, J. *The Real Self. A Developmental Self and Object Relations Approach.* New York: Brunner-Mazel, 1985.

Murray, C., Ed. *The Place of Attachment in Human Behavior.* New York: Basic Books, 1982.

## Periodicals

Bakdash, D.P. "Becoming an Assertive Nurse." *American Journal of Nursing* 78:1710-1712, October 1978.

Bakdash, D.P. "Personality Clash and What to Do About It." *Your Life Health* 97(10):20-21, October 1982.

Boe, G.P. Systematic Guide to Understanding Behavior." *MLO* 15(10):133-134,137, October 1983.

Coynan, A. "Meeting Developmental Needs of Neonates." *Family and Community Health* 1:79,90 November 1978.

Fleming, R.A. "Developing a Child's Self-Esteem." *Pediatric Nursing* 5:58-60, July-August 1979.

Herbner, G.F. "Recognizing Personal Styles to Get Along Better with People." *Nursing Life* 4(1):28-32, January-February 1984.

Parkinson, C.E. "Effects of Home Environment on Child Development." *Midwife Health Visit Community Nurse* 15:236-239, June 1979.

Sullivan, B.J. "Negative Parental Evaluations and How They Affect the Child." *Maternal-Child Nursing* 8:173-179, Fall 1979.

Swisher, J.D. "Cognitive and Affective Learning for Self-Directed Health Behavior. Mental Health — The Case of Preventive Health Education, Part 1." *Journal of School Health* 46:386-391, September 1976.

Taggert, M. "Body Image: Looking Beyond the Mirror, Normal Development," *Journal of Practical Nursing* 27:32-33, July 1977.

Tyler, N.B., et al. "Reduction of Stress Between Mothers and Their Handicapped Children." *American Journal of Occupational Therapy* 31:151-155, March 1977.

Uustal, D.B. "Values Clarification in Nursing: Application to Practice, Part 2." *American Journal of Nursing* 78:2058-2063, December 1978.

## CHAPTER 4

### Books

Applebaum, S. *Stress Management for Health Care Professionals.* Rockville, MD: Aspen Publications, 1981.

Lazarous, R., and Falkman, S. *Stress Appraisal and Coping.* New York: Springer Publishing Co., 1984.

Meddery, T. *Burnout and Health Professionals: Manifestations and Management.* Norwalk, CT: Appleton Century Crofts, 1983.

### Periodicals

Beck, J. "Nurses Have Needs, Too: Take Time to Take Care of Yourself, Part 2." *Nursing Times* 80:30-35, October 10-16, 1984.

Billings, C.V. "Emotional First Aid." *American Journal of Nursing* 80:2006-2009, November 1980.

Davis, R.E. "Stress-related Disorders and Stress Management." *Physician's Assistant* 8(9):75-76, 79-80, September 1984.

DeTornyay, R. "Nursing Decisions. Experience in Clinical Problem Solving, Mrs. G. Helping the Patient with a Colostomy, Part 6." *RN*, March 1976, pp. 39-47.

Elliott, S.M. "Denial as an Effective Mechanism to Allay Anxiety Following a Stressful Event." *Journal of Psychiatric Nursing*, October 18, 1980, pp. 11-15.

Fritz, W.S. "Maintaining Wellness: Yours and Theirs." *Nursing Clinics of North America* 19(2):263-269, January 1984.

Fuller, E. "Behavioral Therapy — Behavioral Approaches to Patient Care." *Patient Care* 13:26-29, April 30, 1979.

Gruber, K.A., et al. "Letting Your Anger Work for You." *American Journal of Nursing* 76:1450-1452, April 1976.

Haggord, M.E., et al. "Patient Anxiety: Teaching Students to Intervene Effectively." *Journal of Nursing Education* 4:19-21, January-February 1979.

Kinsler, D.D. "Relaxation: Key to Stress Reduction." *Occupational Health Nursing* 25:7–8 July 1977.

Moore, J. "Nurses Have Needs, Too: Caring for the Careers, Part 1." *Nursing Times* 80:28–30, October 10–16, 1984.

O'Neal, E. "A Simple Way to Modify Behavior." *Geriatric Nursing* 7(1):45, January–February 1986.

Thorson, J.A., and Thorson, J.R. "How Accurate Are Stress Scales?" *Journal of Geriatric Nursing* 12(1):11–15, January 1986.

———. "Ways to Control Stress and Make It Work for You." *US News and World Report* 96(10):69–70, March 12, 1984.

Trygstad, L. "Simple New Ways to Help Anxious Patients." *RN*, December 1980, pp. 28–32.

Willis, R.W. "Options in Managing Stress." *Pediatric Nursing* 5:24–27, January–February 1979.

# CHAPTER 5

## Books

Ellis, A. *Humanistic Psychotherapy: The Rational-Emotive Approach.* Edited by Edward Sagarin. Julian Press, 1973.

Fagan, J., and Shepherd, I., eds. *Life Techniques in Gestalt Therapy.* New York: Harper and Row, 1973.

Francher, R.E. *Psychoanalytic Psychology: The Development of Freud's Thought.* New York: W.W. Norton and Co., 1973.

Fine, R. *Psychoanalytic Psychology.* New York: Aronson, Jason, Inc., 1975.

Glasser, W. *Reality Therapy: A New Approach to Psychiatry.* New York: Harper and Row, 1975.

James, M., and Jongeward, D. *Born to Win: Transactional Analysis with Gestalt Experiments.* Reading, MA: Addison-Wesley Publishing Co., Inc., 1971.

Polster, I., and Polster, M. *Gestalt Therapy Integrated.* New York: Vintage Books, 1973.

## Periodicals

Carruth, B.F. "Modifying Behavior Through Social Learning." *American Journal of Nursing* 76:1804–1806, November 1976.

Diffenbocher, J.L. "Group Desensitization of Dissimilar Anxieties." *Community Mental Health Journal* 12:263–265, Fall 1976.

Priestly, J. "Music, Freud and the Port of Entry." *Nursing Times* 72:1940–1941, 9 December 1976.

# CHAPTER 6

## Books

Argyle, M. *The Psychology of Interpersonal Behavior.* 2nd ed. New York: Penguin Books, 1972.

Bion, W.R. *Experiences in Group.* New York: Basic Books, Inc., 1961.

Fitts, W.H. *Interpersonal Competence: The Wheel Model.* Research Monograph No. 2. Nashville: Rich Printing Co., 1970.

Gazda, G.M., ed. *Basic Approaches to Group Psychotherapy and Group Counseling.* 2nd ed. Springfield, IL: Charles C. Thomas, 1977.

Lassey, W.R. *Leadership and Social Change.* Iowa City, Iowa: University Press, 1971.

Loomis, M. *Group Process for Nurses.* St. Louis: C.V. Mosby Co., 1979.

Marram, G. *The Group Approach in Nursing Practice.* 2nd ed. St. Louis: C.V. Mosby Co., 1978.

Sampson, M., and Marthas, M. *Group Processes for the Health Professional.* 2nd ed. New York: John Wiley & Sons, Inc., 1981.

Stuart, G.W., and Sundeen, S.J. *Principles and Practice of Psychiatric Nursing.* 2nd ed. St. Louis: C.V. Mosby Co., 1983.

Whitaker, S., and Lieberman, M. *Psychotherapy through the Group Process.* Chicago: Aldine Publishing Co., 1964.

Wilson, H.S., and Kneisl, C.R. *Psychiatric Nursing.* 2nd ed. Menlo Park, CA: Addison-Wesley Publishing Co., 1983.

Yalom, I.D. *Inpatient Group Psychotherapy.* New York: Basic Books, Inc., 1983.

———. *The Theory and Practice of Group Psychotherapy.* 2nd ed. New York: Basic Books, Inc., 1975.

## Periodicals

Adrian, S. "A Systematic Approach to Selecting Group Participants." *Journal of Psychiatric Nursing* 18(2):37, 1980.

Affonso, D.D., "Therapeutic Support During Inpatient Group Therapy." *Journal of Psychosocial Nursing and Mental Health Services* 23(11):21-25, 1985.

American Nurses Association. Statement on Psychiatric and Mental Health Nursing Practice. Kansas City, Mo., 1976.

Authier, J., et al. "Group Interventional Techniques: A Practice Guide for Psychiatric Team Members." *Journal of Psychiatric Nursing* 14(7):19, 1976.

Borriello, J. "Leadership in the Therapist-centered Group as a Whole Psychotherapy Approach." *International Journal of Group Psychotherapy* 26:149, 1976.

Griffin, W., Ling, I., and Staley, D. "Stress Management Groups." *Journal of Psychosocial Nursing and Mental Health Services* 23(10):31-35, 1985.

Hager, R. "Evaluation of Group Psychotherapy: A Question of Values." *Journal of Psychiatric Nursing* 16(12):26, 1978.

Parloff, M. and Dies, R. "Group Therapy Outcome Research." *International Journal of Group Psychotherapy* 23:281, 1977.

Reed, G., and Sech, E.P. "Bulimia: A Conceptual Model for Group Treatment." *Journal of Psychosocial Nursing and Mental Health Services* 23(5):16-22, 1985.

Slimner, L. "Use of the Nursing Process to Facilitate Group Therapy." *Journal of Psychiatric Nursing* 16(2):42, 1978.

White, E.M., and Kahn, E.M. "Use and Modifications in Group Psychotherapy with Chronic Schizophrenic Outpatients." *Journal of Psychosocial Nursing and Mental Health Services* 20:14, 1982.

Williams, R. "A Contract for Co-therapists in Group Therapy." *Journal of Psychiatric Nursing* 14:11, 1976.

Witt, J. "Transference and Countertransference in Group Therapy Settings." *Journal of Psychosocial Nursing and Mental Health Services* 20:31, 1982.

# CHAPTER 7

## Books

Collins, M. *Communication in Health Care: The Human Connection in the Life Cycle.* St. Louis: C.V. Mosby Co., 1983.

Edwards, B. *Communication in Nursing Practice.* St. Louis: C.V. Mosby Co., 1981.

Peplau, H. *Interpersonal Relations in Nursing.* New York: G.P. Putnam, 1951.

## Periodicals

Adamson, L.S. "Strategies For Nurse-Patient Communication." *Supervisor Nurse,* December 11, 1980, pp. 44-45.

Apse, A., and Stetler, G. "Avoiding Terms of Bewilderment." *Nursing 85* 15(12):42-43, December 1985.

Ashworth, P.M. "Staff-Patient Communication in Coronary Care Units." *Journal of Advanced Nursing* 9(1):35-40, January 1984.

Bailey, I., et al. "View from the Horizontal Side of Caring." *Nursing 85* 15(10):53-54, October 1985.

Bennett, H.L. "Why Patients Don't Follow Instructions." *RN* 49(3):45-47, March 1986.

Castle, M.A. "Barriers to Effective Communication." *Professional Medical Assisting* 17(4):8-10, July-August 1984.

Crews, N.E. "Developing Empathy for Effective Communication." *American Operating Room Nurse* 30:536, September 1979.

Goreant, C. "Skills in the Therapeutic Process of Chronic Illness." *American Journal of Nursing,* December 1980, pp. 2166-2169.

Henrick, A.P. "What's Really Bothering Your Patient. Five Ways to Find Out." *Nursing Life* 4(5):62-64, September-October 1984.

Hill, R.L. "Transactional Analysis. A Better Patient Approach." *Focus Critical Care* 11(3):11-16, June 1984.

Hirsch, A.L. "Duty to Stop, Look, Listen and Communicate." *Nursing Homes* 32(5):37-38, September-October 1983.

Johnson, M.N. "Anxiety/Stress and the Effects of Disclosure Between Nurses and Patients." *Advanced Nursing Science* 1:1-20, July 1979.

Kasch, C.R. "Interpersonal Competence and Communication in the Delivery of Nursing Care." *ANS* 6(2):71-80, January 1984.

Lay, T.N. "Personal Awareness: Therapeutic Communication, Part 1." *Journal of Nursing Care* 12:16-18, September 1979.

Mackinnon, S.R. "Health Professionals' Patterns of Communication: Cross Purpose or Problem Solving." *Journal of Allied Health* 13(1):3-12, February 1984.

McGuire, M.A. "You Who Touch Me in Your Passing — Human Compassion and a Gentle Touch May Help Restore a Person's Dignity and Self-Respect." *Supervisor Nurse,* October 11, 1980, p. 72.

McGuire, P. "Consequences of Poor Communication between Nurses and Patients." *Nursing* 2(38):1115-1116, 1118, June 1985.

Pinal, C. "Say What You Mean." *Nursing Mirror* 158(24):22-23, June 20, 1984.

Pouilio, S. "Using Techniques to Improve Nurse-Terminal Patient Communications." *Canadian Nurse* 80(7):16-18, August 1984.

Ramaeker, M.J. "Communication Blocks Revisited." *American Journal of Nursing,* June 1979, pp. 1079-1081.

Raudsepp, E. "7 Ways to Cure Communication Breakdown." *Nursing Life.* 4(1):50-53, January-February 1984.

Smith, M.S., et al. "Empathy Training for Nursing Students." *Journal of New York State Nurses Association* 15(1):17-25, March 15, 1984.

Thompson, R. "Communication Checklist." *Caring* 3(1):37-38, 40, January 1984.

Walke, M. "When a Patient Needs to Unburden his Feelings." *American Journal of Nursing* 77:1164, 1977.

Woods, E., et al. "Do You Talk to Patients." *Nursing Times* 80(37):61-64, September 12-18, 1984.

# CHAPTER 8

## Books

Apgov, J., and Beck, J. *Is My Baby All Right?* New York: Pocket Books, 1974. Brazelton, T.B. *Infants and Mothers.* New York: Delta Books, 1969.

Chester, P. *With Child . . . A Diary of Motherhood.* New York: Berkley Publishing, 1979.

Klaus, M.H., and Kennel, J.H. *Maternal-Infant Bonding.* St. Louis: C.V. Mosby Co., 1976.

Moore, J.L. *Newborn, Family, and Nurse.* 2nd ed. Philadelphia: W.B. Saunders Co., 1981.

Oremlent, E., and Oremlent, J. *The Effects of Hospitalization on Children.* Springfield, IL: Charles C. Thomas Publishers, 1972.

Petrillo, M., and Sanger, S. *Emotional Care of Hospitalized Children.* 2nd ed. Philadelphia: J.B. Lippincott Co., 1980.

## Periodicals

Berger J.C. "When Your Child Goes to the Hospital." *Life Health* 96:4-6, March 1981.

Bergman, A.M. "Living with Progressive Childhood Illness: Parental Management of Neuromuscular Disease." *Social Work Health Care,* Summer 1980, pp. 387-408.

Brown, J.W., et al. "Nursing Based Intervention With Prematurely Born Babies and Their Mothers: Are These Effects?" *The Journal of Pediatrics* 97:487–491, September 1980.

Brown, L. "Negative Feelings Toward Children: Their Impact on Pediatric Care." *JACCH* 19:50–52, Fall 1980.

Browning, D.H., and Boatman, B. "Incest: Children at Risk." *American Journal of Psychiatry* 134:69–72, 1977.

Carter-Jessop, L. "Promoting Material Attachment Through Parental Intervention." *Maternal-Child Nursing Journal* 6:107–112, March–April 1981.

Clatworthy, S. "Therapeutic Play: Effects on Hospitalized Children." *JACCH* 9:108–112, Spring 1981.

Cline, F. "Lack of Attachment in Children." *Nurse Practitioner* 4:35, January–February 1979.

Conn, J.L. "Communicating with the Child Abusing Family." *Topics Clinical Nursing,* October 1979, pp. 141–148.

Cooney, K.M. "Nursing Care of Emotionally Abused and Deprived Children." *Issues Comprehensive Pediatrics Nursing* 3:54–62, September 1978.

Donnelly, G.F., et al. "Parent-Neonate Communication in the Care-Giving System." *Topics Clinical Nursing* 1:1–9, October 1979.

Dean, D. "Emotional Abuse of Children." *Children Today* 8:18–20, July–August 1979.

El Massen, B.J. "A Practical Approach to Communicating with Children through Play." *Maternal-Child Nursing Journal* 4:238–240, July–August 1979.

Fusstenberg, F.F. "Unplanned Parenthood: The Social Consequences of Teenage Childbearing." *Final Report of Maternal-Child Health.* Grant #MC-R-420117-05-0, U.S. Government Printing Office, p. 165, June 1975.

Gillette, C. "Child Abuse." *Journal of Nursing Care* 11:12–13, December 1978.

Green, A.H. "Expanding Psychiatry's Role in Child Abuse Treatment." *Hospital Community Psychiatry* 30:702–705, October 1979.

Hiley, R., et al. "Communication in a Neonatal Unit." *Nursing Times* 74:1771–1772, October 26, 1978.

Jekel, J., and Forbush, J. "Service Needs of Adolescent Parents." *The Journal of School Health,* November 1979, pp. 527–530.

Johnson, E. "Easing Children's Fright During Health Care Procedures." *American Journal of Maternal-Child Health* 1:206–210, 1976.

Keer, N.J. "The Effect of Hospitalization on the Developmental Tasks of Childhood." *Nursing Forum* 18:108–129, 1979.

Kranz, P.L. "The Play Therapist: The Student, The Struggle, The Process." *Journal of Psychiatric Nursing* 16:29–31, November 1978.

Mansen, T. "Bonding: The Newest Options in Childbirth." *American Baby* 40:50–53, November 1978.

Menke, E.M. "School-Aged Children's Perception of Stress in the Hospital." *JACCH* 9:80–85, Winter 1981.

Milliken, D. "Change in the Neonatal Nurse's Role." *Australian Nurse* 8:30–33, October 1978.

Nelson, M. "Identifying the Emotional Needs of the Hospitalized Child." *Maternal-Child Nursing Journal* 6:181–183, May–June 1981.

Ortman, E. "Attachment Behaviors in Abused Children." *Pediatric Nursing* 5:25–29, July–August 1979.

Quink, T.R., O'Donahue, S., and Middlet, J. "The Perinatal Bereavement Crisis." *Journal of Nurse Midwife* 24:13, September–October 1979.

Rae, W. "Hospitalized Latency-Age Children: Implications for Psychosocial Care." *JACCH* 9:59–63, Winter 1981.

Ruffing, M.A. "Mothering and Early Infant Stimulation." *Nursing Forum* 18:69–79, 1979.

Scharer, K. "Nursing Interventions with Abusive and Neglectful Families within the Community." *American Journal of Maternal-Child Nursing* 8:85–94, Summer 1979.

Schaer, K. "Nursing Therapy with Abusive and Neglectful Families." *Journal of Psychiatric Nursing* 17:12–16, September 1979.

Skagg, R.L. "Colors That Help Soothe the Pediatric Patient." *Hospitals* 55:159–60, February 19, 1981.

Skellern, J. "Self-Concept of Children and Adolescents and the Effect of Physical Disability." *Australian Nurse* 8:36–38, December 1978–January 1979.

Taylor, C. "Use of Therapeutic Play in Ambulatory Pediatric Hematology Clinic." *Cancer Nursing,* December 3, 1980, pp. 433–437.
Wilk, J. "Assessing Single Parent Needs." *Journal of Psychiatric Nursing* 17:21–22, 1979.

# CHAPTER 9

## Books

Chaisson-Stewart, G. *Depression in the Elderly: An Interdisciplinary Approach.* New York: John Wiley and Son, Inc., 1985.

## Periodicals

Baker, N.J. "Reminiscing in Group Therapy for Self-Worth." *Journal of Gerontological Nursing* 11(7):21–24, July 1985.
Brock, A.M., and O'Sullivan, P. "Wife to Widow: Role Transition in the Elderly." *Journal of Psychosocial Nursing and Mental Health Services* 23(12):6–12, December 1985.
Fine, M., et al. "Electroshock Exploding the Myths." *RN* 48(9):58–59, 61–62, 64, September 1985.
Hatcher, B.J., et al. "Overcoming Stress-related Depression." *Journal of Gerontological Nursing* 11(11)34–39, November 1985.
Hemshorn, A. "They Call it Alzheimer's Disease." *Journal of Gerontological Nursing* 11(1):36–41, January 1985.
Hollinger, L.M. "Communicating with the Elderly." *Journal of Gerontological Nursing* 12(3):8–13, March 1986.
Janicak, P.G., et al. "An Assessment of Mental Health Professional Knowledge and Attitude." *Journal of Clinical Psychiatry* 46(7):262–266, July 1985.
Lucas, M.J., et al. "Recognition of Psychiatric Symptoms in Dementia." *Journal of Gerontological Nursing* 12(1):11–15, January 1986.
Kiely, M.A. "Alzheimer's Disease. Making the Most of the Time That's Left." *RN* 48(3):34–46, March 1985.
Mawson, D. "Shockwaves." *Nursing Times* 81(46):42–44, November 13–19, 1985.
Nagley, S. "Predicting and Preventing Confusion in Your Patients." *Journal of Gerontological Nursing* 12(3):27–31, March 1986.
Ninos, M., and Makahon, R. "Functional Assessment of the Patient." *Geriatric Nursing* 6(3):139–143, May–June 1985.
Nowakowski, W. "Accent Capabilities in Disorientation." *Journal of Gerontological Nursing* 11(9):15–20, September 1985.
O'Neal, E. "A Simple Way to Modify Behavior." *Geriatric Nursing* 7(1):45, January–February 1986.
Palmateer, L.M., and McCortney, J.R. "Do Nurses Know When Patients Have Cognitive Deficits?" *Journal of Gerontological Nursing* 11(2):6–16, February 1985.
Rader, J., and Doan, J. "How to Decrease Wandering, a Form of Agenda Behavior." *Geriatric Nursing* 6(4):196–199, July–August 1985.
Schwab, Sr. M., et al. "Relieving the Anxiety and Fear in Dementia." *Journal of Gerontological Nursing* 11(5):8–15, May 1985.
Whall, A.L., and Conklin, C. "Why a Psychogeriatric Unit?" *Journal of Psychosocial Nursing and Mental Health Services* 23(5):23–27, 1985.

# CHAPTER 10

## Books

Burkhalter, P.K. *Nursing Care of the Alcohol and Drug Abuser.* New York: McGraw-Hill Book Co., 1975.
Estes, L., and Heinemann, M.E. *Alcoholism: Development, Consequences, and Interactions.* St. Louis: C.V. Mosby Co., 1982.

Milt, H. *Basic Handbook on Alcoholism.* 2nd ed. Scientific Aids Publisher, 1972.
Scott, E.M. *Struggles in an Alcoholic Family.* Springfield, IL: Charles C. Thomas Publisher, 1970.

## Periodicals

Addis E.G., and Jovita, R. "Why Our Children Drink." *Liquorian,* December 1976.
"Alcohol Abuse: Test Yourself." *American Journal of Nursing* 80:919, May 1980.
Baird, K. "Special Unit Treats Problems of Teenagers....Alcoholism." *Hospitals* 54:50-53, February 1, 1980.
Bingham, A., and Barger, J. "Children of Alcoholic Families: A Group Treatment Approach for Latency Age Children." *Journal of Psychosocial Nursing and Mental Health Services* 23(12):13-15, 1985.
Booth, P., et al. "The Windsor Clinic...Alcoholism Treatment Unit." *Nursing Times* 75:547-551, March 29, 1979.
Califano, J.A. "How Alcohol Damages America." *Life Health* 94:19, February 1979.
Callahan, C.L. "The White House Conference on Food, Nutrition and Health." *Nursing Outlook* 18:58, January 1970.
Comer, J.P. "Drinking in Young Adolescents." *Parents* 55:90, February 1980.
Davidson, S.V. "The Assessment of Alcoholism." *Family Community Health* 2:1-31, May 1979.
Davis, R.E. "The Primary Prevention of Alcohol Problems." *Alcohol Health and Research World,* Spring 1976.
DePaola, B. "Emotional Care of the Patient Who Is Also an Alcoholic." *Journal of Practical Nursing* 30:18-19, May 1980.
Doherty, J. "Disulfiram (Antabuse) Chemical Commitment to Abstinence." *Alcohol Health and Research World,* Spring 1976.
Dumstra, D. "Clinical Session Briefs. Alcoholism: A Nursing Dilemma. Part 1." *Journal of Psychiatry Nursing* 28:24-25, August 1978.
Estes, E.R. "Counseling the Wife of an Alcoholic Spouse." *American Journal of Nursing* 74:1251, July 1974.
Fields, B.L. "Adolescent Alcoholism: Treatment and Rehabilitation." *Family Community Health* 2:61-90, May 1979.
Garerl, E.A. "Assertiveness Training for Alcoholics." *Journal of Psychiatric Nursing* 17:31-36, January 1979.
Garrison, T. "Alcoholism Can Be A Family Problem." *Life Health* 94:13-15, May 1979.
Hindman, M. "Rational Emotive Therapy in Alcoholism Treatment." *Alcohol Health and Research Development,* Spring 1976.
Hudson, H.L. "Programs Rehabilitate Alcoholics, Alleviate Personnel Problems," *Hospitals* 52:83, October 16, 1978.
Isler, C. "The Alcoholic Nurse: What We Try to Hide, Deny." *RN* 41:48-55, July 1978.
Knauert, A. "The Treatment of Alcoholism in a Community Setting." *Family Community Health* 2:91-102, May 1979.
Lerner, D. "Consultation on Alcoholism in a General Hospital." *Health Social Work* 3:103-125, February 1978.
Lewis, L. "The Hidden Alcoholic — A Nursing Dilemma." *Nursing '75* 5:20-21, July 1975.
Luke, B. "Maternal Alcoholism and the Fetal Alcohol Syndrome." *American Journal of Nursing* 77:1924-1926, December 1977.
Michael, M.M., et al. "Symposium on the Self-Care Concept of Nursing. Use of the Adolescent Peer Group to Increase the Self-Care Agency of Adolescent Alcohol Abusers." *Nursing Clinics of North America* 15:157-176, March 1980.
Mueller, J.F. "Treatment for the Alcoholic — Cursing or Nursing." *American Journal of Nursing* 74:245-247, February 1974.
Osborne, E. "The Elderly Alcoholic." *Journal of Practical Nursing* 29:25-26, September 1979.
Peek, M. "Alcoholism: The Treatment Phase." *Journal of Nursing Care* 11:16-17, December 1978.

Potter, M.L., et al. "Is Your Patient Also an Alcoholic?" *Journal of Practical Nursing* 30:17–22, May 1980.
Rosien, A. "Alcoholism: Pointing Alcoholics Toward a Recovery." *Patient Care* 12:110–113, October 30, 1978.
Segal, M., et al. "Alcoholism: A Special Crisis Intervention Program." *Journal of Psychiatric Nursing* 28:22, January 1978.
Taif, B. "Preventing Complications of Alcoholism." *Journal of Practical Nursing* 25:18–19, September 1975.
Triplett, J.L., et al. "Children of Alcoholic Parents: A Neglected Issue." *Journal of School Health* 48:596–599, December 1978.
Ufer, L. "How to Recognize and Care for the Alcoholic Patient." *Nursing '77* 77:37–39, October 1977.
Yearwood, A.C., et al. "How Can an Alcoholic Change in 28 Days?" *American Journal of Nursing* 79:1436–1438, August 1979.

# CHAPTER 11

## Books

Brecher, E.M. *Licit and Illicit Drugs.* Boston: Little, Brown and Co., 1972.
Fort, J., and Christopher, T. *American Drugstore (A-Alcohol to V-Valium).* Boston: Little, Brown and Co., 1975.
Raths, L., et al. *Values and Teaching.* 2nd ed. Columbus: Charles E. Merrill Publishing Co., 1980.
Rokeach, M. *The Nature of Human Values.* New York: The Free Press, 1973.

## Periodicals

Barber, E.R. "The Pros and Cons of Methadone Maintenance." *Journal of Psychiatric Nursing* 11:18, November–December 1978.
Betemps, E. "Management of the Withdrawal Syndrome of Barbiturates and Other Central Nervous System Depressants." *Journal of Psychiatric Nursing* 17:31, September 1981.
Caroselli-Karinja, M. "Drug Abuse and the Elderly." *Journal of Psychosocial Nursing and Mental Health Services* 23(6):25–30, 1985.
Caskey, K. "The School Nurse and Drug Abuse." *Nursing Outlook* 18:27, December 1970.
Coletta, S.S. "Values Clarification in Nursing." *American Journal of Nursing* 78:2057–2063, December 1978.
Darity, M. "Drugs: Facing Up to a Problem on Your Staff." *RN* 42:20–26, November 1979.
Finnegan, L., and Mairew, J. "Care of the Addicted Infant." *American Journal of Nursing* 74:685–693, April 1974.
Foreman, N.J., and Zeru, J. "Drug Crisis Intervention." *American Journal of Nursing* 71:1736–1741, September 1971.
Fultz, J.N., Jr., et al. "When a Narcotic Addict is Hospitalized." *American Journal of Nursing* 80:478–481, March 1980.
Gaylin, W. "Caring Makes the Difference." *Psychology Today* 10:34–39, August 1976.
Gossop, M. "The Pattern of Drug Abuse." *Nursing Times* 74:996, June 15, 1978.
Gray, N. "Chemical Use/Abuse and the Female Reproductive System." Tucson, Arizona: A Do It Now Drug Survival Publication, 1974.
Huberty, D.J., and Malmquist, J.D. "Adolescent Chemical Dependency." *Perspectives in Psychiatric Care* 16:21, January–February 1978.
Jaffe, S. "First-Hand Views of Recovery." *American Journal of Nursing* 82:578, 1982.
Lewin, D. "Care of the Drug Dependent Patient." *Nursing Times* 74:621–624, April 13, 1978.
Morgan, A., and Morenao, J. "Attitude Toward Addiction." *American Journal of Nursing* 73:397–501, March 1973.
Nelson, K. "The Nurse in a Methadone Maintenance Program." *American Journal of Nursing* 73:870–874, May 1973.

Nussel, E.J., and Althoff, S.A. "Alienation, Drugs and Social Class." *Health Education* 8:26-28, May/June 1977.

Olson, J., and Johnson, J. "Drug Misuse Among the Elderly." *Journal of Gerontological Nursing* 4:11-14, November-December 1978.

Pillar, G., and Narus, J. "Physical Effects of Heroin Addiction." *American Journal of Nursing* 73:2105-2108, December 1973.

Schonberg, S.K. "Drug Abuse Counseling" *Pediatric Nursing* 4:31-33, July-August 1978.

Singer, A. "Mothering Practice — Heroin Addiction." *American Journal of Nursing* 74:77-82, January 1974.

Smith, L. "Limit Setting." *Nursing Times* 74:1074-1075, June 1978.

Stellefson, W., and St. Pierre, R. "Does Dissonance Work in Consumer Education?" *Health Education* 10:2-4, January-February 1979.

Stone, S.J. "The Meaning of Health: In the Works of Rollo May." *Health Education* 8:2-4, May/June 1977.

Tricone, B., et al. "Perspective on the Combative Patient." *Journal of Nursing Care* 12:15-22, November 1979.

Tricone, B., et al. "Street Terms Defined: A Glossary" *Journal of Nursing Care* 12:22-24, November 1979.

Vourakis, C., and Bennett, G. "Angeldust: Not Heaven Sent." *American Journal of Nursing* 79:649, 1979.

# CHAPTER 12

## Books

Bruch, H. *Eating Disorders: Obesity, Anorexia Nervosa and the Person Within.* New York: Basic Books, 1973.

Burgess, A.W., and Lazarre, A. *Psychiatry Nursing in the Hospital and the Community.* 2nd ed. Englewood Cliffs, NJ: Prentice-Hall, Inc., 1981.

Garner, D.M., and Garfinkel, P.E. *Handbook of Psychotherapy for Anorexia Nervosa and Bulimia.* New York: The Guilford Press, 1985.

Green. H. *I Never Promised You a Rose Garden.* New York: Holt, Rinehart & Winston, 1964.

Irving, S. *Basic Psychiatric Nursing.* Philadelphia: W. B. Saunders Co., 1973.

Jourard, S.M. *The Transparent Self.* Florence, KY: D. Van Nostrand, 1964.

Kalkman, M., and Davis, A.J. *New Dimensions in Mental Health Psychiatric Nursing.* New York: McGraw-Hill Book Co., 1974.

Kesey, K. *One Flew Over the Cuckoo's Nest.* New York: Viking Press, 1962.

Rubin, T. *Lisa and David.* New York: Ballantine Books, 1961.

Sarason, I.G. *Abnormal Psychology, the Problem of Maladaptive Behavior.* New York: Meredith Corp., 1972.

Saxton, D.F., and Haring, P.W. *Care of Patients with Emotional Problems.* 3rd ed. St. Louis: C.V. Mosby Co., 1979.

Sullivan, H.S. *Interpersonal Theory of Psychiatry,* Edited by M.L. Gawel and H.S. Perry. New York: W.W. Norton, 1953.

## Periodicals

Anderson, C., and Meisel, S. "An Assessment of Family Reaction to the Stress of Psychiatric Illness." *Hospital and Community Psychiatry* 27:868-871, December 1976.

Arieti, S. "Roots of Depression: The Power of the Dominant Other." *Psychology Today* 12:54-56, April 1979.

Arnold, H. "Working with Schizophrenc Patients — Four A's: A Guide to One-to-One Relationships." *American Journal of Nursing* 76:941-943, June 1976.

Bemis, K.M. "Current Approaches to the Etiology and Treatment of Anorexia Nervosa." *Psychological Medicine* 85:593-617, 1978.

Bull, A. "Nursing Care Study: Schizophrenia." *Nursing Times* 74:442-444, March 16, 1978.

Burnside, I. "Recognizing and Reducing Emotional Problems in the Aged." *Nursing '77* 7:56-59, July 1977.

Bush, M. "Sex Offenders are People." *Journal of Psychiatric Nursing* 13:38-40, July-August 1975.

Cline, F. "The Adoloscent Manic-Depressive." *Nursing Mirror* 4:34-35, March-April 1979.

Coburn, D.C. "The Experience of Schizophrenia." *Journal of Psychiatric Nursing and Mental Health Services* 15:9-13, December 1977.

Crawford, D.A. "Social Skills Training for Psychiatric Patients." *Nursing Times* 74:1322-1323, August 10, 1978.

Davidites. R.M. "A Social Systems Approach to Deviant Behavior." *American Journal of Nursing* 71:1588-1589, August 1971.

de Silva, D. "Behavior Therapy for Obsessional Neurosis." *Nursing Mirror* 146:15-17, February 2, 1978.

Dickstein, L.J. "Anorexia Nervosa and Bulimia: A Review of Clinical Issues." *Hospital and Community Psychiatry* 36:1086-1092, October 1985.

Diram, M.O. "You Can Prevent Suicide." *Nursing '76* 6:60-64, January 1976.

Doyen, L. "Primary Anorexia Nervosa: A Review and Critique of Selected Papers." *Journal of Psychosomatic Nursing and Mental Health Services* 20:12-18, 1982.

Floyd, G.J. "Nursing Management of the Suicidal Patient." *Journal of Psychiatric Nursing* 13:23-26, February 1975.

Goldberg, M. "Managing the No-Institutionalized Psychotic or Keeping Psychotics Useful." *The PA Journal* 7:103-105, Fall 1977.

Goleman, D. "Who's Mentally Ill?" *Psychology Today* 11:34-41, January 1978.

Gould, E., and Glick I.D. "The Effects of Family Presence and Brief Family Intervention on Global Outcome for Hospitalized Schizophrenic Patients." *Family Process* 16:503-510, December 1977.

Gould, S, et al. "Depression." *Journal of Practical Nursing* 28:19-21, August 1977.

Green, N.C. "A Psychiatric Assessment Tool for Staff and Students." *Journal of Psychiatric Nursing* 17:28, 1979.

Hansell, N. "Services for Schizophrenics: A Lifelong Approach to Treatment." *Hospital and Community Psychiatry* 29:105-106, February 1978.

Hart, N.A., et al. "The Suicidal Adolescent." *American Journal of Nursing* 79:80-84, January 1979.

Hersch, P., and Hersch, C. "Reflections for Rosalynn: Mental Policy and Time Log." *Health and Social Work* 3:12-34, August 1978.

Hickey, B.A. "The Borderline Experience: Subjective Impressions." *Journal of Psychosocial Nursing and Mental Health Services* 23(4):24-29, 1985.

Hopkins S. "Schizophrenia: The Slow March of Knowledge." *Nursing Mirror* 151:37, July 31, 1980.

Kroll, M.L. "Guidelines for Writing Mental Health Treatment Plans." *American Journal of Nursing* 76:236, 1976.

Lancaster, J. "Schizophrenic Patients: Activity Groups as Therapy." *American Journal of Nursing* 76:947-949, June 1976.

Martin, I. "The Intruders." *Nursing Times* 73:244-245, February 17, 1977.

Meinhardt, K. "Nonhospital Alternatives for Acute Psychiatric Care in California." *Hospital and Community Psychiatry* 29:439-442, July 1978.

Mitchell, R. "Hysteria." *Nursing Times* 70:1030-1032, July 4, 1974.

———. "Personality Disorders." *Nursing Times* 70:1153-1155, July 25, 1974.

———. "Anxiety." *Nursing Times* 70:991-993, July 27, 1974.

Murray, J.E. "Patient Participation in Determining Psychiatric Treatment." *Nursing Research* 23:325-333, July-August 1974.

O'Connor, K.K. "Treatment for Adults with Psychosomatic Symptoms." *Health Social Work* 2:89-110, November 1977.

Ostendork, M. "Dan Is Schizophrenic: Possible Causes, Probable Causes." *American Journal of Nursing* 76:944-947, June 1976.

Pepper, B., Kirshner, M.C., and Ryglewicz, H. "The Young Adult Chronic Patient: Overview of a Population." *Hospital and Community Psychiatry* 32:463-469, 1981.

Phinney, R.P. "The Student of Nursing and Schizophrenic Patients." *American Journal of Nursing* 70:790, April 1970.

Pisarcik, G., et al. "The Psychiatric Nurse in the Emergency Room." *American Journal of Nursing* 79:1264-1266, July 1979.

Rohrs, C. "The Many Faces of Schizophrenics." *Journal of Practical Nursing* 27:14-16. June 1977.

Searicht, R. "Being Honest with Gary Was the Least...and the Most We Could Do." *Nursing '80* 10:54-56, February 1980.

Smith, J.B. "Separation Anxiety...A Personal Experience." *American Journal of Nursing* 75:972-973, June 1975.

Smith, L. "To Be, or Not To Be..." *Journal of Psychiatric Nursing and Mental Health Services* 15:36-39, October 1977.

Snyder, J., and Wilson, M. "Elements of a Psychological Assessment." *American Journal of Nursing* 77:235, 1977.

Steiger, T. "Shadow Child." *American Journal of Nursing* 73:2080, December 1973.

Swanson, A. "Communicating with Depressed Persons." *Perspectives in Psychiatric Care* 13:63-67, 1975.

Thornicroft, G. "Group Home — a Success?" *Nursing Times* 75:84, January 11, 1979.

White, C.L. "Nurse Counseling with a Depressed Patient." *American Journal of Nursing* 78:436-39, 1978.

Wiley, L. "Nursing Care of a Suicidal Adolescent." *Nursing '80* 10:56-59, April 1980.

Yarvis, R.M., and Edwards, D.W. "Do Community Mental Health Centers Underserve Psychotic Individuals?" *Hospital and Community Psychiatry* 29:387-388, June 1978.

Zangari, M.E., and Duffy, P. "Contracting with Patients in Day-to-Day Practice." *American Journal of Nursing* 80:451-455, March 1980.

# CHAPTER 14

## Books

Boston Women's Health Book Collective. *Our Bodies, Ourselves.* New York: Simon and Schuster, 1973.

Brownmiller, S. *Against Our Will: Women, Men and Rape.* New York: Simon and Schuster, 1975.

Burnside, I.M., et al. *Psychosocial Caring Throughout The Life Span.* New York: McGraw-Hill Book Co., 1979.

Ehrlich, G. *Sexual Problems of the Arthritic Patient — Total Management of the Arthritis Patient.* Philadelphia: J.P. Lippincott Co., 1972.

Ellis, J.R., and Nowlis, E.A. *Nursing — A Human Needs Experience.* Boston: Houghton-Mifflin, 1977.

Foley, T., and Davies, M. *Rape: Nursing Care of Victims.* St. Louis: C.V. Mosby Co., 1982.

Kaplan, H.S. *The New Sex Therapy.* New York: Brunner/Mazel, Inc., 1974.

Kuten, J. *Coming Together, Coming Apart.* New York: Macmillan Publishing Co., 1974.

Masters, W., and Johnson, V. *Human Sexual Response.* Boston: Little, Brown and Co., 1966.

Mims, F.H., and Swenson, M. *Sexuality: A Nursing Perspective.* New York: McGraw-Hill, Inc., 1980.

Shafer, K., et al. *Medical-Surgical Nursing.* 6th ed. St. Louis: C.V. Mosby Co., 1975.

Woods, N.F. *Human Sexuality, Health and Illness.* St. Louis: C.V. Mosby Co., 1979.

## Periodicals

Adams, G. "The Sexual History as an Integral Part of the Patient History." *Maternal-Child Nursing Journal* 1:170, 1976.

Allen, A.J. "All-American Sexual Myths." *American Journal of Nursing* 75:1770-1771, October 1975.

Anderson, K.J. "The Role of the Nurse. Psychosexual Problems in Gynecology — 3." *Nursing Times* 74:1560, September 7, 1978.

————— . "The Way They Present Psychosexual Problems in Gynecology — 2." *Nursing Times* 74:1537-1538, September 14, 1978.

Anderson, M.L. "Talking About Sex — With Less Anxiety." *Journal of Psychiatric Nursing* 18:10, June 1980.

Andreoli, K., and Foster, S. "Behavior Following Myocardial Infarction." *American Journal of Nursing* 70:2344, November 1970.

Baxter, R., and Linn, A. "Sex Counseling and the SIC Patient." *Nursing '78* 8:46-52, September 1978.

Benjamin, H., and Ihlenfeld, C.L. "Transexualism." *American Journal of Nursing* 73:457-461, March 1973.

Berkman, A., et al. "Sexual Adjustment to Spinal Cord Injured Veterans in the Community." *Archives of Physical Medicine Rehabilitation* 59:29-33, January 1978.

Branson, H. "Nurses Talk About Abortion." *American Journal of Nursing* 72:106-109, January 1972.

Braverman, S. "Homosexuality." *American Journal of Nursing* 73:652, April 1973.

Burgess, A. "Rape, The Rape Victim: Nursing Implications." *Journal of Practical Nursing* 28:13-15, November 1978.

————— . "In Janet's Case...Part 2." *Journal of Practical Nursing* 28:16, November 1978.

Clark, T.P. "Counseling Victims of Rape." *American Journal of Nursing* 76:1964-1966, December 1976.

Costello, M. "Sex, Intimacy and Aging." *American Journal of Nursing* 8:1330-1332, August 1975.

Deni, L. "The Sexually Abused Child." *Journal of Nursing Care* 11:10-11, December 1978.

DiMauro, J. "The Threat of Hysterectomy." *Journal of Practical Nursing* 23:28-29, April 1973.

DiVasto, P. "Measuring the Aftermath of Rape." *Journal of Psychosocial Nursing and Mental Health Services* 23(12):30-32, 1985.

Elder, M.S. "The Unmet Challenge...Nursing Counseling in Sexuality." *Nursing Outlook* 18:38, November 1970.

Frauman, A.C., et al. "Sexuality and Illness. Sexuality in Adolescents with Chronic Illness, Part 2." *Maternal-Child Nursing* 4:371-375, November-December 1979.

Freeley, E., and Pyne, H. "The Menopause: Facts and Misconceptions." *Nursing Forum* 14:74, 1975.

Gedan, S. "Abortion Counseling with Adolescents." *American Journal of Nursing* 74:1856, October 1974.

Grace, M.J. "The Psychiatric Nurse Specialist and Medical Surgical Patients." *American Journal of Nursing* 74:481-483, March 1974.

Griffith, E., and Trieschmann, R.B. "Sexual Function Restoration in the Physically Disabled: Use of Private Room." *Archives of Physical Medical Rehabilitation* 50:368-369, August 1977.

Groth, A.N., et al. "Rape, Power, Anger and Sexuality." *American Journal of Psychiatry* 134:1229-1234, November 1977.

Hall, N.M. "Symposium on Directions in Psychiatric Nursing. Group Treatment for Sexually Abused Children." *Nursing Clinics of North America* 13:701-705, December 1978.

Halstead, Lauro S. "A Hospital-Based Program in Human Sexuality." *Archives of Physical Medicine Rehabilitation* 58:409-412, September 1977.

Hanlon, K. "Maintaining Sexuality After Spinal Cord Injury." *Nursing '75* 5:58-62, May 1975.

Haskett, R.F., and Meir Steiner, M.D. "Diagnosing Premenstrual Tension Syndrome." *Hospital and Community Psychiatry* 37:33-36, January 1986.

Hoggard, M.J. "An Initial Response to Rape Prevention and Control." *Health Social Work* 3:77-78, November 1978.

Huerter, R. "Sexuality: A Universal Human Experience." *Occupation Health Nursing* 25:16-17, March 1977.

Hurt, L.D., and Peregoy, R.C. "Postpartum Disorders." *Journal of Psychosocial Nursing and Mental Health Services* 23(2):15-20, 1985.

Jacobson, L. "Illness and Human Sexuality." *Nursing Outlook* 22:50, January 1974.

Keaveny, M.E., et al. "Hysterectomy: Helping Patients Adjust." *Nursing '73* 3:8-12, February 1973.

Keller, C., and Copeland, P. "Counseling the Abortion Patient is More Than Talk." *American Journal of Nursing* 72:102-106, January 1972.

Kobosa-Munro, L. "Sexuality in the Aging Woman." *Health Social Work* 2:71-87, November 1977.

Krizinosfski, M.T. "Human Sexuality and Nursing Practice." *Nursing Clinics of North America* 8:673-681, December 1973.

Kroah, J. "How to Deal With Patients Who Act Out Sexually." *Nursing '73* 3:38-39, December 1973.

Lass, L. "How Do You Cope With the Patient Who Is Different." *Journal of Practical Nursing* 28:30-33, July 1978.

Levinger, G.E. "Working through Recovery after Mastectomy." *American Journal of Nursing* 80:1118-1120, June 1980.

Lief, H., et al. "Sexuality and Knowledge and Attitude." *American Journal of Nursing* 75:2026-2029, November 1975.

Lindh, K., et al. "Spinal Cord Injury: You Can Make the Difference." *Nursing '74* 4:41-45, April 1974.

May, G. "Sexual Abuse: the Undercover Problem." *Current Problems in Pediatrics* 7:36-39, October 1977.

McKinley, H., and Drew, B. "The Nursing Home: Death of Sexual Expression." *Health and Social Work* 2:180-187, August 1977.

Miller, J.B., and Mothmer, I. "Psychological Consequences of Sexual Inequality." *Nursing Digest* 6:27-31, Fall 1978.

Moore, K., et al. "The Joy of Sex After a Heart Attack." *Nursing '77* 77:52-55, June 1977.

O'Brien, J. "Body Image... Mirror, Mirror, Why Me?" *Nursing Mirror* 150:36-37, April 24, 1980.

Offir, C. "Don't Take It Lying Down." *Psychology Today* 8:73, August 1975.

Olin, B., and Perlman, A. "Sex After Ileostomy or Colostomy." *Medical Aspects of Human Sexuality* 6:23-42, July 1972.

Paradowski, W. "Socialization Patterns and Sexual Problems of the Institutionalized Chronically Ill and Physically Disabled." *Archives of Physical Medicine Rehabilitation* 58:53-59, February 1977.

Polan, H.J., and Hellerstein, D., et al. "Impact of AIDS — Related Cases on Inpatient Therapeutic Milieu." *Hospital and Community Psychiatry* 36:173-176, February 1985.

Roznoy, M.S. "The Young Adult: Taking a Sexual History." *American Journal of Nursing* 76:1279-1282, August 1976.

Scalzi, C., and Dracup, K. "Sexual Counseling of Coronary Patients." *Heart and Lung* 7:840-845, September-October 1978.

Sha'ked, A., and Flynn, R. "Normative Sex Behavior and the Person with a Disability — Part II — Training of Rehabilitation Agencies." *Journal of Rehabilitation* 43:34-38, November-December 1977.

Shontz, F.G. "Psychological Adjustment to Physical Disability." *Archives of Physical Medicine Rehabilitation* 59:251-254, June 1978.

Silbert, D. "Human Sexuality Growth Groups." *Journal of Psychiatric Nursing* 19:31, 1981.

Smith, D.W. "Survivors of Serious Illness." *American Journal of Nursing* 79:441-446, March 1979.

Sredl, D.R., et al. "Offering the Rape Victim Real Help (Care Study)." *Nursing '79* 9:38-43, July 1979.

Stanford, D. "All About Sex . . . After Middle Age." *American Journal of Nursing* 77:608-610, April 1977.

Stephens, G.J. "Creative Contraries — A Theory of Sexuality." *American Journal of Nursing* 78:70-75, January 1978.

Stoller, R., et al. "A Symposium — Should Homosexuality be a Diagnosis?" *Nursing Digest* 3:55-56, March-April 1975.

Timmreck, T.C., and Stratton, L.H. "The Schedules of Recent Events: A Measurement of Stress Due to Life Changes Events, Translated for the Spanish Speaking." *Journal of Psychiatric Nursing and Mental Health Services* 16:20-25, August 1978.

Vernon, A. "Explaining Hysterectomy." *Nursing '73* 3:36-38, September 1973.

Wasow, M. "Human Sexuality and Terminal Illness." *Health Social Work* 2:104-121, May 1977.

Watts, R.J. "Dimensions of Sexual Health." *American Journal of Nursing* 79:1568–1572, September 1979.

Whitley, M.P. "Seduction and the Hospitalized Person." *Journal of Nursing Education* 17:34–39, June 1978.

Whitley, M.P., and Willingham, D. "Adding a Sexual Assessment to the Health Interview." *Journal of Psychiatric Nursing* 17:27, April 1978.

Whitley, M., et al. "Human Sexuality and the Spinal Cord Injured Patient." *Imprint* 24:50–51, April 1977.

Wilcox, R. "Counseling Patients About Sex Problems." *Nursing '73* 3:44–46, November 1973.

# CHAPTER 15

## Books

Epstein, C. *Nursing the Dying Patient.* Englewood Cliffs, NJ: Reston Publishing Co., 1975.

Erikson, E. *Childhood and Society.* 2nd ed. New York: W.W. Norton & Co., 1963.

Kübler-Ross, E. *On Death and Dying.* New York: Macmillan Publishing Co., 1972.

Kyes, J.J., and Holfing, C.K. *Basic Psychiatric Concepts in Nursing.* 4th ed. New York: Harper and Row, 1980.

Lifton, R., and Olson, E. *Living and Dying.* New York: Bantam Books, 1974.

Roberts, S.L. *Behavioral Concepts and the Critically Ill Patient.* Englewood Cliffs, NJ: Prentice-Hall, Inc., 1976.

## Periodicals

"Assumptions and Principles Underlying Standards for Terminal Care." *American Journal of Nursing* 79:296–297, February 1979.

Barnett, K. "A Theoretical Construction of the Concepts of Touch as They Relate to Nursing." *Nursing Research* 21:102–210, March–April 1972.

Barnsteiner, J.H. "Death and Dying — Anxieties, Needs and Responsibilities of the Nurse." *Journal of Practical Nursing* 24:28–30, June 1974.

Brimigion, J. "Living with Dying." *Nursing '78* 8:76–79, September 1978.

Burgess, K.E. "The Influence of Will on Life and Death." *Nursing Forum* 15:239–258, 1976.

Burgess-Kohn, J. "A Death in the Family." *Parents* 53:72–73, October 1978.

Capp, L. "The Spectrum of Suffering." *American Journal of Nursing* 3:491–495, March 1974.

Comerford, B. "Parental Anticipatory Grief and Guidelines for Caregivers." *Nursing Digest* 5:64–68, Summer 1977.

Crill, M.E. 'In Bereavement." *Journal of Practical Nursing* 27:22–25, October 1977.

Crout, T.K. "Caring for the Mother of a Stillborn Baby." *Nursing '80* 10:70–73, April 1980.

Davis, A.J. "Pain q3h... Ethical Issues." *American Journal of Nursing* 80:974, May 1980.

Davitz, L., et al. "Suffering as Viewed in Six Different Cultures." *American Journal of Nursing* 8:974, May 1980.

Decker, D.J. "In the Valley of the Shadow (Care Study) Part 3." *American Journal of Nursing* 78:416–418, March 1978.

Engel, G. "Emotional Stress and Sudden Death." *Psychology Today* 11:114–115, November 1977.

————— . "Grief and Grieving." *American Journal of Nursing* 64:93, September 1964.

Gerber, I., et al. "Anticipatory Grief and Aged Widows and Widowers." *Journal of Gerontology* 30:225–229, February 1975.

Goleman, D. "We Are Breaking the Silence about Death." *Psychology Today* 10:44–47, September 1977.

Gyuley, J. "Care of the Dying Child." *Nursing Clinics of North America* 11:95–107, March 1976.

Hauser, M., and Feinberg, D. "An Operational Approach to the Delayed Grief and Mourning Process." *Journal of Psychiatric Nursing* 14:29, July 1976.

Hollowell, E.E. "The Right to Die: How Legislation is Defining the Right." *Journal of Practical Nursing* 27:20-21, October 1977.

Holman, M., et al. "Family-Centered Care for Cancer Patients." *Nursing '78* 8:42-43, March 1978.

Jozefowski, J. "Paula's Legacy (Care Study)." *RN* 40:81-83, November 1977.

Kossoff, P. "Telling Children About Death." *American Baby* 40:44-45, February 1978.

Kowalsky, E.L. "Grief: A Lost Life Style." *American Journal of Nursing* 78:418-420, March 1978.

Krant, M.J. "The Organized Care of the Dying Patient." *Hospital Practice* 7:101, January 1972.

Kreiger, D. "Therapeutic Touch: The Imprimatur of Nursing." *American Journal of Nursing* 75:784-787, March 1975.

Kübler-Ross, E. "Hope and the Dying Patient." *Nursing Digest* 5:82-84, Summer 1977.

LeRoux, R.D. "Communicating With the Dying Person." *Nursing Forum* 16:144-155, November 2, 1977.

Lewis, F.H. "A Time to Live and a Time to Die: An Instructional Drama." *Nursing Outlook* 25:762-765, December 1977.

Mandel, H.R. "Nurses' Feelings About Working with Dying." *American Journal of Nursing* 81:1194-1197, June 1981.

Martinson, I.M., et al. "Home Care for the Child." *American Journal of Nursing* 77:1815-1817, November 1977.

McCaffrey, M., and Hart, L. "Undertreatment of Acute Pain with Narcotics." *American Journal of Nursing* 76:1586-1591, October 1976.

McLaughlin, M.F. "Encounters with Grief: Who Helps the Living?" *American Journal of Nursing* 78:422-423, March 1978.

Mills, G.C. "Books to Help Children Understand Death." *American Journal of Nursing* 79:291-295, February 1979.

Morris, K., and Forrester, J. "Teamwork: Nurse and Chaplain." *American Journal of Nursing* 72:2179-2199, December 1972.

Nirenberg, A., et al. "The Day Hospital: Ambulatory Care for the Adolescent with Cancer." *American Journal of Nursing* 79:500-504, March 1979.

Paige, R.L., and Looney, J.F. "Hospice Care for the Adult." *American Journal of Nursing* 77:1812-1815, November 1977.

Parks, G.S. "Some Thoughts on Death — 2." *Nursing Times* 73:105-107, August 4, 1977.

Pellman, D.R. "Learning to Live with Dying." *Nursing Digest* 5:27-31, Summer 1977.

Popoff, D., et al. "What Are Your Feelings About Death and Dying?" *Nursing '75* 5:15-24, October 1975.

Schneidman, E.S. "Death Questionnaire." *Psychology Today* 4:67-72, August 1970.

Sharer, P.S. "Helping Survivors Cope with the Shock of Sudden Death." *Nursing '79* 9:20, January 1979.

Shubin, S., ed. "Cancer Widows: A Special Challenge." *Nursing '78* 78:56-60, April 1978.

Simms, L.M. "Dignified Death — A Right Not a Privilege." *Journal of Gerontological Nursing* 1:21-25, November-December, 1975.

Stecchi, J.M. "The Death of a Child: Looking Back, from a Parent's Point of View." *Journal of Nursing Care* 12:13-16, May 1979.

Thompson, D.M. "Thoughts on Bereavement." *Nursing Times* 73:1334-1335, August 25, 1977.

Toth, S.B., et al. "Empathetic Intervention with the Widow." *American Journal of Nursing* 80:1652-1654, September 1980.

Walker, K., MacBride, A., and Vachon, M. "Social Support Networks and the Crisis of Bereavements." *Social Service Medicine* 11:35, 1977.

Wentzel, K.B. "The Dying are the Living." *American Journal of Nursing* 76:956-957, June 1976.

Wiley, L., ed. "The Other Side of Death." *Nursing '78* 78:42-45, December 1978.

Wise, D. "Learning About Dying." *Nursing Digest* 22:42-44, January 1974.

Woodward, K.L., et al. "Living with Dying." *Newsweek* 91:52-56, May 1, 1978.

Yano, B.S. "Group Therapy for Oncology Nurses — What About Us?" *Journal Of Practical Nursing* 27:28-29, March 1977.

# CHAPTER 16

## Books

Beers, C.W. *A Mind That Found Itself.* Garden City, NJ: Doubleday, 1948.

Brill, N. *Working With People: The Helping Process.* Philadelphia: J.B. Lippincott Co., 1973.

Dec, D. "The Abused Child — The Abusing Adult — A Non-Judgmental Attitude." *Journal of Practical Nursing* 28:27-29, September 1978.

Erikson, E. *Insight and Responsibility.* New York: W.W. Norton & Co., 1964.

Fontana, V., et al. "The Abused Child, The Abusing Adult. Both are Victims, Both Need Your Help." *Journal of Practical Nursing* 28:24-26, September 1978.

Fromm, E. *Man for Himself: An Inquiry into the Psychology of Ethics.* New York: Holt, Rinehart & Winston, Inc., 1947.

Garfield, C.A. *Stress and Survival: The Emotional Realities of Life-Threatening Illness.* St. Louis: C.V. Mosby Co., 1979.

Goble, F. *The Third Force.* New York: Grossman Publishers Inc., 1970.

Grace, H., et al. *Mental Health Nursing: A Socio-Psychological Approach.* Dubuque, IA: William C. Brown Publishing Co., 1977.

Guttentag, M., Salasin, S., and Belle, D. *The Mental Health of Women.* New York: Academic Press, Inc., 1980.

Harrington, M. *The Other America: Poverty in the U.S.* New York: Macmillan Publishing Co., 1962.

Harris, T.A. *I'm O.K. — You're O.K.* New York: Avon Books, 1969.

Johnson, M., and Davis, M.L. *Problem Solving in Nursing Practice.* 2nd ed. Dubuque IA: Wm. C. Brown Publishing Co., 1975.

Kirschenbaum, H., and Simon, S.B. *Readings in Value Clarification.* Minneapolis: Winston Press, Inc., 1973.

Leaman, K. "Recognizing and Helping the Abused Child." *Nursing '79* 9:64-67, February 1979.

Lewis, O. *Five Families.* New York: Basic Books, 1959.

Montagu, A. *Touching.* New York: Columbia University Press, 1971.

Nisbet, R.A. *The Quest for Community.* New York: Oxford University Press, 1969.

Otto, H., and Mann, J. *Ways of Growth: Approaches to Expanding Awareness.* New York: Pocket Books, 1971.

Papalia, D.E., and Olds, S.W. *Human Development.* St. Louis: McGraw-Hill Book Co., 1978.

Slater, P. *The Pursuit of Loneliness.* Boston: Beacon Books, 1971.

## Periodicals

Adelson, P.Y. "The Backward Dilemma." *American Journal of Nursing* 80:422-425, 1980.

Aime, D. "Philosophy and Structure of a Day-Treatment Center." *Journal of Psychiatric Nursing and Mental Health Services* 11:27, 1973.

Appell, L., and Baskin, D. "Transactional Analysis — Improving Nurse-Patient Relationships." *Journal of Practical Nursing* 25:24-31, September 1975.

Babcock, D.E. "Transactional Analysis." *American Journal of Nursing* 76:1152-1155, July 1976.

Bachrach, L.L. "A Conceptual Approach to Deinstitutionalization." *Hospital and Community Psychiatry* 29:573-578, September 1978.

Beard, M.T., et al. "Activity Therapy As a Reconstructive Plan on the Social Competence of Chronic Hospitalized Patients." *Journal of Psychiatric Nursing and Mental Health Services* 16:33-40, February 1978.

Bell, J.M. "Stressful Life Events and Coping Methods in Mental Illness and Wellness Behaviors." *Nursing Research* 26:136-141, March-April 1977.

Bowen, W., et al. "Assessing Community Attitudes Toward Mental Illness." *Hospital and Community Psychiatry* 29:251-253, April 1978.

Brenton, D. "Health Center Milieu: Interaction of Nurses and Low-Income Families — Value Differences Between Nursing and Low-Income Families." *Nursing Research* 21:46-52, January 1972.

Britton, J.G., and Mattson-Melchor, D.M. "The Crisis Home: Sheltering Patients in Emotional Crisis." *Journal of Psychosocial Nursing and Mental Health Services* 23(12):18-22, 1985.

Brotman, H. "Income and Poverty in the Older Population in 1975." *The Gerontologist* 17:23-26, January 1977.

Carr, F. "Impact of Improved Living Environment on Health and Life Expectancy." *The Gerontologist* 17:242-249, March 1972.

Craig, A.E., and Hyatt, B.A. "Chronicity in Mental Illness: A Theory of the Role of Change." *Perspectives in Psychiatric Care* 26:139-154, 1978.

Davis, H.R. "Management of Innovation and Change in Mental Health Servcies." *Hospital and Community Psychiatry* 29:649-658, October 1978.

Dickelmann, N. "Staying Well While Growing Old: Pre-Retirement Counseling." *American Journal of Nursing* 78:1337-1338, August 1978.

Dall, M. "Family Coping with the Mentally Ill: An Unanticipated Problem of Deinstitutionalization." *Hospital and Community Psychiatry* 27:183-185, March 1976.

Dowd, J., and Bengston, V. "Aging in Minority Populations." *Journal of Gerontology* 33:427-436, March 1978.

Elwell, R. "Community Mental Health Centers." *American Journal of Nursing* 70:1014, May 1970.

Gammonkey, J. "New Directions for Mental Health Education. *Journal of Psychiatric Nursing* 16(12):40, 1978.

Gardner, K. "Patient Groups in a Therapeutic Community." *American Journal of Nursing* 71:528-531, May 1971.

Gaylin, W. "Caring Makes the Difference." *Psychology Today* 10:34-39, August 1976.

Gilette, E. "Child Abuse." *Journal of Nursing Care* 11:12-13, December 1978.

Goldman, H., and Runck, B. "Social Security Administration Revises Mental Disability Rules." *Hospital and Community Psychiatry* 36:343-345, April 1985.

Gralnick, A. "Build a Better State Hospital: Deinstitutionalization Has Failed." *Hospital and Community Psychiatry* 36:738-745, July 1985.

Guilette, W., et al. "Day Hospitalization as a Cost-Effective Alternative to Inpatient Care: A Pilot Study." *Hospital and Community Psychiatry* 29:525-527, August 1978.

Hanebuth, L. "Behavioral Response to Stress." *Journal of Nursing Care* 13:16-19, September 1980.

Heide, W.S. "Nursing and Women's Liberation, A Parallel." *American Journal of Nursing* 73:824-827, May 1973.

Hein, E.C. "Teaching Psychosocial Wellness in Family Community Health Nursing." *Nurse Educator* 3:22-25, September-October 1978.

Hirsch, C. "Integrating the Nursing Home Resident into a Senior Citizen's Center." *The Gerontologist* 17:227-234, March 1977.

Hitchcock, J.M. "Crisis Intervention: The Pebble in the Pool." *American Journal of Nursing* 73:1388-1390, August 1973.

Huber, H., and Lynch, F. "Teaching Behavioral Skills to Parents: A Preventive Role for Mental Health." *Children Today* 7:8-10, January-February 1978.

Huey, F. "In a Therapeutic Community." *American Journal of Nursing* 71:926-933, May 1971.

Iveson-Iveson, J. "Prevention: How to Stay Healthy...Mental Fitness. Part 5." *Nursing Mirror* 149:84, October 11, 1979.

Janzen, S. "Psychiatric Day Care in a Rural Area." *American Journal of Nursing* 12:2216-2217, December 1974.

Joyce, C.A., and Lipo, B.J. "People Who Need People." *Nursing Outlook* 19:470-472, July 1971.

Kamerman, S. "Community Resources for the Aged." *The Gerontologist* 16:529-537, June 1976.

Klerman, G.L. "National Trends in Hospitalization." *Hospital and Community Psychiatry* 30:110-13, 1979.

Lancaster, J. "Activity Groups as Therapy." *American Journal of Nursing* 76:947-949, June 1976.

————. "Working with the Schizophrenic Patient — Activity as Therapy." *American Journal of Nursing* 76:947-949, June 1976.

LeMasters, G. "The Effect of Bereavement on the Elderly and the Nursing Implications." *Journal of Gerontology* 4:21-25, 1978.

Lenarz, D.M. "Caring is the Essence of Practice." *American Journal of Nursing* 71:704-707, April 1971.

Levinger, M., and Billings, H. "Nursing in a Low-Rent Housing Project." *American Journal of Nursing* 71:314-318, February 1971.

Lipman, A., and Slater, R. "Status and Spatial Appropriation in Eight Homes for Old People." *The Gerontologist* 17:250-255, March 1977.

Marram, G.D. "Patient's Evaluation of Their Care — Importance to the Nurse." *Nursing Outlook* 21:322-324, May 1973.

North, G.E. "The Concepts of Mental Illness and Disability." *Occupational Health Nursing* 25:12-14, July 1977.

Pasquali, E.A. "Learning About a Poverty Budget." *American Journal of Nursing* 72:1419, August 1972.

Pepper, K., Kirshner, M., et al. "The Young Chronic Patient: Overview of a Population." *Hospital and Community Psychiatry* 32:463-469, July 1981.

Petty, B., et al. "Support Groups for Elderly Persons in the Community." *The Gerontologist* 15:522-528, June 1976.

Primeaux, M. "Caring for the American Indian Patient." *American Journal of Nursing* 1:91-94, January 1977.

Rosenberg, G., and Attinson, L. "Attitudes Toward Mental Illness in the Working Class." *Social Work in Health Care* 3:77-85, Fall 1977.

Salerno, E.M. "A Family in Crisis." *American Journal of Nursing* 73:100-103, January 1973.

Scmandt, J., et al. "Information and Referral Services for Elderly Welfare Recipients." *The Gerontologist* 19:21-27, January 1979.

Spratkin, R., et al. "Teaching Interpersonal Psychiatric Out-Patients Using Structured Learning Theory in a Community Based Setting." *The Gerontologist* 19:21-27, January 1979.

Sturges, J.S. "Talking with Children About Mental Illness in the Family." *Health and Social Work* 2:88-109, August 1977.

Talbott, J. "Deinstitutionalization: Avoiding the Disasters of the Past." *Hospital and Community Psychiatry* 30:621-624, 1979.

Treas, J. "Family Support Systems for the Aged." *The Gerontologist* 17:486-491, June 1977.

Wallace, M.A., and Morley, W.E. "Teaching Crisis Intervention." *American Journal of Nursing* 70:1484, May 1970.

Walter, R. "Psychiatric Liaison with Private Facilities Caring for Discharged Patients." *Hospital and Community Psychiatry* 27:33, 1976.

Wasow, M. "For My Beloved Son, David Jonathan: A Professional Plea." *Health and Social Work* 3:127-146, February 1978.

White, E. "Health and the Black Person: An Annotated Bibliography." *American Journal of Nursing* 10:1839-1841, October 1974.

Winslow, W.W. "Changing Trends in Community Mental Health Center's Key to Survival in the Eighties." *Hospital and Community Psychiatry* 29:273-277, 1982.

# INDEX